BRIAR PATCH

The Murder That Would Not Die

Donald Grady Shomette

4880 Lower Valley Road Atglen, PA 19310

Copyright © 2011 by Donald G. Shomette
Library of Congress Control Number: 2010941721

Author's Note: The story presented herein was inspired by actual events. Many of the names have been changed to protect the privacy of the living, and to insure the peaceful repose of the dead.

Designed by "Sue"
Type set in Atlantic Inline/Humanst521 BT

ISBN: 978-0-7643-3782-6
Printed in China

For Kathy and Nancy

*The Book of Life begins
With a man and a woman in a garden.
It ends with Revelations.*

Oscar Wilde
A Woman of No Importance

CONTENTS

Part II: Terry 147

PRELUDE

A s the old man caressed the borders of the fragile, creased newspaper photograph, as he had done a thousand times before, he shivered. The clipping was his companion over the last half-century, and he had looked at it often. A pinhole over the top border attested to years tacked to a wall. The folds bore witness to many more years he had carried it in his wallet. The yellowed clipping was mottled about its torn edges with grime and the vestigial stain of coffee. That mattered little to him now. With heavy-lidded eyes that fought to stay open, he sought to drink in once more the familiar but faded image of the teenager on the precipice of womanhood, lovely and smiling, with high cheekbones and an effervescent aura that still radiated from the ancient paper. His withered hands, fish-belly white and laced with exquisite blue veins, quivered as he struggled to hold the clipping still.

Again he remembered the love, the anger, the pain, and the shame.

The hospital bed that had confined him for what seemed countless months was uncomfortable in its upright position. The room was too cold. Maybe it was the air-conditioning, or maybe just him. Maybe he needed another blanket. Already three lay over him, but his bony frame had grown so frail since the cancer set in, he had been unable to retain body heat. His feet were freezing, and the chill was moving relentlessly up his legs. Discomfort mattered little to him now as he looked into the wide, cheerful eyes of the girl in the picture. He had tried his best. God knows he had tried his best, but he knew it wasn't enough. Not much time left now. He had to talk to someone, tell someone, before it was too late.

The cold moved upwards.

"Ellen," he whispered to the ghost of evening, and closed his eyes.

Part I

ELLEN

"In a while this will all be forgotten."

Chapter 1

BR'ER RABBIT

The baby girl had been a gift. Her parents, Philip and Lucille Chauvanne, unlike most of their many brothers and sisters who married early, had waited out six years of courtship, until they were twenty-three years old, before tying the knot. Their sometimes-volatile relationship began halfway through the Great Depression. Despite the hormonal surges that had overwhelmed many of their less than stoic young friends, they had held out for as long as they could, although both their respective and extended clans agreed that a few years more might not have hurt. Providing for two would be hard enough, but feeding, clothing and caring for an extra mouth was something else.

For Philip and Lucille the delay in starting their own household hadn't been a matter of choice, but plain pragmatism. For the first few years together, they had been obliged to live with Philip's parents, in a small apartment crowded with younger siblings and sundry out-of-work family members who had come up from Texas to Washington, D.C. in search of government jobs. Like many Americans, Philip and Lucille, simply too poor to support children, were obliged to hold off a full five years after tying the knot before beginning their own family. For Lucille, who had secured a job that she hated at the State Department as a switchboard operator, the wait had been desperate, almost unendurable. Then they were blessed. Philip had wanted to delay a bit longer, but Lucille claimed it had been an accident of nature despite the best precautions. Philip wasn't so certain, but it didn't matter, for the deed was done, and that was that.

Ellen Marie Chauvanne was delivered by the family physician, Dr. Merrill Gleason, on July 17, 1938 at Georgetown Hospital in D.C. For Philip and Lucille the world was suddenly right, even if times were still hard. It would be an uphill struggle but that was all right. Moving out of the crowded apartment where they had lived with Philip's parents and relatives, they had rented their own small flat and, despite a world on the cusp of war, somehow survived.

A little over five years later, on October 8, 1943, Lucille gave birth to her second child. His name on the birth certificate at Providence General Hospital, in Washington, read Philip Edwin Chauvanne III, but from the beginning everyone just called him "Eddy." Soon afterwards, Lucille had returned to work at the State Department switchboard.

Then, on February 14, 1948, the couple adopted a third child named Theresa Anne, dubbed Terry from the very beginning. Terry was born at Providence to one of Philip's unwed nieces, the same day as her adoption. Though the Chauvannes chose not to tell the little girl of her origins, at least in the beginning, it mattered little. For all intents and purposes, Terry might just as well have sprung from Lucille's own womb, for she was as deeply loved and adored as Ellen and Eddy. Though it was clear to all that pretty little Ellen, the first-born, was also foremost in the parental pecking order, the primary beneficiary and victim of her mother's smothering protectiveness.

From the beginning Ellen was an amiable child. Thin but well formed, with delicate hands and long fingers, inherited from her mother, her only curse was an occasionally terrifying asthma condition that dogged her since birth. Yet, she was a meld of the best genes of both her parents, and she was from the very start both mama's daughter and daddy's little girl. She bore many of her mother's more dominant traits, and from the moment she could speak, asserted her will through words. Yet it was her natural, wholesome personality, inherited from her father, that charmed and won over everyone.

Both parents were of working-class origins. Lucille descended from a small well-to-do family named Grouse ensconced out in Rockville, Long Island, and a blue-collar clan named Dears. Philip came from a large tribe that had migrated from Texas, then Mississippi, and finally settled in the Washington metropolitan area before World War I. Philip was tall, lanky, muscular and ruggedly handsome. His full head of thick, light brown hair, prematurely graying on the sides, gave him an air of country dignity that two hundred years earlier could have passed him off as a prosperous Virginia squire. By trade an excavation engineer who operated heavy earth-moving equipment, he was a staunch unionist from a family mostly of anti-union construction men.

Philip's own father, Philip, Sr., a tough, taciturn Mississippian born and raised in Texas, had been a wild-eyed, bona fide six-shooter in his youth who rough-necked in the oil fields, herded cattle, and worked as a railroad telegrapher. He had fought in the Spanish-American War, and ran away with Ida Gerdes. Ida was the starkly handsome daughter of a German immigrant schoolteacher who had come to America from a small village in the Black Forest in 1856, and homesteaded in central Texas after the Civil War. A hard man even by the standards of the plains, family legend said that Philip, Sr. had fled east from a trumped-up murder charge for fatally pistol-whipping a union organizer in Mississippi. He ended his days quietly behind a desk as a low-level Washington bureaucrat, a family man, and a respected minor official in the Spanish-American War Veterans Association.

Philip's relations had included ten siblings, counting a brother who had died soon after birth, and an older sister who succumbed to a burst appendix in the early 1920s. Most of his brothers saw military service. The oldest, Tommy had served as a teenager in the horse cavalry on the Arizona-Mexico border with Pershing, and then, at the outset of World War II, though in his mid-40s, re-enlisted in the Coast Guard. Several of his other brothers had fought overseas. Henry, waded ashore on Day-1 at Normandy, and survived all the way through to the occupation of Berlin. Philip, who was supporting five of his family (including his mother-in-law) had been considered by the Selective Service Board as too old for the draft, and had stayed home. Yet he was proud to boast that at the outset of the war he helped build the Pentagon and later, in the 1950s, the Chesapeake Bay Bridge. And to hear him tell it — and he told it to just about anyone who would listen, for his ego was not a diminutive one — he had built both almost single-handedly! Like most of the Chauvanne men, he was happiest when clawing at dirt with a steam shovel or bulldozer, the bigger the machine the better. A bulldozer was embossed on his bronze belt buckle, which he always wore even with formal attire.

Ellen's mother was, at forty-four, a slightly built but well-shaped woman who wore flared rhinestone-flecked glasses with pointed sides. Her father, Jeffrey Dears, had been instrumental in founding the electrician's union in Washington. She, like her husband, was a chain smoker, and ever in control of her brood, ruled the roost in all matters domestic. Some of the extended Chauvanne family considered her domineering, quick to take offense, and indeed at times abusive to Philip or anyone else, including strangers who got in her way on an off day. Others were less generous and deemed her a poisonous scold with a razor tongue who lorded it over her husband and children. One brother-in-law even suggested that Lucille was the feminine nickname for Lucifer.

During the latter days of the war years, while employed as a switchboard operator for the State Department, Lucille had been loaned out to the White House on a temporary basis. Not surprisingly, with the war on she had been obliged to work long hours. Her supervisor, a tough but fair-minded lady named Hackey, had regimented the office in a near military fashion. Quiet moments were few. One summer evening in 1944 Hackey informed Lucille that she would have to work the extra shift as her replacement had called in sick and there could be no break that particular evening, even for a quick meal. About 11 p.m. FDR himself, sitting in a wheelchair with Bennie Steel, his black manservant, behind him, peered into the room and saw the harried operator hard at work handling an almost continuous stream of calls. "Dear, have you eaten anything yet?" he asked her in between calls.

"No, Mr. President," she said, as she plugged in another line. Though working in the basement of the East Wing for nearly six months, she had never even seen the Chief Executive of the United States much less spoken to him, and was a little flushed.

"Well, we can't have that now," the president said with his famous broad smile. "I'll have the White House chef send you up a little something."

Lucille never forgot the kindness. Especially since the President must have had greater worries on his mind than getting a roast beef sandwich up to a harried telephone operator. After all, it was the night of June 5, 1944, the eve of D-Day in Europe, with the fate of the world hanging in the balance. And it was a story she later told her children — or anyone else who would listen — over and over again.

Not long after Ellen's birth, Lucille began to display wisps of gray in her light brown hair, and would eventually succumb to peroxide to stave off the evil signs of aging. After the war, like most women of her times who had been working on the home front, her principal occupation had shifted back to housewife, and she was good at it. Rarely seen at home without her apron on, she was a master seamstress who made her own curtains and clothing for the family. Her children considered her "down home" cooking incomparable. In her rare free time, she knitted, crocheted, embroidered, and enjoyed the newest rage, paint-by-numbers. At Christmastime, she was fanatic about preparations for that magical instant when her children would descend the stairs to find the tree, gifts and decorations all synchronized to provide the most memorable moment of the year.

In 1953, the Chauvanne family moved from a diminutive house on Beale Street in the quiet community of Landover Hills, Maryland. It had been there that Philip and Lucille purchased their first home, and Ellen took her first job, delivering the local weekly community newspaper. They had been the first family on the block to own a television. Yet, owing to a downturn in the construction trade during a brief recession they soon lost the house, and were forced to rent a place on Kennedy Street in another small, bucolic blue-collar community called East Riverdale, not far from the Maryland-D.C. line.

While living in East Riverdale, Ellen became, like many pubescent girls her age, fixated on horses. She was, Eddy would later recall, simply "crazy about horses." Aside from her brother and sister, there were few children in the community, and horses had captured her imagination, and she would often take little Terry to a local stable just to pet them. Her biggest thrill came yearly when the stately behemoths of beer advertising, the Budweiser Clydesdales, arrived in town and paraded on Fletcher's Field near her home. Her love of animals, however, was not limited to horses, and her tendency to round up and bring home every stray cat she could find drew repeated objections from her mother, which were rarely enforced.

With an up-tick in the economy, Philip soon found more work and a resumption of prosperity. The family moved again, this time to a new red brick semi-detached duplex house in the recently built subdivision of Lane Manor, near the University of Maryland. There, during the summer of 1954, Ellen finally learned how to ride and jump on a rented mare, and immediately began pestering her father to buy a horse for her upcoming seventeenth birthday — a rite-of-passage both Philip and Lucille had been obliged to delay for financial reasons. Their daughter's adoration of horses, however, knew no bounds. Some of her new neighbors said she was more interested in horses than boys, and one of her teachers at nearby Northwestern High School, where she was a popular sophomore, observed that she frequently wore costume jewelry in the shape of horses' heads to school.

Lucille often noted that Ellen wasn't a whiz kid or an A student, but she got by. "I don't ask my kids to be geniuses," she would often say defensively, "just average." And academically that's what Ellen was, albeit with difficulty. Owing to her asthma condition, she was often absent and her grades had suffered accordingly. In the first quarter of her sophomore year at Northwestern she had failed or was close to failing four out of six subjects, but she had been out sick for nearly a third of the time.

Ellen's social life was something else. Despite her condition, she was a wholesome girl who always seemed freshly minted with every new day. She made friends easily. Soon after the family's arrival at Lane Manor, she befriended another recent settler, Michael Linn O'Riley, the thirteen-year-old daughter of a Washington, D.C. police officer. Michael, or Mikie as the kids called her, petite and delicate, was as vivacious and attractive as Ellen, and despite the three-year age difference the two quickly bonded into a quasi-sisterhood. Within weeks of the Chauvannes being ensconced in the neighborhood, Ellen and Mikie joined the Prince George's County Parks and Recreation Summer Program together and spent endless hours that first vacation reading stories to pre-school children. Both teenagers resolved to have kids of their own after marrying the movie star of their dreams. No matter that the stars they dreamed of varied from week to week. Ellen religiously maintained a scrapbook, a present from her grandmother, of motion picture matinee idols and recording artists.

In their new home, Ellen shared a small room with Terry, as she had done ever since her sister had been born. Although both now had their own beds, the girls shared a single dresser. Ellen kept her jewelry in a folding boudoir table with a lacy skirt just to the left of a small closet opposite the beds. On the dressing table, she displayed her collection of little glass horse statues, and a face powder container with a glass horse lid. Inside the container she kept a dime — dated 1944 — for good luck. One of the drawers held a small jewelry collection, mostly inexpensive bracelets with decorative horse ornaments, and her sole cosmetic, a tube of dark red lipstick. Over the table was a window that overlooked the house next door. This belonged to the Miller family, one of two unrelated clans of the same name in the neighborhood. The Millers next door were the family of an army colonel whose son, Benny, was one of Terry's friends. Like her, he was a first grader at Lewisdale Elementary, just down the street. Candice Miller, one of Ellen's closest friends, belonged to the second Miller family further down the block.

Little Terry tagged along with her sister everywhere, a Peter Pan shadow attached to Ellen's shoes. In many ways the diminutive child felt closer to her older sister than to her mother. Indeed, like many siblings, the younger child idolized the older. And the older girl was fiercely protective of the younger. Lucille, who may have been somewhat jealous of her youngest daughter's devotion to her older sister, occasionally denigrated her as "Ellen's Little Doll." At bedtime, the two girls would lie together in the dark, and Ellen, who had an odd affinity for the richness of the grotesque, told Terry stories of goblins, witches, and ghosts, as well as princes, magic toads, and enchanted forests until she drifted off to sleep.

Moving to Lane Manor had changed the Chauvannes' lives immeasurably, particularly those of the children. Many other families, most with kids, had taken up residence in the quiet suburb specifically for its middle-class community charisma. The Chauvannes were fortunate to acquire a small but pleasant home at 604 West Park Drive, directly across from a wooded park and playing field. These, along with a modest, unfinished recreation room in their basement, held the chief attractions. It mattered little that the small, working-class, brick duplexes all looked exactly alike, more barracks than residences. For many families on the street, they were their first true homes. Their new home was clean and wonderful, but the park and its enchanted woods were the real prizes.

Northwest Branch Park, administered by a quasi-governmental agency with the laborious name of The Maryland National Capital Park and Planning Commission (M-NCPPC), was bisected by its namesake, a meandering little stream called the Northwest Branch, which fed into the Anacostia River, a tributary of the Potomac River. The park was a gem, handsomely fitted out with picnic tables, brick fireplaces for grilling hot dogs, a ball field, and a basketball court. It meant sunshine and fresh air for the kids. The edge of the Lane Manor sector of the park, hard by University Lane, faced a pretty pond filled with frogs and ducks, and covered by water lilies, which everyone enjoyed. During the first winter the Chauvannes spent in their new home, Ellen, Eddy, and Terry often fed the ducks at the edge of the pond. Tow-headed Eddy, in particular, loved the park, and played there everyday with his buddy, Bobby Barnes, and occasionally little Charlie Bricker from down the street. The boys fished in the creek and caught blue gills, carp, eels, and, on rare occasions, a bass that had wandered up from the Anacostia a few miles to the southeast. They hiked the creek and sometimes traced its reaches for miles either way. Eddy knew every tree and bush in the park and, after he read Mark Twain in school, fancied himself a modern day Huck Finn. And like Huck, he learned early on to smoke and cuss up a storm.

For Ellen, though, the focus of social life revolved around the nearby Riggs Lane Teen Club. Organized by Lucille and a group of local kids, the club was an instant success, and pretty, bubbly Ellen, who by then was several inches taller than her own mother, was elected its first secretary. Thereafter, her life, at least it seemed to her parents, revolved entirely around the club, and her love of horses slowly began to retreat in the teenage sea of priorities. Philip and Lucille were delighted their daughter was so involved, and threw open their home to all of her friends. The Chauvanne household soon resembled Grand Central Station. Philip enlarged the rec room to accommodate the increased traffic, and walled it with an imitation walnut veneer. Both parents were quickly elected as "advisors" to the club.

Every Saturday their parents escorted the teens in Lane Manor to the club dance — the social highlight of the week — held at the nearby Lewisdale Elementary School. Philip and Lucille would drive Ellen over early since she was the one charged with seeing that there was an adequate supply of ice, soft drinks, and potato chips. The Chauvanne rec room was frequently the center of local teenage community life after-school. On warm weeknights, the neighborhood kids clustered on the picnic tables in the park off West Park Drive and talked until dark, and sometimes necked a bit. Then they would emigrate to Ellen's or one of the other houses along the street and play records — Ellen loved records, particularly Theresa Brewer and Eddy Fisher. Philip and Lucille winced at the sounds of the newest craze, Rock and Roll, when the caterwauling of Bill Haley and the Comets issued forth from the kids' inner sanctum, but they endured.

From all outward appearances, it was a wonderful little community where everything one needed was close by, and friends who could be counted on lived next door.

Five houses down the street lived Ellen's best friend, Mikie, who chattered incessantly about her mother Lanie, a beautiful woman by any standard, and her father, Private Thomas W. O'Riley, a taciturn, red-headed Irish station clerk with the First Precinct of the Washington Metropolitan Police Department. If Ellen's new heroes were handsome Hollywood stars, Mikie's were her mom and dad, though boys were beginning to pull a strong second, especially for the nubile Mikie.

Mikie had two younger sisters, Elaine, 8, and Catherine Elizabeth, 3, both of whom, neighbors often remarked in praise, were so cute they could have sprung from a picture book. When Mikie herself was born, the doctor had told the proud parents that their baby was the prettiest one he had ever delivered — a beautiful little doll — and as the years passed, she only got prettier.

The O'Rileys, from the beginning of their marriage, had been hamstrung by a cop's inconsiderable salary, and had lived in an apartment for most of their sixteen years together until finally saving up enough to move to Lane Manor in January 1954. Their modest, new duplex at 614 West Park Drive became their castle. Tom's workroom was his sanctuary. Both parents labored hard to furnish their household as attractively as possible. It was their first true home, replete with a substantial mortgage, a backyard of their own, and friendly neighbors; and they devoured their newfound community status with relish. They, too, loved the kids.

"We all said we'd always keep our homes open to the kids," Lanie later recalled, "so we'd always know where they were. We were glad when the teen club was organized because it gave the children something they could run themselves. And we all helped."

The O'Rileys, devoted Irish Catholics, had seen to it that their eldest, Mikie, attended St. Joseph's Parochial School on 2nd and C Street, NE, in the District, where she would receive the best education possible. The nuns were pleased at the wonderful demeanor of the petite, delicately built girl, and her parents were delighted at her straight A report cards. She excelled all the way through.

On the night of Friday, June 10, 1955, Mikie O'Riley graduated from the 8th grade with a grand ceremony. Monsignor Thomas M. Spicer, pastor of St. John Baptist De La Salle Church, in nearby Chillum, where the O'Rileys attended weekly services, personally presented Mikie with her diploma. Dressed in white, with a garland of flowers in her bright blond hair, "she looks like a bride," some said. Her parents were determined that she would continue her Catholic education and had enrolled her in the not-yet-built Regina High School. They attended the laying of the school's cornerstone two days after Mikie's graduation and watched the archbishop bless it. Mikie knew she was going there and seemed, at least outwardly, happy. It would be a struggle for John and Lanie to make the tuition payments on a police clerk's salary, but as Lanie said, "Not every child has such an alert mind." Sacrifices must be made. Her daughter was special, and she vowed the child would get the best Catholic education possible regardless of cost.

For Mikie, the academic year had already ended, but for Ellen, who attended public school at nearby Northwestern High, there were still final exams and then the good-byes to bused-in friends who she would not see until next fall. Warm weather was at hand, and delicious prospects for the summer had yet to be plumbed. Like many young girls they daydreamed of horses, Hollywood, and boys, albeit no longer in that order.

The Chauvanne household was not extravagant, nor was spare money often in evidence, especially when Philip was between jobs. From time-to-time Ellen earned a little spending money baby-sitting. The same night Mikie was graduating, Ellen was paid two dollars for watching one of the neighbor's children, and carefully folded and stuck it away in the little white purse she always carried, but only after putting her initials on a corner of each bill in the event her little brother snitched one, which he sometimes tried to do. She intended to use it to get her beautiful yellow-brown, shoulder-length hair cut and set. Aside from the money, and the usual collection of personal debris that teenager girls acquired and filed in such small containers, she also carried a pocketknife, "for protection" she once said. In truth, carrying the tiny pearl-handled pocketknife was little more than an heirloom from her semi-tomboy stage rather than a protective measure adopted by the attractive young woman she was becoming.

On the night of Saturday, June 11, the last teen club dance before the school year ended went off without a hitch. Philip and Lucille Chauvanne drove their daughter to nearby Lewisdale Elementary, and the usual crowd assembled. A few older boys arrived in their own or their parent's cars at the chaperoned affair, which was punctually concluded without incident at 10:00 p.m. Or so it seemed. Ellen, for once, had come home in an extremely maudlin mood. Her father dismissed it as teenage angst. It passed.

Eddy Chauvanne, who was only eleven, thought little of such things at the time, and usually managed to worm out of the few social events in which he was obliged to participate. A good-looking boy, with sandy hair and shoulders prematurely broad for his age, he modeled himself after his father's tough construction man persona, replete with all the rough edges. Like his dad, he would rather go fishing or play ball than go to a dance or attend formal functions. That would eventually change, but for now his dad described him simply as "all boy."

For Eddy, life was one big adventure, and anything and everything beyond the fringes of his home were of interest. Academics were definitely not on his must-do list and skipping school was a regimen at which he excelled. As with many boys his age, he occasionally exhibited a streak of pubescent rebelliousness and would disappear for hours on end, hanging around in the park or playing pickup ball with his friends at the ball field. He had long yearned to own his own BB-gun, the kind advertised on the backs of comic books. After he finally got a handsome Red Ryder Sharpshooter, which he kept in the downstairs closet, he was rarely seen without it, whether after coming home from school or on weekend excursions far a field.

Lucille and Philip, unlike their neighbors the O'Rileys, were not regular churchgoers, although they weekly ferried their kids to Bible school. Sunday mornings were for taking it easy and attending to weekend chores. For the kids, after Bible school, it was always a free day. It was not abnormal for Eddy to grab his BB-gun and take off for the park with a few buddies. On the Sunday morning after the dance, he had picked up his gun, and bounded through the front door with a very quick goodbye lest he be interrogated endlessly about his intentions. Linking up with a 14-year-old friend, he took to an unpaved lane near Northwestern High. It was the same route his big sister walked every day to school, through the park.

Eddy's tendency to gallivant around Lewisdale Elementary and Northwestern High on weekends was usually frowned upon by his parents, not to mention the local authorities, especially since someone had taken to shooting out school windows. No one had ever pointed a finger directly at the boy, but many neighbors had their suspicions. Neighborhood rumors and parental disapproval notwithstanding, however, the two youths again headed for the school for a little bottle "plinking" behind the ball field. Shooting at bottles, squirrels, or anything that moved in the woods was all the same to Eddy. They were fun.

This day would be different.

As the two boys neared the school, they saw a car approach. Eddy immediately hid the BB-gun behind him, but it was already too late. They had been spotted. There was a man inside and, as the car approached, the boys quickly discerned him to be pointing what appeared to be an old western style six-shooter at them. A cop? They froze like a pair of deer in the headlights. The man stopped, lowered the gun, got out, and approached them. Fear soon gave way to curiosity as the stranger, who they could now see was definitely not a cop, began laughing. He told them that he had noticed Eddy's BB-gun and therefore had assumed the boys might be curious about real guns. The boys loosened up a bit, for the stranger, who had a curious accent, seemed genuinely interested in nothing more than discussing weapons. A friendly five-minute conversation ensued, during which the man showed them two real guns, a six-shooter, and another weapon, an old caplock pistol, and proudly discussed their history.

"Have you ever shot anybody?" Eddy asked.

The man's face erupted in a wide grin, and then a laugh, this time more of a deep, ominous cackle.

"If I told you I had," he replied, "then they'd have to arrest and hang me, wouldn't they? Yust like in them westerns. Guess I yust can't answer that then, can I?"

Then, with another laugh, he was off.

When Eddy returned home, he said nothing of the incident to his parents. He later thought he should have.

Building was going on everywhere. The stretch along University Lane leading to the University of Maryland campus, which intersected with the beginning of West Park Drive, had in recent years witnessed a construction boom. In the previous decade, post-war expansion from metropolitan Washington had grown almost exponentially by the week into the rapidly disappearing countryside. Between 1900 and 1950, the government reported, the county had increased in population by an astonishing 548 percent, with most of the growth after World War II, and the greatest concentration along the northern border of the Maryland-D.C. line. New communities, shopping centers, roads and the very bearers of the most amiable levels of the new civilization — the emerging post-war American middle class — seemed to be swarming locust-like with unvarnished zeal into the new suburbs along the University Lane corridor.

Not a few miles to the west of the university was the enormous Langley Park complex. Even directly across the highway from Lane Manor bulldozers moved the virgin earth to make way for new roads and retail shopping — all within convenient access to new housing developments in the once pristine Maryland tobacco lands and countryside.

Tall, lean, soft-spoken, and movie-star handsome, Henry Chauvanne had been dubbed by his brothers "The Duke of Marlboro" after the namesake of the county seat of Upper Marlboro, where, with composed grace, albeit laced with sublime braggadocio and testosterone, he "presided over" the most attractive ladies of Southern Maryland. Yet, like many young men shipping out for the European Theater in World War II, Henry, 20, had married his sweetheart, Mary "Bootsy" Clagett, 19, a local tobacco farmer's beautiful young daughter. The one thing they had in common was Abraham Lincoln. Bootsy was a descendant of Mary Surratt, who had been executed as one of the Lincoln assassination conspirators. Dr. Samuel Mudd, son of the physician of the same name who had treated the broken leg of John Wilkes Booth, Lincoln's assassin, had delivered several Chauvanne boys, including Henry, at birth.

Henry, a heavy equipment operator working on a construction project on University Lane, only a mile away from his elder brother Philip's house, was nearing the end of another long workday. As with most of the six surviving Chauvanne brothers, Henry had dropped out of school during the Depression to help support the family. He had taken up the construction trade as a teenager. At the urging of his eldest brother, Tommy, at that time a steam-shovel man, Henry had become an oiler, and then graduated to heavy equipment operator.

Building and heavy construction machines, bulldozers, steam shovels, and the like, had been his life.

Not long after Pearl Harbor he had been drafted into the Army Engineers, and saw constant combat, from Omaha Beach to the surrender of Germany. A crack shot since childhood, he could drop a moving rabbit at a hundred yards with a .22-caliber rifle fired from the hip. The skill served him well throughout the war. In Europe, he had witnessed every horror of ground combat possible. As one of the first American grunts to enter Buchenwald, it had been the most searing, unsettling episode of his life, and one that left scars that would remain with him until his dying day.

Upon his return from the war, Henry fathered a pair of wonderfully blonde identical twins named Dorothy and Debby. His wife Bootsy liked to remind him thereafter, with no little sarcasm, that twins ran in his family. Indeed, four of his own siblings had also been twins, including his brother Philip and sister Marissa, and brothers Tommy and Roderick. He often told the youngest of his brothers, Fred, that twins had been why there were no more children in his own brood. Bootsy simply didn't want to chance another set.

The late afternoon of Tuesday, June 14, was unusually hot and dry. The sun was setting and shadows were spreading across the construction site as Henry concluded his work for the day, and climbed down from his machine. While standing at the water-cooler, wiping the dust from his face, he happened to glance across University Lane toward Northwest Branch Park. He did a mild double take as he saw a figure, six foot or so tall, armed with a rifle and wearing a sheath knife on his belt, walking into the wooded park. Wrapped diagonally across the figure's chest was a bandolier of bullets — or was it only a rolled blanket? He couldn't tell from this distance and quickly dismissed it from his mind. Men with guns were of little interest to him now. He had seen too many who had tried to kill him on the battlefield, and he certainly wasn't interested in local yokels showing off. Probably just a hunter, he thought as he punched out for the day.

The telephone rang in the Chauvanne house and, as usual, it was Ellen's chum Mikie. The two girls had been known to tie up the phone for hours on end with what seemed to their parents' mindless chatter. As it was 9:30 p.m., and close to bedtime, the conversation was unusually abridged thanks to Lucille's raised right eyebrow, which bespoke volumes to her daughter. The two girls were planning a barbecue picnic with a few friends in the park after Ellen returned from Northwestern the next morning to pick up her report card on the last day of school, which was to be only an hour long. Details had yet to be worked out. Mikie, already out for the summer, eagerly suggested that she accompany Ellen to school. They could discuss the barbecue on the way. Mikie had always wanted to see what a real public high school looked like on the inside. She had wanted to go to Northwestern rather than Regina, because that's where her best friend went, but her parents wouldn't hear of it.

Mikie also wanted to go with Ellen tomorrow for another reason. Though she didn't tell her friend, that's where she knew her former boyfriend Sammy Stokes might be tomorrow. She hadn't seen or talked to him for several weeks, and then only against her father's direct orders. John had strictly forbidden their budding relationship on the grounds that the boy was after only one thing. Sammy, who was of no particular religion, hadn't been at all like most of the Catholic boys she had met, and this was probably another reason why her father hadn't liked him. The fact that he was four years older than she, had his own car, had just graduated from high school, and had a less than enviable reputation as a troublemaker had not helped matters, but she could still hope. Going along with Ellen might give her another opportunity.

They agreed to take off about 8:00 a.m., unless something came up, and would be back in an hour or so to put things together for the picnic. Rudy Slattery, Carlin Bulmer and Candice Miller, kids from the teen club, were coming by later to help set things up. Mikie hoped Sammy might even join them.

Soon afterwards, Ellen and her little sister Terry lay in their twin beds. For both the children, the next day would signal not only the last day of school for Ellen, but also the beginning of the summer vacation, a savory prospect. For seven-year-old Terry, though, it had produced one irritating aspect about which she was growing increasingly angry. A week earlier, Ellen had promised to take her to see her high school on the last day, and Terry had been overjoyed by the idea of at last visiting her big sister's dominion. For a moment it had been uplifting, like a birthday balloon let go. Her mother, though, for some mysterious reason, had outright forbidden it.

"I still want to go with you," cried the little girl.

"I'll take you there," consoled Ellen, "just not tomorrow. Maybe in the fall."

"Promise!" Terry begged.

"Yes, I promise. In the meantime how's about I tell you a story?"

Ellen told her sister the tale about Br'er Rabbit and the briar patch, and then the two children fell asleep together for the last time in their lives.

Chapter 2

THE REPEATING KIND

The headlines in the *Washington Post* and *Times Herald* on the morning of June 15, 1955 were disconcerting, but no more so than usual. A mock bomber raid on the nation, simulating a surprise Soviet attack, had revealed the United States to be terribly unprepared for nuclear war. President Eisenhower and dour-looking Secretary of State John Foster Dulles were meeting with Indian Prime Minister V. K. Krishna Menon on how to resolve an impasse with Communist China over Formosa and the offshore islands of the Chinese mainland.

Closer to home, the AFL-CIO, recently joined together, had called for a strike by construction workers at select building sites in the Washington area to test its muscle. Philip Chauvanne, temporarily unemployed, had already been told down at the union hall that he would have to wait for a notice from his steward before he could look for work. Today was to be the first day of the strike, predicted to be long and difficult, and he worried how he was going to make the next house note. It had been, ironically, one year earlier to the day that the Chauvannes had moved to Lane Manor.

Lucille Chauvanne had little time to pay heed to the news, however, as she bulldogged her kids from bed and readied them for the day, even as Philip lazed over his coffee and the newspapers. For Ellen, it was a special day: the last day of school. She was delighted classes were finished, but not particularly happy about how much of the year had passed. She had attended junior high school at nearby Bladensburg, before transferring to Northwestern, and often wished she were still there. Not much she could do about it, she had resolved to tough it out. Now the final semester was finally over and summer beckoned.

The last day of school required something extra, so she selected one of her favorite dresses and blouses — an orchid-colored affair that accented her light skin. She put on just enough of her mother's makeup to cover the few remaining teenage pimples that once blanketed her face in vast numbers. She hated her recent yearbook photo because the terrible, grainy black and white seemed to accentuate her blemishes, though now they were, thank goodness, all but gone. She applied a smidge of lipstick, took a sideways glance in the mirror at her figure, all 5'8" of it and a duplicate of her mother's, and smiled. She was not a fastidious girl, but she did try to look her best in the presence of friends and especially the boys who were increasingly drawn to her.

Boys. Some, such as her little brother Eddy, seemed the bane of her existence. She loved her brother, but he could be pugnacious and she was always coming to the defense of her little sister Terry, whom he picked on relentlessly. That was the natural order of siblings. Yet, other boys, such as Samuel Raymond Stokes, an 18-year-old Northwestern graduate who lived a few blocks away over in Lewisdale, were something else. Samuel, who preferred to be called "Sammy," had taken a shine to Ellen, dated her on several occasions, and once asked her to go steady, but she had demurred. They had fought, made up, fought some more, and from time to time the romance heated up, only to fizzle again. Neither Philip nor Lucille cared for the boy, whom they characterized as a ruffian. He had a bad reputation in the neighborhood, as Ellen discovered. The last go-round she had dumped him and started dating Jimmy Combs, from Bible school. Sammy, though, kept turning up like a rusty nail and even sent her a nasty letter warning her not to see the other boy again. Recently, Sammy had taken to secretly seeing Mikie against her father's orders. Ellen had repeatedly counseled the younger girl to avoid him.

Ellen wasn't sure about either Sammy or Jimmy, but she consoled herself that there were plenty of other boys better than either. Some were content to merely worship her from afar. She liked that. At the beginning of the school year, she had been going with Harmon Simons, whom she had met while in junior high at Bladensburg. The experience hadn't been pleasant, and she had even briefly considered running away to New York as a dramatic gesture. Yet, as she had matured nicely — and rapidly — the retinue of young peacocks who developed an interest in her had grown almost geometrically by the month. On the brink of womanhood, she was unquestionably attractive and growing more so by the hour, a fact not lost on her siblings or her parents. Not surprisingly, like most fathers, Philip feared her maturity, along with the loss of his little girl's innocence. With a heavy heart, he had agreed to teach Ellen to drive, and she promptly secured her learner's permit. She had already begun to master the mysteries of the family's beat-up old black De Soto. Wheels were one thing, but Philip worried about the backseat. He knew what boys like Stokes really wanted, but he also resigned himself to the fact that he couldn't protect either of his daughters forever.

Then, there were some boys Ellen simply couldn't stand. A few of her suitors, such as skinny Teddy Dubinski from over in Hyattsville, had on occasion grown obnoxious, but she could usually handle them. Teddy, however, one of four sons of Alexander and Helena Dubinski, Polish immigrants, was an ungainly tall punk with greasy, slicked back hair, and had become an increasing nuisance. Last Saturday, at the teen club dance, when Teddy began flirting with both Ellen and Mikie, and then asked Ellen out, right in front of Jimmy, she had verbally crushed him like the worm he was. This was a humiliation tactic she had learned from her mother and it had given her substantial leverage whenever it came to unwelcome overtures. Dubinski hadn't liked it, of course, but the pimple-faced wimp — and she had called him that to his face in front of a crowd — had, as usual, angrily retreated into his shell, and that was that.

Now summer was actually here, with other potential suitors around. Who could tell what great things the future held in store?

When Ellen bounded down the stairs and into the kitchen barefooted, carrying her bobby sox and black-and-white saddle shoes in one hand, her hair was still up in curlers. Terry was already sitting on the speckled linoleum floor next to the cupboard, a few feet from the door leading to the basement, with her Raggedy Ann, hoping upon hope that her sister had forgotten last night and would still be taking her to Northwestern regardless of her mother's edict. Philip sat at the breakfast table, his nose buried in the newspaper.

"Morning Pop," chirped Ellen even as she pulled on her bobby sox, rolled them down to her ankles in the current fashion, slipped into her saddle shoes, and then began removing her curlers.

Without moving his head from behind the newspaper wall, he grunted in recognition.

"When are we going?" asked Terry expectantly.

"I'm sorry, doll," replied her sister. "I know I told you that you could go with me, but like mom said, not this morning. Next time, I promise."

"But why?" moaned the child.

"Listen, honey, I'll only be gone an hour. When I get back from school, I'll make pancakes for you. I promise."

Grudgingly, Terry acquiesced, albeit with a pout that seemed glued to her face.

A bit before 8:00 a.m., Ellen checked her wallet to make sure that her two dollars earned babysitting were still there, and then inspected the contents of her little white purse for her asthma pills. She never left without them, for her asthma attacks, although less frequent as she grew older, could still be brutal. Every night for the last fifteen years, the Vicks® Vaporizer had provided an ever-present stench in her bedroom. In one such attack when she was fourteen, she had almost died, and stayed in the hospital for two solid weeks. That was more than two years ago, and she had borne her condition stoically. "Just do it," had been her response to meeting any problem, and her little sister called her a "just-do-it person." Then she left the house for the last time.

Terry was sitting on the front stoop, pulling ticks off Tweedle Dee, one of her twin pet spaniels, and moping because she couldn't go to see the big kids' school. What made it even worse was that Ellen's companion would be her acolyte and closest friend Mikie, who seemed to be taking up more of her big sister's time of late and leaving her with less. Terry felt she should have been accompanying her big sister, not that girl from down the street. Mikie had shown up wearing a pretty pink skirt and matching jacket that made the occasion even more irritating for Terry. The girl in pink was just too perfect. She looked perhaps three years older than she really was, and could have fooled most of Ellen's classmates about her age, or at least thought she could.

As she watched, the two teenagers leaped down the steps in a most unladylike fashion. Still wearing her best Shirley Temple pout but to no avail, Terry remained ensconced on the lowest step of the three-step front stoop. The sulk had always worked in the past, but not this time. The performance, however, did not go entirely unnoticed by Ellen, who stopped, turned, and promised again in her most sincere voice to make the little girl some pancakes as soon as she returned home. The tactic once again temporarily assuaged Terry. Then, with little more than a "see-ya," the two teenagers were off.

Five houses down the street, Mikie's little sister Elaine also sat on her front stoop watching. After the happy teenagers bounded across West Park Drive, both Elaine and Terry saw them disappear arm-in-arm along the path leading into the shady park. Their well-traveled route, used by all the kids on the west side of the park who walked to Northwestern, would take them through a picnic grove to a small footbridge and a short-cut across the Northwestern Branch to the University Hills neighborhood, and then on to the high school grounds on Adelphi Road.

It would be the last time either Terry or Elaine would see their big sisters alive.

Deloris Pfeizer's daily schedule had been the same ever since she and her husband Bruno had moved in at 625 Twenty-Fifth Avenue, a block over from the Chauvannes. Bruno was a bookbinder who worked for the Dabney Printing Company in nearby Hyattsville. Deloris made breakfast for him, and he left for work promptly every morning at 7:30 a.m. As soon as he left, she got her two children, Michael, 3, and Lyn, 2, out of bed at exactly 7:40 and between 7:45 and 8:00 a.m. she fed the children and cleared the table; then, for the next quarter hour, she washed the dishes. It was a Teutonic morning ritual that never varied.

At 8:15 a.m., as usual, Deloris was finishing the breakfast dishes. The morning was pleasant, but warm in the house, and she opened both windows in the kitchen to let in the breeze from the nearby park. Michael was playing in the next room, producing the normal noisy tumult not uncommon to three-year-olds.

Suddenly, Deloris heard it, sharp and clear. Someone was firing a cap gun, "like one of the repeating kind," in rapid succession. The sound was distinctive and could be plainly heard over the racket in the next room. Kids in the park. She dismissed it, and automatically returned to her work.

Down the street, a laundry truck driver standing on University Lane had also heard what initially sounded to him like a burst of gunfire, followed by a few moments of silence, and then another burst of shots. Though they seemed to be coming from the park, he assumed they must be from a car backfiring. Without another thought, he returned to his business.

Candice Miller and Anita Slattery were neighbors who lived around the corner from each other, and were on their way for the last day of school at Northwestern High when they saw Sammy Stokes at the little footbridge in the park.

"Hey, Sammy!" said Anita. "What're you hanging around here for at this time of the morning. You've already graduated. Gosh, if I were off, I'd be sleeping right now."

"I'm waitin' for Ellen," he replied nervously.

He looked more than a little edgy. Both of the girls knew of the recent on-again-off-again romance between Ellen and Sammy, and from what they had heard, it was strictly off now, as was his dalliance with Ellen's best friend Mikie. Candice liked Sammy, and she wouldn't have minded dating him herself if it weren't for Ellen, though her own brother was one of Sammy's best pals. Besides he had his own car, a blue 1946 Packard sedan. He loved blue, wore it all the time, and his clothes and car matched his eyes, which Candice thought were beautiful. With his shirt collar turned up at the back, he reminded her of James Dean, although he certainly wasn't nearly as good looking. Perhaps it was something in his self-confident swagger? She couldn't put her finger on it.

"Why you waitin' here?" asked Candice, although as one of Ellen and Mikie's friends she already knew.

"This is the way she always walks to school," he said. "Have you seen her?"

"No. She's probably already left and is at school right now. She's always early."

"I guess you're right," he replied.

Anita looked at her wristwatch. It was 8:20 and they had only ten minutes to get to school, clean out the detritus of the last semester from their lockers, report to homeroom, then the only class of the day, to pick up their report cards and call it a year. "Hey, Sammy," she said demurely. "Since Ellen's already gone, how about a lift to school."

He grimaced, and then thought better of it. "Sure. No problemo. My wheels are parked up on Stanford."

Five minutes later, they were at the school.

At the Northwestern High School parking lot, Sammy Stokes stood beside his car smoking and talking for nearly half an hour to younger former classmates coming to pick up their grades. He had already graduated a few days earlier, and it was in many ways a final goodbye, but it was also a way of securing the last bit of esteem that his mere seniority would buy.

The younger boys admired Sammy for his hot car, his age, seniority, and coolness. After all, how many guys could boast having two good-looking girlfriends at the same time?

"What brings you back to this dump?" said one of his friends standing around him as if he were holding court. Smoking cigarettes on school grounds was strictly against the rules for students, but Sammy wasn't a student anymore, and he reveled in indulging in the once-forbidden Lucky Strike while playing the big man.

Leaning nonchalantly against his car while taking a drag, he replied, "I'm waiting for Ellen and Mikie. They'll be coming out soon." He seemed skittish.

At 9:00 a.m., the school bell sounded its familiar ring, and the hallways of Northwestern High, a new school only three years old and anything but a "dump," were suddenly crowded with shouting and laughing students en route from the only class of the day, where they received their report cards. Then, on schedule, a veritable deluge of youth spilled from the school's three main exits — but no Ellen or Mikie. One of Sammy's former classmates observed that the rail thin boy dressed in blue was still standing by his car all alone when the final school bell sounded.

"You still here," said a friend as he scurried by.

"Not for long," replied Sammy. In an instant he had started the car and peeled out of the parking lot. A few minutes later he had returned to the deathly silent park, but not a living soul was there. Not a sound. He headed back to the school again, where he hung about for another hour talking to a few friends still lingering. He smoked more cigarettes in the parking lot. Suddenly, he was overcome with a sense of being alone even while surrounded by others. His youth was over, but he did not yet know it. More importantly, innocence had fled, and that he was well aware of.

Henry Chauvanne got down from his big orange HD-2 Caterpillar tractor for a morning break about 10:30 a.m. It was a bright, sun-swept day and already unseasonably warm. The sweat marks on his dusty khaki shirt already enveloped a vast area around the armpits, and the cuff of his hat brim with the big Caterpillar logo was stained with perspiration as well. Some distance away, in the shade beneath the only copse of trees left on the job, three black laborers had gathered around one of two water-coolers. One cooler was for the whites and, separated by a distance of about 150 feet, the other for the "coloreds." He passed them on the way to the white man's cooler with little more than a grunt of recognition, paying little heed to their crude jokes and banter. Like many Marylanders who had been raised amidst the tobacco culture of the Old South, he had little use for "colored folk" except as laborers, and considered himself in every way superior to them. He was running the heavy equipment, making the big bucks, and they were down in the hole with picks and shovels. And that was the way it should be. After filling a pointy-bottomed Dixie cup with ice water he sat for a few minutes in the shade of an ancient oak, not far from the white man's cooler, and leaned against its rough base smoking a Pall Mall.

The heat, as sultry as in any hothouse, was reflecting off the pavement of University Lane and the grassless, hard-packed ground of the construction site. Invisible waves were rising in the air, making every object in the distance shimmer. It was the stuff of mirages, of the hallucinations heat-stroke victims often experience after collapsing. Henry was intrigued by the distortion, but more so by the image of the person who appeared to be emerging from the ripples. An apparition, he thought. No. A man with a gun. His mind flashed back eleven years to the Cotien Peninsula in France when a German soldier emerged from the July heat with a fixed bayonet on his rifle and death for the enemy of the Fatherland in his heart. Henry had put a clean hole through his head without another thought — until now.

The figure crossing University Lane and walking directly toward the three black men lounging about the water cooler was lanky and disheveled. He was a young white man, between 5'10" and 6' tall, with a wild look about him. Henry guessed he probably weighed about 160 pounds, although, with the sun directly behind the stranger, it was impossible to make out any singular features. From a distance, his complexion seemed weather-beaten, his dark hair rather bushy in front but slicked back on the sides, all of which only added to an untamed appearance. He carried a rifle in one hand and, like a hunter, wore a sheath knife on one side of a web belt and an Army canteen on the other. Either a blanket roll or a bandolier, Henry couldn't tell which from so far away, was draped around his lean body, clad in a blue shirt and dark khaki pants. In some ways, his appearance was not unlike the once notorious Mexican bandit Pancho Villa his oldest brother Tommy had chased while serving under Pershing. Henry instantly recognized him from the day before.

The stranger appeared courteous and asked the laborers for permission to drink water from the cooler. "Nigger lover," thought Henry, who would never ask permission from a black man for anything, much less drink from his cooler.

"Man, you look like the damned devil done beat up on you," said one of the laborers. "You been hunting?"

"Naw," replied the stranger. "I jest been over in the picnic grove in the park. Pretty place, you know. And a heck of a lot cooler there than here!"

Henry tried not to pay much attention since the man—or perhaps it was a tall teenager—was talking directly to the laborers and not him; he took offense, but said nothing. When the laborers and the stranger moved out of earshot, he didn't budge. Then, a few minutes later, Pancho Villa's double walked off to the west, along University Lane.

Despite his feigned disinterest, Henry could not long resist asking the three blacks what the man with the gun had said.

The laborers told him the stranger hadn't said much, but did mention something about either once being or knowing a patient in an armed services mental hospital. This was something Henry could relate to. While he had been fighting in Europe, his own father, Philip Chauvanne, Sr., a Spanish American War veteran, had died in 1944 in a miserable VA facility at Perry Point, Maryland, near the head of Chesapeake Bay. The family had kept his father's death a secret from him lest it bring more worry to a man already dodging bullets to stay alive, but Henry had known in his heart, for in their letters from home there was never a mention of "Pop." It didn't help when he returned home only to learn that his father had "lost his senses" and died of "dementia."

He watched as the stranger disappeared down University Lane and felt a twinge of empathy. Though not for long.

By 10:40 a.m. James Forman, a bulldozer operator from Laurel, Maryland, had been working on the construction job across University Lane, opposite Northwest Branch Park, for less than three hours. He counted himself lucky, first, that he had a job, and second, that he wasn't among the commuters who came this way since he started work well ahead of the morning rush hour. He chuckled, knowing his work was what was causing many of the delays in the first place. Traffic dominated the scene. There was nothing else, until he

noticed two very tall teenage boys walking along the highway near the north end of the park. One was carrying a rifle. Strange, he thought. What would two boys be doing at this time of the morning walking along this road with a rifle? Then, as they disappeared, he shook his head, returned to his work and dismissed the whole thing.

"Kids!"

Twelve-year-old Shelly Huffington lived on Wells Boulevard, on the east side of Northwest Branch from the Chauvanne home, and regularly cut across the park to visit the spanking new Adelphi Shopping Center on University Lane. Accompanied by her neighbor's dog, a little mongrelized black-and-white English Spaniel named Midge, she had gone to the shopping center early, and decided to return through the park. About 10:45 a.m., as usual, she crossed the rustic footbridge, passed a grove of trees, and was heading west toward West Park Drive with Midge padding along some distance behind her. Suddenly the dog began barking furiously.

"Here, Midge," she called repeatedly, but the dog continued his staccato yelping. A summons.

"What now," she fumed, and turned to trace the sounds of barking. Then, partially hidden in a briar thicket, the dog yapping furiously fifty yards from the footbridge, she discovered the bloody body of a girl in an orchid dress.

The horror was immediate and overwhelming. Little Shelly Huffington, who had never seen a real dead person before, rushed home to tell her mother, Mrs. Thomas A. Huffington.

"Mommy," shouted the girl as she slammed the screen door behind her, "there's a dead girl in the park."

"Hold on, now Honey. There isn't any dead person in the park. You must be imagining things. You know, you've been watching too many westerns on TV lately, too much of that Gunsmoke."

"No, mommy. It's true. Midge found her by the picnic grove. I'm not making it up. I swear, I swear."

"All right, but you had better not be lying."

Within minutes, led by her daughter, she too had crossed the bridge and entered into the shady grove. Shelly had not been imagining anything and her mother discovered the body lying alongside some logs just as the girl had described it. The first thought that crossed her mind was that the body was a dummy or mannequin.

"It didn't look real," she later said. "I went right up to it. Then I knew for sure. I thought maybe the girl had fallen from a tree." It was immediately apparent, though, that her first impressions were wrong. The once pretty orchid skirt was in disarray and the dead girl's face and body were covered with blood. There was a small hole right between her eyes. Almost fainting, Mrs. Huffington grabbed her daughter's hand and stumbled home to call the Prince George's County Police. The call was logged in at 11:20 a.m. and a response was issued immediately. Barely forty-five minutes had elapsed from the time Midge had found the body.

The new Langley Park apartment project was less than two miles west of Lane Manor and Northwest Branch Park. The majority of residents there were mostly recent arrivals because the apartments themselves were relatively new, some buildings still undergoing the contractor's finishing touches. Construction men and rough-looking laborers were a common presence in many areas of the development. Thus, just before 11:00 a.m., as she stood on a street corner, one resident spied a weather-beaten-looking stranger who passed by her, and entered the basement laundry room of an apartment building near Merrimac Street. She thought little of it. She had seen him in the neighborhood a week earlier, not far from Northwest Branch Park: perhaps a local laborer working on one of the many building projects in the area. Yet, when he emerged from the basement a few minutes later, walked past the Langley Park Elementary School and then disappeared into a nearby grove of trees, she took note. He appeared quiet and incredibly weary, as if he bore the weight of the world on his shoulders — as well as a rifle and...could it be...a bandolier of bullets. She judged his height to be about six feet, about the same as her own son, and his waist, about 32-inches, which approximated her husband's. The encounter did not soon fade from her mind. Or so she would later state.

Rudy Slattery, Anita's brother, and Carlin Bulmer, both members of the teen club, arrived at the Chauvanne house promptly at 11:15 a.m., as they were to join Ellen and Mikie for the picnic planned for that afternoon. Both Rudy and Carlin lived over on Chapman Road, a few blocks from the park, and both were a little pissed to discover, when Lucille answered the door, that her daughter hadn't returned home. The two girls were way behind schedule.

"The picnic is at noon," whined one of the boys, "and everybody's supposed to bring something. Ellen was supposed to have put it all together."

"Maybe the teacher kept her for a little while," Lucille frowned. "You know she's been out a lot because of her asthma. Her marks weren't so good."

The walk through the park from the Chauvanne house took no more than five minutes, and the girls had been gone for more than three hours. Lucille, who had been busy washing and hanging slipcovers, was not so much angry as concerned. Not like her daughter to be late. She decided to send Philip out to find the girls. He immediately drove over to Northwestern High, taking one of the boys along, and sent him into the school. The boy spoke with Miss Amelia Clench, Ellen's homeroom teacher, who told him that the girl hadn't appeared all morning. The boy hurried down the school stairs to inform Philip.

"Something must have happened to change Ellen's plans," said Philip while driving back to the house. "She said she wouldn't be gone more than an hour." Nevertheless, he was of the opinion that Ellen and Mikie had simply hopped a bus to D.C., which they had done quite often, to go shopping and spend Ellen's baby-sitting money. Maybe she just didn't want to have to show her lousy report card to her parents and was putting off picking it up until the last possible moment. She was a big girl and could look out for herself, and he wasn't the least bit concerned about her safety or whereabouts. Lucille was, and sent out another expedition.

"Would you kids see if you can find Ellen and Mikie?" she asked the two boys.

They immediately consented.

Almost as soon as they reached the corner of West Park Drive, however, they encountered Sammy Stokes, who had just driven up after failing in his own "search" for the two girls. Joining forces with the two boys, Stokes set off once again, this time with more than a hint of panic in his demeanor.

Within minutes after Sammy's well-polished Packard pulled away from the curb, a brown-and-gold Prince George's County Police cruiser arrived at the edge of the park.

Privates R. B. Musk and Wilhelm Goetz were unprepared for the grisly site they would encounter. Guided by Mrs. Huffington, who had been awaiting their arrival at the park entrance, the two officers walked to the spot the dispatcher reported.

About eighty feet along a dirt path, at the edge of a cleared grove with picnic tables, they found what they had been seeking: the body of a pretty, young girl lying on her back, with her right side slightly raised, at the perimeter of a briar patch and beside a log. A thin, white arm was flung out like a broken rag doll. Her clothes were pulled up over the upper body, suggesting that she may have been dragged over the ground by her feet. Twigs and small branches had been thrown across her, almost as if in a hasty effort at camouflaging the bloody head from the world. Musk at once called the Homicide Unit, and within minutes, shortly after noon, Detective Sergeants James T. Barnwell and Thomas A. Bearson arrived at the crime scene. Barnwell quickly began photographing the dead girl's body, a routine move in all probable homicide investigations. Then, something else caught his eye.

Handing the camera to his chubby colleague, Barnwell went to check a peculiarly matted grassy spot nearby. As he walked slowly along a faint trail deeper into the woods, he noticed a pair of feet projecting directly in his path, exactly thirty-two feet from the body he had just been photographing.

The second body, another once beautiful young girl, was lying on its back. Her pink skirt and jacket was in disarray as if she, too, had been dragged across the ground. Blood covered the girl's face and legs, and twigs had also been partially arrayed across her body as if in a hurried attempt at concealment. The crushed grass, blood smears, and marks on the earth, near the dirt road into the park and a hundred and fifty feet across the grove from the bodies, reinforced the initial assumption that one or both victims had been dragged to their current positions.

Sergeant Barnwell immediately notified headquarters. Chief Gregory Panadapoulis, head of the Prince George's County Police Department, and his second, Captain Julian Patrick Edwards, were quickly underway. In the meantime, a M-NCPPC park police private named Daily appeared on the scene while conducting his regular rounds and was immediately put to work roping off the whole area with red plastic tape. By the time Panadapoulis arrived, the officers at the crime scene had determined that the girl beside the log was the older of the two girls. Soon Prince George's County Medical Examiner Dr. Robert R. Macubbin arrived and made his initial assessment. Owing to the enormous amount of blood covering both bodies, and the many modest puncture wounds in each, especially the girl by the log, he first believed the victims might have been repeatedly stabbed, perhaps by an ice pick. What was unique, however, was that in most sharp instrument assaults, the entry wounds were concentrated. In this case, the punctures in the body of the girl in the orchid dress were spread all over from head to calf, with a concentration of fatal entries in the left chest and one place in the head.

Closer examination, however, suggested that they had been shot, probably by a very small-bore weapon, which caused equally small entry wounds. Laboratory analysis would soon provide the specifics. From the condition of their bodies, it was clear that the victims had been dead less than three hours. Dr. Macubbin ventured a guess of 10:00 a.m. as the probable time of death. That meant the killer could well still be in the immediate vicinity.

As the police went about their preliminary work at the crime scene, a small crowd of boys began to gather around the newly roped off area. Charlie Bricker, a friend of Eddy's, picked up a small blue piece of cloth before the police chased him away.

Seven-year-old Terry Chauvanne was still sitting on her front stoop patiently awaiting the return of her big sister from school. Her best friend, Betty Steiner, who lived over on the corner of West Park and Chapman, had joined her in her vigil. They watched with curiosity as an unusual number of police cars arrived and parked near the trail entrance. Terry had never seen a police cruiser up-close before and it excited her to watch them arrive, with their loud sirens blaring and the lights on their roofs spinning. It was almost like a circus. Then two boys, whom she immediately recognized, came up and told her: "There's a girl in the park who's unconscious. It looks like your sister . . ."

In an instant Terry rushed through the front door and told her father. Philip Chauvanne ran to the stoop, viewed the commotion down the street, and then charged towards his car. Within a matter of seconds he had driven the short distance to the trail entrance, with Terry and Betty running breathlessly behind. For them, it all seemed like a game.

When Philip stopped the car, without turning off the ignition, he got out and rushed straight ahead, bypassing the police, raced across the rustic bridge, and then, passing the baseball diamond, the basketball backboard, the stone fireplaces and picnic tables, 1,500 feet down the bank of the creek. He could feel his heart pounding, beating in his ears, as he sprinted alongside the little waterway. In his panic he had somehow failed to see the knot of policemen assembled close to his house, in the grove festooned with picnic tables and a brick fireplace, and ran back again. Then he found them, and charged directly into their brown clustered assemblage, where an officer weakly wrestled to stop him.

"My daughter Ellen... Where is she? Is she all right?"

"Who are you, sir?" asked one of the officers.

"My name's Philip Chauvanne. Where the hell is my daughter?"

"There's a body in the grove over there, sir. Can you take a look at it with us."

Philip rushed into the grove. "My God. It may be my daughter. Please don't let it be," he shouted, almost in tears.

Shaking off the arresting arm he pressed on toward the edge of the briar thicket. There, he suddenly saw the body, with Dr. Macubbin leaning over it. He couldn't bring himself to look at the blood-smeared face. He didn't have to. He saw the billowing orchid skirt, and he knew. He heard someone say that there was a second girl's body in the woods, and he knew instantly it was Mikie.

Lanie O'Riley had been having coffee with a neighbor when she was also drawn to the sidewalk by all the commotion. She had seen the police cruisers, and then Philip rush to his car and drive down the street. She instantly froze white with fear. A neighbor ran over to her as Lanie began crying out, "Something's happened to Mikie! I know something's happened to Mikie!"

In the meantime, Terry had managed to elbow her way through the police. "I see it as a movie," she recalled many years later. "I see it very clearly. I saw Ellen on her back. One leg was bent, crossed on the other leg, and there was blood on her orchid-colored skirt and top. And Pop was standing over her."

Unable to comprehend what she had just seen, she turned instantly, and ran all the way back home with Betty trailing behind. "It was just still a big game, to see who could beat the other back up the dirt road to the house." Her mother was standing alone on the street corner, pensively awaiting the news when her daughter arrived.

"Mommy," gasped Terry. "Ellen's dead!"

His gaunt face was drained of blood, tears streaming down his cheeks, as Philip also wheeled about, and started back up the dirt trail, ignoring his still running car as he ran all the way home. Lucille stood waiting for him on the steps.

"They're both dead," he said in a quivering voice.

Lucille walked blindly into her husband's protecting arms.

"It's Ellen," she said over and over. Murdered not a hundred yards from her home. Turning away from Philip, she took a few steps and collapsed.

Lanie O'Riley ran towards her house screaming, "Mikie's dead! Mikie's dead!" Minutes later, her husband, unaware of the events, arrived home from his shift. His wife looked at him with eyes red from weeping. "Mikie's gone," she said without further explanation. "Mikie's gone."

Near the Chauvanne stoop, little more than three blocks from the crime scene, the two boys who had been waiting for Ellen and Mikie to come home so the picnic could start, stood on the street and cried. When Candice Miller arrived a few minutes later with hot dogs for the barbecue and learned of the killings, she too wept.

Many of the women had gathered their children about them, hen like, all along the borderline formed by the road between their secure homes and the park — a park which only hours before had been welcoming and friendly to the children of the community, but had somehow morphed into an evil forest from a Grimm's Fairy Tale nightmare. Some called their husbands who told them to stay inside and lock their doors. Others shuddered in fear.

Eddy Chauvanne was in a daze. When he finally looked upon the bloodied bodies of his brutally slaughtered sister and her best friend, his mind went blank. Without a word, he walked across the park to the ball field, sat on a bench, and just stared. For the next three hours, he didn't move. He didn't cry. He didn't know how to act or what to do. All he could think of, as the rage grew in him, was "Why?"

When Eddy finally returned home, he set foot in a madhouse filled with detectives and reporters interviewing his mother and father. He vaguely heard something about diaries and letters as he entered the front door and, without stopping or acknowledging anyone, walked across the living room, opened the closet by the stairs, grabbed his BB-gun and started back for the front door. "I'm going to get that bastard," he shouted to no one in particular as his father grabbed him, struggled to stop him, and then hugged him firmly.

"I'm going to get that bastard!"

Sammy Stokes returned to West Park Drive about 12:15 p.m., after an hour of cruising the community with Rudy Slattery and Carlin Bulmer in search of the two missing girls. They were surprised when they arrived on the road and saw a large crowd around the entrance to the dirt trail, not far from Ellen's house.

"What's all the commotion about?" Rudy asked.

"I don't know," Sammy replied, "but I hope to hell it ain't got anything to do with Ellen and Mikie."

"We'd better see what's going on," Carlin suggested.

Sammy pulled his car over to the curb and the three boys hopped out and walked toward the gathering crowd. A number of police officers were assembled off to one side, heatedly discussing something. Sammy recognized Mikie's father among them.

As the boys approached, John O'Riley looked out from the circle of officers and pointed at the three boys. "That's him," he shouted, singling out Sammy with his finger. "The guy in the middle."

In an instant, Sammy Stokes found himself surrounded by a sea of policemen and men in suits, several with guns drawn and pointed directly at him.

"Son," said Sergeant Bearson as he reached for the handcuffs. "You're gonna have to come with us."

Chapter 3

SEVENTEEN TIMES

It was Prince George's County Police Detective Captain Winchester "Winnie" G. Sweitzer's job to direct the roping off and survey of the murder scene, including the footbridge about one hundred and thirty feet from where the bodies were found. After seventeen years on the force, he had learned to ignore the peripheral commotion of a crime scene, which most normally consisted of scores of neighbors, clustering in tight little groups, whispering and watching the unfolding events.

Sweitzer's detectives and officers, a score or more, worked with speed to comb the murder scene, while a growing multitude of local residents pressed along the police barrier line. Just before Chief Panadapoulis's arrival, Ellen's small pearl-handled pocketknife had been discovered under a log. Its blade was closed and no blood evident. Her white pocketbook was found some thirty feet from her body, almost as if thrown there. There was nothing inside but a comb. Her wallet with the two dollars she had earned from baby-sitting was missing. When the police questioned Lucille Chauvanne, she was certain her daughter had it when she left the house. Had the butcher taken it? Could robbery have been a motive? A murder for a measly two dollars! It was an important question, for when murder is linked with another crime, such as drugs, rape or robbery, it was normal procedure for investigators to look at the other crime first to establish motive. Yet, the murder of two teenage girls in the park for a couple of bucks seemed illogical, especially in a county that experienced only three killings a year. And those had usually happened as by-products of stick-ups or domestic quarrels. Double homicides, especially without apparent motives, simply never occurred.

Sweitzer was particularly interested in what seemed like a crude attempt by the killer or killers to hide Ellen and Mikie's bodies, an effort apparently interrupted before it was finished. There were the several small branches and twigs splayed across parts of both bodies, but of equal interest was a heavy picnic table nearby. The table had apparently been dragged fifty feet from its original spot near a fireplace beside the creek, to the site where Ellen's body was found. Had the killer moved it to conceal his handiwork but failed in the attempt? Had he been frightened off before completing the move? A large spot of blood had been found on the dirt path leading to the bridge, across the way from Ellen's corpse. The bloodstained spot beside the path, undoubtedly the point at which the girls had been shot, suggested efforts by the killer or killers to move both bodies. However, the most important question was: what type of weapon had he, the killer, used, and where was it?

Sweitzer caught himself in mid-thought. "Why the hell am I so sure it's a male, or for that matter, just one person?" Perhaps it was incomprehensible to think a woman could be capable of committing such a heinous crime. It was possible, he admitted, just not likely. It would have taken a man, maybe two, to move the corpses, not to mention the heavy picnic table if it had, in fact, been moved to hide the bodies.

"Yeah," he said out loud. "It's got to be a guy."

Sweitzer's men were thorough, but not perfect. It was almost impossible to address a crime scene of such a large scale, for they would have to record every footprint, every piece of evidence, every feature in the park that might help solve the crime, all with the press soon relentlessly breathing down their necks.

Soon after the canvassing began, little Charlie Bricker, who had been watching the investigation, handed an officer a piece of blue cloth, possibly torn from a jacket sleeve, which he had picked up soon after the area had been roped off. He agreed to show the officers where he had found it — a spot one hundred yards away, but equidistant from the two bodies. Was it important? Perhaps. Was Sweitzer embarrassed by the way in which the find had been made? Absolutely. After all, if the press ever learned that some kid had simply walked away with evidence from a crime scene festooned with county cops, it could be downright humiliating. At worst it could cost him his job, and at least prompt a tongue lashing from Panadapoulis! The captain determined that neither the find nor how it was acquired would be leaked to the media, but it would be.

About 1:00 p.m., Sweitzer broke for a quick lunch of a couple of peanut butter and jelly sandwiches his wife had made, and a Tru-Aid orange soda. Before he could remove the wax paper from his first sandwich, a private with a most serious look on his face approached.

"What now, Lindsay?" Sweitzer said in exasperation.

"Sir, I got a call for you from the dispatcher. Looks like more trouble."

"Aw, hell. Be there in a minute."

After rolling off the stump where he had just sat to eat his lunch, he walked quickly to the cruiser, reached in the window, and cupped the radio.

"Sweitzer here."

"Sir," replied the voice on the radio, "we just got a report about five minutes ago that a girl, about seven-years-old, has just been molested off Riggs and Ager Road, not far from East-West Highway. A possible young adult male suspect exposed himself to several children, including the victim, grabbed one, and then tried to disrobe her, but she escaped. She was down near the Northwest Branch playing in the park when it happened. That's barely two miles from you. Request that you send one of your cars to check it out."

"Got an address?"

"The girl's mother is standing beside the intersection of Riggs and Ager now, holding the girl and her two boys. Said she would wait. She's right shook up."

Sweitzer smiled ever so slightly. What were the chances the perpetrator of the murders and the pedophile were one and the same. The coincidence was almost too good to be true.

"Lindsay," he shouted. "Get over to Riggs and Ager and check this out now. Get a description of the suspect from the little girl and start to canvass the area. He's probably still in the neighborhood. We might have a hot one."

As newspapers, television, and radio spread news of the brutal murders across the region, the developing story of the crime and the evolving manhunt was soon gaining a life of its own. Rumors circulated with unvarnished speed throughout Lane Manor, and many more curiosity seekers came down to look. Men from the neighborhood, who carpooled to work, talked soberly together about the crime; a few recalled that in recent weeks they had been disturbed late at night by loud talking and possibly drinking parties in the park. One or two dutifully informed the police.

Some residents, who had been home when the story was first broadcast, locked their doors and windows: the bloody killer, even some Frankenstein, on the loose, might next select a more domestically situated target. Others, alone in their homes, called friends begging them to join them. Someone said the coroner had determined that the girls had been stabbed about 10:00 a.m. Others had heard that a suspect named Sammy Stokes, Mikie's ex-suitor and Ellen's sometimes boyfriend, had been seen in the park about the time of the murder and was taken into custody. Nevertheless, along West Park Drive, three neighbors went from door to door, collecting money for flowers for the families of the two victims.

Among those who had come down to the police barricade early in the day was Deloris Pfeizer, who had heard what she at first believed to be the reports of a cap gun going off in the morning, at about 8:15, and wanted to report her observation to the police. She found the entire area around the murder scene roped off and an ever-growing crowd of onlookers pressing hard against the barricade line. No sooner had she arrived at the scene and attempted to speak to an officer, however, than a police loudspeaker began to blare a repeated message: "Everybody out of the park who has no official business here." Again Pfeizer attempted to speak to the policeman.

"I haven't got time to talk to you now, lady," snarled the officer. "We're busy here. You'll have to leave the park right now." Dutifully, she left.

The data from the murder scene seemed to grow exponentially by the hour, but so had the questions. Dr. Macubbin, careful not to disturb the corpses until the immediate crime site area had been fully documented, observed that Ellen's body had eleven entry wounds, and Mikie's had three, suggesting that the older girl had been the primary target. Then detectives crawling in close formation on their hands and knees discovered two small holes in the earth. They dug up two .22-caliber slugs near the blood spot and not far from the road edge, leading to speculation that the murder weapon was a rifle. The press was soon reporting, much to police displeasure, that a third, misshapen slug, matted with blood and a strand of hair, was found under Ellen's body, indicating that at least one shot was fired into her at relatively close range as she lay dying. They picked up two cartridge casings for a .22-caliber long-rifle about twenty-five feet from the blood spot. It was a start, but shell casings and slugs were as good as useless without a gun to match them.

Fixing the precise time of the murder was also a conundrum. A neighbor of the Chauvannes, walking her dog in the park only minutes before the two victims had started through, had not seen nor heard anything. Ellen's two schoolmates, Anita Slattery and Candice Miller, who had also started out about 8:15 a.m. to get their report cards, some fifteen minutes after the two victims set out, entered the same grove three or four minutes later, but had seen nothing before meeting Stokes. Had the killer, or killers, noticed them and hidden? A road construction crew at the far end of the park had heard neither shots nor screams. And where was the murder weapon? If it had been disposed of, it had yet to be found in the immediate area.

In the late afternoon, volunteer firemen from the Chillum-Adelphi Fire Department arrived to begin damming up the Northwest Branch beside the road to facilitate dragging for the murder weapon. The police brought in a tractor to speed the project along. Farther upstream, 1,500 yards from the crime scene, two boys playing in the park discovered an old automobile seat-cover, a rumpled pillow with a hole in it, and a pair of tiny blue tennis shoes and brought it to the attention of the police. Could the site have possibly been the murderer's campground? The find was initially dismissed as irrelevant to the case, but after some consideration all of the artifacts were sent off to the FBI laboratory in Washington for testing and possible fingerprints. By late afternoon, the finds had assumed increased importance, but by dark, the murder weapon, the most significant piece of evidence, as well as the green wallet, had still not been found. It was obvious to all that the search had just begun. It was now equally obvious that it must be expanded over a much larger area.

A police guard was stationed at the crime scene for the night. Elsewhere, the hunt for any eyewitness to the murder, or anyone who had observed any suspicious activity, moved into high gear. Canvassing of the neighbors began almost as soon as the inch-by-inch search of the crime scene was organized, but in an embarrassingly disorganized manner.

The press was everywhere in the neighborhood, conducting its own interviews with practically anyone encountered. Sweitzer considered them parasites looking for sensational human-interest leads replete with appropriately distressing sob stories. "We all bought here," one mother told a reporter, "because we wanted our children to have the park. Now we're all afraid of it."

The most prized interview targets of all were the victims' aggrieved parents. One reporter for a Washington daily managed to gain access into the O'Riley home, but secured little testimony before being scuttled out. The scene that he witnessed, though, was heartbreaking. John, pale and drawn, was sitting beside his sobbing wife. Young Elaine gently smoothed her mother's hair. Little Catherine Elizabeth, who neighbors were caring for in the next room, would stick her head in the door and ask: "Are you all right, mommy?"

"I hope that whoever did this will realize the heartache he's caused two families," said Mrs. O'Riley, her tearful face puffy and red.

In the Chauvanne household, Terry was sitting in her mother's lap, cradled by arms clasped tight around her, and rocking from side to side. Serious-looking men in uniforms and in suits were standing all around, some with guns. A photographer began taking flash-bulb pictures of mother and child until a short, heavy-set man wearing a fedora and thick black-rimmed glasses stopped him.

"Time to butt out, Casey," said the man.

"Listen Buber, I have a right to be here, you know. The public's got a right to know. Madonna and child here . . ."

"Get the hell out of here before I have to throw you out!" warned the man in the fedora.

Terry didn't like either of the men, and began to cry. She knew something had drastically changed — and she hurt inside.

When Prince George's County Police Chief Gregory Panadapoulis was first informed of the morning's savage murders, like most officers in the force, it touched a spot in a heart not yet fully hardened to criminal acts. He had joined the Prince George's force as Chief only in mid-February, and this was the first case of such major significance he had encountered, and also the first homicide of the year. However, when he learned that one of the victims was the daughter of another officer, albeit a member of the Washington Metropolitan Police, the crime took on new meaning. Murder was one thing. A brutish double murder like the Lane Manor slayings was another. Nothing, though, aroused the blood of a police officer more than the violent killing of a fellow cop or a member of a cop's family, for there was no known fraternity closer than that of the law enforcement community.

Washington Metropolitan Police Chief Harold T. McAdams, John O'Riley's boss, had learned of the murders almost as soon as the bodies were found. In D.C., a wave of indignation had swept through the police department in a half hour. Hundreds of off-duty cops from both D.C. and Maryland volunteered almost instantly to help.

Panadapoulis was well aware the District police enjoyed superior resources. Within hours of Mrs. Huffington's call, he consulted with his deputy, Captain Julian Edwards, about the propriety of requesting McAdams's assistance. The legal ramifications of such a request, especially as they might effect the later prosecution of a suspect, were entirely ignored. Panadapoulis decided that immediate help from the D.C. police was imperative.

Captain Edwards called McAdams, who, out of professional courtesy to John O'Riley, immediately assigned his top detectives to the case. These five men, Chief McAdams pledged, would remain on it as long as necessary. They were to join two nine-man teams of Prince George's detectives, the county's entire plainclothes force, that had also been assigned to the case. Moreover, the D.C. chief offered the Prince George's police full use of the District's identification bureau and sophisticated crime laboratory facilities. Cooperation between the two police departments was vital. Jurisdictional lines between the District of Columbia and neighboring Prince George's County, Maryland, evaporated almost instantly and, in the passion to catch the perpetrator of such a heinous act, the red tape was thrown out.

McAdams initially assigned to the case Lieutenant Terrance Hendricks and Sergeant B. G. Smyth of the Homicide Squad, Detective Sergeants Russell Black and Jonathan Holder of the Robbery Squad, and Sergeant Joe Roma of the First Precinct. Detective Sergeant James D. McManus, a polygraph specialist, was ordered to provide his services as necessary. The assignment of Black and Roma was as much a personal as a professional selection, since Black lived in the same neighborhood as the O'Rileys and Chauvannes, and the latter worked in the same precinct as Mikie's father. Both were John O'Riley's close friends. Hendricks, second in command of the Homicide Squad, and Smythe, a veteran homicide investigator, were considered the two top homicide detectives on the Washington force. "We wanted to send them the best," Chief McAdams later explained to the press regarding his decision, "not only because one of our own men was involved, but also because it is important that a killer on the loose be apprehended as quickly as possible."

Sammy Stokes shivered in the back seat of the police cruiser racing toward the Prince George's County police substation in nearby Hyattsville. He was told that he had been taken into "protective custody" and that John O'Riley identified him as a former boyfriend of Mikie's. O'Riley had never liked the lapsed Protestant dating his daughter, a good Catholic girl. Mikie was a beautiful, bubbly, and outgoing kid who had just started going to parties, and she had entered her teen years with all the panache that usually frightens parents. She looked far older than thirteen, and the lanky Stokes, four years her senior, had been smitten with her the previous summer. When she wore her tight green short-shorts with rolled up cuffs, all the boys took notice.

It was Sammy, though, with his turned-up collar, rolled up short sleeves, and Brylcreamed hair, who boiled John O'Riley's ass. John was well aware of the effects of youthful testosterone. He knew what the boy was after, and told him in no uncertain terms to stay away from his daughter. Sammy was intimidated by John, a police officer, and had backed off. To O'Riley's knowledge, the boy and his daughter had not met since.

Later, when Sammy had returned his attentions to Ellen, Mikie's best friend and mentor, the equation had changed, but it didn't remove the father's disapproval.

Earlier in the afternoon, O'Riley had not been surprised to learn from Candice Miller that she and Anita Slattery had encountered Sammy in the park near where the bodies were found a short time later. If there ever was a prime suspect, O'Riley thought, it had to be Sammy. And John O'Riley wasn't slow in communicating his opinions to the detectives assembled at the murder scene. They had begun looking for Sammy Stokes only a few minutes after O'Riley's arrival. When Sammy suddenly reappeared with two other boys, parked his car near the Chauvanne house shortly before 12:30 p.m., and John quickly pointed him out to Sergeant Bearson, the youth was immediately taken into custody for questioning.

Now, as the police cruiser, siren blaring, rushed purposefully through the suburbs, Sammy Stokes considered exactly just how much he should tell them about himself, Ellen, and Mikie. At the Hyattsville substation, he was interrogated for only a short time, and became completely tongue-tied when he tried to explain his presence in the park near the murder scene. It apparently wasn't good enough, for soon they moved him to the new county police headquarters at Seat Pleasant. Then, about 4:00 p.m., two detectives drove him to the Metropolitan Washington Police Department. He was nervous and, not having eaten since breakfast, complained that he was hungry. To put the prisoner at ease, the officers stopped off at a Chinese restaurant in D.C., where he consumed a hearty meal. The officers joked about what death-row inmates ate for their last supper.

"This will be a first for Chinese food," snorted one of the detectives as Sammy washed a mouthful of chow mein down with a Pepsi.

"Hey," snapped the youth. "That ain't funny."

"No shit!" replied the detective. "Neither was what you did to those two girls. Now shut up, you little fuck, and eat."

Sammy completed the rest of his meal in silence. After dinner, about 6:30 p.m., they left the restaurant and drove to D.C. police headquarters. Sammy was more nervous now than ever in his life, including the first time he got laid. He would be allowed to stew in his anxiety for the next hour and a half. Then, he was told, he would take a lie detector test. The county didn't have a polygraph unit, and the District did.

"What if I refuse?"

"If you don't take the polygraph," suggested the detective, "it might be shown as an admission of guilt in court. You can refuse if you want. That's your decision, but, if I was you, I'd take the test."

The murder scene was documented as if it had been an archaeological survey. Investigators studiously recorded the position of the bodies, the probable trajectory of the bullets, even the blades of crushed, bloodstained grass and dirt. Soon after the field analysis had been completed at the crime scene, the bodies were moved to the county morgue for an official autopsy. Late in the afternoon, county coroners John Macubbin and John A. Bales began their grisly labors. They immediately confirmed that the victims had not been stabbed as initially suspected, but shot to death.

Ellen had been injured by gunfire eleven times, three times just to the left of the middle of her chest, twice in the right thigh, in the abdomen, under the jaw, in the left forearm, in the left calf, in the spine, and at relatively close range in the head, with the bullet exiting between the eyes.

"The bullet found beneath Ellen Chauvanne's body," reported Dr. Macubbin, "shows that she was shot by someone standing over her. The fact that she was shot in the back suggests that she first faced her killer, and then tried to run away. Whoever killed her put the last shot through her head while holding her down with his foot on her rear, and then turned her over on her back."

Mikie was killed by a bullet through her left breast, which entered the chest from left to right. She had also been shot to the left of the spine, and above the left ankle. From the fatal chest wound that had killed her, Dr. Bales surmised that powerful bullets must have been used because the slug passed entirely through the body. Most of the wounds were to the head and upper parts of the bodies, and their points of entry showed that the victims had been shot from both the front and back. A number of .22-caliber slugs or fragments were recovered from the bodies. No powder burns had been found on either of the victims, or their clothing, indicating that the shots, except for the one in Ellen's head, had come from some distance away. Neither girl had been sexually molested. The autopsy findings had also revised the earlier stated fixed time of death from 9:00 a.m. to 10:00 a.m., plus or minus one hour, reducing the period in which the murders had been committed from as early as 8:00 a.m. to as late as 10:00 a.m.

An accounting of the wounds and slugs indicated that seventeen .22-caliber shots had been fired, in quick succession, suggesting (albeit not confirming) a rapid-fire long rifle rather than a handgun. The killer was undoubtedly a fine shot, missing only three times. From the evidence it now appeared that, intent on ambush, he had concealed himself in or near the picnic grove. As the two teenagers emerged from a clump of trees and around a bend on the path to the footbridge, the killer, or killers, opened fire at a range of between 100 and 150 feet. It was surmised that Mikie had probably been hit first and Ellen started to run for the thicket when the killer turned his full attention upon her. Both Mikie and Ellen, staggered and wounded by the barrage of gunfire, struggled for their lives. He, she or they, had then gone over to administer the coup de gras to the back of Ellen's head.

The crime had been one of pure viciousness. Could it have been a personal vendetta? Chief Panadapoulis was determined to cap the case as quickly as possible. Not only had it been an egregious crime that ended the life of the daughter of a fellow law enforcement officer, but now the entire community was suffering from a growing sense of panic. He was also certain there would be political pressures to be addressed. Soon after the coroner's report was in, Panadapoulis canceled leave for his entire detective force and scheduled them to work in sixteen-hour shifts until they had hunted down the killer or killers.

Alerts went out through the entire metropolitan area and surrounding suburbs in both Maryland and Virginia. Even with Sammy Stokes in hand, the chief was not about to let any suspect slip away. Anyone who might be under the slightest cloud of suspicion would be rounded up and questioned. The fraternal brotherhood of law enforcement had suffered a loss and someone was going to have to pay. And it better be soon.

The dragnet produced almost instant results. Within hours, on the Virginia side of the Potomac River, Arlington police arrested a second suspect who was carrying a .22 caliber revolver and two boxes of ammunition. The suspect, one Billy Ray Martin, a 23-year-old man from the nearby hamlet of Vienna, had been picked up in a drugstore telephone booth at Wilson Boulevard and North Rhodes Street in Arlington. The Arlington police were holding him under a $1,000 bond on a concealed weapons charge, but what interested

Panadapoulis was that the suspect had purchased the gun in nearby Falls Church, Virginia on Monday, June 13, just two days before the murders.

Gregory Panadapoulis, of medium build, high forehead, and sloped shoulders, was dressed extremely well for cop on a $11,000 a year salary. He tended to wear expensive, well-cut, gray suits, dark ties and white shirts. He looked almost dapper, but was always deadly earnest. When he looked left or right without moving his head, he presented an almost furtive appearance, ironically not unlike a crook in a lineup. His large eyes were buttressed by bags of bountiful size, which cast shadows in press photos and bore testimony to many long hours on the job in the last three months since he had been hired.

Panadapoulis was a hard-edged, blunt man who rarely minced words. A graduate of the University of New Hampshire, he had come to Maryland in 1934, the peak of the Depression, in search of employment. The racetrack, where he spent most of his free time, had been an added bonus. Unlike most of the cops on the force, he was well-educated and loved the ironies he often found in literature, especially in the works of Alfred, Lord Tennyson, whom he loved to quote to his staff, most of whom knew little or nothing of such matters.

Now, he was in charge of the 112-man force required to protect more than 350,000 county residents. The job, he told his wife, was head and shoulders above his old post, where he headed up a three-man force for the little suburb of Beltsville, but a hundred times more demanding. He had been brought in at a time when the department case-closure rate was at an all-time nadir, and he was expected to turn it around. Yet, his selection for the position owed as much to being an acolyte to County Commission Chairman Jessup Leggett as it was to his police experience, which was admittedly limited. That was the way things were done in Prince George's. As Leggett would famously say, "It's not only who you know, but who you blow that gets you ahead."

Now Panadapoulis was faced with the first murder case he had ever presided over, and he had been understandably nervous and irritable when the crime was initially reported. But tonight, he felt lighter, for a prime suspect was already in custody and undergoing intense interrogation at D.C. police headquarters, and there was even a backup candidate in Arlington.

Yet, problems abounded. Principle among them was the unfortunate matter of the missing murder weapon that had to be dealt with. Panadapoulis wasn't at all sold on the possibility that the revolver picked up in Arlington could be the instrument used in the two killings, since the autopsy suggested that the bullets had been fired from a rifle. For the time being, though, it would mollify the press and his boss, Chairman Leggett, that there was forward motion. Panadapoulis considered it more likely that the killer had ditched the murder weapon somewhere in the park, the Northwest Branch, or in one of several local ponds. He blanched at the thought that they would probably have to be searched. That would take time and money. It was also possible the killer still had the weapon in his possession. Manpower was short. Most of the chief's own men, as well as the D.C. detectives and volunteers, were already or would soon be tied up canvassing the neighborhood door-to-door for witnesses. The weather was holding, but for how long? Evidence might be compromised by the next big thunderstorm.

Earlier in the afternoon, when he bounced his concerns off Julian Edwards, his second-in-command, his deputy had offered several solutions. Why not request assistance from the Army, and more volunteers from the local fire department?

"Call the commander at Fort Meade, up in Anne Arundel County," Edwards suggested. "He might be able to loan us not only some men but a few mine detectors as well. Hell, if the killer dumped or buried the murder weapon, a mine detector might be just the thing to find it. After all, these guys can detect deeply buried explosives, and Civil War nuts use them to locate old guns, bullets and other relics on all them old battlefields. Why couldn't we use them to find a murder weapon? We can also probably get the Chillum-Adelphi Volunteer Fire Department to provide volunteers for the search. If we line the mine detector guys and the volunteers up, along with our own investigators, elbow-to-elbow, we can cover the entire park in no time doing radial search patterns. Winnie's already in charge of the field investigation, and I think he would welcome the help."

"I like it," said the chief. "Get on the horn and make it happen."

The captain grimaced as he looked at his watch, which said 8:32. "Yes sir."

Despite the late hour, Edwards roused the commander of Fort Meade from a late dinner, and intercepted the local fire department chief just before he left his station house, and made the appropriate arrangements. Within a short time, the captain had been promised six soldiers and two mine detectors from Fort Meade, and more volunteer firemen to be on site at 8:00 a.m. Together with the police assigned to the crime scene itself, Winnie Sweitzer would have a search team of thirty-one men to systematically comb the park, as well as officers already assigned to the house-to-house canvass in the neighborhood.

Detective Sergeant James D. McManus, the Metropolitan Police polygraph specialist assigned to lead the interrogation of Sammy Stokes, knew he had a long night ahead of him. He was an expert in naked psychological warfare, and his polygraph was his principal weapon. He had already called his wife to tell her he wouldn't be coming home. She had heard the news and for once had not made a stink. Before he began, as he always did, he spent a few moments intently examining the skinny subject opposite him. Sammy was no young Clark Gable. His V-shaped face, high forehead, weak chin, and ears that hung vertically from the side of his head, were almost cartoon-like. His blue eyes were widely set and shadowed by heavy, dark eyebrows. His nose was narrow but flared at the nostrils, which almost seemed joined as one orifice rather than two. His lips were pursed and narrow. Though he displayed outward signs of nervousness, his body language was defiant and confident. He was scared, but not intimidated. That was good, thought the sergeant. McManus wanted him at his ease, even a bit overconfident. Overconfidence of a subject, he knew from experience, was the investigator's best ally.

As the lie detector was being readied, McManus sought to lower the suspect's guard and chatted amicably with him. Sammy exhibited little interest in the equipment. "You know," he said as they taped the sensors to his wrist, "I also know a fair amount about psychology and I read a lot. I know a good bit about this criminal stuff and lie detectors. I even know how that thing works. Heck, I can even tell you the states where evidence from lie detector tests ain't even admissible in court."

"Yeah," McManus laughed. "What does your little red guidebook to law enforcement tell you about polygraph evidence in Maryland?"

"It don't mean a thing," Sammy said defiantly. "This is D.C., ain't it? Maryland don't accept it, and Ellen and Mikie were killed in Maryland, not D.C. Right?"

"Big deal. Anybody can read detective stories and learn that crap," replied McManus, his demeanor turning serious. "This is real, I can assure you. Your two girlfriends are dead, and we're gonna find out one way or another if you killed 'em."

Despite Stokes' outward tough-guy stance, McManus was intrigued. The kid was definitely not stupid and, as he would soon learn, was actually well-read on the subject of polygraph analysis. But the test was not going to be delayed. The technician on the machine waited for the go ahead. At 8:00 p.m., the questioning began. It would continue unabated for the next eight hours.

By nightfall nearly a score of potential witnesses had been questioned by the Prince George's police, but it was clear that the cops were pinning their hopes on Sammy Stokes for a quick closure to the case. It was Sammy that Panadapoulis wanted — and it was up to McManus to deliver him.

At the Chauvanne home, Dr. Merrill Gleason, the family physician, gave both Philip and Lucille a sedative for sleep. The Gorsuchs, old friends and neighbors from Landover, had picked up Terry and taken her to their home for a while. Philip's younger brother Fred and his sister-in-law Lois also came by to offer whatever assistance they could, and ended up staying the night.

Lois had learned of the killings while riding the bus home from her work at American Express in D.C. and had immediately notified Fred. When they arrived at Philip's home later in the evening, neighbors, curiosity seekers, and reporters surrounded the place, and they had barely been able to squeak their way in. Once inside, Lois had been obliged to go from window to window drawing down the Venetian blinds to prevent people from peeking in. Not long afterwards, she went to sleep at the foot of Lucille's bed.

Chapter 4

LONG ROUNDS AND SHORT

At 4:00 a.m., June 16, the polygraph interrogation of Sammy Stokes was finally terminated and the eight-hour-long psychological combat ended. The exhausted, sleep-deprived detainee was hustled from the interrogation room to a waiting police cruiser, and driven back to the Prince George's County police headquarters at Seat Pleasant.

McManus and the officers who had conducted the "interview" were almost as bone weary and drained from the night's work as was their subject. Their findings were anything but promising. Sammy had been consistent in his story and appeared to have an alibi that he was with others most of the time. Yet he had also opened another but intriguing avenue of investigation.

Stokes claimed that he had indeed been hanging around the park on the morning of the murder, to impress Ellen but specifically to make Mikie jealous. His cocky, self-centered attitude had disgusted McManus, who neither liked nor trusted the suspect. He had found out that the relationship with each of the girls had been rocky, and on one occasion Sammy had written a letter to Ellen in a somewhat intimidating tone, but without a direct threat. The interrogators had perked up, however, when the boy added a new line to his story.

"When I first got to the park," said Sammy, "I seen a guy with a rifle across his knees sitting on a log, a few feet from where you say the murders had taken place. I didn't think anything of it. Kids are always shooting off their BB-guns in the park. I didn't know Ellen and Mikie had already gone into the park. When Anita and Candy showed up a minute or two after I had arrived, I looked around but he had gone."

"Why didn't you say anything about this earlier?" queried McManus quietly.

"I knew you wouldn't believe me."

McManus looked at the technician on the polygraph, who nodded his head. The boy wasn't lying. Or so the machine readout indicated.

"Did you recognize the guy?"

"Couldn't tell who he was. He was in the shade, and I only seen him a few seconds."

"What happened then?"

Sammy shifted uncomfortably on the wooden chair. "I took Anita and Candy to school. They said Ellen and Mikie had left well before them and were probably already there. So I drove 'em over and looked for Ellen, but I couldn't find her anywhere, and she hadn't showed up at her homeroom. So I drove back to the park, about 9, I guess, to look again, and when she wasn't there I went back to the school. I hung around 'til about 10. I knew it was 10 'cause the bell rung even though most of the kids had left. But she still hadn't come so I went back to the park yet again. Ellen and some of the kids from the teen club were gonna have a picnic and I thought they might be there. When I got there and found that Mrs. Chauvanne had asked Teddy and Carlin to look for her, I told 'em I would help 'em. We cruised for an hour in my car and couldn't find the girls, and when we come back again to tell Mrs. Chauvanne, that's when you guys picked me up."

"You sure about the times you were at the school?" asked McManus.

"Sure. There's a bell that rings at 8:30. You got a half hour till school starts. At five minutes before 9 the bell rings again and everybody's got five minutes to get to homeroom. Then at 9 the bell rings again and you gotta be in your seat. It rings five minutes before the hour to end each class, and then on the hour by which time you got to be seated in your next class. I heard five bells. The first was at 8:30, right after I let Anita and Candy off. I hung around the parking lot with some friends and heard the 8:55 and 9:00. Then I drove back to the park, and then came back to the school. I heard the 9:55, and 10. And there were plenty of kids around I can name for you that saw me there every time. And you can ask Anita and Candy about when we were in the park."

"How long had you been at the park the first time before Anita and Candice arrived?"

"Only a minute or two at best."

"What time did they arrive?"

"Well, only a minute or two before we all left together. Anita had looked at her watch and said it was 8:20 when we left 'cause I only had ten minutes to get them over to the school."

"What was your relationship with Ellen and Mikie?" McManus asked.

"I dated 'em both."

"Wasn't Mikie a little young for you?"

"No way! If you saw her in those short-shorts you wouldn't think so, know what I mean? I mean if you ask around, you'd find she had quite a reputation, if you get my drift. She had these short-shorts she rolled right up to the crotch. Only fourteen, but she looked nineteen. She didn't want to go to no damned Catholic school either."

"Did you ever have sex with either of them?"

"No!" the boy retorted.

The polygraph operator raised his eyebrows and looked at McManus who looked back without a word.

"Did you ever want to?"

"Who wouldn't? But I respected them too much. Besides, if I'd done something like that, Mikie's dad was a cop and he'd have killed me if he found out. Old man Chauvanne would have plastered me all over the wall if I ever screwed Ellen."

"Ellen had other boyfriends, or at least a lot of guys who wanted to date her. Were you jealous of them?"

"Naw. What she did was her own business."

"That's not what this letter you wrote to her last week says," McManus taunted, holding up a hand-written document, albeit too far from Sammy to see clearly.

Sammy turned white.

"How'd you get that?" he shouted. "That's between Ellen and me."

"Not anymore," replied the detective quietly. "Remember, she's dead now."

McManus wasn't about to tell him that the police had not only Ellen's letters from him, mostly maudlin teenage stuff, but they also had her diaries as well as Mikie's, in which Sammy Stokes figured prominently. This specific letter, warning her not to date another boy, had been potentially incriminating, and provided a possible motive for the murder.

"I only wanted to warn her," said Sammy, who was now on the border of tears. "If she wouldn't go steady with me, I wanted my ring back. Besides, she had two-timed me and was going with Jimmy Combs."

"You think she was seeing other boys, like maybe Teddy Dubinski?"

"That kid Dubinski and his punk brother are both twerps. Teddy ain't worth a crap. I just wanted to scare Ellen a little. I don't know if she was interested in him, but I saw him putting the squeeze on her last Saturday night."

And so it went throughout the night. McManus probing, and Sammy repelling. He had stuck to his story, and unflinchingly stayed with it, without variation, for eight long hours. He hadn't fallen for the many traps that had been laid, nor had he allowed himself to be railroaded.

Had he told the truth? The lie detector said yes. Did the police believe him? The answer was a firm no.

Sergeant Bearson recommended that he be retained in custody and a second polygraph test be administered.

"And, oh, by the way," Bearson said to the officer escorting the prisoner back to the police cruiser, "don't let him get too much sleep."

By mid-morning of the second day of investigation, hundreds of neighbors, spectators, and thrill seekers had again begun to assemble along the periphery of Northwest Branch Park, and were quietly milling about the once-lively play center. None were admitted to the area. Most had been drawn to the scene by the blaring, page-one, column-one headlines in the morning *Washington Post and Times Herald*. "2 Schoolgirls Murdered in Park; Dog Leads Girl to Bodies." The sub-head had been no less dramatic. "Police Hunt Killer of 2; 20 Questioned In Double Tragedy." Below were pictures of the two victims, both taken from school yearbooks, and run in a two-column format usually reserved for mug shots of heads of state of international importance. Ellen looked right out from the page at the reader, her incredible smile still fresh as life itself. Mikie's portrait was subdued but elegant, presenting the image of a child-woman far more advanced than age fourteen. The story shoved even the President of the United States off to the side. On television the same images of the two girls dominated the airwaves.

The initial news reports, broadcast on local radio and television the night before, had generated substantial interest, but nothing like the morning *Post* story. It was instantly picked up by both the Associated Press and United Press and spread across the nation. Yet, the gathering wave of fear, sensationalism, and public fascination had yet to reach the tsunami stage except at the local level. On the University of Maryland campus, less than half a mile from the murder scene, the crime had become the topic of the day. No one on the campus was more interested, however, than William Galt Trueman.

Born in 1933, the same year Philip and Lucille Chauvanne had been married, Billy Trueman was a Korean War vet. He entered the university on the GI Bill and was paying his way through school by working as a grocery clerk. Billy loved conspiracy stories, and cloak and dagger stuff, detective who-done-its, and spy novels. But he took a very personal delight in the Chauvanne-O'Riley murder case. Ellen's picture in the morning paper made him shiver. Both of the girls were attractive, but there was something in Ellen's portrait, the very one she had hated, that somehow had captivated him. Maybe it was her innocent smile, or her pure white collar. She had been purity itself until she became soiled. Now she was dead. He frowned as he tacked the picture to the wall over his bed right beside the hanging plaster statute of the Virgin Mary. As the investigation continued, and as more pictures were published, he would collect them all. He would make a scrapbook of them. In fact, many scrapbooks. The scrapbooks and other artifacts related to the crime would become his personal shrine to poor tragic Ellen. Over time, they would capture the citadel of his soul and in the coming years he would grow to love her. And he knew, had she been given half a chance, that she would have loved him.

In the park, Winnie Sweitzer's small battalion of searchers trod carefully. Every potential piece of evidence was located, recorded, and if moveable, retrieved for later fingerprinting and testing. Plaster casts of a man's footprint and random tire marks were made. Bits of paper and numerous other items were photographed *in situ*, bagged and tagged. On both sides of the park, detectives had fanned out through the adjacent neighborhoods, in Lane Manor, Adelphi Manor, University Hills, Rosemary Park and Chatham. By forenoon, the weary, red-eyed man-hunters, warned by their superiors not to speak to the press, had already questioned more than 400 persons, many of whom also gave their stories to reporters.

In the early afternoon, Captain Edwards, Sergeant Bearson, and Lieutenant Lloyd R. McGowan, in charge of the District police firing range, held a joint press conference in a vain effort to quench what was clearly becoming an voracious public appetite for the murder story. There was silence as Edwards described some of the recent findings. But he held back on revelations of critical data that might later be used in court or to eliminate possible suspects. There were murmurs, however, when he provided the stunning news that the police had acquired a .22-caliber gun that would soon undergo ballistics tests to see if it were the murder weapon. He refused to reveal where the gun had been acquired or whether it was a pistol or a rifle. Yet the suggestion that "the" gun had been found sent reporters into a feeding frenzy hard to curb.

The late afternoon Washington newspapers, *The Evening Star* and a four-cent-a-copy tabloid called *The Daily News*, ran the Chauvanne-O'Riley story on page-one and, like the *Post*, knocked the big national news stories into second place. Speculation in both papers now focused on the murder weapon that, along with the story of Sammy Stokes's lie detector test, had become the leads. The indication that seventeen shots had been fired in rapid succession, was leading police firearms experts to speculate that the murder weapon was of a type that was illegal under District of Columbia law. Specifically, the law classified a machine gun as any gun that fired more than twelve rounds without reloading. Rifles, said Lt. McGowan, such as .22-caliber weapons capable of firing seventeen rounds of "long" bullets or twenty-five rounds of "shorts," were formally classified as semi-automatic. On such rifles, it was necessary to press the trigger to fire each shot, unlike fully automatic weapons, which would continue firing as long as the trigger was held down. The accuracy of the shots that had brought down Ellen and Mikie also indicated that a rifle had been used rather than a .22-caliber pistol. With no powder burns on the victims' clothing, it was almost certain that the gun had not been fired at close range, except for the coup-de-gras shot administered to Ellen's head. McGowan believed the murder weapon to be a semi-automatic "because the bullets were fired at a distance and it is much easier to be accurate with a rifle than a pistol."

Ironically, on the same day as the murder, D.C. Police Chief McAdams had just issued a memorandum to Washington police indicating that the sale of any .22-caliber rifles that could fire seventeen cartridges without re-loading might also be illegal. The memo had stated that the United States Attorney's office had questioned the legality of sales of such weapons, recently available in the area. He had urged his men to survey their districts, and to warn dealers that this class of rifle could not be sold except under special regulations.

The slugs and shell casings recovered were of the "long" type, but the use of other weapon types was not being ruled out. Even as the press conference was underway, ballistics comparison tests were being conducted on slugs fired from the revolver taken from Martin the day before and the slugs found at the murder scene and those removed from the victims' bodies. Moreover, the Prince George's police had asked other law enforcement agencies nationwide to forward information on any .22-caliber rimfire weapons that might come to their official attention during the investigation of other crimes.

Were there other suspects besides Stokes? asked one reporter.

"There are other suspects, either in custody or to be picked up later," said Sergeant Bearson knowingly. That Panadapoulis's back-up suspect over in Virginia, Billy Ray Martin, had just been eliminated as a prime candidate by virtue of the ballistics findings, which failed to match bullet markings with those from the crime scene, was entirely overlooked. In truth, Stokes was now the only suspect in sight, and a questionable one at best.

A clamor in the room instantly ensued as dozens of reporters all asked the same general questions. "Who are the other suspects?" "Have they already been picked up for questioning?" "What have they said?"

Raising his hands to quell the crowd, Bearson responded as obliquely as possible. "You know how these things are. One thing leads to another."

"That's all the questions for now," interrupted Edwards. And with that the press conference was concluded.

Sammy Stokes had enjoyed no sleep, except in the back seat of the D.C. police squad car that had taken him back to Seat Pleasant, where he dozed. Nor was the jail cell at county police headquarters a place conducive to rest. His mind was churning with frightening thoughts. Anguish and anxiety had caused his stomach to tighten so that he couldn't even shit. His fatigue was now almost too much to endure. Both Ellen and Mikie were dead, and the cops seemed certain that he had killed them. Maybe he had and had blocked it out of his mind! Where were his mom and dad? Did they even know he was in jail? Were they getting him a lawyer? He hadn't seen them or, for that matter, anyone else except cops since he had been taken into custody. He wasn't even certain he was under arrest since he had yet to be formally charged with anything. The police were obviously not playing games, though, and he had already been put through the ringer once. They had repeatedly asked him why he had killed the two girls. When had he killed them? Where had he dumped the gun? What was next?

About 10:00 a.m., a guard entered the lockup room, and opened his cell. "Come on, boy," he said as he again fastened the handcuffs. "You're going for another ride."

An hour later, they again escorted Sammy, still handcuffed, into D.C. police headquarters for another round of lie detector tests. One of the cops seemed genuinely sympathetic to his plight, brought him a Coke, and even gave him a cigarette. Sammy's parents didn't know he smoked, and he had been careful not to let them find any evidence of his habit. But now, in front of the cops, it somehow made him feel older, more in control of himself. He appreciated the kindness from the officer who gave it to him. The other cop, however, was a son-of-a-bitch who said he wanted nothing more than to tie the boy's balls up to a post and cut them off for killing the two girls, but his partner had interceded.

For the next sixty minutes, without being hooked up to the detector, Sammy was interrogated first by one, then the other of the two officers. He kept to his story, though, regardless of who questioned him. At noon, a wave of relief swept over him when he was told the testing was to be canceled, but he stiffened again when informed the interrogation would continue without the polygraph, but across the hall. At 4:00 p.m., after more rigorous questioning, he was again moved, this time to a room adjacent to the main cell block in the station house. A half hour later, the two officers shuffled him out to a waiting police cruiser for the trip back to Seat Pleasant. By 6:00 p.m. he was again in a cell at county police headquarters.

Soon after his arrival, Sammy had his first personal contact with the outside world in thirty hours when the guard notified him of a telephone call, and that he would be permitted five minutes. To his surprise, the call was not from his parents, but from Mitchell Bulmer, Carlin's brother, who was chairman of the Riggs Lane Teen Club and one of Ellen's closest buddies.

"How you holding up, Sammy?" said Mitchell. "We're all worried about you."

"Man, is it good to hear from you," replied Sammy. "They've had me all over the place. I ain't slept in days, and I feel like crap. Where are my folks? I ain't seen or heard from 'em since they locked me up."

"I don't know about your folks, just what I read in the papers and they haven't been mentioned. Your picture made the front page in the *Post*. All the talk with the kids is 'bout you and Ellen and the fight you had the other night. What happened, Sammy?"

"I didn't do it, if that's what you mean. The police seem to think I threatened one of her goddamned boyfriends, too, but I didn't. Why don't they ask him? I think the guy I saw in the park when I first got there was the bastard that did it."

"What guy you talking about? I haven't heard a thing about anybody in the park except you. Heck, the only one they's looking at hard is you."

"Well, when I first got to the park, you know, down by the bridge, the first time, just before I seen Anita and Candice, I seen some guy sitting there with a rifle resting across his knees. He didn't stay there but a few seconds after he seen me, and I didn't think nothing of it. Heck, Ellen's little brother, and half his fucking friends are always in the park with their damned BB-guns shootin' at anything that moves."

"Did you see him real good? What's he look like?"

"Don't know," said Sammy. "It was only for a few seconds. I looked away for an instant when I heard Anita and Candy coming, and when I looked back he was gone. He was sitting when I saw him, but I got the impression he was kinda tall. He could've just been a big kid, but he looked kinda ratty, wild lookin', you know like a bum. Looked like he hadn't combed his hair in a month. I think he had on a dark shirt. Could've been blue, and brown or khaki pants."

"D'ja tell that to the police?"

"Yeah, over and over, but they didn't believe me at all. I could tell. They think I did it, and that I'm lying to 'em about the bum. That's why they wanted to give me another lie detector test."

"You sure you're telling the truth?" Mitchell slowly asked.

"You think I'm lying to you too?"

"No, man. I just thought . . ."

"Go screw yourself!" shouted Sammy into the phone as he slammed it down onto the wall receiver.

"Got that?" asked the sergeant in the next room.

"Yes sir," said the officer monitoring the call. "Got it on tape, but it's what he's been saying all along."

Deloris Pfeizer read the headlines of the evening newspaper with keen interest, the murder story that was so close to home. She felt extremely sorry for the two girls, but more so for their grieving mothers and fathers. She noted that Michael Linn's parents had already arranged for the burial of their daughter on Saturday, June 18. There was to be a closed service at 9 a.m. in their home, and a requiem mass an hour later at St. John Baptist de La Salle Church, off Chillum Road. Burial was to be in Mount Olivet Cemetery in Washington. Should she attend, even though she didn't personally know either the Chauvannes or the O'Rileys? She wasn't sure, but they were, after all, neighbors.

The police, according to the first news reports earlier in the day, were theorizing yesterday that the shooting had happened around 10:00 a.m. That was an hour and three quarters later than the cap gun sounds she had heard. In any event, the officers at the scene of the crime were certainly not interested in what she had to say, and she had dismissed the matter from her mind. But now, according to the papers, they were looking for anyone who may have heard shots between 7:00 a.m. and 10:00 a.m. Maybe, she thought, I should call them!

"No," she reconsidered, "they probably wouldn't be interested in cap guns." Besides the officer in the park had been quite rude to her. She went back to her cleaning.

Not long after Mitchell Bulmer's call, Sammy's heart leapt into his throat as the cell door was opened and his father, Samuel Richmond Stokes, was admitted for a visit. "Dad. Thank God you're here. You've got to get me out of here," he blurted out. "I don't belong in jail. I didn't do anything, and they won't believe me."

"Calm down," his father responded. "I know you didn't do it. Your mother and I have been worried sick about you. They wouldn't let us see you until tonight, but I've gone and hired a couple of good lawyers in Upper Marlboro, a guy named MacIntire and his partner, and they think they can get you out soon. One of 'em should be here anytime now to talk to you. He's going to try and get to the court tomorrow."

"I didn't do it, dad," repeated the boy, now almost in tears, his words tripping over themselves. "Ellen and I had a few fights, but I couldn't kill her or Mikie. Do you understand? I didn't do it. When I first went into the park to wait for them, I saw a guy sitting near the fireplace with a rifle across his lap. I told the cops but they wouldn't believe me. It was Mikie's dad that's the cause of all this. He's hated me ever since I took her out last winter. Don't you see? I told them over and over, but they just stared at me and the damned lie detector."

His father lowered his head. "I know, son," he reassured him. He didn't tell the boy that he had given two county detectives named Barclay and Clelland permission to search the house, upon attorney MacIntire's advice, without the required permit albeit with the proviso that the attorney be present at all times during the visit. He was well aware that they were likely to haul off Sammy's .22-caliber squirrel rifle for ballistics tests. "Try to take it easy. We'll get you out of here soon."

The five minutes allocated for the visit passed quickly after which the guard escorted Samuel Richmond Stokes from the cell without further ceremony. After thirty hours of detention without contact with the outside world, Sammy Stokes was again alone. Not for long, though. Soon after his father's departure, he was again cuffed and taken by squad car to D.C. Police headquarters where an important meeting was about to get underway, and Sammy was key to its proceeding.

Prince George's County Commissioner Blair Sasscer was about as powerful as they come in the good-old-boy system of local politics that had reigned in the county since the Civil War. Known to his inner circle of friends as "Bud," Sasscer had been in Maryland politics for more than twenty years. His family name was as familiar and influential in Southern Maryland as the Lees in Virginia. Backed by the powerful county Democratic Party machine, he had conducted his first successful run for the State House of Delegates in 1934 and served until 1941, when he was elected to the Prince George's Orphans Court. The following year he became Chief Judge of the Court and served in that capacity until 1954. His political popularity was formidable. In 1952, the year when Dwight D. Eisenhower and the Republicans swept the nation in the tidal wave that changed the American political landscape, Bud was one of the few county Democrats who had held on to his office. Two years later he was elected to the powerful five member Prince George's County Board of Commissioners.

In Maryland, it was an aphorism that with local political power came business success if the seat holder was a Democrat — and Bud was no stranger to either power or success. Besides owning two stores, one in Upper Marlboro and another in Aquasco, he operated two large cattle farms in Upper Marlboro and in Thurmont, a bonding business, and an insurance company. In 1950 he was made director of the First National Bank of Southern Maryland, and vice chairman of its board of directors. In his role as a leader of the state Democratic Central Committee he was described by friends as an honest, careful politician, and by his enemies as "King Maker."

And one of the "Kings" he had helped make, the only one theoretically more powerful than himself on the County Board of Commissioners, was its outspoken Chairman, Jessup St. James Leggett. Sasscer had wisely positioned himself as the eyes and ears of the Chairman, a hulking man, with a gruff, Southern Maryland accent who spoke his mind, and then some. Chairman Leggett had once been a stonemason, owned a monument business in Hyattsville, and had begun his own political career on the town council and then mayor. As a mover and shaker, he was without equal. Within a short time after entering the political scene he had become president of the Hyattsville District Democratic Club, and vice-president of the Prince George's County Young Men's Democratic Club, and the Prince George's Kiwanis Club and Elks Lodge No. 1778, among others. One of his political cronies, Frankie Amato, once described him as a politician "you could go to with a problem and he would solve it. He wouldn't do it by committee. Things aren't done like that anymore in the county."

This was a tried and true governmental arrangement practiced in Prince George's for years, a spoils system where one's power was determined by the number of votes he or she could deliver to the party, and political favors were bought and sold every day. Patronage was everything. Jess, as the man on the street called him, had become the king of patronage and a master back-room county manipulator, a post that won him a position as a major cog in the county Democratic machine run by powerful State Senator Webster "Web" Marbury. The Marburys and Sasscers were so interrelated by marriage they might have been a single family—a single powerful family whose main operative was Jessup Leggett. Anything that went on in the county, from zoning approvals to fixing parking tickets, and everything in-between, required Leggett's blessing to go forward. And to get to Chairman Leggett, it was first necessary to pass through his point man and gatekeeper, Sasscer.

Bud Sasscer was seldom seen at police briefings, but when he made an appearance — always unannounced — it meant that Leggett or Marbury were on the warpath.

Now, the Chauvanne-O'Riley murder case, though only a day old, had the potential of turning into an embarrassing episode politically, especially with elections looming, and Chairman Leggett wanted it put to rest immediately. Innocence and guilt were not at issue. A quick arrest, conviction and a return to public order were. It was, after all, at Leggett's instigation that Panadapoulis had been hired as Chief of Police, bypassing the more experienced and popular candidate, Captain Julian Edwards, who had been with the force for seventeen years. Chief Panadapoulis was entirely aware of the delicate path he must tread.

Leggett was blunt about the situation. The chief had called for an evening briefing of all of the senior detectives involved in the case, including the District's detectives, as well as Lansdale A. Marbury, Web Marbury's son and State's Attorney for Prince George's County. Sasscer informed Panadapoulis that he was only there as an "observer." In fact, he was sitting in to insure that through his mere presence, the Chairman's desire for a speedy resolution to the crime was explicitly clear. The message was not lost on Chief Panadapoulis, even though the meeting was being convened, at Chief McAdams's suggestion, at D.C. headquarters.

At 7:00 p.m. sharp, the participants filed into the conference room. Sasscer scanned the assemblage; some he knew, others he had read about in the papers. Present were Chief Panadapoulis, his principal aide, Captain Julian Edwards, and Chief of Detectives Dennis Thompson, all from the Prince George's County Police Department, Lieutenant Hendricks, Detective Sergeants Smyth, McManus, Black, and Roma, Precinct Detectives Daniel G. Winston and Jonathan Holder of the D.C. Metropolitan Police Department, and finally State's Attorney Marbury. Chief McAdams, in a tactical move, did not attend.

As the briefing got underway, each of the police officers presented his findings and then discussed developments in the case to that time, even as a uniformed armed officer stood at the door to hold at bay a small legion of reporters. During at least part of the conference, Sammy Stokes, the primary suspect, was present to answer questions, but reporters outside managed to secure only tantalizing glimpses of him when the door opened to let someone in or out. He was sitting alone at one side of the room. They were unaware that he had just been joined by one of his newly secured attorneys, Jeffrey MacIntire.

The meeting was finally concluded at 9:35 p.m. Within minutes the officers filed from the conference room one by one, but refused to issue any statements. States Attorney Marbury stopped only briefly to say that police did not "at this time" have sufficient evidence to place a murder charge against anyone. He had, in fact, little alternative, for when Jeffrey MacIntire appeared, he informed the press that he would produce Sammy Stokes in court the next day to answer a writ of habeas corpus. But the consensus of almost all convened was summed up when one officer murmured to another as they exited: "That skinny bastard is guilty as sin."

For Sammy Stokes, it seemed there was to be no relief, for after the conference he was again hauled back to Maryland to face another six solid hours of interrogation. Not until 3:00 a.m. was he finally escorted back to his lonely cell, exhausted, drained and thoroughly pessimistic. For the first time, he considered the unthinkable: "Give them a confession, stop the incessant torture and get it over with."

Chapter 5

REVELATION

The Prince George's County Courthouse, situated smack in the center of the county seat of Upper Marlboro, was about as emblematic of the ante-bellum Old South as any Georgia plantation. Built and rebuilt on the site of the one-time home of Charles Carroll of Carrollton, one of the Maryland Signers of the Declaration of Independence, it was both stately and decrepit. With its tall Victorian columns and brick 1840 façade firmly establishing the primacy of the American judicial system, all that was lacking to confirm its antiquity was a good coverage of creeping vines and the removal of the ugly electrical cables and telephone wires that crisscrossed sections of its exterior.

Upper Marlboro, founded in 1706 at Belts Landing, was one of the oldest surviving towns in the state, and it showed. Named after the Duke of Marlborough but a few years after his victory at the Battle of Blenheim, during the long-forgotten War of Spanish Succession, it had not acquired the preamble of "Upper" until a competing hamlet in nearby Calvert County had also usurped the same name. Thus, the county seat of Prince George's became "Upper" and the rival downriver town became "Lower." No one, however, seemed to know just when the name Marlborough had been abridged. It was indeed doubtful whether the tobacco farmers in the surrounding countryside, who provided the principal source of county tax revenue, had ever heard of Blenheim, the Duke, or the War of Spanish Succession. What counted to them was the market price of Calvert Gold, the richest brand of tobacco farmed in the nation, bought at auction at the edge of town every September. It hadn't been a spurious decision, claimed one local farmer, that the R. J. Reynolds Tobacco Company had named its most prestigious cigarette "Marlboro."

Situated on a once navigable waterway called the Western Branch, which fed into the nearby Patuxent River a few miles downstream, Upper Marlboro had once been not only the center of county government, but also briefly a thriving international seaport. That had ended early on with the silting up of the tributary and then the main river itself. Despite futile efforts to keep both open to commerce, which was funded as early as 1759 by the first state-authorized lottery in Maryland, the maritime traffic soon disappeared, and Upper Marlboro's reason for being was reduced to serving as the hub of a rural county government. Now the old town's business, with its vestigial remnants of colonial days, could boast of little more than a few dozen lawyers' shingles on Main Street, a barber shop, tobacco warehouse, grain and feed store, a few shops, a drugstore, an ancient hotel, a jail, a bug-infested movie theater, a few run-down churches and both a public and a parochial school. When the summer set in, with sweltering temperatures averaging in the mid-90s, the streets were usually devoid of traffic save for the county police cruisers coming and going to the courthouse.

At 10:00 a.m. on Friday, commitment papers for Sammy Stokes, dated the day of the slayings, were finally signed at the courthouse and witnessed by Detective Sergeant Thomas Bearson of the Prince George's Police. On the papers to officially commend Stokes to jail was written: "Held for investigation of murder." It was, however, but a formality justifying the previous two days of incarceration and questioning without benefit of warrant or formal arrest. It was a "gentle bending" of procedure that was usually applied to "uppity" blacks that got drunk on Saturday nights and tore up property, but such practice was rarely employed for the holding of a white man except in the most extenuating circumstances. Stokes was one of those special cases.

Sammy Stokes had been turned over to County Sheriff S. Lee Hall for processing, with full knowledge that the prisoner's attorneys had just served a writ of habeas corpus on the county police, and would soon file one with the sheriff. Nevertheless, procedures were procedures and a belated examination of his hands and arms had been ordered at the last minute by Deputy District Coroner Dr. Andrew L. Riesberg to check for recent traces of bloodstains. The results proved negative, but the processing continued. A half hour after the commitment papers had been signed, Ball ordered that the prisoner be taken to Prince George's General Hospital in nearby Cheverly for further testing.

Soon after midday, Stokes' attorneys, Jeffrey MacIntire and W. Gale Boynton, whose offices were just a block down Main Street, had obtained a formal writ of habeas corpus ordering the police to produce the detained youth before the County Circuit Court at 1:30 p.m. at the county courthouse. The presentation before Judge Thomas B. Cloberry in his chambers was brief and to the point. With his head pointed down and his shoulders drooped against his slim frame as if he had already been convicted, Stokes was flanked by the two lawyers. A wispy two-day growth of youthful beard made his face look dirty and drawn. He had not bathed in several days, and the short-sleeve blue sport shirt and matching slacks in which he had been picked up were both smelly from perspiration and rumpled. Puffy lines of red from lack of sleep, and perhaps crying surrounded his blue eyes. It was just the appearance the attorneys hoped to present, not of a young man, but a victimized teenage boy.

The unsmiling youth poured a glass of water as one of his attorneys asked on what grounds the boy was being held.

Cloberry looked up from his chair, and then toward States Attorney Lansdale Marbury without saying a word.

"Your honor," MacIntire said without waiting for an answer, "our client has been held in various unknown places in what I am told is called 'protective custody', without a formal arrest or charges being filed, since 12:30 p.m. June the 15th, following the murders of Ellen Marie Chauvanne and Michael Linn O'Riley in Northwest Branch Park. Indeed, only two hours ago were commitment papers formally submitted, although they were dated two days ago. He has been questioned almost continuously for more than forty-eight hours."

"Yes, I know," replied the judge in a subdued tone.

"Moreover, he has been held incommunicado, with no contact permitted with anyone, including legal counsel, for most of that time. Indeed, he was not even allowed to make or receive a phone call for thirty hours after his detention, or to see either of his parents until last night. Your Honor, I am terribly concerned that not only has he been transferred numerous times from place to place against his will, but that he has also been transported across the state line into Washington, D.C., not once but twice to undergo polygraph tests without being charged with anything. The crime was in Maryland and not the District of Columbia. My client was taken into custody immediately after the murders occurred and never had time to cross the D.C. line himself. All of his activities have been in Maryland. Your Honor, you must be aware that the entire Metropolitan Washington Police force is emotionally aroused since one of the victims was the daughter of one of their own, and may not be acting within the letter of the law. Not only are all of these actions violations of my client's civil rights, the actions of the Prince George's County Police are violations of numerous federal and state statutes."

"Mr. Marbury?" said the judge.

The States Attorney cleared his throat. "The State will consent to this writ. We do not wish to retain Samuel Raymond Stokes any longer."

"Thank you Your Honor," MacIntire said.

The proceedings, which had taken less than two minutes, were concluded. Sammy Stokes was free to go. Managing a wan smile, he turned to leave.

As Stokes, his parents, and the two attorneys exited the judge's chambers, the gaggle of reporters waiting outside rushed them as if the President or the Pope had suddenly appeared.

"Sammy, did you kill your two girlfriends?" shouted one reporter.

"How'd you do it?" shouted another.

"What'd you do with the gun?" demanded a third.

Sammy's father stopped and turned to face the cameras, a plaintive look on his face. "Haven't we been through enough?" Samuel Richmond Stokes shouted, and then resumed his march down the hall. The Stokes had been scheduled for an immediate meeting with the attorneys in W. Gale Boynton's nearby office on Main Street and they would not to be deterred.

MacIntire sought to ensure the getaway by diverting the press with a few comments: "Insofar as this particular suspect is concerned," he said slowly and deliberately, buying as much time as possible, "I am thoroughly convinced the police had the wrong person. I am convinced of my client's innocence."

"How'd the cops treat him?" asked a reporter from the *Washington Star*. "They had him hid for a long time."

"The boy has no complaints whatsoever on his treatment while in police custody. He will be available through his attorneys at all times, but he needs rest and quiet and he's going somewhere we hope he'll get it. We have advised the Stokes to take a trip somewhere for a rest. God knows they need one, too."

The telephone clerk at the Seat Pleasant police headquarters received the call from the unidentified informant at 12:35 p.m. and thought it was another crank caller. He assigned the caller a number, 238, and though at first suspicious of the validity of the informant and his "tip," proceeded to register the information. He had already fielded at least two-dozen such calls offering false leads before noon, among the hundreds of bona fide but generally worthless messages that had come in since he had been assigned to take tips on the Chauvanne-O'Riley case. This one, though, seemed different. It sounded like the voice of a teenage boy, but not a prankster. Although the caller refused to identify himself, there seemed to be some veracity in what he had to say.

The clerk had never personally visited Northwest Branch Park, although he had been provided with a thorough description during briefings, and he discerned that the caller seemed to have more than a passing familiarity with the scene of the crime. The clerk recalled that his sergeant had told him that in the event there was any question of an important possible lead, he was to route it directly to the appropriate detective. The clerk immediately patched in the informant to Winnie Sweitzer, who was in the field at the park.

"Sir, can you identify yourself?" asked the detective from his car phone.

"No," replied the caller succinctly. "And don't ask me again, okay!"

Sweitzer, too, thought the caller sounded like a youngster, probably a male teenager, one who was deliberate and serious. He couldn't be certain, though.

"Sure. What is it you want to tell me, sir?" replied the detective.

"You guys ain't doin' your job," the caller snickered. "You've been lookin' in the wrong place."

"What do you mean? Can you tell me where we should be looking, and what we should be looking for?"

"Yeah," said the voice. "I saw a guy standing behind a tree in the woods you been looking in. He was firing a rifle. Fired ten times, then waited, and fired again. Look close to the cherry tree, near the picnic table and the bridge. I think you will find what you're looking for."

"Like what?"

"Just find the cherry tree and look." Then the phone went dead.

"What the hell!" said the detective, looking into the radio speaker. "Tucker," he shouted to an officer just coming up the park path with a bag-full of debris raked up from the streambed. "Get Whittington and Galbraith, find every cherry tree in the vicinity of the picnic table, and do another radial search around each one, and I mean a thorough one. Now!"

Within thirty minutes, the search team had found a shell casing, then another and another. Within an hour, a total of eleven casings for a .22 caliber rifle had been found near a young forked cherry tree. The site formed an approximate equilateral triangle with the spot near the path where the bloodstains had been discovered, and the thicket where the bodies had been found. Each side of the triangle was about 150 feet in length. The young tree itself was very near the bank of a meander of the creek. The killer had mowed down the two girls in an ambush while hiding behind the tree, and had probably used the low branch crotch as a rest for his gun. He had waited until the girls were in sight and then opened fire as they approached. The eleven shell casings and the three shells previously found matched the total of the fourteen shots now known to have been fired into their bodies. The puzzle was beginning to fit together.

By afternoon, ballistics evaluation of the slugs and casings that had been recovered two days earlier, and the known number of shots fired in rapid succession had substantially narrowed the parameters of search for the murder weapon. Bullets fired from the murder weapon were the lead equivalent of fingerprints. Each gun left identifying grooves on the slug as it left the barrel. Firing pins and ejectors also left marks on the shells. Match the bullet with the gun and you had the murder weapon. The FBI's firearms experts informed the county police that the accuracy of the shots and the number apparently fired now confirmed that the weapon was a multiple-action automatic or semi-automatic piece, almost certainly a Marlin .22 repeater. Ironically, the bullets were marketed under the name "Revelation."

Scores of detectives had already fanned out through Maryland, the District, and Virginia to examine local police reports of recently stolen weapons, and to thumb through sales records at gun shops and sporting goods outlets. The preliminary results were numbing, for it was readily apparent that the task ahead would be gargantuan. A single area gunsmith reported that his records alone indicated purchases made for as many as ten different Marlin models, the earliest of which had been put on the market in 1953. The only catalogue Marlin that was a semi-automatic, however, was a Model 88 D-L, which fired fifteen long bullets without reloading. It was two less bullets than had been accounted for in the Northwest Branch Park, but it was a start. In D.C. a police inspector named Aubrey Manson had learned from character check records on file with his department, required by law for gun purchases in the city, that no fewer than one hundred and fifty .22-caliber Marlin repeaters, mostly new guns, had been sold in the last eighteen months. All would have to be traced, as would guns identified by similar records in Maryland and Virginia. Yet, the FBI report had reduced the typological search to a specific gun type that had been manufactured within the last two years.

Near the crime scene, in the meantime, police and volunteer firemen continued their relentless quest for clues in the park, but a quarter mile from the murder scene. The shallow but scenic lake at the edge of the park on University Lane, usually covered by squadrons of ducks and geese, was soon under intensive scrutiny by officers wearing hip wanders and armed with garden rakes. Soldiers from Fort Meade, wearing camouflaged field gear and waders, hefted their bulky mine detectors along the lakebed, and on the streamed of the dammed up branch itself.

On the neighborhood streets, police continued to systematically canvass the residents for information. Park employees cutting grass early on Wednesday were questioned, but with negative results. In late afternoon, members of the task force began intensive interrogation of a semi-literate laundry truck driver who reported hearing shooting in the park on the morning of the murder. A little intimidated by so many uniforms, his story was nevertheless convincing.

"I can't say for sure what time it was. You see, it was in the early morning when I was on my way to make my first pickup. Sometime between maybe 8:00 and 9:00 a.m. — I remember the time because I was running a little late 'cause of traffic, you see — I was coming down University Lane just to the north of the park and had just got out of my truck when I hears what sounded like a burst of shots. First thought is that it was a car backfiring. Then there was a few seconds of silence, and then another bursts of shots. Then I kinda knew it was a gun done made the sounds. Seemed to be coming from the park, but I couldn't tell the exact area. You know, too many trees."

Fifteen-year-old Constance Steiner, who lived over on Chapman Road, little Betty's older sister and a friend of the two victims, provided a few more bits of information in the evening. She had been on her bicycle on the morning of the murders, and at 9:45 a.m. she had passed a dark sedan parked on West Park Drive not far from the path the two victims took. At 5:00 p.m. she was brought to the park to show police the precise spot she had passed the car. It was close to the murder scene. It was also the spot Sammy Stokes had parked on his second return to the park in search of Ellen and Mikie.

At precisely 7:30 p.m., Chief Panadapoulis convened his second briefing on the Chauvanne-O'Riley case. This time, Commission Chairman Leggett himself would be sitting in, and there was no getting around his visible impatience for a quick resolution to the situation. The sensationalism generated by the murder of two innocent teenage girls in a supposedly safe county park was the worst publicity Prince George's had encountered during his entire administration, and he didn't like it one bit. Commissioner Leggett had already made himself quite clear in a pre-briefing meeting with Chief Panadapoulis that with a killer still on the loose in his county, it was imperative that they find him — or a reasonably acceptable facsimile — and fast. Bad fanfare in the county paid out poorly for the incumbent at the voting box. Election day was barely six months away, and a candidate named Spealman, running on a platform of government anti-corruption, clean up, law and order, was already making waves. Finish it now, and the public will have forgotten the whole thing before they placed their ballots. Let it linger, and there might be the devil to pay.

Unlike the meeting the previous evening, the briefing was held at the county police headquarters in Seat Pleasant, and twenty-five detectives from Prince George's and D.C. were present. Outside, the press waited patiently, but in vain, for anything they could phone in to their respective night desks. Finally, at midnight, an officer opened the door to the conference room, and more than two dozen bleary-eyed men spilled out, eager to get home for a few hours sleep before resuming the investigation the next morning.

Both Panadapoulis and Leggett at first attempted to avoid engaging the half dozen reporters who blocked their way as the two officials emerged, apparently still engaged in a heated debate.

"Chief, can you tell us about the meeting? Have you learned anything new?" one of the reporters questioned.

"I can only tell you that we had more than two dozen of the best detectives in the county and D.C. at the briefing. We have a number of suspects lined up for questioning, and have turned up certain new information that we will begin to explore tomorrow. Today alone, we have already questioned more than two hundred individuals in the neighborhood, and have found a witness, a laundry truck driver, who claims to have heard firing in the vicinity of the killings Wednesday morning. He reported hearing a burst of shots, then silence, and then a second round of shots. We have also sent certain articles found at the scene of the crime to the FBI's laboratory in Washington for analysis."

"How many men you got on the case?" asked another reporter.

"The Prince George's County Police Department has been using nearly half of its entire personnel in the investigation of the case," replied Panadapoulis. "These men are working sixteen to twenty hours per day. The department has received the finest cooperation and assistance from the Federal Bureau of Investigation and the D.C. Metropolitan Police Department who have assigned five detectives to assist our department. In addition, the department has received offers of assistance from the Montgomery County Police Department and numerous nearby Virginia police departments. The crime scene has been searched thoroughly each day since the day of the crime. The valuable services of the volunteer fire department in the area have been used in the search. We will proceed on a round-the-clock basis until the killer is caught. I would appeal to the public that anyone having information relating to the crime, or that might in any conceivable way have a bearing on the case, be relayed to us as soon as possible. I have assigned four officers to accept calls at the Seat Pleasant station and to immediately relay information or relevant calls to detectives in the field. Every call will be checked out, and the strictest confidentiality will be maintained in our effort to capture the guilty party. And, I assure you," said the chief, "he will be apprehended. Beyond that, I cannot elaborate."

"Commissioner Leggett," shouted a reporter from the back of the crowd, "can you tell us what the county government plans to do about the situation?"

"Sir," said jowly, white-haired Leggett, forcing a smile, "I promise you that the County Commissioners will do everything in our power to aid in the apprehension of the slayer of those two poor young girls."

The media feeding frenzy was accelerating. The Chauvanne-O'Riley murders were now a national news item.

On Highway 80, just outside of Chicago, Tommy Chauvanne looked at his truck radio set with disdain. "Damn it," he muttered. "The next time around they'd better get me a rig with a goddamned radio that works."

The reception had been terrible ever since he left Richmond bound for Chicago with a truckload of Pall Malls, Lucky Strikes, and Chesterfields. He seldom got anything but broadcast static interrupted only occasionally by short periods of good reception. He hated the silence, but hated static even more. After twenty-six hours without sleep, however, he had to have something to keep him awake besides No-Doze.

Tommy Chauvanne was on his second run across the United States as a professional trucker; he had been forced to temporarily abandon work in the construction field, he claimed incessantly, thanks to the unions. Unlike his younger brother Philip, he hated all unions, especially those attempting to establish themselves in the D.C. area, and more specifically an engineers local that had tried to organize his little excavation contracting company. He had chosen to shut down rather than cave in. His wife Dorothy likened him to his late father, a pig-headed man who would mop floors on the principal of the thing rather than surrender. He had paid her no heed.

Tommy had been many things in his forty-seven years, from horse soldier, mounted D.C. cop, construction contractor to Coast Guardsman, heavy equipment operator, and long-distance freight hauler. Almost anything it took to make a living. Now, as an independent trucker, he was getting heat from the Teamsters, and was considering what to do next. Never mind. Like most of his brothers and sisters, his credo had been, and always would be: "I'll deal with it tomorrow."

Absent-mindedly, he tried the radio again. "Maybe this time it'll work," he said to himself. The radio came to life in mid-sentence.

". . . terrible murders. The two victims, Ellen Marie Chauvanne and Michael Linn O'Riley, will be interred tomorrow near Washington. Both Mrs. Philip E. Chauvanne, who has lapsed into unconsciousness several times since the slayings, and Lanie O'Riley, parents of the two girls, are under doctor's care."

Tommy Chauvanne stared at his radio for but a minute, then turned his big rig and $167,000 worth in lading around in mid-highway and headed back to Washington.

Chapter 6

REQUIEM

Mourners began arriving at St. John Baptist de La Salle Church, in Chillum, well before 8:30 a.m. on the morning of Saturday, June 18, even though the requiem for Mikie O'Riley was scheduled for 10 a.m. By 9:30, her former classmates from St. Joseph's Parochial School had already assembled in the rear. The girls were beautifully attired in their white graduation dresses, and the boys in new summer suits. Their congregation gleamed brightly in the morning sun.

On precisely the stroke of 10 a.m., between 250 and 300 mourners watched as the Reverend Paul J. Toomey, Reverend John C. Raider, Vice Chancellor of the Diocese, and the Reverend Michael B. Lade, chaplain of the county police and fire departments, walked slowly and solemnly onto the speakers platform.

Six boys from Mikie's neighborhood, Carlin Bulmer, Rudy Slattery, Carlos De Sousa, Harmon Simons, Donald Quickston and Warren Grady, all members of the teen club and good friends, served as pallbearers. They carried her white casket up the steps and into the church through an aisle formed by ten boys and sixteen girls, all members of her eighth grade graduating class.

Reverend Toomey conducted the Mass, in which both Raider and Lade participated. John and Lanie, and their two daughters sat in the front row, weeping quietly.

Following the Mass, Monsignor Thomas M. Spicer, pastor of the parish, offered a remembrance, a prayer, and an appeal to the audience. "Just eight days ago," he began, "I had the privilege of superintending the graduation of Michael Linn O'Riley. Little did I know then that she would have such a short time to prepare for eternity. Please pray that whoever is responsible for the terrible crime that snuffed out her life so prematurely will be brought to justice and be put properly behind bars so that the people of our fine community may again walk in the sun and allow their children to romp in the park. Please pray that we may also be able to remove all thoughts of vengeance from our hearts, for God will touch the soul of whoever was responsible for this terrible tragedy so that he may repent and be forgiven."

He paused and looked at the audience. Then, speaking directly to John and Lanie O'Riley, he continued. "I hope and believe that your faith will help you accept the Will of God in taking your daughter from you. God bless you and protect you. Amen."

John supported his wife as they left the churchyard, but she slipped from his grasp and fell in a faint to the sidewalk as they neared the black funeral limousine. A half-dozen friends instantly rushed over and soon revived her. Struggling to stand, she was helped into the limousine for the trip to Mt. Olivet Cemetery, where Mikie was to be laid to rest. By the time the limousine had arrived, Lanie O'Riley had regained her composure, as she walked slowly to seats arranged before the graveside.

In full uniform, a platoon of John's fellow officers from the First Precinct stood at attention at the flower-banked grave as Reverend Toomey read prayers for the deceased. Then it was over.

Little Terry Chauvanne sat at the piano in the living room of the Gorsuch's house on Beale Street in Landover Hills, plinking away at the white keys with zest. She liked staying with the Gorsuchs, just as she had many times before when her own family lived next door. Sharon Ann Gorsuch, though several years older, had been one of her best friends, and for the last few days had sheltered Terry from the ongoing news coverage of the murders. About 11:00 a.m., Sharon Ann came down from her room upstairs dressed up as if she were going to Sunday school.

"Where are you going?" asked Terry, surprised to see her friend so attired.

"I'm going to see Ellen," replied Sharon Ann.

Terry looked at her in surprise and then with excitement. "Is she alive again?"

For the first time in her life, owing to the explanation that followed, Terry Chauvanne learned of the finality of death. She did not accept it, though.

Shortly after noon, a few miles to the northeast of Mt. Olivet Cemetery, just across the Maryland-D.C. line, friends and relatives of the Chauvanne family began arriving at Gasch's Funeral Home in Hyattsville. By 2:15 p.m. three hundred or more mourners had filled two large chapels in the home. Unlike Mikie's funeral, where the deceased's casket had not been opened, the Chauvannes had chosen to see their daughter one last time before burial. The wounds on her body had been dressed so well that they were no longer visible. She was clothed now for eternity in a blue taffeta-and-tulle party dress that in happier days she had often described as her favorite.

The funeral home was not yet provided with air-conditioning, a luxury still unaffordable for most business establishments. With so many people confined to the two small chapels, and the afternoon heat increasing, many of the mourners had removed what outer garments they could. Men loosened their ties and took off their suit coats. The hundreds of flower bouquets surrounding the casket had already begun to wilt. All of the quiet chatter amidst the crowd seemed to center on the recent crime and what was being done to capture the killer. The entire Chauvanne clan and related families, numbering well over forty individuals, with the exception of Philip and Lucille, were in attendance. Tommy Chauvanne, red-eyed and weary after being forty hours on the road, and his wife Dorothy, sat in the second row. Beside them sat his brothers and sisters, Henry, Fred, Roderick, Gilbert, Mary Katherine, Marissa, and Marva, their spouses, and assorted relations, though most of their younger children had been left at home. In the rear of the church, a half-dozen plainclothes detectives scanned the crowd for suspicious persons.

Just before 2:30 p.m., when the service was to begin, Philip and Lucille arrived in a shiny new, fiery red Cadillac specifically rented for the occasion, and walked slowly into the chapel and directly up to the casket for a last, loving look at their daughter. The Cadillac had been Lucille's idea, saying she thought her daughter would have loved the gesture of extravagance. To show off the family's beat up old De Soto would not have been fitting. The fact that Philip was out of work and couldn't afford such luxuries, much less the funeral itself, mattered little to Lucille. Ellen would have loved it. After all, she consoled her husband in justifying the unorthodox flare of their arrival, his well-off brother Roderick had generously offered to loan them the money for the funeral (although he knew nothing of the car rental). They would worry about repaying the loan later.

Both Philip and Lucille dressed in black. Lucille wore short white gloves and a white hat. Her dark glasses could not hide the puffy redness of her eyes. Philip appeared drawn and gaunt, but was the pillar upon which his wife leaned. Eddy stood behind them, uncomfortable in his seldom-worn sport coat, still dazed by the immensity of the evil that had befallen his family. Within seconds of viewing their daughter for the last time, Lucille broke into loud gasps. "My baby, my baby." With loving care, Philip took her left arm and steered her from the casket to her seat. Eddy lingered for a few seconds, the anger again welling up inside him as he saw his sister for the last time, but refused to let the tears come. He promised himself they never would again.

The Reverend Vincent B. Wilding, pastor of the nearby Mt. Rainier Christian Church, offered a brief eulogy. The pastor knew Ellen from his Sunday school class, at which she was a regular, and characterized her as "a little girl filled always with abundant good hope." He prayed for God "to comfort all who mourn her loss" and told those assembled before him to "be thankful that the end came quickly, with no molestation that would have been so hurtful." Casting his eyes down to his Bible, he quoted: "Be not afraid of death, only believe in God." Among the many mourners, reported the *Washington Post* the next day, grown men wept.

Burial was to take place at Fort Lincoln Cemetery, less than a half mile away. As the grieving parents arrived, Lucille stumbled and nearly fell as she walked slowly from the rented Cadillac towards the casket. When she was safely seated beneath a canopy that sheltered the grave and surrounding seats for the immediate family, Pastor Wilding read the burial services, concluding with the verse: "And he said to her, I am the resurrection and the life."

Even as the final words were being said over the casket at Fort Lincoln Cemetery, the police interviews of local residents along the park, and of anyone who personally knew the victims, were proceeding full tilt. Pandora's Box was slowly but methodically being pried open, and its contents sorted before escaping to the press. Lt. Terrance Hendricks, one of many Washington policemen working on the case, teased the reporters with a statement saying only, "We have something new and it looks good." He refused to amplify his comment. All Panadapoulis would say was that "certain new information" had been acquired, and would be checked out during the day. Only later would it be leaked that the investigation was coming to focus on reports of an unidentified man who carried a rifle, a sheath knife, and a bandolier of cartridges. Neither Henry Chauvanne's nor Sammy Stokes's reports of the stranger were mentioned.

When the press attempted to question Sammy at his home in Lewisdale, they were able to engage only his mother. All she would tell them was that she also had two small children, and she, like the police, could not rest with the knowledge that the murderer was still at large. Sammy's attorney, Jeffrey MacIntire, closed the brief interview by informing the pack of journalists camped on the Stokes lawn that the boy was not at home, but "at a place where he can get a lot of rest and will not be bothered."

Immediately after the funerals, word leaked out that fresh clues had emerged, but had been tossed aside after close examination. One of the most promising among them had been the testimony of a seventeen-year-old student, a friend of both the victims, who attended Bladensburg High School, two miles to the south of Northwestern. Police had picked him up at the cemetery shortly after the services were concluded, and informed them that on June 9th, only six days before the killings, Ellen had come over to his school with Sammy Stokes. She had shown a diamond ring to him and confided that she was secretly engaged, but that Sammy wasn't the fiancé. A Chauvanne family spokesman immediately denied the boy's story, and told the police that the piece of jewelry she had been showing around was an old family ring given to her by her grandmother.

Miscellaneous tips flowed in almost hourly. All had to be checked out. One typical lead was brought in by a cabdriver for the local Diamond Cab Company, one Vernon Biggers, who reported that earlier in the day a passenger named Leon H. Dudley, from Irving Street, NW, in the District, had gotten in his cab with a rifle in a bag, and had told him in no uncertain terms that he "knew who killed those two girls in Maryland." Police immediately investigated and within hours Dudley, who was found to be armed with a .22-caliber rifle and fifty-six cartridges, had been arrested and charged with carrying a deadly firearm. Though he denied Biggers's statement, police promptly hauled the suspect before Judge Gladys Landis in Municipal Court; she ordered him held for mental observation following the hearing.

Meanwhile, the search for the murder weapon and other clues continued unabated. In the park, twenty-five volunteers, primarily from the Chillum-Adelphi Volunteer Fire Department and off-duty D.C. cops, had begun chain-sawing trees to expand the damming of the Northwest Branch so that even more of the streambed could be searched. Their primary targets were the murder weapon and Ellen's tiny green wallet that she was believed to be carrying when ambushed. The wallet contained $2 and a vial of asthma pills, all still missing. Grasping at even the slimmest murder motives, police could not rule out robbery as the killer's objective. So thorough was their search for even the most meager clue that the on-duty and off-duty men, on their hands and knees, scrambled through the tangled underbrush around the roped-off murder scene.

It was the third day of the investigation, and throughout the county the murders had by now become the focal point of interest. The perimeter of the Northwest Park crime scene again became the gathering place for hundreds of onlookers. Time and again officers were obliged to appeal for citizens to stand clear. Though only authorized personnel were permitted inside the search area, where Winnie Sweitzer and his men were centering their efforts, the public attention often became unnerving.

The field investigation had been methodical and labor-intensive. At no time during the day did the searchers get more than an arm's length apart from one another, and were frequently on their hands and knees crawling through heavy underbrush in ever widening circles. By the day's end, Sweitzer took little consolation in the fact that his men and the volunteers had scoured every inch of eight to ten acres of park woodland before he was finally obliged to called off the hunt. As on the previous day, when they left, the blood-spattered murder scene was again roped off and left under police guard.

The only potential evidence had been discovered by Detectives Jonathan Holder and Ron Fornost who had again been canvassing the park and the adjacent Christian Heurich estate, this time on horseback. Notebook papers, one bearing the inscription "Ellen C." and other handwriting on the rest, and a filthy blue sleeveless gabardine jacket, had been found in Fireplace No. 4, more than one hundred yards from the slaying site. The jacket seemed to match the piece of cloth Charlie Bricker found by the crime scene soon after the murder. Neither the papers nor the jacket showed burn marks. Though nothing apparent linked either to the crime, they were nevertheless catalogued, photographed, and sent to headquarters for fingerprinting and study.

With the narrowing of the field to gun type, brand, and period of production, the methodical check of sales of such rifles in D.C., Maryland, and Virginia was beginning to bear fruit. Although no weapons were overlooked in the investigation, police had focused on the .22-caliber Marlin repeater. During the day, no fewer than three individuals carrying rifles were either stopped on county roads or brought in for questioning.

About 4:00 p.m., Corporal C. C. Musk and Private T. J. Budding spotted a fourteen-year old boy walking with a rifle along Route 202, near a development called Kent Village, four miles to the east of Hyattsville. When sighted by the two cops, the boy had tried to hide the gun behind him. The weapon, however, proved to be a bolt action Stevens repeater. The youth was not brought in for questioning, but the rifle was held at Seat Pleasant.

Acting on a tip soon afterwards, Musk and Budding picked up another youth and his .22-caliber rifle at his home and brought him into the station for questioning early the same evening. The boy, clad only in a blue T-shirt and khaki trousers, was discharged after a brief interrogation. About 7:15 p.m., another .22 rifle was brought in, wrapped up in a newspaper. Later, a 20-year-old man was hauled in with his .22 and questioned for an hour and then dismissed. Their guns, along with three other similar weapons rounded up during the day, were held for examination. In all, six weapons had been confiscated in twenty-four hours from the vicinity of the killings.

Over on Adelphi Road, at the now empty Northwestern High, detectives had spent hours searching the school and every nook therein even remotely associated with Ellen. Lockers, classrooms, the gymnasium, and cafeteria, were all examined for possible clues "from top to bottom." One of the principal areas of investigation was the school rifle team's squad room. When a school official erroneously commented that one of the locked-up guns might have been missing, a gaggle of detectives descended on the room in a swarm, but found the inventory of weapons untouched since before the murder. Nevertheless, a full inspection of the collection, and examination of anyone who had access to it, was soon underway. Of the eleven members of the rifle team, six of whom were female, five had known Ellen, but as no more than passing acquaintances, and all had solid alibis. However, within a few days, the search was enlarged to incorporate the entire school and surrounding grounds. Every room, locker, filing cabinet, nook and cranny was examined and scrutinized, but to no apparent avail. Simultaneously, other detectives launched a mass questioning of students at the school, both those who knew the victims and others who did not.

The intensive campaign to interview residents of the neighborhood, both adults and youths, as well as business owners in the area, had begun to turn up information that was beginning to provide a temporal framework for the crime. Though it was a Saturday night, and his men were tired, at 9:15 p.m. Panadapoulis called in nearly a score of detectives for another note-swapping session and review of the day's work. The meeting was long and, for the men who had been in the field all day, fatigue was extreme. Charts and diagrams worked up of the murder scene, the neighborhood, and possible movement routes of the victims and the killer were laid out and discussed. The location of every witness was marked in red on a large area map. Dr. Macubbin, the county medical examiner, had refined his assessment of the time of death to 9:00 a.m. plus or minus an hour. That meant that Ellen and Mikie had been murdered between 8:00 and 10:00 a.m.

The most promising news, however, was Henry Chauvanne's account of the mysterious "Pancho Villa" character who had entered the park on June 14 and come out the next day, soon after the murders had been committed, according to the medical examiner's new time frame. The information seemed to corroborate Stokes's account, which he had also related to Mitchell Bulmer. Interviews with Anita Slattery and Candice Miller had fixed Stokes's presence in the park at between 8:18, when he arrived, and 8:20 a.m., when the three of them departed. If Sammy had actually seen "Pancho Villa" in the park near the footbridge, as he claimed, the ambush must have occurred before

8:18 a.m. Unfortunately, several witnesses had testified that they had heard shots, or what sounded like shots, coming from the park, but could not pinpoint the time. Others, who lived closest to the scene, had heard nothing.

Three hours later, the meeting broke up and for the first time in three days the detectives went home before midnight.

"I want you all back here at 1:00 p.m. tomorrow for an evaluation of what we have gone over tonight," said Chief Panadapoulis, well aware that the following day was the Sabbath. "Sleep well."

Chapter 7

THIS CAN'T BE KANSAS

Unlike those sixteen-hour shifts of the preceding four, the fifth day of investigation for the Prince George's police, commenced on Sunday afternoon, June 19, at 1 p.m., permitting a much-needed, if short respite for the fatigued officers. Panadapoulis began anew with an hour-and-half long strategy meeting at the Seat Pleasant headquarters, where plans were laid out to question more promising witnesses and potential suspects. A giant map of the murder scene was tacked to the gray wall and scanned in detail. Sifting of the massive data collected thus far, consolidation of the reports of the nine two-man teams of detectives, and weeding out irrelevant information gathered by many scores of others, began with renewed intensity.

The main objectives were daunting. Panadapoulis and his officers began backtracking to reassess what had been uncovered so far. The murder weapon, believed to have been a Marlin repeater or semi-automatic, had yet to be found or its specific typology identified. Moreover, Ellen's green wallet containing her asthma pills and $2, all once tidied away in her white purse, which had been found opened and thirty-five feet from her body, were also missing.

Panadapoulis was anything but dismayed as he listened to the reports and discussions from the officers assembled. He had definite plans on how he would proceed if he could steer clear of the political flak. What bothered him most was the phone call he received from Jessup Leggett just before the session began. The chief had been grateful for the commissioner's pivotal role in elevating him in the blink of an eye, from head of the lowly three-man Beltsville Police, to command of the 112-man county police over a career veteran of the force, Julian Edwards. Panadapoulis had been aware from the beginning that his personal loyalty to his patron, Leggett, was all-important and would soon be tested. He was also quite conscious of the way the system worked in Prince George's County, indeed throughout Maryland. What he had not expected was that his first test, a sensational crime now splashed across the front pages of most newspapers on the Eastern Seaboard — the first murder case he had ever engaged in — would come so soon after his appointment. To say that he was charged up by the challenge would have been an understatement.

Panadapoulis did not personally care much for overweight, jowly Commissioner Leggett, whose deep voice, which always seemed to have a rasping quality, grated on him. Nor did he look forward to the commissioner's calls, which were usually about fixing someone's speeding ticket, borrowing a cruiser for some private reason, or having a uniformed officer perform some menial personal task for Mrs. Leggett, their obese children, or some well-heeled fellow politicos. He was well aware of the rumors of the commissioner's powerful influence in zoning matters and of possible kickbacks from developers, especially along the corridor for the planned Interstate 95 Baltimore-Washington superhighway, but he had dutifully turned a blind eye whenever complaints came his way. The call this morning had not been unexpected.

"Morning Commissioner," Panadapoulis had begun.

"Major," replied Leggett without bothering a greeting, "I'll cut to the goddamned chase. This murder case is getting to be an embarrassment for the county, and the negative media attention ain't exactly what I was hoping for as we begin to approach the elections. We need some forward motion and fast. What've you got in the hopper?"

"Sir, we have not been able to find the murder weapon yet, and some of the victim's belongings have yet to surface. Edwards and I are both of the opinion that the gun was probably dumped in the branch or in one of the nearby duck ponds, maybe even hidden in a tree. The old Christian Heurich estate, just down the way, is also a possible dumping spot and we are going to begin combing that today. I believe quite strongly that the weapon was ditched in the water somewhere nearby. We've got fingerprints from Chauvanne's purse, all of which are hers, and from a picnic bench that was dragged across the park, possibly to hide the bodies, but none of which can be matched. We haven't ruled out robbery as a motive, but for two bucks? Not likely."

He waited for a response from Leggett, but gleaned only silence, and thus continued with his summary.

"I've got one of my detectives, Ron Fornost, who has a pilot's license, going up tomorrow morning with Sergeant Holder of the D.C. police, to conduct a flyover of the park and neighborhood. He wants to scan the rooftops for the murder weapon, which I think is a good move. And I'm firing off a request for the FBI to begin ballistics tests on the bullets recovered from the site. They have already told us that we are probably looking for a Marlin manufactured within the last two years. We're on the lookout for anyone who even remotely fits a description of the man seen sitting on a log in the park with a rifle across his knee about the time of the murder. He seems to be our best bet. My men have taken to calling him 'Pancho Villa.' But we're still trying to pin the exact time of the murder down more tightly. Moreover, we think we might have a lead or two in some of the victims' personal journals and letters we discovered earlier."

He was, in fact, hopeful that the papers, particularly those belonging to the Chauvanne girl, might shed some light on the mystery. Two of his men, Lieutenant Detective Lee Humphrey and Sergeant Thomas Bearson, were bringing them in this evening. There was some interesting material in them regarding one of Ellen's old schoolmates who now lives in New Jersey, and the two detectives were driving up "to look for another piece in this jigsaw puzzle" and to interview the lad.

"How long's all this crap going to take," demanded the commissioner, "before we get somebody?"

"We're moving as fast as humanly possible, sir," replied the chief almost apologetically.

"Well, dammit. I want the public to see some forward motion now. And I don't want the damned FBI involved anymore than absolutely necessary. That son-of-a-bitch Hoover would like nothing better than to make it a bigger media thing than it already is just so's he can look good. The bastard loves to see his mug in the papers."

"Sir, we don't have a crime lab to do even the basic ballistics tests. We have already scheduled testing to begin. We've got to use the FBI!"

Deputy Chief Edwards had been lead man in the effort to incorporate the services of the FBI's firearms and ballistics experts, who had already pointed out that the minute firing marks found on the slugs recovered from the crime scene did not stem from any recent development in firearms manufacture. The rifle marks on the bullets were simply a by-product of the spiraling grooves inside the gun barrel; these were designed to make the bullets spin as they exited, thereby providing greater accuracy and distance — and with considerable accuracy they could be matched to the gun they had been fired from... if the weapon were in hand! The FBI ballistics lab was the best in the nation.

"Oh, dammit," said the commissioner, caving in. "Go ahead, set it up with them, but keep it low-key. As for the public's so-called need to know, why don't you release the stuff about that guy seen sitting in the park? You know, some bits and pieces that Stokes kid told you about. Anything to at least give the impression that we're doing something."

"I hadn't intended on it so early in the game and it could be harmful to the investigation."

"Well let's put it this way. I think the game's already too goddamned long. Interest in this case among my constituents is picking up rather than subsiding. It's the damned topic of conversation on the street and at every corner drugstore. Newspapers are being sold as soon as they reach the stands. Everybody's got his or her own theory and I don't like it. It draws too much attention to the government, you and me, and we can't afford that, and you know precisely why. I want some goddamned forward motion, and I mean now! I don't care if you have to arrest everybody in the state that owns a .22. Hell, I couldn't give a rodent's rectum who did it. I just want an arrest and for this thing to blow over within the next month, by mid-July at the latest. Do I make myself clear?"

"Yes, sir."

The sound of the phone on the other end of the line hitting its receiver was audible even to Deputy Chief Edwards, who had just come in and sat down opposite Panadapoulis.

"Guess we got to get something tantalizing out to the press," said the chief with a smirk, "but not until after the morning briefing."

2:00 p.m. Private Emmet Kudnal had been answering the phone all afternoon. The special line was set up for the Chauvanne-O'Riley case, fending off the obvious quacks, and forwarding the few seemingly compelling ones, to the appropriate officers in the field. Most of the latter were attended to promptly, albeit with little to show for the effort except more time-consuming footwork and paper shuffling. The long-distance call that came in from Kansas City, however, was different, and the desk clerk put it directly through to the chief himself.

"I think I got a hot one," Kudnal said on transferring the call to his boss.

"Panadapoulis here. What can I do for you?" the chief said as he picked up the receiver.

"Thanks for taking my call," the voice said on the other end of the line. "My name is Wesley N. Walters, and I'm a civilian engineer with the Navy Department. I heard over the radio out here in Kansas about those horrible murders in Northwest Branch Park. My wife and I, you see, are out here on vacation, visiting relatives. But I live at 322 Stanford Street, a short distance from the edge of park. When I heard what happened, I thought I should call you right away."

"Well, Mr. Walters, what is it you want to tell me?" replied the chief.

The caller cleared his throat, and began. "On Wednesday morning — that would be the day of the killings — I began loading up my car for the trip out here. At about 8:25 a.m. I glanced over toward the park and noticed a dark blue or black sedan near the scene with a teenage boy standing beside it. I know it was 8:25 cause I wanted to leave by 9:00 a.m. and I looked at my watch because I was worried about running late. And I think I saw two girls in the park at the same time, but I can't be certain."

"You sure about the time?" the chief said excitedly.

"Certain of it. Dead certain."

Panadapoulis managed a near smile on his thin lips. Besides Stokes, here was the first possible witness to the presence of someone actually at or near the crime scene, and perhaps someone who had actually seen the two victims while they were still alive. After a few minutes more, the questions and answers ended.

"Musk," shouted the chief out into the station, "get in here!"

Corporal C. C. Musk appeared instantly. Within five minutes he and his partner, Private T. J. Budding, were en route to Stanford Street to canvas Walters' neighbors and check out the engineers' story. Within two hours they had radioed back to the chief that in an interview with one of Walters' neighbors, Mrs. Harvey R. Coney, Jr., who lived two houses down from him, at 318 Stanford, they had confirmed his story. Indeed, Mrs. Coney had been helping the engineer load up between 8:00 and 8:20 a.m. and they had made a number of trips from the house to the car, carrying clothes and luggage and stowing away vacation paraphernalia in his trunk, and thus had an opportunity to view the park a number of times. Her own house was the nearest of all in the neighborhood to the park, but while helping out Walters she had seen neither the teenager, the girls nor the car that the engineer saw twenty-five minutes later. Nor had she heard any gunshots. In fact, the police had already questioned her twice before about not hearing gunshots, but she had failed to mention Walters.

"I'd know a gunshot if I heard one," she had told Musk, wagging her bony finger to make the point. She was a skinny, gaunt woman who reminded Private Budding of the Wicked Witch of the West in the Wizard of Oz. "The kids often fire their rifles target-practicing in the park, and I can tell you their shooting is quite loud and clear. I never let them walk through my lawn when they are traipsing down there. No telling what they're likely to carry off from my yard, but I swear to God I didn't hear a thing on Wednesday morning."

For Panadapoulis the information was intriguing, but far from conclusive. The youth Walters observed might well have been Stokes driving his dark blue Packard sedan. The two girls could have been Slattery and Miller, but they had already left by 8:20 a.m., which would make Walters' statement erroneous, for the difference in time between their departure and his sighting was a full five minutes. Had his watch been off? Had he, indeed, seen Stokes, Slattery, and Miller? Or could he have actually seen the killer and the two victims just before the crime was committed? Mrs. Coney had seen no one in the park between 8 and 8:20 a.m. from the identical vantage point Walters had made his observation. Both the two new informants were adamant about the time, and there was no reason to believe they were not credible. But something just didn't fit.

The victims had left their homes shortly before 8:00 a.m. and their sisters had seen them, arm-in-arm, enter the park immediately afterwards, indeed no more than five minutes later. They had apparently never exited. The actual murder — the firing of seventeen shots — and the subsequent effort to drag the bodies into the briar patch must have taken at least twelve to fifteen minutes. Coney had seen no one between 8:00 and 8:20 a.m. Stokes had arrived a minute or two after 8:15 and had just spotted a male, presumably an adult, sitting with a rifle across his lap when Slattery and Miller appeared. When he looked again, the figure in the park had disappeared. At 8:20 a.m., having seen neither Ellen nor Mikie, the three youths had left for Northwestern. If Ellen and Mikie were not lying in the briar patch at 8:20 a.m., where the hell were they? They hadn't been seen at the school, and if they had deviated from their route, or stopped somewhere, not reaching the murder scene until after 8:20 a.m., where had they gone? Then, at 8:25 a.m. Walters saw a youth, a car, and two girls, all unidentified.

Something was screwy. The timing was simply inconsistent with a growing consensus among investigators that the killings were carried out within a few minutes on either side of 8:00 a.m., and that the killer's aiming, firing seventeen shots, fourteen of which hit their targets at least one of which was moving, from a range of about fifty yards, and dragging one body, but probably both, nearly 150 feet, was completed by 8:15 a.m. One thing, however, seemed certain. The killer was no novice with a gun.

The chief took a sip of black coffee, and then bit off a hangnail that had bothered him all morning. With his head tilted to one side and a quizzical look on his face he peered at Edwards. "Gee Toto. This can't be Kansas, can it? We haven't even found the yellow brick road yet."

"Chief," interrupted the desk officer from out front, "you should come down to the lockup. Sheriff's deputies down in Leonardtown got a kid they picked up this morning with a .22 rifle. Sheriff down there said he had been seen firing it 'indiscriminately' and thought he looked suspicious, so they sent him up here."

Leonardtown, Panadapoulis knew, was the county seat of St. Mary's County, and a good forty miles out in the heart of Southern Maryland tobacco country, at least two hours drive from Seat Pleasant. And everybody down there owned a gun or rifle of some sort.

"Well that's something, anyway," responded the chief morosely. "Get him into interrogation right away."

The young man, a tall, handsome 20-year-old clad in denim jeans and a white tee shirt, was thoroughly terrified by his situation. He was grilled behind closed doors for more than an hour and was then whisked off in a scout car to the crime scene, after which he was brought back for further questioning. The man's alibi, which was quickly confirmed by witnesses who were with him on the day of the murder, proved rock solid and within a few hours he was driven home and released, although his gun was retained for further evaluation.

No sooner had he gone than another potential suspect was brought in for questioning. The new arrival, approximately 55-years old, wore dirty work clothes, and a five-day growth on his face. The only reasons for his being picked up were his disheveled appearance and proximity to Northwest Branch Park when a police cruiser passed by. He was also released after questioning.

Detective Sergeants Ronald D. Fornost, and D.C. Detective Sergeant Jonathan Holder's early morning hour-long flyover on June 20 of Lane Manor, Lewisdale, University Hills, and adjacent neighborhoods, and over the play areas in the park, was interesting but unproductive. Fornost, a Civil Air Patrol wing commander, had secured approval to fly as low as 150 feet to scan rooftops in search of the murder weapon or anything else that might prove of interest in the case that could possibly be lying on a roof. The exercise, carried out in a Cessna 140, however, had generated little more than a few irate residents waving their fists up at the aircraft as it passed noisily — and repeatedly — overhead. A few spots were logged in for further checking, and upon landing, the two detectives set off by car to run down the leads. All proved of no value.

Near the crime scene in the park, Detective Carroll F. G. Black of the Prince George's police and Sergeant Russell Black of the D.C. police conducted an unannounced test-fire experiment while a group of neighborhood children stood and watched in utter curiosity outside the police barrier. The purpose of the experiment was to determine the audible range of the sound of a Marlin semi-automatic rifle being fired. The Prince George's officer expertly loaded a sample Marlin, hunkered down behind a low bank at the periphery of the Northwest Branch, and fired several shots through a screen of shrubbery at given time intervals. As he pumped shot after shot into the bushes, he noted that the ejected shells were flying off at a thirty-degree angle, and were landing in the stream a full ten feet away. Several hundred yards off on Stanford Drive, Sergeant Russell Black moved in synchronized fashion from position to position as each shot was fired and simply listened. Every shot was audible.

Yet not one call from any neighbors — all of whom were unaware of the experiment — was received at police headquarters.

The physically exhausting search in the park for the murder weapon had continued without letup, but now took on an even more daunting area than the park itself. Little more than a half mile from the murder scene stood the once grand estate, built in September 1935, of an American success story named Christian Heurich. A German immigrant who had started with $1,000 from his savings account, Heurich had erected one of the great American brewery empires of its day, with headquarters in Northwest D.C. He had dallied heavily in real estate as well, and built a formidable manse at what was now the region between Colesville and Queen's Chapel Roads. Following his death in 1940 at the age of 97, Heurich's empire had begun to crumble and along with it the grand estate, the largest portion of which was sold off to developers. Indeed, most of Lewisdale, Lane Manor, and Northwest Branch Park, had been carved out of his once great holdings. Of particular interest to the police was a substantial man-made lake, which covered five acres, and an adjacent pond about 150 feet by 20 feet. Both were popular meeting places for students at Northwestern High.

Soldiers from Fort George G. Meade, near Jessup, Maryland, this time belonging to the 19th Engineers, again returned to assist the police. First, though, a twenty-ton county crane was employed to dig a drainage ditch from a cement-walled finger of the lake on its eastern extremity, even as a demolition squad placed a dynamite charge to blast a four-foot hole in the wall to drain the waters. Then, they went in with metal detectors and rakes to search for the murder weapon amidst the black goop and slop of the lake bottom. By dark, the effort had produced no results, and the search was called off until the following morning.

By late evening a total of six more .22 rifles and one pistol had been taken into custody, though most, such as a Higgens automatic seized by D.C. police during a liquor raid the previous evening, were not Marlins. The owner of the Higgens had claimed that he had bought it to shoot the rats proliferating in his Southeast D.C. neighborhood almost as fast as the crime rate there. The .22 pistol from the suspect Martin in Arlington a few days before had definitely been eliminated as the possible murder weapon. Captain Richard J. Felber, head of the Homicide Squad, had nevertheless been assigned to conduct a routine check on the gun though it was almost certain the murder weapon had been a Marlin repeater or semi-automatic. Based upon the accuracy of the shots and their number, firearms experts at the FBI had emphatically declared it virtually impossible for anyone to group the shots so closely with a sidearm. Another gun, a Marlin, had been voluntarily brought in by a resident of nearby Carmody Hills on the slim but "highly improbable" chance that someone might have removed it from his house without his knowledge. The only promising Marlin taken in had been a .22 picked up by detectives Brian Barclay and George Clelland during their search of the Stokes home during the day. The kid might not be out of the woods yet!

At 8:00 p.m. the chief finally released a statement for the morning papers. He informed them of the interrogation and release of two potential suspects, but the real teaser, one that would more than meet Commissioner Leggett's directives for creating an appearance of "forward motion" — no matter how possibly injurious to the case — came over the protest of Deputy Chief Edwards. Panadapoulis maintained a rigid demeanor when he informed the gaggle of reporters assembled in the conference room that the principle witness thus far, Sammy Stokes, had seen a man, wearing a bandolier style ammunition belt, sitting in the park with a rifle across his knees on the morning of the slayings. A noticeable murmur rippled across the room when he informed them that his detectives were even then examining a sheaf of mysterious letters for possible clues. Finally, to humanize the whole affair, Panadapoulis noted that Private Thomas W. O'Riley was going to take a personal part in the ongoing investigation. With that, he concluded the briefing.

The next morning on the front page of the *Washington Post and Times Herald*, in 72-point type, the banner headline read: "Police Check Findings in Slayer Hunt. Two More Men Are Questioned In Park Murder And Released."

Chapter 8

FORWARD MOTION

On Tuesday morning, June 21, the work at the Christian Heurich lake began afresh. A two-inch centrifugal pump drained off the remainder of the now four- to eight-inch-deep water, while the crane deepened the drainage ditch. The four-man crew of Army soldiers wearing hip-waders stood at the ready with their metal detectors, prepared to go in as soon as the residual water was gone. Once the lake was emptied, Captain Sweitzer, who was superintending the operation, ordered that two forty-foot cisterns discovered at each end of the nearby pond also be pumped out, and a strong searchlight be brought in to examine the empty wells.

Back at the Seat Pleasant station, five of the .22-caliber rifles, some of the slugs from the crime scene, bullets that had been test-fired from each of the guns, the victim's bloodied clothes, the blue gabardine jacket and the matching portion of sleeve, the papers found in Fireplace No. 4, and blood-stained sod from the murder scene — indeed everything gleaned thus far — were packed for shipment to the FBI crime lab in Washington. There they would undergo bloodstain analysis and microscopic scrutiny. At the same time, an FBI agent, escorted by several Prince George's detectives, visited the crime scene to conduct a detailed examination of his own so that he could personally familiarize himself with the provenance of the evidence being sent in for testing.

There were, of course, some intriguing properties and potential clues still in development. Edwards had suggested that the department undertake a re-enactment of the crime in the park, and that they test fire another Marlin during the course of the effort. In this way the physical realties, the actual logistical requirements needed to perpetrate the crime itself, might be better understood, and provide investigators with more on the killer's thought processes. The dry-run would also give investigators an approximation of the time it took to drill eleven shots into Ellen Marie Chauvanne, and three more in Michael Linn O'Riley, then run fifty feet, drag at least one, but probably both, of their bodies 150 to 160 feet each into the briar patch, attempt to drag a picnic bench seventy-five feet, and gather twigs in an attempt to cover both bodies, and then successfully flee the scene. A more precise knowledge of minutes, even seconds, necessary to complete the crime, was vital to the case. If the process of the murder had been such a contest against time, the race to solve the crime was an even more furious one.

Both Panadapoulis and Edwards anxiously awaited forthcoming reports on the cast of a man's footprint and tire marks taken in the park. Fingerprints had been successfully lifted from the picnic table that had been moved, presumably in an abortive attempt to hide the bodies. Moreover, two leather-bound diaries belonging to Ellen and Mikie were undergoing intense scrutiny, and preliminary analysis revealed a number of names of interest to investigators. Though neither officer would identify ownership of the two volumes as belonging to either girl, the chief was quick to state that the new evidence "is very important to a solution of the case."

Henry Chauvanne had done about all he could to ease the pain and anguish of his older brother and sister-in-law. The Chauvanne brothers, all six of them — Tommy, Henry, Fred, Philip, Gilbert and Roderick — and their four sisters, Mary Katherine, Marissa, Marva, and Clair, even in the best of times, had for years been a contentious lot, given to infighting and family feuding far beyond the norms of sibling rivalries. Conflict reached a peak in 1924 when one of the sisters, Clair, married a Syrian-Lebanese immigrant named John Picola, the handsome son of a prominent immigrant Christian Syrian theologian and author. For many in the Chauvanne clan, olive-skinned Middle Easterners, Christians or not, were no different than Maryland "coloreds" or "high yellers." The marriage had driven a wedge between many of the family members and the couple had been immediately ostracized by one side, but warmly embraced by the other.

The product of their union was a beautiful, raven-haired child named Emilia. The Picolas had struck out on their own and the future looked bright. In 1926 John, a well-educated naturalized citizen, joined the U.S. Treasury Department's Bureau of Alcohol, Tobacco, and Firearms as a field agent. Clair also took a part time job to help support the family. Then, on October 4, 1928, Agent Picola sustained severe injuries in a crash during a heroic high-speed pursuit of rumrunners through the little Maryland town of Laurel and died soon afterwards. Two years later, Clair died of a burst appendix while visiting relatives in Texas. Three-year-old Emilia was orphaned. There seemed little alternative for the family patriarch, Philip, Sr., and his wife Mary but to raise the girl that they considered a half-breed and cared little for. During the terrible years of the Great Depression, they received a government stipend for housing the orphan, and because of the money, had little interest in turning the girl over to her Syrian-Lebanese relatives living in New York.

Despite her Cinderella status in the household, Emilia rapidly matured into a stunningly beautiful teenager, who had emerged perfectly, though neither loved nor counseled in the ways of the world. Perhaps not surprisingly, during her first week on her first job as a secretary for a trucking company, the raffish good-looking company owner, Gilbert R. Nicewarner, seduced and impregnated her. The Chauvanne clan was horrified at the prospect of an out-of-wedlock birth in the family, and by a half-breed at that. Nevertheless, Emilia Picola refused to have an illegal abortion.

After considerable anguish, and at the instigation and encouragement of her uncle Fred and aunt Lois, she agreed to turn over to Philip and Lucille her unborn child as if it were their own offspring. There would be no formal adoption, for with the collusion of the family doctor, the birth certificate would be made out as if the child had been naturally born of Lucille. Emilia also agreed never to see the child again. Baby Terry, born on a rainy Valentine's Day in 1948, was to be told nothing of her true origin.

The birth of Terry Chauvanne and the conditions of her adoption had caused a horrific tear in the fabric of the Chauvanne clan that would never heal. Indeed, not until Ellen's funeral, more than seven years later had one faction even spoken with the other. Henry had been on the side allied with Philip and Lucille, and he had readily offered to take the child in for a few weeks until things around Lane Manor retuned to a semblance of normalcy.

Seven-year-old Terry had spent the first day or two after the murder with the Gorsuch family in Landover, but with Lucille in a near state of collapse, it was evident to the entire family that she was in no condition to take care of the little girl. Eddy could manage himself, but fragile Terry needed attention. Henry again quickly volunteered to take her in for a few weeks. This time the offer was accepted.

Henry had a small twenty-acre farm near the diminutive hamlet of Bristol, once called Pig Point, a thriving river port of the colonial era, on the Patuxent River in Southern Maryland. Though he made his living as a heavy equipment operator, he had supplemented his income to help support his wife Bootsy and his seven-year old twin daughters, Dorothy and Debby, by raising tobacco, chickens, horses, and a few head of cattle. "I can take Terry for a few weeks," he volunteered to Philip, "get her away from all this chaos, and get her mind off Ellen. Besides, my girls would love to have her, and she loves horses like her sister did."

Over the next two weeks Terry, Dorothy, and Debby became almost inseparable playmates on Henry's farm. The farmhouse itself wasn't much to look at, and needed a lot of work. A few derelict pieces of farm equipment, reapers, and scourers, covered by a thick coat of honeysuckle vines behind a calamitous tobacco barn, along with a scattering of rusting cars, bulldozer parts, a blade or two, steel cables, several broken-down cement mixers, a dozen empty fifty-gallon steel drums, and other detritus of the construction industry. Henry affectionately referred to the junk heap as his "Golden Yard."

To one side of the decrepit-looking barn, and about three hundred feet from the pasture fence, behind which grazed cattle and a single nasty-tempered but nearly lame bull named "Fluffy," was the outdoor privy. Bootsy called it "The Crapper," but Henry always referred to it simply as his "Seat of Ease." Terry had never used an outhouse before and was immediately put off by the experience, fearing that she might fall through the wooden seat hole and drown in the awful glop below, and did her best to hold off visits as best she could.

The days on the farm had passed quickly. With her two blond cousins, Terry, usually clad only in her red bathing suite and a pair of old Shirley Temple shoes, had cavorted about thinking little about her dead sister. On hot days they would climb through the barbed wire fence that girdled the cow pasture and race across the field to a duck pond on the other side. There they could frolic around the edge, or paddle about in a wooden rowboat Henry had found floating down by the river. Once, possibly spotting Terry's red bathing suit, Fluffy had chased them all the way across the pasture to the outhouse. The chase had frightened Terry so that she redoubled her efforts to refrain from visits to the Seat of Ease.

Many years later Terry would relate the story about the subsequent return trip home to West Park Drive in Henry's truck and the consequences of her fear of visiting the outhouse. "I had my hand in Uncle Henry's lap all the way home. And I remember looking up and seeing kind of like floaters — you know the kind you sometimes get in your eyes. And I told Uncle Henry 'I see Ellen. She's an angel.' He laughed hard and said, "No. I think you're just constipated."

Terry's return home proved as traumatic as the day of the crime itself. When she entered the front door it was as if a pall had been draped across everything. Her devastated adoptive father and domineering mother were as one now, both pasty looking semi-automatons going through the motions of living, but neither really alive. Still folded newspapers had been piled by the inside door. When she entered her room, everything had changed. Ellen's bed was gone and her clothes had vanished. Almost all of her belongings had disappeared. Most had been given to Philip's sister and brother-in-law, Marva and Rufus Pearson, a retired D.C. fireman who lived in a shack down on the Potomac and received a monthly allotment for raising foster children. The single dresser was still there as was the folding dressing table laced with the feminine skirt where Ellen had kept her jewelry. Only one or two of her glass horse statues and the container for face powder with the glass horse lid and a tube of her favorite lipstick remained. She looked inside the powder jar. Ellen's 1944 good-luck dime was still there. Terry took it out and put it in her pocket for safekeeping, then looked out the window at the Miller house next door, and started to cry.

Julian Edwards, for one, was not a happy man. At every turn his men had been worked to the bone and little of substantial interest had been turned up. The investigation at the Christian Heurich pond and in the adjacent wells and even in the sewer system was exhaustive, as the mine detector team began systematically to search the bottom in preset survey lanes so as not to miss a single audible signal. An afternoon thundershower failed to halt the work more than a few minutes. The results were nevertheless frustratingly negative. The only find had been a recently-buried paring knife with no apparent connection to the crime. Despite its inconsequential nature, the tool was bagged, tagged, and sent off for analysis.

Edwards had scarcely been home over the last week and his wife, Alice, though normally supportive, was also fraying. Their friends and neighbors had bombarded their teenage children with questions every day, as if they were insider traders in informational commodities. Moreover, Panadapoulis had been bugging him to provide the press with daily dollops of the course of the investigation and the most recent discoveries, no matter how they might jeopardize a later prosecution. He had long believed that the people's right to know every detail of a case came second to law enforcement's mission, to protect the public and to bring criminals to justice. It didn't help that the politicians were pushing the chief. He was also well aware that Leggett and his cronies were more anxious than usual to make the negative news disappear any way they could. Not that they, like most politicians, didn't enjoy the limelight now and then, it was just that they feared such attention might inevitably turn to the less desirable aspects of their activities, in particular their cozy dealings with several heavy-hitting real estate developers.

Edwards flinched a bit as he began to draft the daily press release for his clerk to type and distribute. This time it concerned the laundry truck driver over on University Lane, to the north of the park, who had heard two distinct fusillades of shots about the time of the killings. The driver's statement, which could not be corroborated and was in places contradictory, was in his own opinion questionable. Edwards had told Panadapoulis that he was against dispensing such information, but had been rebuffed, Again, as he had done in all earlier releases, he included a line appealing to the public, indeed to anyone who might have been in the area and heard shots to call in with whatever information they could provide.

Deloris Pfeizer had read with renewed concern the Prince George's Police Department's latest appeal for information regarding the murders in Northwest Branch Park in Thursday's *Washington Post and Times Herald*. What if she had been wrong, and the cap gun shots she had heard had actually been gunshots? The issue had troubled her for several days, and her anxiety had festered and grown with each new appeal. When she mentioned it to her husband Bruno, he at first dismissed her concerns without even lowering his evening newspaper. "It's none of our business," he said. "And even if it is, we could get in some kind of legal trouble for not coming forward earlier."

Deloris's anxiety nevertheless continued to worsen and her badgering soon reached exceptional heights. Finally, on Sunday, June 19, Bruno agreed to inform the police — but only after he had secured legal counsel. The attorney advised them in no uncertain terms to go immediately to the police and relate Deloris's story.

On June 22, Deloris and Bruno Pfeizer walked down to the park, believing the police would still be searching the area. Within a short time they came upon a Prince George's private, Wilmer V. Sams, who had been working on his days off to help solve the case. They found Private Sams walking barefoot, looking for the murder weapon, in the wake of an afternoon thundershower. He immediately referred the couple to Lieutenant Humphrey and Sergeant Bearson, to whom Deloris related her tale. The informants were immediately driven to the Seat Pleasant stationhouse where they were questioned for two hours. "You know, by fixing the time at 8:15 a.m. you have provided us with an important part of the puzzle. Why didn't you come forward earlier? Your four days of hesitation may have allowed the killer to escape."

"We know that now," said Deloris, "but your man at the police line on the day of the killings had rather forcefully told me to move on and wasn't the least bit interested in what I had to say. And when they kept saying over the radio that you fellows believed the killings were about 10:00 a.m. I just dismissed the whole thing. What did you expect?"

Within hours of the significant new information, Chief Gregory Panadapoulis had released to the press word of the findings, shedding new light on the investigation — information that had "cleared a major point" in the hunt for the killer of Ellen Marie Chauvanne and Michael Linn O'Riley. Moreover, an unnamed laundryman and two other purported witnesses, all of whom would remain anonymous, had reported hearing shots, confirming the Pfeizer report that the apparent time of the murder was before 8:20 a.m. and possibly at or about 8:15 a.m.

Edwards was furious. It had been his policy to maintain a blackout of all data pertaining to the time of the murder, but he had been repeatedly blind-sided by his boss. Even with a partial blackout, the media seemed to be putting two and two together with little difficulty, and the press seemed to be pabulum-fed every bit of critical data.

Meanwhile, the suspect roundup continued unabated, as the police groped for more and more leads.

When an eighteen-year-old youth from Schenectady, New York, hitchhiking to Florida, stopped off at the Hyattsville Station, seeking a place to sleep, he was held for questioning, but was finally released after a night in jail.

Not so fortunate was a 24-year-old former resident and habitué of the Landover Hills area, where the Chauvanne family had once lived. He was picked up and charged with the rape of a 25-year old woman. Booked as "held for investigation" on the rape charge, he suddenly also found himself a suspect in the double homicide because of his former residency near the onetime Chauvanne home. It was a slim lead that would soon go nowhere.

Forward motion, Commissioner Leggett had demanded, but the case seemed to be moving in circles.

Chapter 9

THE WORST CRIME

The U.S. Army mine detector crews were back on the job early on June 23, beginning a second and even more thorough examination of the same terrain they had already searched, even as Deputy Chief Edwards laid down plans for an intensive underground investigation of the local storm-sewer system.

The sewer system, which ran through all of the developments surrounding the park, was an incredibly complex warren of 36- and 48-inch concrete pipes fed by an even more intricate maze of terra-cotta pipes, basins, and drains that had been laid as the fringe suburbs of the Washington Metropolitan region grew like topsy-turvy.

At Edwards's suggestion, the Prince George's Police Association started a reward fund for information leading to the arrest and conviction of the slayer, or slayers. A little over $200, donated by officers, had already been posted at the main office of a local thrift, the Suburban Trust Company, on Baltimore Boulevard, in Hyattsville. Benjamin Ogle Bowie, a vice president of the company and confidant of Commissioner Leggett, had agreed to personally handle all the donated money, which it was anticipated would eventually grow to a substantial amount, through any or all of the bank's branches.

Despite the potential incentive of a reward, which was admittedly still small, and the constant calls for public assistance and information regarding the crime, Edwards had begun to feel the effort was for naught despite the numerous — but usually wasted — calls coming in. However, one major outlet had never been tried by the police before — this was the new medium of television that was sweeping across the nation. Edwards himself had just purchased his first set, a Muntz, with a twelve-inch screen. His kids had immediately become addicted, especially to a fifteen-minute puppet show called "Sam and Friends" put on by a former fellow classmate of the Chauvanne girl at Northwestern, a young man named Jim Henson. If puppets could hypnotize so many people over a cathode ray tube, why not make a public address to appeal for public aid on the most popular of several local television stations? Panadapoulis was anything but keen on the idea, but after some diplomatic promoting and a few calls to the executives at the broadcast center in D.C., the appearance was set for mid-day, June 24, on station WRC.

Neither Panadapoulis nor Edwards had ever been on television before and the experience was interesting. Both men had informed their families of the impending appearance, and soon all of their friends and acquaintances had gathered around their own or neighbors' sets to watch. The appeal was both concise and sobering as Edwards, who did most of the talking, described the twin homicides as "the worst crime in the history of Prince George's County." Concerned that the gray pall of fear over the communities surrounding Northwest Branch Park might darken, he assured viewers that Lane Manor and its neighbors were now adequately protected and the residents need have no fear that the killer would strike again. Then it was Panadapoulis's turn to speak.

"I appeal for any citizen having any knowledge of any aspect of this heinous crime to bring it to the attention of the Prince George's County Police Department," said the chief. "I am certain that there are still some among this viewing audience who know something which would prove of value to police, but have as yet to come forward with their stories. If there is anyone out there who might have heard or seen anything in the area between 7:30 a.m. and 9 a.m., I urge you to get in touch with police and call this number." Then, dropping out from under the headshot appearing on the screen was a white telephone number to the Seat Pleasant station.

The appeal had been succinct and to the point. The span given had covered a 45-minute leeway both ways from the time the police had set for the crime — 8:15 a.m. — but did not, thanks to Edwards, reveal the critical exact time. Then the chief closed with a line that took even Deputy Chief Edwards by total surprise.

"This evening," Panadapoulis said grimly, looking straight into the camera, "we will be releasing a description of the individual that has become our prime suspect. We urge anyone who has seen this man, or anyone that fits his description, to come forward at the earliest possible time. You may be saving a life."

When the red camera light went off, indicating the close of the live interview, Edwards accosted the chief with an air of total incredulity.

"What the hell was that all about?" He shouted. "We don't have a verifiable description of anyone! All we have is the extremely questionable narrative of the Stokes boy, which isn't — in my book at least — worth a warm bucket of piss. We got this weird character Philip Chauvanne's brother and the three colored laborers down the road saw before and afterwards, but each one of them has described the man they saw differently. Henry Chauvanne's story seems to change every time he tells it. When he first saw the guy, he said, he was wearing a blanket rolled up over his shoulder. Later it became a bandolier full of bullets. The laborers have each described him in a different way. And that's all we got! My God, if we start broadcasting a composite description of this guy without a little more solid information, we are going to be snowed. Every Tom, Dick, and Harry with a canteen and back pack seen walking down the street is going to be called in."

"Now, hold on just a goddamned minute, captain. I'm running this operation and it's my head on the chopping block. First off, the initiative for this has come from the Metropolitan Police, not us. I got a call from Chief McAdams of the D.C. force just before we came over here that one of his officers is going to release a composite description of the guy Stokes, Chauvanne, and the laborers saw. They put this together without consulting us, but I think it's in our best interest right now to facilitate them. After all, they have as many men in the field out here now as we do! And most of them are also volunteering their own time, without pay, as well. How am I going to tell Chief McAdams to shut up? It's a trade off, and thus far we haven't done so well on our own. Maybe it will stir up the pot a little more."

"Long as it doesn't boil over," responded the captain sullenly.

What had begun as a single strategic planning session at the beginning of the case had, by June 23, become almost an evening ritual, with most of the key investigators attending, usually at Seat Pleasant headquarters. Several hours would be consumed in information sharing, then discussion. Finally assignments for the next day's work would be laid out in detail. With the composite description of a possible suspect, Panadapoulis had decided it was time to "reevaluate all the circumstances in the case." And, as always, a briefing for the press by the chief or another senior Prince George's officer or official would follow.

This evening, however, was different. After Panadapoulis's almost ritualistic appeal to the public for information, Lt. Terrance Hendricks, of the Metropolitan Police, stepped forward to the array of microphones erected outside the conference room.

He spoke in a quiet but firm voice. "Tonight," he began, "we are seeking a definite suspect in the June 15 double murders committed in the Northwest Branch Park picnic grove."

The hallway filled with reporters was suddenly quiet even as flashbulbs flashed and then fizzled with amazing rapidity. It was the first time in the nine-day-old search for the mysterious assassin that police had employed such a label — "a definite suspect." Now, it seemed, there was something solid to go on.

"The individual we are now seeking is a white male, between 16 and 30 years old, from 5 feet 10 inches to 6 feet tall, and weighing about 160 pounds. He has a dark, full head of hair, bushy in front and apparently in need of a shave when last seen. He has a weathered complexion, like he spent the best part of his time in the open. At the time he was wearing a blue shirt and dark khaki pants with a web belt. On one side of the belt was a sheathed knife or dagger, and on the other an Army canteen. He carried a .22 caliber rifle that may have been new. We have credible information from at least one witness that he was carrying a bandolier of cartridges slung across his shoulders, although three other witnesses say the bandolier may have, in fact, been a blanket. This individual was seen wandering around in the woods at or near the park before and shortly after the crime. A drawing of the suspect will soon be available. His description is being relayed by teletype to all police on the Eastern Seaboard, and more than a dozen states, fifteen to be precise, are on the hookup, and are being relayed via Ohio to points west as far as the Mississippi."

Panadapoulis stepped in to complete the presentation. "I would like to call on all gun dealers in the District of Columbia and surrounding Maryland and Virginia suburbs who may have sold a Marlin .22 caliber rifle to any such character to report it to the authorities as soon as possible. We would also like to learn of all reports on stolen Marlins, and to request all Marlin gun owners to check their weapons to make certain they have not been stolen."

"Does this character have a name?" a reporter from the *Evening Star* asked.

"Well, my men have taken to calling him 'Pancho Villa' because of the bandolier."

Captain Edwards cringed as the crowd of reporters murmured loudly. The villain had a name and a description. He could see the sensational headlines now: "Police Search for Pancho Villa Killer."

"Exactly why is this man being sought?" asked another reporter lamely.

"We can place him close enough to the scene. That's why we want him for questioning."

As Edwards feared, a deluge of calls on potential 'Pancho Villa' suspects began to roll in within hours.

The 22-year-old serviceman walking in civilian clothes down Marlboro Pike, a heavily forested route between Upper Marlboro and District Heights, a suburb on the southeast side of Washington, intended on doing a little deer hunting. He had carried with him a brand new .22-caliber Marlin rifle, replete with telescopic sight, and had the misfortune of meeting the physical description of Pancho Villa, minus canteen, bandolier, and knife. When he was picked up, despite protestation that he had been several thousand miles away at the time of the murders, and was only in the area to visit his girlfriend, he was the first of a veritable legion of Pancho Villa look-alikes to be quickly spirited off to police headquarters for interrogation. After many hours of grilling, and numerous calls by police to addresses in California given by the suspect confirming his story, he was released, but his gun was retained for ballistics tests.

In Spotsylvania County, Virginia, another suspect, a 39-year old dishwasher from Baltimore, was picked up by Virginia State Trooper T. R. Browlee and Fredericksburg Police Officer Russell Lily, booked on suspicion of murder, and lodged in the town jail. The officers had been acting on a tip. Though the suspect admitted to owing a single shot .22 caliber rifle, but had neither a rifle nor a bandolier in his possession, a sergeant at the Fredericksburg jail declared that the man's physical resemblance to the description provided by the D.C. and Prince George's police made him a "definite suspect."

After a hurried consultation at the Prince George's detective bureau at Seat Pleasant, two officers, Detective James Carvile and Private E. G. Musk, were dispatched to Fredericksburg to question the hapless dishwasher. The man, as it turned out, had purchased the rifle at a Baltimore sporting goods store the day before the murders, but pawned it two days afterward for $4 cash and later sold the pawn ticket for $2. After his story was checked out, he was quickly released, albeit without any apology.

In the meantime, Arlington, Virginia, police had received three noteworthy reports of Pancho Villa characters in their county. One had been spotted hitchhiking north on U.S. Route 1 on June 17, another on the same day between 1:30 and 3:00 p.m. on Shirley Highway hitchhiking south, and a third walking on Route 236 on June 22. None had been brought in, but manhunts for the suspects had already begun.

In Baltimore, acting on a tip from a cabbie, city police picked up a 43-year-old man, a fugitive for over a year from the state mental hospital at Spring Grove, on a street corner. They found in his possession a few razor blades, a penknife, and a set of keys. Questioned by Prince George's police, he was taken into custody for further interrogation before finally being released and returned to appropriate hospital authorities.

By the evening of June 24, more than three hundred tips had been received, many from anonymous callers, thirty-five of which were Pancho Villa sightings phoned in to the Seat Pleasant headquarters, all of which had to be checked out. How many of them had actually been about the same person? Several teams of detectives began knocking on every door in the neighborhood to interview potential witnesses to find out. More than five hundred persons had already been interviewed. The manpower drain was telling. Edwards had little choice but to delay the intended re-enactment of the crime until he could free up several detectives for the job. Thankfully, the soldiers from Fort Meade had taken up some of the slack in the fieldwork at the park, and investigated more than thirty storm sewers in the University Hills and Lane Manor sections, albeit with little results. One soldier had found a rifle. Unfortunately, it proved to be a toy lost by a five-year-old from 25th Avenue a few months earlier.

A report had also just come in that a thirteen-year-old boy found a dollar bill at the fireplace where papers containing Ellen's name had been recovered. Unaware that the item might be important, the boy had promptly spent it. Had it been one of Ellen's, and if so, did it have any relationship to a possible motive of robbery? Of equal importance was why the item had been overlooked at all and why was the boy there within the roped off police investigation area in the first place?

If there was anything positive to be said, it had to be about one of those most shattered by the whole tragedy. Private Thomas O'Riley, Mikie's father, had just revealed in an interview with the *Washington Post and Times Herald* that he had just signed up his two remaining daughters, Elaine and Cathy, for the supervised summer recreation program in Northwest Branch Park.

On the morning of Sunday, June 26, perhaps the longest police crime scene barrier ever erected in Prince George's County came down. Yet the investigations in the park would continue full bore.

Chapter 10

THE CALLER

The healing process for the families of the victims of the Northwest Branch Park murders, given the unceasing media coverage, and the constant comings and goings of police, soldiers, firemen, and countless other volunteers participating in the manhunt, had been static, even anesthetizing.

For Terry Chauvanne, who had taken to sitting by the telephone in the hall of her house, awaiting a call from her sister in heaven, the grief, which she could barely comprehend, seemed at first to come and go without order, drifting in and out, like a radio station on the edge of its broadcast range. Over and over she would revisit those last moments on the front stoop as she watched her older sister, her mentor, her protector, her guardian, almost her second mother, walk toward the dirt path. She had no understanding of the demon that had stalked her Peter Pan, or for what purpose? All she could think of was why did this have to happen to Ellen. Why hadn't she, Terry, been there instead of Mikie? Why hadn't she gone with her wonderful sister to wherever she was now? She felt both cheated and angry at being left behind, and a little guilty.

She kept mentally recounting when she had her first inkling of what dying meant. It was a vivid memory that would cling to her throughout life, a memory of the time Ellen had literally almost breathed her last in an asthma attack at age fourteen. Her parents had rushed her to Prince George's General where she was resuscitated and where she would remain for several weeks. Patients were not allowed visits by children, and when Philip and Lucille had taken Terry to the hospital, she was allowed only to stand on the street corner with a friend of the family while they visited her sweet sister. She could still visualize Ellen looking down from her second story hospital window, almost beatifically, and waving vigorously to her as if to say, "Everything's all right." Nothing would ever kill her, thought Terry. Nothing could ever stop her sister, her Madonna, the "Just Do It" girl.

When the phone rang, Terry almost didn't hear it, so enveloped in thoughts of her sister had she been. Then, with both of her tiny hands slightly trembling, she lifted the heavy black receiver to her ear.

"Hello," she said cautiously.

"Hello," responded a youthful voice from the ether. "I want to speak to Ellen."

"She's not here right now," said Terry, tears welling up in her eyes. "She's dead."

"No she's not! I want to speak to her now, do you hear me?"

There seemed no rest for the weary, Detective James Carvile thought as he drove towards Washington, en route home from investigating a potential suspect at Fredericksburg, Virginia. He had just received word, while in the police station in the town most famous for the great Civil War bloodbath that had taken place there, to go through Alexandria on his way home, and pick up yet another .22 Marlin for testing by the FBI. This time the weapon was from a gun shop called the Old South Sporting Goods, at 120 King Street. The owner, one Hugh Davidson, who had called the Prince

George's police strictly as a "routine," was voluntarily submitting it for examination. A youth, "a very young boy," had allegedly sold the piece to him. Having taken the kid's name, Davidson thought the police should take a look. "Musky," said the detective to his car-mate, Private Everett G. Musk, "we've got one more stop to make before you can go home to your sweet little old wife."

"Sergeant, I'm guessing I ain't gonna be that lucky. I bet soon as we get to the station they send me right back to the damned park."

Musk was right. As soon as they checked in, he was ordered to patrol the Northwest Branch Park even though the police ropes had been removed. When he arrived late Sunday afternoon, he found the grounds, until the day before a scene of brooding desolation, now alive with picnickers from Lane Manor, University Lane, and the communities around the University of Maryland.

At sunset, as the picnickers gathered their families together, packed away their food in wicker baskets, and headed home to prepare for the workweek ahead, Musk marveled at how quickly the removal of the police lines seemed to have set the world right, even though the investigation was still continuing in certain sectors of the park. Almost as if nothing of any consequence had happened there. Nothing at all.

Then he saw the lights.

Within a matter of minutes, Private Everett G. Musk had rounded up yet another batch of suspects, the largest thus far — five boys armed with three flashlights who told him "they were just looking around" the murder scene. The boys, completely frightened out of their wits, were taken to the Hyattsville stationhouse for questioning, and then, after endless hours of intense interrogation, released.

Monday, June 27. The morning began as usual at Seat Pleasant, with calls stimulated by the latest Sunday coverage in the two major D.C. newspapers, *The Post* and *The Star*. One call, however, seemed quite promising. An anonymous woman informant from Langley Park had phoned in to report having definitely seen the "Pancho Villa" character enter an apartment basement laundry room on Merrimac Street at 10:50 a.m. and leave a few minutes after 11 a.m. on the day of the killings. The area described was a mile north of the crime scene and a mile and a half from the same construction job on which Henry Chauvanne and the three black laborers had spotted an identical character the same day at 10:30 a.m. Captain Edwards immediately dispatched several detectives to check out the apartment project. The lead, like all those leads before, provided little more than another dead end.

In the park itself, soldiers from Fort Meade, again armed with mine detectors, returned to the familiar murder scene to continue checking and rechecking, even as another team of detectives was again sent to Virginia on yet another false lead. No fewer than eight "Pancho Villa" sightings had come in the last twenty-four hours. One suspect picked up near the White House by National Park Police proved to be a drunk who only vaguely resembled the mystery man's description. Another call-in reported having been walking in the park with her dog between 7:00 and 7:50 a.m. on the day of the murder, but had not seen anything suspicious.

The investigation was, by now, taking on a distinct life of its own. A quasi-permanent police center was established in the Lewisdale Elementary School, within a mile of the crime scene, at which all data could be conveniently gathered and investigated.

Meanwhile, the search for the murder weapon pressed on relentlessly in Northwest Branch Park. On June 28, a detail of twenty-six U.S. Army Signal Corpsmen from Fort

Meade began climbing every tree in the park, under the direction of Captain Sweitzer, searching through the foliage for the elusive Marlin .22. On the ground, unformed county police and plainclothes officers from D.C. joined in as the mine detector teams combed the ground yet again. One nineteen-year-old soldier, Private Ansel R. Hutchinson, got tangled in a copse of matted vines and accidentally slashed his right heel with his climbing gaff, and had to be taken to Prince George's General Hospital for stitches.

By afternoon, the searchers moved to a thickly wooded section on the west side of the stream. In a dense thicket, one party soon came across a piece of cardboard with holes in it that might have been made by bullets. The item was photographed *in situ*, tagged, bagged, and sent off for analysis. The location in which the cardboard was found, not far from where the bodies had been discovered, was then subjected to intensive scrutiny by the mine detector teams. A drain opening in the field, already explored, was again investigated, but for naught.

The activity was far more than Winnie Sweitzer had anticipated, and once again he decided to postpone staging a re-enactment of the shooting until the next day, owing to potential confusion with so many operations going on at once. Moreover, he had scheduled a comprehensive search by Army troopers of the outbuildings on the rambling old Heurich estate on the slim chance that the killer might have been concealed the rifle somewhere therein.

Finally, Sweitzer decided to seek permission from the M-NCPPC to bulldoze some 1800 feet of extremely dense creekside brush to allow search in a hitherto impenetrable area. He had been reluctant to do so fearing the bulldozers could bury more evidence than might be found, but he had little choice now. After nearly two weeks of intensive search, he was beginning to doubt if any of his efforts were worth it. Yet he refused to display anything less than a positive front for his men and the press. After literally thousands of man-hours of unending legwork invested in the hunt, he and his men could only pray for a break in the case. Yet the killer's trail seemed to grow colder by the minute.

Prince George's County Commissioner Brad J. Fastner was gregarious, quick to praise and to shake a hand if it might prove of benefit to him. He had little interest in the Chauvanne-O'Riley murder investigation or, indeed, much else except county politics, in which he had been embroiled in one way or another during most of his adult life. But Commission Chairman Leggett, who was becoming ever more anxious to disassociate himself from the whole negative affair, was adamant about keeping tabs on what was going on. Leggett had no interest in showing his face or making any more public statements again in front of the gaggle of reporters that had almost taken up permanent residency at police headquarters. Fastner, whose record was squeaky clean, especially when it came to the quietly simmering backyard rumors of Leggett's kickbacks from developers for zoning favors, would have to serve as point man.

Unlike Leggett, Fastner was also able to talk with the chief of police or a lowly cop on the beat on a man-to-man basis, without either intimidating or engendering sycophantic ass kissing. Whenever he walked into police headquarters unannounced, he was greeted with approving nods, a few warm handshakes, an offer of coffee, and nothing more.

"Morning, major," Fastner said as he ambled into Chief Panadapoulis's office. "Just thought I would see how the Lane Manor case is moving along."

Well aware of the commissioner's mission, after a typist on Leggett's staff who owed him a favor for a fixed parking ticket informed him, Panadapoulis was ready.

"Morning, Commissioner. We are, indeed, making considerable progress. Though we've got nothing new to report from police departments along most of the coastal cities — Baltimore, Philly, or Wilmington, North Carolina — or from some of the states we've established links with, such as Connecticut, we have a number of potential leads. Of course, the switchboard has been deluged with calls reporting the damned Pancho Villa suspect. Just today we've received seventy-five calls, thirty-eight of which we've already followed up on. So far all have proved negative, but we can always hope. D.C. is getting the same response as we are. Besides the Pancho Villa suspect, who we still think is our best bet, we also have a lookout for a College Park man, a mental case, whose been evading child support payments for weeks. We just received the results from the FBI exam on the victim's clothes, blood samples, and chunks of the blood-stained sod taken from a point about 150 feet from the briar patch thicket where the bodies were found. The blood in the sod matches that of the Chauvanne girl. Unfortunately, the analysis of the bloody clothing hasn't shed much more light on the case than we already know. Of eleven guns FBI ballistics are working on, ten have proved negative and there is still one more to go, but I don't think it's going to tell us anything."

"What else have you got, major? I've read all that already in the papers."

"Well, it's not for public consumption," Chief Panadapoulis said, leaning across his desk, and lowering his voice ever so slightly, "but both the Chauvannes and O'Rileys have been getting mysterious telephone calls for several days now. Sometimes they come in as late as midnight. All of the calls, when someone on the other end speaks, sound like they have been made by a youth, probably a male teenager. Sometimes the caller hangs up without saying a word. When the little Chauvanne girl picks up the line, the caller insists on speaking to Ellen. We've set up a tap, but the caller is never on the line more than a few seconds. It's really sad because that little girl is beside herself and still thinks her sister is alive! I think the calls are from some crank, but that poor kid . . ."

"How long can this go on, chief?" the commissioner said almost sympathetically.

"Not much," Panadapoulis answered. "In fact, in my briefing to the press tomorrow, I'm announcing that we are going to have to reduce the number of detectives assigned to the case. We simply can't let everything else go in the county for the sake of this one. We can still follow up all our leads, but it will be at a somewhat slower pace. However, I think we've come up with a plan to take some of the heat off — that's likely to pick up — when we make the announcement. The D.C. police had an artist from the *Washington Star* present during their recent interviews with all of the prime witnesses to the Pancho Villa character, and he's prepared a wonderful composite drawing. They're going to publish it first in the *Star* on Thursday, June 30, and then it will be circulated to all of the press, television stations, and distributed to all of the states east of the Mississippi. That should compensate a bit, don't you think?"

"Chief," Fastner said with a slight smirk, "if you think you've been swamped with callers up 'til now, in the immortal words of the great Jimmy Durante, 'You ain't seen nuttin' yet!'"

"Commissioner," responded the chief, "maybe you would like to say a few words on our behalf yourself this afternoon!"

Chapter 11

POP, POP, POP

Lucille Chauvanne scowled at the electric washing machine in the corner of her tiny laundry room. It had cost Philip $69.95 new at Sears and Roebuck, far more than he could afford. But Lucille had been adamant about getting one from the beginning, and, as usual, won out. Now, barely three months later the machine had already begun to falter and Lucille attacked the problem in her usual manner, namely by cursing her husband for buying an inferior model and banging the machine with her fist. "Damn you, Philip," she shouted, even though her spouse was nowhere about, "this piece of garbage ain't worth crap!" Another bang with the palm of her hand, and a kick with the side of her foot. "Goddammitall. Start, you bastard."

Suddenly, the machine came alive, as the wash cycle mysteriously commenced, and Lucille smirked, just as the doorbell rang.

"Be there in a minute," she shouted above the clattering sound of the washer.

At the door was Private Lester "Reds" Daily, of the M-NCPPC Police. Lucille liked Daily, who had begun to stop by frequently to see how she and Philip were doing, and to inquire about Terry and Eddy. He wasn't anything like the PG Police, who, for the most part, had always seemed terse and unfriendly. Young Daily had formed something of a bond with her husband over the last few weeks, both men finding common ground in talking construction and heavy equipment, and occasionally riding about the park in Daily's cruiser to watch the ongoing investigation therein.

"Just thought I'd stop by for a few minutes and let you know what's going on down in my park," he said.

"I'm appreciative," said Lucille, standing in the vestibule. "Come on in and have some iced tea?"

"No thank you, Mrs. Chauvanne. I just wanted to tell you and your husband that the Hyattsville Fire Department's started pumping out the farm wells and cisterns down on the old Heurich place and they'll be working there for the next couple of days. The Army mine detector guys are going to be walking over the park creek north of Ager Road, and near the footbridge, one more time. That's because the police department has asked the Park and Planning Commission for permission to bulldoze the thick creekside brush in that area, probably next week. We're gonna cut a swath about 1,800 feet long and 200 feet wide, which will take some doing. So don't be alarmed by the noise. They're hoping to scrutinize the bare earth for cartridge cases, bullets, and any other clues they might have missed."

"Officer Daily," Lucille responded, "my husband's a bulldozer operator, and heavy equipment noise comes with putting up with a man like him. I gotta tell you, though, I think they're wasting their time. The murder weapon ain't in that park. Any idiot could tell you that. Why in the hell they think the goddamned warped monster that took my daughter's life didn't take his gun with him is beyond me. I told Detective Sweitzer I thought he was barking up the wrong tree, and he just looked at me like I was a dumb piece of wood."

"I'm sure that's just your imagination talking," said the park policeman, attempting to quell the woman's rising sense of anger. "You've been under one heck of a lot of stress, ma'm, and I know . . ."

"These PG cops," she interrupted, "think they're so smart and efficient. Well, if that's the case, why haven't they found anything yet? They haven't got a suspect they can hold, no weapon, and they can't figure out why anyone would want to kill the girls in the first place. They arrest every Tom, Dick, and Harry that comes down the street, but they still haven't got a clue. Literally! I think Chief Panadapoulis is just out to make a name for himself. His mug is in every damned newspaper article that comes out. I understand the FBI offered to step in and help, but Panadapoulis said no. I swear to God Almighty! Who in his right mind would turn down an offer from J. Edgar Hoover. An idiot! That's who. An idiot like Panadapoulis!"

Daily nodded politely, but refused to get pulled in by the tirade. He glanced toward the kitchen and saw little Terry sitting on the congoleum-covered floor reading newspapers beside Tweedle Dum, one of her two pet cocker spaniels. "What's she reading, the comics?"

"No," said Lucille. "She has been completely preoccupied with the investigation. Her teacher says she's precocious, whatever that means. All I know is that for a seven-year-old, she reads as well as her older sister used to. She has a really smart head on her shoulders and I think she's still trying hard to comprehend it all. She misses her sister. . . and truly believes she's gonna be coming back any time now. We just let her go on. It's easier that way."

"Hello, Terry!" said Reds to the child. "Remember me, Officer Daily?"

"Yes sir," replied the little girl looking up from her newspaper. On one side of the page Reds could see the story that had so engrossed her, about a police search for the murder weapon, a search about to be widened to include the University of Maryland campus. A picture showed the campus police chief, Captain Dave Best, who was to direct two teams of volunteer soldiers from Companies A and B of the 601st Anti-Aircraft Battalion stationed at Forrestville and Landover, Maryland. Adjacent to the story was one on Queen Elizabeth of England celebrating her birthday by bestowing titles on the famous actor Alex Guinness, sculptor Henry Moore, and Admiral Earl Mountbatten. Another photo showed the Queen's devilish-looking six-year-old, Prince Charles.

"Would you like to be a queen someday, honey?" Reds asked in mock seriousness.

"Well, Ellen says I'm already a princess."

"Honey," said Lucille, bending to stroke Terry's raven locks from her eyes. "Ellen isn't here any more. She's gone to heaven."

"I know, but she told me again I was a princess when I went to bed last night. And you know what?" she said, sticking her chest out proudly. "She said I was 'a just do it girl,' just like her."

The press conference at Seat Pleasant police headquarters went much as Gregory Panadapoulis suspected. "As is natural in cases of this type," he informed the assemblage, "the descriptions given by the witnesses vary at certain points. There are, however, several points of general agreement. Though you have already been handed a slightly revised written description of the so-called Pancho Villa character, I would like to announce that we have now been able to pull together a composite sketch of the suspect thanks to our friends at the *Evening Star*. They have provided an artist who has accompanied our detectives during interviews with key witnesses. Copies of the sketch will be distributed tomorrow morning to all of you, although the *Star* will be publishing it first this evening."

News of the composite drawing of "Pancho Villa" had caused such a stir that the reporters present hardly noticed the one-line sentence that followed announcing the reduction of personnel assigned to the case. By the time Commissioner Fastner had chimed in with a loud assurance "that the county is sparing no expense to solve one of the most malicious crimes" he ever heard of, most of the newsmen had already rushed off to phone in their reports.

The composite was pulled together by a young staff artist named Zang Auerbach, brother to the famed sports broadcaster Red Auerbach. The artist was known in sports circles as well, as the designer of the logos for the Washington Senators baseball team, the Boston Celtics basketball team, and others. Such details mattered little to the public, however. All that really counted was that there now was a picture of the man most believed to be the killer.

Commissioner Fastner had been right on the mark in his prediction. That same evening, the first crude visage that was to become cemented in everyone's mind as the Pancho Villa Murderer appeared on page one of the Washington *Evening Star*, and a veritable cascade of calls swamped the Prince George's and D.C. police phone lines. But that wasn't all.

At precisely 9:30 p.m., less than six hours after the *Evening Star* hit the street, a shabbily-dressed black man walked into the Second Precinct Police Station in the District of Columbia and presented himself to the tending desk sergeant.

"What can I do for you, sir?" the officer asked.

"I come here to surrender myself," said the man.

"For what?"

"I killed those two girls out there in Maryland."

Lincoln Vane, 24, the truck driver who had walked into the station, said he lived, sometimes, at 112 V Street, in N.E., in the District, and had been out of work and down on his luck for six months. When Lieutenant Terrance Hendricks entered the interrogation room in the Prince George's Police station at Hyattsville, where Vane had been taken, the offensive smell of cheap whiskey evaporating from the prisoner's pores invaded his nostrils. Stains and the pungent aroma of dried urine were in ample evidence. The suspect's clothes had not been changed for weeks, and personal hygiene obviously had been abandoned. Within a minute or two of Vane's entry, Captain Julian Edwards also came in and was equally repelled. Both, however, were all business and the questioning soon commenced.

"You say you killed the two girls out here in Maryland." Edwards began. "Did you know them?"

"No, sir. I just shot 'em dead."

"Why?" asked Hendricks.

"Because I felt like it. I hates bitches. All of 'em."

"Okay. How did you do it?"

"Well, I just took my pistol and shot 'em. Pop, pop, pop. Just like that. Just like I used to shoot rats over at 14th and U in D.C."

"You say you used a pistol," said Edwards. "Tell me something about it. What kind and caliber of gun was it and how many times did you pull the trigger? Pop, pop, pop. Just like that."

"Well, I found the gun in a trash can down on Kennedy Street, beside the Miami Bar and Grill. I don't recall what kind it was, or nothing like that. Just found it wrapped up in newspaper while I was rootin' around for somethin' to eat. As to how I done it, I pulled the trigger real slow and shot 'em five, maybe six times. I don't recall too much about it though 'cause I was fucking tanked, if you know what I mean. I ain't been home in a while, cause my old lady done throwed me out, so I been mov'n around a bit."

"You still living over on V Street?" asked Hendricks.

"Naw. Been sleeping, most of the time, downtown, know what I mean, out on the grates on the Mall, down by the museums. But I done seen'd the stories in the papers and thought you could get one of them high fallutin' writers to do a story on me, take my photograph and put it in the papers just like that Mexican guy. Maybe even front page. Maybe make me famous too, just like him. You do that and I'll even show you and all of 'em just how I done it! That'd show my old lady! She done thinks I can't do nuthin'. I'll show her! Hey, man, I need to take a crap."

The two detectives and the drunken suspect stared at each other for a long moment before Edwards spoke. "You can go take a shit after you tell us where you killed the two girls. We want you to take us there for your demonstration. Now. Tell us where to go, and you can take your dump."

"Well, you know. Out in Maryland, out by the District line."

"No, sir, where exactly. And how do we get there?"

"Come on, I gotta go bad. I know you got a can here!"

"Not until you tell us where the murder was done."

"Please. These be the only pants I gots."

The two detectives just looked at the pathetic creature before them. Within minutes, he quietly confessed that he didn't know where the slaying had taken place, and that his story was false. All he wanted was a little notoriety, three squares, and a roof over his head. He didn't care if it was a jail cell or not. Just a roof over his head.

Lincoln Vane was charged with making a false report and held on $500 bond pending a hearing on July 5 in the Hyattsville Trial Magistrate's Court. Within two weeks he had achieved at least part of his wish for the next three months.

Within the space of a month, false confessions, willfully given by two other street people and another by an alcoholic shopkeeper on a binge, would also be recorded by the D.C. police.

The day the bulldozer had been scheduled to arrive at Northwest Branch Park to begin cutting the heavy brush along the creek, two more suspects, both resembling the Pancho Villa character, were picked up in D.C., one at Meridian Hill along posh upper 15th Street, and another at the Tidal Basin, near a popular paddle-boat rental consortium opposite the Jefferson Memorial. One was a 43-year-old Baltimore drifter who claimed to be a crack shot, gave a fictitious home address at Perry Point, east of Baltimore, and said he was in D.C. to visit his sister and a girlfriend. A records check revealed the drifter had two robbery convictions and had spent most of his nights in homeless shelters and missions. A third suspect was picked up soon afterwards. All three were interrogated for hours before being placed in a lineup and viewed by Henry Chauvanne.

None fit the description and all were released.

That same evening, several more men were picked up, questioned, and released after no fewer than thirty-one tips were called in. The following morning, three more men were likewise hauled down to Hyattsville, interrogated for hours on end, and finally released.

By dusk in Northwest Branch Park, it was quiet after the noise generated by the small army of uniformed men crawling about the park in search of a .22-caliber rifle, that most now believed had never been dumped there in the first place, vanished. The bulldozer work had been cancelled for unknown reasons for several more days. Children were already returning to the baseball diamond, a scant four hundred yards from the site where Ellen and Mikie had been murdered just two weeks before. One among them was Eddy Chauvanne. His gaunt, suddenly gray-haired father Philip sat on a nearby picnic table and watched. He was the only adult in the park until a reporter from the *Washington Post and Times Herald*, who had ghosted the Chauvannes for days, saddled up beside him.

"You know," said Philip quietly. "This sure has wrecked our lives. It's very quiet at our house now. When we sit down to dinner there's just my wife and me. Terry and Eddy eat by themselves. My wife is still under a doctor's care."

The two men sat there for a while longer, saying nothing, until darkness fell and the game broke up. As Philip turned to leave, he said softly, almost to himself: "In a while this will all be forgotten. The kids will come back to the park . . . in time."

Suspects were picked up, questioned, and released in an almost unending stream. For the next week, a steady flow of "ill-fitting" Pancho Villa look-a-likes and a veritable flood of telephone tips continued to pour into police stations throughout the Washington Metropolitan area and in neighboring suburbs. On July 1, at least 150 sightings were reported. By July 2, no fewer than 1,100 persons purporting to have either seen the mysterious bandolier-drapped man or to have knowledge about the case had been interviewed.

If the police departments seemed to be baffled, it was not for want of aggressiveness by field officers. From some distance away, a legion of children watched with rapt attention Detective Winnie Sweitzer's long-delayed re-enactment of the ambush at the crime scene itself. Sweitzer, who had been putting in ten and twelve hour days without a break since the case had been opened, had hoped to discern at least something new from the effort.

Little had been learned, but the kids clapped and cheered with every shot fired, as if they had been watching a Wild West show.

And for every scrap of data that was gleaned from informants, field work, and forensics, new riddles continued to appear. One such enigma surfaced just before Independence Day when a report came in from Woody's Esso on the corner of Ager and Riggs Roads, about a mile from the Lane Manor subdivision. Station employees reported that in a small patch of recently poured concrete someone had etched in two sets of initials, five first names, and the name "Michiel Linn O'Riley" while it was still wet. Attendants weren't at first sure when the concrete was poured except that it was "within the past month." One employee, however, recalled that it was poured by a truck driver who dropped by one evening approximately three weeks earlier, and said he had some concrete left over from a job. Another attendant then chimed in that he had seen a teenage boy drawing in the wet concrete. Soon afterwards, a woman in a nearby snack bar said she had also seen the youngster and yelled at him to stop defacing the concrete, and the youth had fled. Neither Lucille Chauvanne nor Lanie O'Riley were able to recognize any of the other names or initials as acquaintances of Ellen or Michael Linn, but the misspelling of Mikie's surname was of considerable interest.

Were the imprints made before or after the murders? And why? Had the notoriety of the crime grown to such an extent that someone was memorializing one of the victims? No one seemed to have an answer.

Least of all Lanie O'Riley. When asked about her future plans and if she intended on leaving the neighborhood for a safer place, Lanie was adamant. "I can't see pulling up stakes now," she told a reporter, as she and several of her neighbors watched Cathy and Elaine gamboling with their friends in the O'Riley yard. "The neighbors have been so wonderful. It's an ideal neighborhood." As for the murder investigation itself, she was less positive. "It seems so strange they can't find anything at all."

The tips continued to flow. Then, on July 2, several anonymous callers reported hearing shots in the park. Three more, one of whom sounded like a teenage boy, told police that they too had seen a man shooting a rifle in the park. In the background could be heard either a radio or phonograph playing the newest recording hit, "The Ballad of Davy Crockett." None of the callers would identify themselves. Only the youth's description matched data that the police had not released for public consumption.

As the Independence Day festivities approached, at Prince George's detective headquarters there was anything but a holiday mood. After two and a half weeks of tireless search, Captain Winchester Sweitzer and his men were exhausted.

By July 3, Captain Dennis Thompson reported that the Prince George's County Police Department had logged in a record shattering 4,104 man-hours in following up leads, of which 3,500 had been spent in questioning more than 1,100 people, most of them at least twice. The military and volunteer fire departments had put in 1,042 hours of metal detecting, climbing trees, searching sewer systems, and crawling to hunt for the murder weapon. Some fifty-three .22-caliber rifles had undergone ballistics tests in the FBI laboratories. Since the television appearance by Chief Panadapoulis and Captain Edwards, the department had logged in an average of two hundred calls per day, nearly 2,000 tips, some from as far away as Newport News, Virginia, Ohio, South Carolina, and California. Three hundred were deemed substantial enough to investigate. Nine two-man teams of detectives and uniformed officers pressed into plainclothes duty had covered 25,000 miles in a dozen scout cars running down leads, many of them claimed sightings of Pancho Villa. Hundreds of overtime hours, without pay, had been donated by county officers, and many more by the D.C. police in the round-the-clock investigation.

On Saturday afternoon, Gregory Panadapoulis authorized Captain Edwards to announce a much needed day-long breather for the beleaguered plainclothes and uniformed officers of the county police, the first in two and a half weeks, even as a 21-year-old Texas hitchhiker, purportedly sighted wearing a bandolier, was picked up while walking through Hyattsville. Like those before him, he was taken in for questioning, but proved to be a drifter moving from job to job, in New York, Philadelphia, and other Eastern Seaboard cities, but whose story checked out. Another slim possibility doomed to failure.

That evening, Chief Panadapoulis summoned his senior staff. Commissioner Leggett was there as well, sitting quietly in the rear of the conference room.

"Gentlemen," the chief said in a low, dark voice, "this hunt for Pancho Villa's going nowhere. It's eating us up and we are no closer to a solution than we were two weeks ago. Hopefully something will break, but I doubt it. The case is already cold. The media attention has started to die down a bit and we have already announced that we are going to be cutting back on man-hours. We are going to have to get back to the daily business of law enforcement for the whole county, not just the folks along Northwest Branch Park, no later than July 15. Is that understood?"

A quiet murmur arose among the officers and staff in attendance.

"Well, good. Have a rest, and I will see you bright and early on July 4."

As the last of the officers shuffled out of the conference room, Leggett stood up and began to walk toward the door, a flaccid smile draped across his jowly face. "Thank you, major. You done good. That's just what I wanted to hear."

"Commissioner," the chief said, "you know I'm not happy about this. We have a monster out there somewhere, and there's no assurance he's just going to go away. You know what a pretty sharp guy once said: 'Man is the hunter; woman is his game.'"

"What the hell you talking about?" the commissioner huffed.

"Tennyson. You ought to read him sometime."

Chapter 12

Kiss

For the next week, the Prince George's County and Washington Metropolitan Police Departments continued with their plodding and increasingly sterile investigation. Suspects even vaguely matching the description of the Pancho Villa character were routinely brought in for questioning, without access to legal counsel, and released after a day or two.

On the Fourth of July, thirteen county and Washington detectives spent a blistering hot holiday running down possible leads. One team, Detective Sergeants Emmet F. G. Gray and Ronald Fornost, was even flown to Staunton, Virginia, to interrogate a sixteen-year-old being held by local police and described as "looking older than his years" who had vaguely matched the composite drawing of the major suspect circulated throughout the region. The youth, a Falls Church, Virginia, resident, had been spotted while camping near Lake Shenandoah, a short distance from Staunton; and he had been wearing a web belt, canteen, and knife. The terrified boy was finally released to his father after his story, of never having been near the scene of the murder, was verified.

The following day, another hitchhiker, a fifteen-year-old, carrying a .22 rifle, a mess kit, and canteen strapped on his shoulder, thumbing his way south from New York, was picked up near Thurmont, Maryland, by Maryland State Trooper T. B. Gray, and held in the juvenile detention quarters of the Frederick County Jail in Frederick, Maryland. Prince George's County Detective Sergeants George A. Clelland and James G. Carvile were dispatched to question him. The youth's story was quickly verified.

Not until Friday, July 8, was the M-NCPPC finally able to start bulldozing to remove almost two acres of thick underbrush. By then, it was being estimated by the agency's director of parks, Peter L. Wolfe, that it was likely to take work crews at least several days to clear the brush away. Along already cleared areas along the creek, the Army mine detector teams followed in the wake of the bulldozer to investigate the newly exposed terrain only to discover a dense concentration of empty beer cans — which kept their equipment humming — but nothing more. For Philip Chauvanne, the opportunity to watch the ongoing work offered a chance to escape from the gloomy confines of his house and to wander down to the creek, sometimes accompanied by his friend Reds Daily of the park police. There he would offer his own advice, mostly ignored, on just how the project should proceed. For Philip, however, it was a way of participating, helping in the only manner he knew to bring to justice the slayer of his precious daughter.

The project was proving as fruitless as all the previous efforts. It was now becoming clear to the police, to the media, to the public, and most of all to the victims' relatives, that the case was growing ever colder. The futility was becoming unbearable, especially among the D.C. police, who had lost the daughter of one of their own. In a desperate effort to keep the case going, members of the 2,000-man Metropolitan Policeman's Association proposed a volunteer campaign to raise contributions for a reward for the killer's apprehension and conviction. The Prince George's police immediately chimed in with the $200 donation collected earlier, which, it was hoped, would soon help generate a pot of $2,000.

It wasn't going to do the trick. Even as the M-NCPPC's big HD-3 bulldozer plowed thousands of yards of brush from the shores of the Northwestern Branch, a summit meeting of the D.C. and Prince George's police was convened at the Metropolitan Police headquarters to evaluate progress and discuss future action. The county officers included Panadapoulis, Edwards, and Chief of Detectives Thompson. Chief Harold T. McAdams, Deputy Chief Norman T. McGrath and Homicide Captain Parker J. Feller of the Metropolitan force also attended. Though well intentioned and crank calls alike had continued to come in, albeit at a rate that had dropped to approximately one hundred per day, useful leads were almost nil, and the repeated dragooning of literally scores of Pancho Villa look-alikes had begun to raise eyebrows in both the media and the public. After several hours of intensive review and discussion, it was apparent the case had grown frigid.

Panadapoulis informed his colleagues what everyone already knew: that he could no longer afford to divert most of his men to a single case. He tactfully said nothing regarding his own boss' directives to close the investigation down as soon as possible, or his reasons for doing so. The Metropolitan force had also felt the pinch caused by the diversion of a substantial amount of its manpower to the Northwest Branch Park investigation. After weeks of futile efforts, McAdams bluntly stated, he was soon going to have to call his men back to their normal work in D.C.

The case was winding down, but not everyone present believed it should be abandoned. "We can't just walk away from this thing," said Edwards. "We've spent too much time and effort, blood, and sweat to let this thing die. For Christ's sake, we already look bad enough. If we just walk away from it, the son-of-a-bitch that killed those two poor girls will also walk away, Scot free, maybe to kill someone else. How much confidence do you think the public is going to have in us if we let this guy just slip away."

"Look, captain," Panadapoulis responded, "we're dead in the water. You know it and I know it. We are no closer to a solution now than we were on June 15. Yeah, we're still getting call-ins, but they're all useless. We've dragged in so many poor smucks, mostly kids and hitchhikers, that it's starting to look like Super Circus. The media, thank God, has finally started to pull away from the story. Jesus, we're about ready to go to war with Russia. That's what's on the front page now. We can keep the case alive, officially, but we are going to have to let it die a natural death. We've already demonstrated a Herculean effort to find this bastard, which the public has commended. Now its time to move on."

After pausing for a minute to light a cigarette, Panadapoulis continued. "I think we should issue an official joint statement that both the Prince George's and Metropolitan Police have agreed that a contingent of detectives from both forces will stick with the case indefinitely. That will assure the public of our intentions, but allow us to return most of the men involved back to their normal duties. Moreover, I suggest that we help cement an appearance of continuity by jointly distributing circulars, the drawing and description of the Pancho Villa suspect, to all major police departments as far west as the Mississippi. Since our own operation is too small and ill-equipped to handle such an undertaking, I would appeal to you, Harry, for some help in this area. I know it looks like we are expanding the manhunt half way across the country, but there isn't much more we can do here."

"We can do that for you, George," replied Chief McAdams. "Won't be a problem, but I doubt that we can make anymore progress than we already have. We're at a dead end. You know it and I know it. I recommend that we quietly slip this one in the files. Maybe something will turn up down the road."

On July 10, the Prince George's Police quietly closed down the field headquarters it had established in the elementary school in Lewisdale. Officially, eight teams of detectives were still allotted to the case, but in reality, most were simply employed in moving the massive files containing data from the now more than 5,000 interviews. Two detectives had been briefly dispatched to fly to New Haven, Connecticut, to meet with executives of the Marlin Firearms Company to determine the precise model of the gun employed in the murders and narrow the area in which the gun may have been sold. The effort, like all the rest, proved to be in vain.

In Baltimore, a 23-year-old Morgan College coed named Carmen James was mysteriously shot in the back, but not seriously wounded, by a .22-caliber gun while sitting in class with sixty other summer students. For a brief instant, the shadow of Pancho Villa had been resurrected, but only for a moment as police soon began to theorize the girl had been struck by a stray bullet from someone target practicing.

At the Northwest Branch crime scene, the park looked denuded as M-NCPPC employees neatly stacked the debris and underbrush ripped asunder by the bulldozer. Sifting through the tons of crushed and shattered vegetation, and pouring over the terrain from which it had been torn, would take several days. In the end, this effort too failed miserably to produce the slightest result.

By July 14, District Police Private Bruce H. Scheibel, financial secretary of the 2,740-member Metropolitan Police Association, in charge of the reward fund, reported dejectedly that only $349.50 had been raised thus far and deposited in the Suburban Trust Company bank in Hyattsville. Even the police were losing heart. Despite the last public announcements to the contrary, the Northwest Branch Park murder investigation was being quietly filed away and would be soon forgotten.

That same afternoon, approximately fifty adults and more than one hundred children turned out for an annual "Family Day" picnic in Northwest Branch Park. The joyful shouts of children melded easily with live accordion music and records played over a public broadcast system less than three hundred yards from the once bloody murder site.

The Riggs Lane Teen Club, with the assistance of the Prince George's Recreation Department, had organized the gala picnic in a candid effort to "re-instill the neighborhood's faith" in the park. A teen talent show was to be the highlight of the day. Among the many spectators were Lanie O'Riley and her daughters Elaine and Cathy. Their mere attendance symbolically bolstered the spirits of everyone present. Unlike the legions of journalists that had clustered about a few weeks earlier, only one reporter was present in the park on this particular day. Murder was news, and redemptive picnics were not. The reporter shared his lunch with a family man named Wilhelm Coblenz, from Chapman and 25th Avenue, two blocks from the park. Coblenz admitted his apprehensions over letting his three kids play there after dusk, but on this day his anxieties had disappeared. "This was one of those things that don't happen more than once in a hundred years," he said cheerfully. "Things are returning to normal in our community."

Terry Chauvanne had not attended the picnic in the park. She was placed under her brother Eddy's care that day because her parents had driven into the District to look for work. The AFL-CIO strike was finally over and Philip's shop steward had summoned him down to the union hall to discuss a job. Lucille was hoping to pick up secretarial work at a charity organization in downtown Washington.

As usual, though, as soon as his parents left, Eddy took off with his BB-gun and his buddy Bobby Barnes, leaving Terry ensconced in front of the television. Within minutes of the boys' disappearance, Terry too left the house, drawn outdoors by the happy sounds from the park across the street. For a while she sat on the front stoop, thinking of her sister and how she would have liked to have been at the picnic she had planned.

Terry wanted to be in the park with her friends, whom she could see even from her stoop, but she had been given strict orders, not to leave the house. "What," she thought, "would Ellen do?"

"Just do it. That's what she would have done."

And so she did. As she walked barefoot down the street towards the dirt road leading into the park she felt, for the first time, like a grown-up.

"Just do it," she muttered happily to herself, as she walked a little faster.

As she entered the park, she stopped for a moment and looked down towards the dark, tree-shrouded area by the footbridge.

"Just do it," she said again, and turned right towards the bridge and away from the picnic to her left. She began to run now.

Suddenly, she felt an intense, sharp pain. "It was," she would recall years later, "like a sharp punch on my neck, at the base of my skull on the left side, right there. I mean sharp."

A panic overtook her. Suddenly the park looked dark and the joyous sounds of the nearby picnic had been swallowed by a great void. She turned back towards home and ran as fast as her little bare feet could carry her, ignoring the street gravel that was cutting into them.

Within a minute or two she reached the house, and rushed into the half-bath at the foot of the stairs. Climbing up onto the sink, she looked into the mirror. Tears were streaming down her face.

"Just do it," she repeated.

Quickly she tore her yellow and brown tee shirt off while holding firmly to the sink top with her right hand and turned her back towards the face mirror. For a moment she struggled to get into the right position to see where the pain had been. Then she saw it. She was stunned and delighted, for on the back of the left side of her neck, which she could barely see, was the perfect imprint of a lipstick kiss. Instantly she rushed up the fourteen-step stairway to her bedroom and found the tube of lipstick in the drawer of Ellen's dressing table. It matched.

"She kissed me," Terry squealed, in a moment of exquisite, beautiful joy. "Ellen kissed me!"

Chapter 13

RACETRACK HILL

In the weeks following the quiet termination of the murder investigation in Northwest Branch Park, the Chauvanne family moved ever so slowly from beneath the cloud of loss that had enveloped them. Philip finally found a job, and Lucille, secretarial work at the United Givers Fund in Washington. She also resolved to immerse herself in local politics to keep her mind off the tragedy. Eddy, who had withdrawn into a somber, dark shell, never smiling and seldom talking except in expletives, had disciplinary troubles at school and home.

Little Terry, though, seemed to have returned to a superficial normalcy the fastest of all, wrapping herself up in a Howdy Doody make-believe world. She was catching fireflies, finger painting, watching after her pets, playing with the neighborhood kids, and at night talking to her sister in heaven. The transition appeared seamless to some, but was in no small measure owing to the conscious efforts of Philip and Lucille. As Terry would later explain to one of her closest confidants: "I'm always, in a sense, amazed after Ellen was killed, how mom and dad did not become so-called overly protective of Ed and myself. They didn't. It was, I'm sure it was . . . something that was a conscientious effort they had resolved upon together."

The O'Rileys too, bit by bit, also emerged from the protective cocoon they had unconsciously woven around themselves. John drank far more than before, sometimes on the job, which caused problems at the station house, but his superiors understood and looked the other way. Lanie became obsessed with replacing the loss of her eldest daughter with another as quickly as possible. Despite occasional regurgitations of the horrible events in Northwest Branch Park in several popular detective magazines, month-by-month the tragedy of Lane Manor receded into the distance.

Then, on the first anniversary of the double murders, the fear returned.

Mary Jane Brigham, an eighteen-year old graduate from Northwestern High and a resident of Beltsville, and her closest friend, sixteen-year-old Sharon Jean Vanderslice, of North Laurel, Maryland, were considered about as pretty as they come. On June 1 both girls started out about dusk on an adventure they would never return from as they began hitchhiking down Maryland Route 1 to visit a friend in Florida, without their parent's knowledge or consent. The last anyone saw of the girls alive was when they entered a blue Ford sedan on the highway in Laurel. Eight days later, Mary's nude body was found in a pond near the Potomac River not far from Brunswick, Maryland, riddled with bullet holes from a .38-caliber pistol. She was then raped after death. On June 14, Sharon's nude body was discovered in a quiet eddy of Catoctin Creek, nine miles away. She had been raped and strangled to death.

The following day, June 15, the first of many mysterious telephone calls began at the Chauvanne home. All were directed toward Terry, and then to the O'Riley daughters. And again, the county police were summoned to the scene and phone lines tapped for over a month. At least six extremely brief calls came in, all from the same caller, sounding much like a teenager whose voice was in the process of changing. The police made recordings and analyzed them for signs of stress, language, dialect, slang, indeed any usable clue, but for naught. Police patrols in the neighborhood intensified, and the M-NCPPC police made a point of cruising through Northwest Park during the closing days of the school year, especially in the mornings and afternoons as children again cut through the glade from Lane Manor.

Yet, this time, the daily cycle of life in the neighborhood went on as if nothing notable had occurred except in the Chauvanne and O'Riley households. There, a dark dread appeared with every morning paper and the latest news that the killer, perhaps the same who had murdered Terry and Mikie — was still on the loose. The stress was palpable. Lanie O'Riley, who had become pregnant, suffered a miscarriage and nearly died before being rushed to the hospital.

The patina of normalcy, however, continued to thicken throughout Lane Manor, even as the composition of the region evolved. The first wave of pioneer residents in the neighborhood had already begun to move out as upward economic mobility became the social order of the day. The Dubinskis, who lived down the street, headed for the eternal summer climes of the Deep South, at the end of the month. The Millers, down at the end of the street opposite the duck pond, followed soon afterward. Others, having little choice but to remain, dug in, expanded their kitchens, built front porches, modernized their furnishings, and prepared for a long stay, until they too could move upward and outward.

Lucille's incessant nagging led Philip to keeping up with the Joneses by building a sunken, liver-shaped concrete pond and fence in the backyard for Terry to raise her fish and frog collection in safety. However, when not engaged in such yard work, he usually retreated to the basement rec room to avoid his wife, who was rapidly evolving into a veritable harpy. Arguments began to erupt daily, always with Lucille taking the noisy offensive. They were usually one-sided combats that inevitably resulted in Philip leaving the house and driving off somewhere for several hours. Both Terry and Eddy were often witnesses to the verbal bloodlettings, which could be as brutal as a gladiatorial fight to the death.

Though maintaining strategic neutrality by simply staying out of the war zone, Terry gradually began to nurture a desire to somehow protect her father from the occasionally venomous onslaughts of her mother. Ever so slowly, she was weaned from Lucille, and ever so slowly, the memory of Ellen became her maternal shield. In her mind, her sister began to replace her mother.

Without her sister to counter her wilder side, and with both her parents working, during the school year Terry Chauvanne was largely left to the care of neighbors and her brother Eddy. As with most little children in a grown-up world, her neck had spent much time looking up in a respectful craned position, but in her own, she had become a smiling extrovert whom everyone liked. Enjoying competitive athletics, in which she excelled, she was usually among the first picked for softball games in the park. She had soon begun to imitate her brother's more rebellious nature, and when left in his care, was frequently abandoned to her own devices, a tomboy bounding about in sandals and shorts, occasionally with dire consequences.

Once, when the boy next door, Benny Miller, playfully pointed his BB-gun at her, Terry rushed into the house and pulled Eddy's Red Ryder from the closet, grabbed a blanket, and raced out the back door to do battle. Throwing the blanket over the porch railing for protection, she began pumping BBs at her assailant with a fury that soon had him crying and begging for mercy. Overtaken by a strange frenzy that she later could not explain to anyone, least of all her parents, Terry refused to stop and was soon shooting him at point blank range as he cowered, shouting and screaming in abject terror. Wearing only shorts and a tee shirt, Benny was bruised and bleeding from the encounter. Terry faced certain retribution from Lucille and Philip and counseling from the school psychologist who claimed it was a product of subdued rage at the loss of her sister. The boy, said the counselor, in the girl's mind, had served as a stand-in for the killer who had deprived her of her beloved sister and mentor. Lucille didn't buy it, and punished both her daughter and son with a sound thrashing, one for committing the crime, and the other for providing the weapon.

Terry had received a shiny new Schwinn bicycle on her eighth birthday, Valentine's Day, and she quickly mastered it with all the aplomb and bravado of a child who knew no fear. The art of riding, even without holding the handlebars, became almost second nature. Moreover, the bike gave her access to a world she could now discover on her own, and the frontiers of the neighborhood begged to be invaded. Philip and Lucille, who, after Ellen's murder, had at first been overprotective of both their children, worried endlessly about their whereabouts. When they sought to establish borders beyond which their daughter was forbidden to explore, they were always met with fits of pouting and, in the end, the pretty little girl with raven tresses, who could manipulate her father with little more than a well-timed whimper, always won.

The bike would provide the means for a nearly disastrous event. During one of her outings near Lane Manor, Terry had discovered on the other side of Northwest Branch Park, not far from the high school, a long hill that she and her playmates began to employ as their personal racetrack. At the bottom were a stop sign and an intersection, but few cars during the day. The catastrophe occurred on a hot mid-August afternoon when Terry and several friends had left the daily M-NCPPC summer crafts program put on in the park for the neighborhood kids. Eddy, who was assigned to watch her, went off to play basketball with his friends at the other end of the park. His absence provided yet another golden moment for Terry and one of her cohorts, Betty Steiner.

They took the usual short cut through the park, passing the murder site and over the little bridge across the branch. The foliage cut down during the lengthy police investigation had returned to the fertile shores of the little waterway and to the briar patch into which Ellen's body had been so brutally dragged over a year before. Now, as the two girls walked along the dark, shaded pathway, Terry's companion, Betty, worried about leaving their familiar surroundings without permission.

"We could get in trouble, you know," Betty said as they began to walk their bikes across the bridge, knowing full well that since the murders the creek always marked the limits beyond which they were forbidden to go.

Terry, too, worried, but she had learned from her brother to show no fear. Looking back over her shoulder at the briar patch she said, "Don't worry. We'll be all right. Nobody knows where we're going and my mom and dad won't be home for another couple of hours."

Ten minutes later the two girls had reached "Racetrack Hill" as they had dubbed it. On the first race down, the chain on Betty's bike came loose. Now, they would have to stop racing and she pouted that she couldn't even ride home.

"That's okay, Betty," said Terry, trying to cheer up her friend. "You can ride with me. Hey, I know! Why don't we both ride down the hill on my bike? You can sit on the handlebars and I'll steer. It'll be safe and fun. I promise."

Betty wasn't so sure.

"You're not scared are you?" said Terry.

"No," replied her companion with mock bravery. "Of course not."

"Then let's just do it, okay?"

Thus cajoled and intimidated by her younger comrade, who refused to play anyone's acolyte, Betty finally agreed and both girls walked the bike to the top of the hill. Betty got on the handlebars after Terry took the seat; then they shoved off and soon were hurtling down the quarter-mile stretch at a breathtaking speed. Their eyelids struggled to stay open against the vortex of air. The moment was all too exhilarating. Terry let go of the handlebars and flung her arms out like an eagle ascending into the clouds. It was pure ecstasy, a moment divine, as she closed her eyes and soared. Then, suddenly, all was darkness and pain.

When Terry awoke, she was still lying on the ground. A small crowd of adults stood over her. She could taste blood in her mouth, and her head and upper body hurt all over. Her tongue could feel the badly cut flesh around it. Her two front teeth had gone clear through her lower lip. A police officer was leaning over her.

"She'll live, I guess, but the other girl is a mess. Both of her legs and one arm are broken, and she's losing a lot of blood. We need to get them both to a hospital and quick."

Ten minutes later, both girls were in an ambulance en route to Prince George's General. Terry was barely conscious of the siren that opened a swath of driving space on Bladensburg Road. She was fully cognizant for a few moments as they rolled her gurney towards the sliding ER doors. Then, for a brief moment she looked up at a second story window in the building overlooking the entry bay. There, just before she again slipped into the shadow of unconsciousness, she saw waving at her a familiar image that looked almost exactly like her sister. And the returning darkness seemed comfortable.

The "Racetrack Hill" catastrophe had, for a time, made Terry something of celebrity among her school chums, and she relished showing off her scars as if they were medals earned on the battlefield. She had emerged from the hospital with a prominent array of stitches on her face and limbs, extensive black and blue marks, a temporary inability to whistle, and the grandiose feeling of having matured five years in a single day. Even Eddy was envious of the attention heaped upon his little sister.

As the months passed, and the temporal distance grew between the horrific events of June 1955 and the subsequent fears wrought by the Brigham-Vanderslice murders, normalcy largely resumed in the Chauvanne household, albeit with a few problems common to many families. Eddy, whose physiology was advancing well ahead of the norm for his age, had, by degrees, begun to emerge from his shell, but not in ways that pleased everyone. By the time he entered his teens, he had the athletic musculature and size of a well-developed eighteen-year-old, and often a rebellious, anti-social attitude to match. On the playground, he became the de facto leader of a band of younger kids whose tendency towards mischief had earned him an unenviable reputation among the teaching staff, and a certain roguish popularity among his classmates. Though excelling at school sports, especially basketball, his academic showing was far below average. His numerous visits to the school counselor, and not infrequently the principal's office, were matched by the number of times he was awarded detention for misbehavior. Always, though, he was cut slack owing to the acknowledged trauma suffered from the loss of his older sister.

Terry, on the other hand, had begun to blossom into a somewhat impish-looking but precocious and diligent student, far advanced for her age in intelligence and curiosity, and generally adored by grown ups. Though nine, she began attending the teen club with her brother, learned to jitterbug, and was an instant hit with the boys. She read anything and everything as if possessed by some literary demon, which her parents found hard to comprehend. When not studying, her nose in some book, magazine, or newspaper, or playing with her friends, she devoted her time to her pets. Her love of animals knew no bounds. By her ninth birthday, she had added to the family zoo, originally consisting of her two cocker's, Tweedle Dee and Tweedle Dum, an aviary of three wounded birds (two wrens and a starling) that she nursed back to health after they had flown into closed windows, plus a wounded turtle picked up in the park with a hole in its shell, three stray cats, a rabbit Uncle Henry gave to her as a gift, an ant farm, a bloodworm farm, two hamsters, two gerbils, six goldfish, and, second in favor only to her dogs, a great green frog named Mr. Bluster. While other little girls played with their Raggedy Anns, Terry tended to her pets as if they were her own flesh and blood, speaking with them as some children did with their dolls at a playtime tea party. And sometimes, still much to her parent's dismay, she talked to her dead sister. They were counseled to let such idiosyncrasies take their course; the passage of time would cure all.

Somehow, the world slowly did return to normal. That is, until the June afternoon in 1957 when the mysterious telephone calls resumed. The following day, the front page of the *Washington Post* reported another horrible homicide.

Chapter 14

SEX BEAST

June 26, 1957. Margaret Henry and Sergeant John Bunting, USA, were at a decision-making point in their lives as they drove along a rural stretch of Maryland Route 450 near the outskirts of Annapolis. John was on a weekend pass from Fort Meade, and the couple had been exploring the bucolic Anne Arundel County countryside, stopping here and there to admire the alluvial fields of tobacco, corn, and the occasional patches of wildflowers.

Margaret had graduated from the University of Maryland two years before, and had been dating John for the last eight months. Though both had repeatedly declared their love for each other, neither, they proclaimed, had any intentions of marriage in the immediate future. Both had resolved to pursue their separate careers for a few years, she as a teacher and he in the military, before someday settling down together. Other issues contributed to the decision. Margaret's parents were both ill, and she had to take her sister Marlene, 14, and brother Tommy, 10, under her wing until things at home improved. To John this seemed an issue that might never be resolved. Devout Catholics, the couple wanted a large family of their own someday, but it was first necessary to begin with a clean slate by rescuing Margaret from her college debt load before taking the plunge. Given the hormonal urges of youth, that was going to be a difficult road to follow.

Margaret was an attractive young woman, with long black hair, a superb figure, and a warm, cheerful persona that made it difficult for John to stay the celibate course that his church required. On several occasions they had nearly consummated the deed before Margaret restrained him. It was almost too much for John to bear, and in late May he resolved to propose formally and purchased a simple gold engagement ring, debt be damned.

Now, as the couple drove along in John's second-hand Nash Rambler, he dithered endlessly attempting to work up to the proposal. It was a warm night and though the windows were rolled down, beads of sweat had formed on his forehead as he nervously approached the subject of marriage. The ring was in his shirt pocket. It was nearing evening before he could summon up the courage and turned the car off onto a lonely side road for the big moment. Now or never, he thought to himself, but it was already too late.

At first neither John nor Margaret paid much attention to the beat-up blue Ford following them down the narrow macadam road, until it began to ride close to their rear bumper.

"Crazy bastard," John said out loud as he watched the car in the rear view mirror weaving wildly back and forth barely ten feet behind him.

Suddenly, at a long open stretch on the road, the tailgater gunned it and sped by the Rambler on the left, moved ahead some fifty yards, then suddenly jackknifed diagonally across the road. John smashed his right foot on the break peddle to prevent crashing, swerved, and came to a stop barely a few feet from the driver's side of the Ford.

"Maybe he's drunk, or needs some assistance or is in trouble and had to stop us," Margaret suggested.

"I doubt it," John replied, as he watched a tall, thin-faced man with long dark hair jump from the Ford and saunter over to him.

"You're on a private road. This is my property," the man said. "Don't think I don't know why you're back here."

"No sir," Margaret said nervously but courteously. "We were just out for a drive through the countryside."

"My ass," the man said in a rising voice. "You're looking for a place to pull over and fuck."

"No, no!" Margaret retorted apologetically. "It's not like that . . . "

Interrupting, John leaned across the seat. "Listen, we weren't up to what you think, and we'll leave your property right now if . . ."

"Shut the hell up," said the man as he quickly opened the back passenger door and slid in behind them. Both Margaret and John, stunned at the brazen entry, turned to face him.

"You!" she exclaimed in shock as she saw his face, and then the nickel-plated .38 pistol pointed right between her eyes.

"I said shut the hell up, or I'll blow your fucking brains out," shouted the man. "But first things first. Got a cigarette?"

"Neither of us smoke," John said.

"Too goddamned bad for you. Empty your pockets and purse, and give me all your money," the man demanded. "But don't look back. Just pass it over your shoulders."

"John, don't give him anything," Margaret said imperiously, calling the intruder's bluff. "He's probably going to kill us for it anyway."

The man leaned forward and began caressing Margaret's head and neck running his fingers through her dark hair. His fingertips were hard and unforgiving.

"Too bad you had to say that lady," he said, pulling her head back by the hair with his left hand and raising the gun to the right side of her head with his other hand.

The bullet ripped through the side of Margaret's forehead, passing through her brain and exiting from the left side of the head just above the eye, taking with it fragments of skull, hair, viscera and gray matter, which splattered across John, the steering column, and dashboard.

As Margaret's body fell sideways, John saw his chance, and threw open the door, rolled onto the ground, and ran down across an open field and into the twilight, weaving back and forth to avoid being killed. But there were no shots. After running for a mile or so John found a small farmhouse near Route 450, and called the police. The response was swift. Within fifteen minutes a pair of squad cars from the county sheriff's office appeared, sirens blaring.

When the police arrived, they found Sargeant John Bunting shaking uncontrollably and still breathing hard. Running up to the squad car, even before one of the officers could get out, he babbled repeatedly: "He just stopped our car and shot her." Within a short time, he had calmed down enough to relate his story and provide a broad brush description of the attacker: average build, tall, somewhat long dark hair, clean-shaven, thin face, and otherwise rather ordinary in appearance. There was nothing overtly threatening about the way the assailant looked, only in his cold, brutal manner. After describing the vicious attack John lead the police back to the Nash Rambler.

The assailant was gone, but the Rambler, with Margaret's body inside, was still there. The front passenger door was open and the corpse had been partially pulled out, feet first. Her dress, undergarments and shoes had been ripped off. It was apparent that the killer had lingered long enough to rape her in death.

Within an hour, a half-dozen patrol cars and more than a dozen officers were on the scene, taking fingerprints from the Rambler and fanning out throughout the immediate area. They hoped that the "maniac driver" had not gotten far, or may have left behind some clue.

Throughout the night, following the immediate issuance of an all-points bulletin to law enforcement agencies in the region, police kept a watch for a battered late-model blue Ford. Even more officers combed the nearby terrain for signs of the killer and possible evidence. About 2 a.m. Anne Arundel County Police Chief Bobby Joe Glade, who had arrived on the scene to personally superintend the search, was summoned by his second in command, Lieutenant Jerry Simkins, to a dilapidated cinderblock building about a quarter of a mile from the murder site, hidden amidst dense forest, weeds and underbrush.

As they cautiously walked with drawn weapons around the building, which appeared to be dark, unoccupied, and locked up tight, they discovered a broken basement window on the side. Shining a flashlight through the window they could make out portions of pictures of nude women tacked to a wall.

After some discussion about the legality of entry into an apparently abandoned building, the two officers squirmed through the basement window opening. Dropping to the floor, they flashed their lights on the walls around them, and were astonished to find plastered all about hundreds of explicit pornographic pictures of women in every lewd pose imaginable. At least half of the photos showed naked women cowering, being whipped, tortured, or posed in humiliating postures of subjugation and bondage. Several dozen morgue photographs were also taped to the walls, showing the bodies of women who had been murdered. The cellar was completely black, except where the spears of light moved about on the lurid, tortured women on the wall, and, as Lieutenant Simkins later said, seemed as if they had suddenly been dropped into some medieval, sexual torture chamber of death.

It was clear that whoever had collected the images was obsessed with sadistic fantasies and made the isolated cinderblock hideout itself a place for his sexual pleasure. The only normal picture to be found was a formal posed portrait of a pretty girl in a sweater with a lacy white collar, and printed on heavy glossy paper. No fingerprints or other evidence were found, even on the pictures themselves. Later search of county records failed to even note the structure on the property, the ownership of which belonged to a large real estate development corporation in the process of going bankrupt.

After documenting the cinderblock building and its contents, Chief Glade sent the picture of the girl in the sweater to the FBI for analysis and possible identification, even as fingerprints from the car were being analyzed. The only prints there proved to be from John and Margaret. For a brief time, Sergeant John Bunting himself had become a suspect, but not for long.

The FBI soon determined that the portrait photograph was of the type used in yearbooks. As the woman in the picture appeared to be a young adult, it was decided that teams of agents would be sent to check out the yearbooks from colleges, trade, and secretarial schools in and about the Annapolis area. Though local and state police normally conducted such operations, the FBI justified the Bureau's direct involvement on suspicion that since the crime was committed barely twenty miles from Washington, and the killer "might" have crossed the state line into the District, it was "possibly" an interstate crime. Owing to the sensational newspaper coverage, some critics charged, Director J. Edgar Hoover himself, ever cognizant of press exposure for his agency and self, had given the order to garner some of the limelight. Whatever the motive might have been, the end product justified the means. Within a few weeks the mystery girl in the sweater had been positively identified.

While pouring over more than a decade of yearbooks from all of the universities, colleges, junior colleges, and trade and secretarial schools in the Washington-Baltimore-Annapolis triangle, they found the right one from the University of Maryland at Baltimore, thirty miles from the crime scene. The photograph was of a 1955 BFA graduate named Amanda Liston, but when located and questioned, Liston denied having known anyone that fit the Bunting description of the killer, although she had dated several young men with long dark hair. It was a disappointing turn of events, for everyone had felt certain they would garner at least some information from her that might lead to an arrest, but to no avail.

Despite an intensive investigation and the round-up of several suspects, all of whom were immediately released, the solution to the Henry case remained, like the Chauvanne-O'Riley and Brigham-Vanderslice murders before them, unsolved and, in a short time, were all but forgotten. That is, until discovery of yet another in the growing series of brutal homicides in the Maryland-Virginia region.

January 11, 1959. The weekend dinners at the home of Custis J. Lee, in Louisa County, Virginia, were always models of family togetherness, Norman Rockwell Americana in the flesh. Custis' brother, Everett T. Lee, Jr., and his wife Carol, would be there with their two kids, Wendy Ann, 5, and Hilda, 18 months. Custis' wife Marcie had prepared a sumptuous turkey, while their adopted daughter, ten-year-old Marie Granger, helped with the trimmings. Later, Everett and his tribe would drive out to visit for a while with Carol's elderly housebound parents, who lived just south of Fredericksburg, in Spottsylvania County.

Everett, 29, was by occupation a feed truck driver, and a quiet, retiring man, liked by all of his neighbors. Every Sunday morning, with his wife Carol, 28, and two children he regularly attended the local Baptist church where he served as president of the missionary society. And each Sunday afternoon they took their two girls to Sunday school. Their little home in Apple Grove, on the South Anna River, off Virginia Route 609, was modest but they lived within their means, and seemed the perfectly happy couple, neighbors said, who never fought among themselves, nor had any enemies.

The drive home along the lightly traveled rural Route 609 from Carol's parents to Apple Grove on Sunday evenings was usually without incident. Carol was in the back seat, cradling her dozing baby Hilda, while Wendy Ann sat beside her engrossed in play with several dolls.

As they drove along, a car appeared in Everett's rear view mirror and appeared to be coming up at a high speed, his high beams blinking off and on as if there was some emergency and asking to pass. Everett slowed and pulled slightly to the right, but the car behind him followed suit. When he increased speed, the mystery car did so as well. On a long open stretch of the road, the mystery car suddenly sped up and passed. Then, without warning, the passing car abruptly jackknifed obliquely across the road several hundred yards ahead, forcing Everett to hit the brakes and skid off to the side.

At first assuming the mystery car had some malfunction or had come to its abrupt halt for some unknown reason, Everett jumped from his own vehicle and ran forward, even as the other driver was emerging with a nickel-plated .38 revolver in his hand.

January 12, 1959. Carol Lee's mother was concerned. She was a diabetic, and every morning, regular as clockwork, her daughter called to check on her. This morning she had failed to call, and by mid-day Carol's mother had begun to fret. A call to her daughter's house yielded no response. Increasingly worried, she called her sister, Mrs. L. G. Couch, who lived near the Lee home, to check on the family. As Mrs. Couch drove along Route 609, she spotted Everett's car on the roadside, apparently abandoned, with skid marks behind the vehicle, and another pair directly in front. She immediately called Louisa County Sheriff Buddy R. Moffit.

Upon his arrival, Sheriff Moffit discovered the car with the keys still in the ignition. Carol's purse and the children's dolls were in the backseat. The sheriff was puzzled. He knew Everett Lee personally to be a strong, burley, tough man who was not easily angered, but who would not have succumbed readily to any possible assailant. Yet, aside from the skid marks, which appeared to have indicated a near collision, there was nothing to suggest foul play, no blood, no signs of a struggle, or trail for police to follow. There were no prints on the car other than those of the Lee family.

The disappearance of the Lees was soon reported in the local press, replete with photographs of the smiling, happy family, in hopes that someone might have information regarding their whereabouts, or had seen or encountered some suspicious person or activity on Route 609.

Within a few days, Tim and Linda Burkowsky, a young married couple, had come forward and informed police that on the afternoon of the same day that the Lees had disappeared, they had been driving on the same road. Out of nowhere a beat up late model blue Ford had driven up behind them, frantically flashing its lights. Suddenly, the driver of the car gunned it and passed them on an open stretch of road, not far from where the Lee car had been found. As soon as the Ford passed, the driver suddenly stopped, forcing them off to the side of the road.

For a few pregnant seconds the Burkowskys waited expectantly as the driver of the Ford got out and walked toward them. The stranger was tall, with a thin face, heavy eyebrows, long, dark hair, and abnormally long arms. He seemed to be walking with a peculiar gate, as if he had pebbles in his shoes, and appeared to be carrying something in his right hand, perhaps a weapon.

Tim Burkowsky didn't wait around to find out, but shifted his car into reverse and escaped back down Route 609. The couple later told police that the man's manner "was threatening and they were certain that if he managed to reach them before they escaped, he would have harmed them. They assumed that he intended to rob them, but now they believed he was bent on far worse things."

March 4, 1959. James Bench and Bill Stott, neighbors of the Lee family, were walking along a shallow ditch near a deserted sawmill not far from Apple Grove. Bench had been here many times over the last two years, ever since the mill shut down, usually to gather sawdust as mulch for his rose garden, which he began to tend to earlier in the spring than most. Stott had come along to assist. As the two men neared the abandoned mill, they noticed what they at first believed to be the smell of a dead animal, perhaps a deer, but then encountered the putrefying body of a man. The corpse was lying face down in the brush near the depression. His hands were tied behind his back with a blue necktie.

When police arrived on the scene and removed the corpse, they found another, an infant girl, lying beneath. The autopsy soon afterwards revealed that the man had been shot in the back of the head with a single bullet, from a .38 pistol, and had fallen forward onto the infant, which was alive at the time, having apparently been thrown into the ditch before the killing, and then suffocated by the body that had fallen on top of her. The deceased were quickly identified as Everett T. Lee and his infant daughter Hilda.

There were no other clues. Both the local and state police were baffled.

March 21, 1959. The box kite that Jamie Trussell and his buddy Johnny Klinger, both 13, were flying not far from Maryland Route 450 on the outskirts of Annapolis had all but disappeared when their string broke. Trussell was determined not to lose the colorful high-flyer purchased with his slender allowance, and he and Klinger immediately set off in pursuit across the open fields, passing copses of dangerous kite-eating trees along the way but never losing sight of their target, though it was growing smaller by the minute.

Finally, the kite disappeared, but the two boys pressed on with their search down a lonely macadam road until they came to a dilapidated and apparently abandoned cinderblock building. Klinger was first to suggest they climb onto the shaky-looking tin roof for a better vantage point. After some difficulty, they achieved the summit, from which they could readily survey the surrounding terrain.

Although neither boy could see any vestige of the lost box kite, they did spy an interesting anomaly that demanded investigation in the ground nearby. From the roof, it looked like a large rat's nest or, more likely, gopher hole. When they climbed down and examined the site more closely they discovered what appeared to be long, black human hair covered by dirt. Frightened that they may have discovered a body, they ran home as fast as their legs could carry them and informed their parents, who immediately called the police.

Again Chief Glade and Lieutenant Simkins arrived on the same scene they had visited twenty-one months earlier to investigate yet another possible crime. Directed to the buried-hair site by the two boys, they began to dig. Within a few minutes they discovered the decomposing body of Carol Lee with a silk scarf tightly knotted around her neck. Lying on top of her corpse were the remains of her five-year-old daughter Wendy, whose skull had been brutally fractured.

Forensic analysis of the bodies by the Maryland medical examiner revealed that both victims had been severely beaten to death with a blunt instrument, which had split the child's head nearly in half. Though numerous blunt trauma marks covered Carol's head, body, and limbs, they initially thought that the woman had been strangled. Based upon later findings, though, they conjectured that the scarf knotted around Carol's neck had been applied to force her to have oral sex with the killer. Re-examination of the abandoned cinderblock building nearby resulted in the discovery of a button from Carol's dress on the floor of the basement, and both old and fresh car tire tracks outside.

With the evidence clearly indicating kidnapping across state lines, the FBI was immediately called into action on the Lee case. A nationwide manhunt was launched for a thin-faced man in a late-model blue Ford. Special squads of both Maryland and Virginia law-enforcement agencies were quickly brought into service. Again the newspapers were filled with descriptions of the grim and seemingly fruitless day-to-day search. Despite thousands of man-hours and countless resources poured into the federal, state, and local efforts to find the murderer, whom the more scandal driven media quickly dubbed the "Sex Beast Killer," within the space of several months the Lee murder case, like its predecessors, had grown stone cold.

By mid-spring 1959, it was becoming clear to the FBI and all of the law enforcement agencies involved that the nationwide manhunt for the so-called "Sex Beast Killer" was going nowhere. Even Hoover himself had admitted privately to his number-two man and life-partner, Deputy Director Clyde Tolson, that it would be necessary, despite the inevitable avalanche of useless information and red herrings, to request assistance from the public-at-large for any data that might lead to the arrest of a suspect. The response became a tsunami that began to tax even the Bureau's substantial resources.

Finally, in May an anonymous letter arrived at the *Washington Star* from a most unexpected source — the "Sex Beast" himself. Immediately forwarded to the FBI, the letter revealed that the killer was following the manhunt with a detached and almost morbid fascination. He took obvious pleasure not only in the acts he had committed, but also in writing about them with a certain smugness that bordered on arrogance. In describing his rape and murder of Carol Lee, he left nothing to the imagination, and attached to the shocking description a photo of the victim clipped from a newspaper.

"Caught on a lonely road," he wrote, " . . . After pulling them over . . . I leveled the pistol . . . I ordered them out and him into the car trunk . . . bound both . . . drove to a select area . . . and killed the husband and baby. Now the mother and daughter were all mine." Following a lurid description of several efforts at rape and sodomy, and how the victim had failed to satisfy his sexual desires, he concluded: "And so . . . I killed her . . . I gagged her, and lead her to her place of execution . . . and buried her . . ."

The similarities of the modus operandi of the Lee and Henry cases could not be ignored. In both, a tall, thin-faced, dark haired man driving a battered late model blue Ford, had systematically used his vehicle to drive his victims off the road, then attack them, using a .38 pistol in both acts. His female victims had been viciously raped and brutalized. The common denominator was the run-down cinderblock building outside of Annapolis that apparently served as his sadistic pornographic *pro forma* base of operations.

The FBI was stymied and the public horrified. Yet another new round of terror was ushered back to the community of Lane Manor, into the households of the Chauvanne and O'Riley families.

Immediately after Terry Chauvanne's eleventh birthday, on Valentine's Day 1959, Lucille suggested her daughter start looking for a summer job after school and before the end of the school year in June. She would be graduating from the fifth grade to the sixth and, as Lucille repeatedly reminded her, a year after that would be junior high school. Although work permits were required for kids under 16, Lucille's motto had been: "You know it's never too early for such things." Ellen had taken her first job at an early age, and it was, Lucille felt, high time that Terry did so too.

"You know your sister never shied away from the work ethic," Lucille told Terry repeatedly. "And you know what her favorite phrase was, don't you?"

"Yes ma'm," Terry answered obediently. "Just do it."

By early May, a local bakery in the newly built Prince George's Plaza had promised Terry a menial job. The father of Candice Miller, one of Ellen's old friends, who lived down the street, with whom Philip had become friendly, owned and operated the bakery. Terry was to work for two hours in the afternoons, two days a week, after school, and on Saturdays, until the end of the school year, and during the summer for fifteen hours a week. She would receive 75¢ an hour. For Terry, it seemed the world was her oyster, and she was about to become fabulously rich.

Then the threatening phone calls began anew, at both the Chauvanne and O'Riley homes.

For Philip and Lucille, the irregular, short, always frightening calls, set against the daily newspaper coverage on the search for the Sex Beast Killer, served only to revive the horrors of the summer of 1955, four years earlier and a lifetime ago. Now the voice on the other end of the line was no longer that of a teenager, but of a man. No longer were they the mystifying requests to speak to poor, dead Ellen. They were now outright threats to rape and kill Terry, Cathy, and Elaine. Like before, the police were informed, lines were tapped, and an investigation launched, all to no avail.

This time, however, protective measures were taken for Terry and both the O'Riley girls. Prince George's County Police Chief Gregory Panadapoulis quickly ordered a stakeout at both homes. All three children were to be driven to and from school in unmarked police cars, and a surveillance team of uniformed and plainclothes officers stationed at key points in and around Lewisdale Elementary.

Several decades later Terry would recall, ironically with some amusement, those last few weeks of fifth grade. "Given the circumstances," she said, "it was kind of exciting for a little kid, you know, going to and leaving from school, under special police escort, what with all the traffic around the school, and the cops coming in and going out. I recall that one morning there was a woman in her car, dropping off her son, who blocked the parking lot entrance to the unmarked car I was in. She was being obstinate and refused to back up. The officer in the car, who was not a uniformed cop, wanted her to back out. She refused. So he turns the siren on. Got her attention pretty darned quick, and she backed up damned fast. I laughed like crazy. In many ways it was a period I will never forget because I felt like Cinderella, being delivered every day to school in my own royal pumpkin. Some of the kids resented the special attention I was getting, and a few of them got down right nasty with me, but they were usually disciplined by the teachers. What I remember most distinctly, however, was the intensity of those few weeks. I don't recall being afraid, but I do recall being told to be circumspect. Then it all came to an end with the arrest of the so-called Sex Beast Killer."

The letter that arrived at FBI headquarters on Pennsylvania Avenue, in Washington, D.C. on May 10, 1959, postmarked from Norfolk, Virginia, unlike most flowing in regarding the investigation, took less than a day to be vetted before making its way up to Director J. Edgar Hoover. The unsigned document, written by hand in pencil in a loose script on common loose-leaf binder paper was legible, but just barely. The letter claimed that a young jazz musician from Hyattsville named Bernard David Breese, Jr., was behind the Lee murders.

Apparently written by a friend of the musician, the letter stated that the author had been with Breese for a while on the same night as the Henry murder, and he had been on a Benzedrine high and acting wildly. The anonymous writer had later become suspicious following newspaper reports of the Lee murders and had asked Breese, who had made some suspicious comments regarding the crime, if he had been the killer. The musician did not deny involvement, but evaded answering the question, and, the anonymous writer said, though in the middle of a gig in D.C., disappeared almost immediately afterwards without a trace.

Within a day of receiving the letter, the FBI began an intensive investigation of Bernard David Breese. A Maryland native, born in 1933, he had served a two-year hitch in the

Air Force during the Korean War and in 1953 attended the state university on the GI Bill, but dropped out before graduation to pursue a career in music. Known to most of his musician friends only as Dave, he had married while in the service and fathered a son, but the marriage hadn't lasted, despite the efforts of his best friend and best man at his wedding, a young county police rookie named Marvin McQueen.

Breese's first professional gigs had been at church socials, weddings, and local club venues, where he was described by one his fellow musicians as "a pretty nice boy . . . rather cold and reserved . . . but a gentleman." Others in the Hyattsville community where he had grown up described him as having "a kind and sympathetic nature . . . who wouldn't hurt a living thing." His closest friends called him a well-mannered and intelligent artist, a musician of considerable talent who played the piano, guitar, saxophone, and clarinet equally well. Not surprisingly, his taste for modern jazz and his employment had often taken him far afield, although he had usually played the local scene.

That Breese was anything but a saint, however, was suggested by his police record. On March 12, 1955, the FBI learned, he had been arrested for assault after offering a 36-year-old woman a ride in his car, which she had refused, and then forcibly dragged her in and assaulted her. It wasn't clear why, but the victim had preferred to drop the charge. Suspicions intensified when Amanda Liston, again questioned and this time confronted with his picture, confessed that she had dated him while both were attending the University of Maryland, but had given up the relationship after she discovered he was married. After his divorce, he had taken to dating exotic dancers from upscale downtown D.C. clubs such as The Blue Mirror, where he occasionally played, and strippers from the Gayety Burlesque Theater, on one of the sleazier city streets.

Teased by Breese's shady profile, the FBI was relentless in its search for the suspect, certain now that he was their man. Yet, other than the Liston connection, and lacking hard evidence, they knew it would be difficult making any charge stick — if they ever found him. Nevertheless, they visited the address they'd received in the anonymous letter from Norfolk, but without luck. They canvassed jazz clubs where he'd once frequented or had played, but no one, including his parents and relatives who were interviewed extensively, seemed to know where he had gone. Perhaps, the Bureau reasoned, someone had tipped him off that the police were looking for him, or he had simply anticipated the possibility after being confronted by the anonymous letter writer. The simple truth, however, was that, though much of the puzzle itself had begun to come together, he had disappeared, and his trail had grown extremely cold.

Nearly a year later, in May 1960, the FBI received a second letter from the anonymous Norfolk writer, who this time signed his name. The correspondent, one Tilman Stower, a salesman in Virginia Beach, again informed the Bureau that he had once been friendly with Breese, whom he was now certain was the assailant in the Lee family killings. Though he had at first been unaware of the suspect's whereabouts, he said, he had just received a postcard from him postmarked West Memphis, Arkansas. It was all the Bureau needed.

On May 29, even as Terry Chauvanne was bringing her elementary school career to a close, FBI agents located the suspect working as a piano salesman in a music store in West Memphis. As he was being formally arrested and charged with flight to avoid prosecution in the Margaret Henry murder, the tall man with the thin face and long, dark hair cried out as if in some trite TV police drama: "But I'm innocent. Innocent."

Soon after the suspect was taken into custody, federal agents interviewed the store manager, who showed them a pile of books Breese had stacked against the wall in his cubicle, all of which suggested a definite Freudian twist to his interests. Included in the pile were: *A Constructive Study of Neurosis*; *Our Inner Conflict*; *The Future of an Illusion*; and *The History of Frustration*, as well as a number of raunchy underground pornographic comic books and sex magazines.

Upon his return to Washington, Breese was placed in an FBI lineup and quickly identified by Sergeant Bunting as the man who had killed Margaret Henry. The following evening, June 24, a gaggle of federal agents descended upon the Breese family residence in Hyattsville, again questioned the suspect's parents, and this time searched the premises. Discovered hidden in the attic was an instrument case for the suspect's saxophone. Stashed inside was a nickel-plated .38 revolver, and various notes describing assorted sadistic acts he had committed over several years. One such act was clipped to a newspaper photo of Margaret Henry, and proved to be the very words sent to the *Washington Star* a year earlier: "Caught on a lonely road... Drove to a select area and killed husband and baby. Now the mother and daughter were all mine." Ballistics tests on the gun proved a perfect match for the bullets that had killed both Everett Lee and Margaret Henry.

The following day, FBI Director Hoover announced that the long-sought Hyattsville musician was to be held and charged in the Henry murder case. Hoover added, in the bland fashion that had become his trademark, that Bureau agents in Baltimore had also filed a Federal complaint charging Breese with the double kidnap-murders of Carol Lee and her five-year-old daughter Wendy Ann. Moreover, the Bureau was continuing the Breese investigation in connection with similar unsolved crimes. High on the list were the Chauvanne-O'Riley and Brigham-Vanderslice killings, which Director Hoover was personally convinced had also been committed by the suspect. Within hours of the FBI statement, the Executive Director of the Virginia State Police, Major J. W. Rockwell, announced that warrants were also being drawn up in Richmond charging Breese with the double homicide of Everett T. Lee and his daughter Jane.

The June 26 front-page headlines of the *Washington Sunday Star*, in a story by staff writer Rebecca Minderhouser, said it all. "Breese Held in Multiple Lee Slayings. FBI Obtains Warrants in Grisly Kidnap Deaths. Possible Links With Other Mystery Killings Being Investigated."

Bernard David Breese, Jr. was tried by jury for the first-degree murder of Margaret Henry in Baltimore District Court in February 1961. The courtroom was sardine packed with reporters and cameramen in what some critics of the punishment later declared was a media circus conducted by an incompetent judge. It was, nevertheless, a brief open-and-shut case in which the results were never in doubt. The defendant was quickly convicted and sentenced to life in prison without parole. Immediately following the trial in Baltimore, he was again tried, this time in U.S. Circuit Court in Spotsylvania County, Virginia, for the first-degree murders of Everett and Hilda Lee. Condemned by his notes, found in the saxophone case in his parents' home, a jury again found him guilty and condemned him to death by electrocution, but it was not to be.

In 1966, after years of seemingly endless appeals by his attorneys, Bernard David Breese, Jr., was ordered to undergo psychiatric testing. Six years later, after a further string of appeals in his behalf, the sentence was commuted to life in prison when the U.S. Supreme Court suspended all death sentences to evaluate the constitutionality of the death penalty.

In 1985, during an interview with a reporter from the *Richmond-Times Dispatch*, the "Sex Beast Killer" confessed that he had also killed Mary Jane Brigham and Sharon Jean Vanderslice. He said nothing, however, about the Chauvanne-O'Riley murders.

J. Edgar Hoover was convinced that Bernard David Breese was guilty of the Northwest Branch Park killings, despite a lack of evidence and contradictions relative to the killer's acknowledged modus operandi. Most notable in the "MO" was his consistent use of a car and a .38 pistol in committing his crimes, and the perpetration of multiple sadistic rapes, all of which failed to resemble anything like the Chauvanne-O'Riley case in June 1955. Espousing a similar belief to Hoover's, federal, state, and county law enforcement agencies were only too eager to close the books on the Northwest Branch Park murders and move on, but for the Chauvanne and O'Riley families, though a serial killer had been brought to justice who might have been associated with the bloody assassinations of their precious daughters, there could be no closure.

Chapter 15

MUSCULAR CALVES

The capture of Bernard David Breese, Jr., the living personification of Dr. Jekyll and Mr. Hyde, may for some have marked the end of an era, an age when out-of-the-blue killings in rural America were much beyond the norm. Yet it was also an era where a growing fear of communism began to cast a malicious shadow across the landscape making such horrific crimes pallid by comparison. McCarthy's "Red Baiting" witch hunts, though long past, had introduced a sense of paranoia difficult to eradicate. As many Americans struggled to control their lives in the aftermath of World War II, the start of the Cold War, the Korean War, and the possibilities of nuclear holocaust, exacerbated by the rise of racial tensions and dynamic social change, only inflamed anxieties. Many teens were attracted to rock stars and the greaser life style, while the emergence of Beatnik philosophy, popularized by writers such as Jack Kerouac and Allen Ginsberg, was just beginning. There was a palpable, albeit infant, revisionism regarding the fate of Everyman, the underprivileged, the poor, the disenfranchised, and the physical and mentally handicapped, including even societal deviants such as the "Sex Beast Killer."

To the police, press, and public, Breese was, plain and simple, a homicidal sex maniac. To some, though, such as Dr. Timothy G. Farrsman, a noted psychoanalyst, who wrote in the *Washington Star* during the nationwide manhunt, the killer was "not a pervert" but a victim of a "much deeper social disease." The man was not operating in the normal pattern of sex criminal; he suggested he had never "encountered a case of a sexual pervert who killed a whole family for no overt reason . . . Mental illness undoubtedly enters the case . . . and some sexual factors may be involved." But, there were deeper issues that needed to be looked at. As the Greek philosopher Seneca had written, "The whole concord of this world consists in discords." If such killings were manifest in discord, the world and its myriad denizens would nevertheless continue on their troubled ways as always. So it was with the Chauvanne family of Lane Manor.

Philip Chauvanne, who had gone into the sewer and water construction business with three of his siblings as Chauvanne Brothers, Inc., paid little attention to the political scene, but after Ellen's death Lucille immersed herself in local politics. Within a short time she was serving as a Prince George's County election judge, and became a veritable Democratic Party fanatic whose local icon, ironically, was gruff-spoken populist Jessup Leggett, Chairman of the County Board of Commissioners. Perhaps fortunately, she was unaware that it had been the chairman, for whom she had become a staunch supporter, who ordered an end to the investigation into her daughter's murder.

In 1962, when the Prince George's Democratic Party "Old Guard," which had operated in the county on the "spoil system" almost without a break since the Civil War, came under attack by a band of upstart reformers, Lucille remained steadfastly loyal. The insurgents, led by one Phyllis M. Spealman, ran on a platform of "ending bossism." Spealman and her colleagues also promised to fire Leggett's one-time acolyte and now equal, Police Chief Gregory Panadapoulis, who was charged with not only ignoring but also being instrumental in promulgating kickbacks from developers to the chairman, and won several county seats. Yet, in the beginning, the insurgents were unable to accomplish either of their announced goals.

In autumn 1964, the Chauvanne family was at last financially able to pick up stakes and move up the status ladder from their semi-detached home in Lane Manor to a fully detached house in nearby Riverdale. After enduring months of considerable hen-pecking from Lucille, Philip also borrowed enough money to purchase a new car, a black Pontiac that looked more like a Hearse than a family vehicle. He held on to his old De Soto for Terry's use, and unwittingly bought membership in a new American social phenomenon, the two-car family. The household was by that time dwindling. Eddy, who had grown into a ruggedly handsome young man like his father, had already graduated two years earlier — albeit just barely — from Northwestern High's vocational education program, with a major in surveying. He had benefited from Philip's connections down at the union hall, joined an Engineers Local, and promptly hauled in a job as an assistant surveyor with a sewer and water construction company in Bladensburg. He was rarely seen around the Chauvanne household now, except when coming home to sleep, and within a year of graduation had secured his own apartment in the blue-collar community of Colmar Manor, near the Anacostia River and close to his job.

Terry, who had taken Driver's Ed in school, managed to get her license at fifteen. By her sixteenth birthday, despite Philip's understandable paternalistic fears, she had been granted use of the old De Soto. With wheels, she soon became a regular fixture at Hot Shoppes, a drive-in restaurant in Hyattsville, where teenagers convened on weekends. Almost overnight she had blossomed, not surprisingly, from an adorable child into a strikingly attractive young lady — a metamorphosis replete with its magisterial benefits and myriad drawbacks. Her stunningly good looks, shapely figure, dark complexion, and long raven hair could, as Lucille bragged, "draw any boy's attention from a mile away."

While Lucille was right, sometimes Terry's striking physical appeal could be troublesome. Once, while sitting in a booth with two girlfriends at Hot Shoppes, sipping cherry cokes and laughing, the trio was accosted by four greasers from Bladensburg High who came in and began making noisy advances. The girls attempted to snub them, but the ruffians refused to be ignored. Then, as the boys tried to force themselves upon the girls, Eddy appeared, almost like a comic book hero, grabbed one of the punks by the throat and told him to get lost or he would kill him right there. Within seconds, the four greasers had left, and Terry Chauvanne's big brother became a local legend overnight.

Unlike many of her friends, Terry had not succumbed to most of the usual teenage diversions and vices that had sidelined countless others. Having kept her part-time job at the bakery, she had money but was never a spendthrift. Like many kids, she had put up posters in her room, but not of the usual subjects, pictures of Elvis and the like, but of animals, especially dogs. Like her late sister, she had learned to ride horseback, and almost religiously kept her large private menagerie intact, adding a new critter every time an old one died. She had maintained a high academic standing, with a goal of becoming either a veterinarian or a lawyer — the former because of her love for animals, and the latter because someday she wanted to personally send the fiend who killed her sister to the electric chair. Although she dated occasionally, and had more than the usual number of suitors, she had steered clear of "going steady" with anyone. She kept her sights on college.

Terry was not averse to boys or immune to the attractions. On a hot summer weekend in 1965, on the advice of a schoolmate, she drove out to Annapolis with several girlfriends, including her best friend, a wild child named Tracy Bowers. Tracy said they wanted to cruise for good-looking middies from the Naval Academy. They parked for a while outside the playing field fence and watched the football team scrimmage. One player, in particular, caught Terry's eye. She later stated, with some amusement, that it had been his extremely muscular calves that first attracted her attention. The blond, blue-eyed fellow was also good-looking and obviously athletic. After a number of trips over the next several Saturdays, they finally met, albeit fleetingly. His name was Carl Anderson, and he was in his second year at the Academy. Concurrently, Tracy, too, honed in on one of Carl's classmates named Christian Felcher.

Carl Anderson had been an all-state high school quarterback from Taylor, Texas, before he had been spotted by the Naval Academy football scouts, and recruited primarily for his athletic ability which, some said, would one day carry him to the pros. Terry, Carl, Tracy, and Christian would meet briefly every weekend thereafter, the young men on the field in one sport or another, drilling, or on parade, and the girls usually watching from as close as possible. Carl was the first man that Theresa Anne Chauvanne ever actively pursued. The setting, with the majestic campus ensconced against the scenic Severn River, filled with midshipmen's boats with their colorful spinnakers, could not have been more perfect. When she finally brought him home to meet her mother and father it was, for the parents at least, love at first sight. However, it was college and a career that Terry had set her primary sights upon. Carl was secondary.

Unfortunately, family finances had again taken a slump when Chauvanne Brothers Inc. began to suffer from a recession downturn. The resultant bickering between the four siblings, Philip, Henry, Tommy, and Fred, over rank, money, and the management and dispersal thereof, soon reached a level of poisonous animosity, heartily nurtured by the four principal's wives. The firm was ultimately forced into bankruptcy and, with Philip's loss of employment again, seemingly went all hopes of Terry's college career.

Yet she doggedly refused to quit. She quickly secured a menial job as a "candy striper," or nurse's aide, at Holy Cross Hospital in nearby Silver Spring, and sometime afterwards moved to a full-time secretarial position at an engineering firm. Having graduated from Northwestern with honors, she enrolled in night school for the 1966 fall semester at Montgomery Junior College, a short drive from her new job, and far less expensive than the University of Maryland. From time to time, people would recognize her name and ask if she were related to the victim of "that horrible murder" more than a decade earlier, and on each inquiry she would simply answer yes, but never anything more.

Even as Terry Chauvanne commenced the first stage of what would become a long and truncated college career, the United States began to commit its national treasure and finest young men into what some were already calling an unwinnable war on the far side of the world. For the first time in her life, Terry Chauvanne began to become politically active. At the outset, echoing her parents' pro-war views regarding American participation in the ongoing Vietnam conflict, she favored intervention, but, in direct opposition to Lucille, within a year she had become a strident student anti-war activist. The consequences were explosive.

During one of the frequent bitter exchanges with her mother, she blurted out: "Haven't you already seen too much killing here? My God, wasn't Ellen's death bad enough?"

For perhaps the only time in her life, Lucille was speechless. The confrontation engendered an ever-widening split between herself and her adopted daughter that would never fully heal.

The Prince George's County political season was in full bloom when Terry began dating Carl Anderson on a regular basis, despite opposing political views that rivaled the split between herself and her mother. A Republican candidate for Congress named Ralph D. Horan had aggressively attacked the jugular of the gasping county Democratic machine by accusing Chairman Leggett of regularly accepting kickbacks from developers for rezoning favors, and Panadapoulis for routing them to him. The charges were, of course, loudly denied, but, as the handsome young Republican repeatedly stated, "Where there is smoke, there is fire."

The charges, some suggested, would be difficult to make stick. Panadapoulis was extremely popular among officers and men alike, as well as the majority of more conservative law-and-order residents of the county. Moreover, few could criticize his overall job performance, albeit often heavy-handed. Even his political enemies, such as Phyllis Spealman, called him "a policeman's policeman." Yet, it was the social divisions sweeping the nation between young and old, black and white, rich and poor following the assassination of Martin Luther King, the race riots, and the so-called "hippy revolution," that made Chief Panadapoulis's appeal to old line traditionalists readily apparent. He publicly denounced "power hungry college students . . . fuzzy faculty members . . . illegal demonstrators . . . and movies like The Graduate." He made headlines after the Washington riots by declaring that any looters found in Prince George's County would be immediately shot, and endeared himself to a substantial portion of old-line white county residents. Moreover, his close ally Leggett still had his thumb on the pulse of the county, countless political debts owned him, and ardent Old Guard supporters, such as Lucille Chauvanne, were still legion.

In 1968, as expected, both Leggett and Panadapoulis, key players in the search for Ellen Chauvanne's killer, were indicted on charges of manipulating rezoning cases after accepting bribes from a local builder. Both were exonerated after the chief agreed to testify before a grand jury, which made him immune from prosecution. By the narrowest of margins, Leggett, too, was acquitted in a jury trial, but it had been too close for comfort. Some party stalwarts began to abandon the chairman's camp while others celebrated as if it had been the Second Coming. Commissioner Leggett's fate, however, would be neither as favorable nor as long-lived as many party loyalists predicted.

Leggett's reign as Chairman of the Prince George's County Board of Commissioners, continually tainted by a host of scandals, finally came to an end in 1970. Two years later, he would be formally indicted and convicted of violating federal bribery laws, specifically on charges of accepting gifts, a tractor and several thousand dollars from a developer named George F. Malkcus in return for zoning favors. Jessup Leggett, late kingpin of county politics, for accepting bribes and transporting them across state lines, was sentenced to fifteen months in the federal penitentiary at Leavenworth, Kansas, and fined $5,000. On

December 17, 1983, the last of the Prince George's County Old Guard, whom some had once likened to a local Maryland version of the Louisiana demagogue Huey P. Long, would die of cancer in Smyrna Beach, Florida, his reign soon forgotten.

Unlike Leggett, Gregory Panadapoulis had seen the writing on the proverbial wall and, under substantial behind-the-scenes political pressure, was permitted to retire with honor. Some wags suggested he had been allowed to do so because he knew where too many political skeletons were hidden, which was probably true. Others declared it was all just part of the insurrectionist's clean sweep of county government, and further indictments would be instituted unless he departed the scene. The chief would not leave, however, without having the last word. At his retirement dinner, attended by over seven hundred persons, including representatives of all Washington area police departments and many of his former political enemies, he gave a scathing speech denouncing everyone from student activists and long-haired hippies to Hollywood. After leaving, he practiced criminal law in Greenbelt until 1980. Nine years later, on April 19, 1989, at age 78, Gregory Panadapoulis died of a heart attack at the Magnolia Gardens Nursing Home in Lanham, Maryland.

For Terry, the void between her mother and herself had become increasingly hostile. Living in the Chauvanne household had become a suffocating experience that by 1968 she could no longer bear. Escape to her own independence, for her own peace of mind, became essential, even if it meant interrupting her college career. Any means to achieve that end seemed acceptable. Soon after the Leggett acquittal, she applied to become a United Airlines stewardess and was immediately accepted for the training program. The same day she informed Carl of her decision, he proposed to her on the shady steps of historic St. Mary's Church, on Duke of Gloucester Street in Annapolis. Many years later she informed a close friend that she always believed he proposed because he feared "he would lose her working as a stewardess and meeting lots of guys." Nevertheless, she accepted, but with the stipulation that she might pursue the course she had decided upon, whatever it might be. Grudgingly, Carl agreed. And Terry became a stewardess for United Airlines.

From the beginning, the marriage between Carl Anderson and Theresa Anne Chauvanne, stewardess, was strained. Carl was a devout Roman Catholic, and Terry, who no longer followed any particular religious belief, had been obliged to convert to Catholicism before taking their vows. Unfortunately, between his military assignments, which took him far afield, usually to the Pacific, and hers, which carried her to the four corners of the earth, there were precious few times together. The marital stress, on those rare occasions, was conspicuous to all concerned.

Terry had begun taking birth control pills soon after marriage at Carl's suggestion, although in clear defiance of Church doctrine, on the grounds that neither were yet ready to raise a family. The clear violation of the Pope's directives regarding birth control mattered little to Terry who, by her own admission to everyone, was a member of the Church in name only, but by 1971 it was apparent that her relationship with Carl would not last unless changes were made.

"Just do it," her late sister had often told her, and during a flight layover, in a dinghy hotel room in Cincinnati, Ohio, Terry determined upon a major course correction in her life. Two days later she quit her job, stopped taking the pill, and resolved to become pregnant the next time she saw her husband. It was the opportune time, for Carl was coming home to San Diego, California, where they had rented an apartment, for an extended leave from his duty station in the Philippines. But nothing happened.

Desperate to increase her fertility, and on the advice of a close friend, Terry began taking massive doses of vitamin E and soon swore that she started "to feel things move." During one visit to an obstetrician, who was informed of her effort to enhance her fecundity, the doctor expressed his amazement, much to Terry's amusement, that she hadn't already given birth to an eight-pound Vitamin E pill. Nevertheless, Terry resolved on having Carl's child whatever it might take and relentlessly pursued her objective. Her campaign was without results, even as the marriage began to slowly dissolve in front of her.

In early spring 1973 Terry flew to Manila, Carl's duty station, for one last try, having resolved that if her husband disagreed that she would inform him that "she didn't want to be married anymore." The meeting was one of fire and ice, ultimatums and tears, but Terry finally conceived. Soon afterwards she returned to San Diego where she began taking classes in American government and law at the University of Southern California. Two months after her return, Carl was transferred to a duty station in Puerto Rico, but suggested she remain in California until the baby was born.

In early winter 1973, Sean Robert Anderson was born at San Diego General. Carl was in San Juan at the time and would not see his new son for more than four months, then only for several days. For nearly two years, husband and wife remained separated except for two or three weeks a year. Finally, in the fall of 1975 Carl was again transferred, this time to the Annapolis Naval Academy, to assume a teaching position in mechanical engineering. Coming full circle, Terry and her son flew east in an attempt to form, for the first time, a normal family life in her home state of Maryland.

After renting a two-story unit at the Annapolis Road House condominium complex in Annapolis, the Anderson family struggled to set down roots. Yet, as before, the relationship was shaky at best. Having never really grown together, the distance between the couple seemed to expand with every difference, including political views, child rearing, money matters, and most importantly, sexual liberation. Carl refuted Terry's demands for more independence as "feminist lib drivel." Moreover, the rapport between Terry and her strong-willed mother-in-law, who in many ways was a mirror image of Lucille, and her docile father-in-law, whom she had dubbed "The Woosie," was strewn with land mines at every meeting. The most egregious difference, though, revolved around Terry's desire to resume her academic career by taking classes at St. John's College, directly adjacent to the Naval Academy. Carl, who controlled the family purse strings, strongly opposed.

"The only damned thing the Johnnies can do," the conservative ex-football star would say derisively, "is play croquet," which was, in fact, the only approved school sport at liberal St. Johns.

Inevitably Terry would retort, "At least they can read something other than football playbooks, which is more than I can say for some of the jocks you work with."

The only saving grace in the relationship was Sean, adored by both father and mother, but usually left in the hands of the latter. Although Terry had been unable to nurse her son in his infancy owing to complications from a respiratory infection she had suffered, her favorite institution nevertheless was motherhood, especially during Carl's frequent absences. And she was good at it. Carl called her a drill instructor who was always overprotective of the boy, to which she replied: "When you see a small bird pecking and chasing a larger bird, the smaller bird is usually a mother protecting her young. I may be a small bird, but nobody's ever going to do Sean any harm, not like they did to my sister."

By spring 1976, Terry had resumed contact with some of her old high school chums, including Tracy Bowers, who had married Carl's classmate Christian Felcher. Unlike most officers' wives at the academy, Tracy was still something of a wild child, anything but a military wife, and soon became Terry's one true confidant, friend, and ally. At Tracy's suggestion, Terry aggressively began, as she called it, a campaign to "find some space." She found a part-time job, against Carl's wishes, waiting tables at a popular downtown Annapolis watering hole called Fran O'Brien's. She took care of Sean by day, and Carl would grudgingly tend to him in the evenings while she was at work.

By late fall Terry had scheduled a meeting with a marriage counselor, but Carl failed to appear. She scheduled a second meeting, but again her husband didn't show.

"You know, Mrs. Anderson," the counselor said bluntly, "unless he comes with you, counseling will be of no use to either of you." After that, things got worse. Terry began sleeping on the living room couch.

In the spring of 1977, Terry and Tracy decided to take up tennis, and signed up for instructions at an indoor court in Arnold, Maryland, north of Annapolis. Both were instantly taken by the handsome, tanned young instructor, a native Californian named Jerry Bostwick, but it was Terry that the instructor responded to. Their affair would last off and on for the next four years.

Carl Anderson's assignment to a duty station in Utica, New York, in 1978 came as a surprise to both himself and Terry. The move did not sit well with Terry, but with her husband's promise that she might resume her studies, perhaps at some local college, she acquiesced. Her lover was bereft.

They made the move during a snowstorm in December, a portend, Terry later mused, of things to come. Carl drove the family Buick and Terry her second-hand air-cooled Volkswagen Beetle with no heat. Within a month of their arrival in Utica, they had separated, Terry taking Sean with her. Soon, she found work, and was attending junior college, with her son usually in tow.

Although she had severed communications with her former lover, Bostwick soon learned of the separation, resigned from his job in Arnold, and headed north. Within a short time he had secured a position with the Syracuse University athletics program as a coaching assistant to the school's tennis team, moved into an apartment east of town, and began to visit Terry on weekends. Espousing his eternal love, he repeatedly begged to move in with her, and she just as repeatedly refused, preferring her independence to what was increasingly becoming a suffocating conjugal relationship.

Terry hated Utica with a passion, she later said, perhaps for what it stood for in her life, perhaps only for the winter cold, probably both. Whatever the reason, in February 1981, when Carl made what appeared to be a heartfelt overture to her for one last chance at reconciliation, and asked her to move back to Annapolis with him for his next assignment, she was only too ready to accept. "I guess, in retrospect," she would note two decades later, "I was fickle, but I knew if I didn't get the hell out of Utica, I was going to kill myself. And at the time, that wasn't an option. I had too much left to do."

Once home, and again living with her husband, the same old wounds were opened; once more Terry sought escape. Again she found employment at Fran O'Brien's, watching Sean during the day while Carl took over in the evenings. This time, the rift had finally become so large that a mutual agreement to separate ensued. Again, Jerry Bostwick, who had trailed Terry back to Maryland, called. The affair was resumed, but was to be short-lived.

Years later, Terry would inform a close confidant that her lover had wanted to marry as soon as she could secure a divorce from Carl. "I loved Jerry, but I still wanted to go to school," she said. "Get my law degree, and become a professional woman even more. If I had learned anything, it was that Jerry was like Carl. All he wanted was an obedient stay-at-home housewife — and I didn't want to be under his control any more than under Carl's."

When Terry finally secured a divorce on March 31, 1983, she asked for neither alimony nor child custody. She wanted nothing from the marriage but her freedom. It was mutually agreed that Sean was to be raised by his father. Five days later, on April 4, Terry, and her best friend Tracy Bowers Feltcher, who had also divorced her own husband, headed west bound for San Diego, California, and a new beginning. For the next seven years, Terry Chauvanne Anderson would live the life she had always dreamt of, only to be followed by a seemingly endless eternity of hell on earth.

Chapter 16

FRUITCAKE

The obituary desk at the *Washington Post's* 15th and L Street offices in Washington, D.C. was not usually the center of attention on any given day, unless some notable or celebrity met their maker. For those public faces, politicians, and socialites who were either elderly or in ill health and likely to pass, canned obits had already been written and held in readiness for instant updating whenever the death finally occurred. For the most part, it was the average citizen, the funeral homes, fraternal organizations, and sometimes businesses, but mostly individuals that placed the majority of obits. Backgrounds were often checked if the deceased were of local importance or the data provided by relatives, or whoever else might have submitted the notice, contained biographical material needing verification. Addenda to the obits, which in Sunday editions typically ran several pages, were the brief "In Memoriam" pieces, usually placed by family members on a particularly important anniversary date, to celebrate the memory of a loved one (no pets please). Most notices were either phoned in or mailed to the desk, and, if provided before noon, would run two days later, three days if it came in the afternoon. Walk-in submissions were usually few, but not unknown.

No one paid much attention to the man in the London Fog raincoat at the obits desk on the afternoon of February 8, 1990. The obits editor was still out to lunch, but a young intern cheerfully asked if she could help the man. The visitor, trim and fit, was not unattractive, his sandy-colored hair thinning and graying about the edges. His soft, blue eyes, set close together behind wire-rimmed glasses, were almost neutral, as was his fair complexioned skin. The intern thought to herself; except for his eyes he would be nothing to write home about, probably a government drone at State, Labor, or the like.

"I'd like to place a memoriam notice," he said in a barely audible whisper.

"Yes, sir," replied the intern. "What would you like to say and when do you want it to run? We can't get it in until the eleventh, 'cause it's already too late for the tenth. And that will be ninety-four cents a word for under one hundred words. No charge for punctuation marks."

"I'd like it to run on the eleventh," he said, "and I'd like you to say, 'Michael (Michelle) Linn O'Riley. . .'"

"We always place the family name last, sir," interjected the intern, "so we can publish them in alphabetical order. Easier for the public to find folks that way."

"Oh yeah, I see," replied raincoat man. "Well then, say 'O'Riley, Michael (Michelle) Linn' and under that put 'Chauvanne, Ellen Marie. On June 15, 1955 the tragic end of your lives caused many tears to follow. You have been forgotten by some, you will be remembered by all.'"

"Will that be all?" queried the intern.

"Yes."

"That will be $31.96. How do you wish to pay? Cash, check, or credit card."

Without answering, the man fumbled nervously for his wallet under his coat, and in pulling out a number of bills, spilled the billfold's contents upon the desk. Quickly he scooped everything up, replaced it in the wallet, and placed a $100 bill on the table, turned and walked out without waiting for change or speaking again. He neglected, however, to retrieve the business card that had fallen to the floor.

Catherine O'Riley Bettancour rarely came to Washington, D.C. At 48-years old and a long-time resident of the West Coast, she had developed a healthy business that occasionally took her on jaunts back to the East Coast. However, her family, two kids, and the good life had securely anchored her far from the home she had known as a three-year-old in Lane Manor near the Northwest Branch Park in Maryland. Her presence in the city on business on February 11 can only be described as pure coincidence. Even more coincidental was her buying a local newspaper, scanning the obituary pages, and seeing the memoriam posted under the names of her sister Mikie and Ellen Chauvanne.

She remembered little of her late sister, although she carried a picture of herself as an infant wrapped in Mikie's arms. Had some O'Riley family member or one of the myriad Chauvanne's placed the notice? She immediately rushed back to her hotel, the Washington Hilton, on Connecticut Avenue, and phoned her older sister, Elaine, then living in France with her aging mother. Neither Elaine nor her mother had placed the notice, and both advised she first contact the Chauvannes, then the *Washington Post*.

The first Chauvanne with whom Catherine spoke by phone was Ed, who neither read newspapers nor paid the least attention to world events, much less those in his own neighborhood, unless they affected him directly. This was an exception. Equally as stunned as Catherine, he immediately checked with his father and the rest of the family in the Washington metropolitan area, but with negative results.

Catherine's initial calls to the *Post* bore little fruit. The obits people could only tell her the notice had been placed by a walk-in who left no name or address and had paid in cash. Unable to find satisfaction with the obit editor, she contacted a *Post* reporter named Kenneth McClennahan, explained the situation and events leading up to it, the extreme feelings the notice had provoked, and requested that he look into the matter.

"The in-memoriam is a mystery," she told him. "We know no one who would have placed it . . .It is additionally confusing because of the name. My sister was blessed with an unusual one. Friends and family knew her as Mike or Mikie, or her birth name Michael. She was proud of her name. No one who knew her would ever call her Michelle."

"I'll do what I can," said the reporter, "but I can't promise anything."

June 15, 1990. Ed Chauvanne was pitching horseshoes in his backyard with a neighbor when his wife Maggie called him to the phone. "Some guy named Trueman wants to talk to you," she shouted from the back porch of their home in Ijamsville, Maryland, in the shadow of the Blue Ridge Mountains.

"I don't know any damned Trueman?" Ed yelled back. "Get his number and tell 'em I'm busy. I'll call him when I've got time."

A few seconds later, Maggie shouted out again, cupping the phone with her right hand. "Says it's important. About your sister."

"Godammit Maggie, I'm right in the middle of a game with Bobby. Unless Terry's dead or something, tell him I'll call him back."

"It's not about Terry. It's about Ellen."

Ed stopped in mid-pitch, dropped the horseshoe from his hand, and turned toward the porch. "Is it some reporter? If it is, I got nothing I want to say that hasn't already been said."

"No, says he ain't no reporter. Says he knows something about her murder."

Within a matter of a minute, Ed was at the phone.

"This is Ed Chauvanne," he said, wasting no time or words. "Who the hell is this?"

"Sorry to bother you, Mr. Chauvanne," said a soft-spoken voice on the other end. "My name is Trueman. William G. Trueman. I live in Cheverly, Maryland, and I have a few things I thought you should know about your sister Ellen's murder. This is the brother of Ellen Marie Chauvanne, isn't it?"

"Yeah. You with the police?"

"No, sir," said Trueman with a slight laugh. "No, I retired from the Central Intelligence Agency a few years ago. Career guy. You know, office type. But I am definitely not associated with the police."

"Well, you're not family, so what do you have to do with my sister's murder?"

There was a long silence before the quiet voice continued. "I became deeply interested in the case in the early 1970s when I saw an article about unsolved murders, one of which was about Ellen and Mikie. You see, I was attending the University of Maryland when your sister was killed. Indeed she was murdered not very far from the cheap little room in Hyattsville I was renting at the time as a student. In fact, I followed the crime in the newspapers from the beginning. And I have to say that both of those girls were eye candy. I couldn't imagine why anyone would have wanted to kill them. Eye candy. Yes indeed."

"I read the papers too, not as much as my sister Terry, but I kept up on what was going on," said Ed in a coarse tone. "My parents were kept informed of about everything the police knew, so I have to tell you, unless you actually know who did it, you're wasting your time and mine."

"Hold on there, Ed. . . May I call you Ed?"

"Yeah, but it better be good."

"You know, today is the thirty-fifth anniversary of that horrible event. I waited till now to tell you. You see I know who killed your sister and the O'Riley girl."

Ed could barely believe what he was hearing. Out of the ether, a disembodied voice over the phone saying he knew who, in a hail of gunfire, had cruelly erased two beautiful young lives from the earth. The word "Revelation," flashed through his mind.

"I was at the old Woody's Esso at the corner of Riggs and Ager, a few days after the murder. You remember that place? Well, I had just pulled in to fill up behind a dark blue sedan, a 1939 Packard, with a tall guy at the wheel. I still remember what he looked like. In fact, he very much resembled that kid the cops arrested right off, you know, Ellen's ex-boy friend."

"You mean Stokes?" said Ed.

"Yeah. Kind of tall and thin, sloped shoulders, hair slicked back, weak chin, sideburns. But kind of Eastern European looking. I can tell you it wasn't Sammy Stokes. There was a very strong resemblance to the police sketch of the Pancho Villa character Stokes and your uncle claimed to have seen. Anyway, a few seconds after I pulled in, he got out and opened his trunk to get something or other, and then went to the front of his car to watch the attendant check his oil. He hadn't closed the trunk completely, and it kind of sprung up a bit. When I got out to use the restroom, I walked around in front of my car and could see a rifle in his trunk. It was a Marlin .22 caliber semi-automatic, a Microgroove I think. I knew my guns 'cause I had just finished a hitch in the Army, you know, as a weapons specialist, before I started school on the GI Bill. The stock had a blue cloth, looked like an old torn-up shirt or jacket, wrapped around it. And there were brown stains on it. I am sure they were dried blood. I'd seen plenty of it in Korea."

"What the hell did you do?" said Ed. "Call the cops?"

"Well," said Trueman, "the guy caught me looking, and walks around and slams the trunk door down and glares at me. So I just walked into the gas station office, snatched a piece of paper and wrote his license number down as he drove off. Still remember it. Maryland tag number 35687. When I came out, he'd already left. I called the PG police at least a dozen times before I got someone to listen to me, but they just took my story down and that was that."

"What did you do then?"

"I dropped it. Not until the early 1970s, when I saw the article on unsolved cases, did I resume any interest." Trueman paused for effect, well aware now that he had Ed's attention. "By that time I was employed at the CIA doing background checks and had the means to run down a few leads, such as the tags, car make, and the owner's name, and so forth, but then that would have been stepping out of bounds and I might have been out on the street with a big boot up my ass. Hell, even now I'm not supposed to tell you or anyone who I worked for or what I did. Not allowed. But fuck 'em. Anyways, I went back to the police at least six times and contacted them by phone another six. Right down there at the station house in Hyattsville, I tried to tell them everything. They wouldn't even listen to me, and the one time they did they paid little attention to what I was actually saying. They thought I was a nutcase, a kook, a pest. One of the detectives, a guy named Bevens, said he had checked the guy out who owned the car, and he was clean. Dumb county mounties!"

"Who the hell was it?" Ed shouted.

"They asked me if I thought I was psychic," Trueman went on, his voice rising in anger. "Imagine all the gall. Here I am trying to help those pitiful Hoover wannabees and they consider me a fruitcake. Who in God's name, I ask you, do they think they are anyway?"

"Goddammit, who the hell was it owned the car!" screamed Ed.

"Hell, I could have conducted my own investigation then, but the Company would have frowned on it. Years went by and I even tried to interest the *Washington Times*, but had no takers. Finally, after I retired in '88, I started my own case file and did my own tracking."

Ed, who was always short on courtesy and long on profanity, finally lost it. "Listen, you sonofabitch. Either shit or get off the pot. You gonna tell me who owned the car or not?"

"Well, Ed, if you're going to get nasty about it, all I..."

Ed slammed the phone down and trudged out the door with a stream of expletives trailing behind. Before he reached the horseshoe pits, however, he had turned about face and marched back inside. "I'm gonna teach that fucker a thing or two," he said to Maggie as he picked up the phone and began to dial. "I got a friend I have to call."

Charles Bricker was not an affable-looking man. Though average in height and build, his overall countenance seemed perpetually gloomy, indeed menacing. His naturally dark complexion accentuated a dour pockmarked face and gargoyle grimace. At 47 his coarse hair was still wavy and black but seldom combed. A brushy, untended moustache running more to salt than pepper, and a croaky voice with irritable, occasionally stentorian utterances erupting at inappropriate moments, helped perpetuate the image of a large surly persona who should never be taken lightly. It was just the image that had taken him years to intentionally cultivate.

As an eighteen-year veteran detective with the Prince George's County Police, Bricker was about as tough as they come — or liked to think he was. For as long as he could remember, he had wanted to be a cop, and after finally making the grade, had flourished. There had been a few bumps in the road, mostly charges of using unnecessary force when dealing with black druggies, pushers, and hookers while with the Narcotics Squad out of Seat Pleasant. The wave after wave of bad guys with guns migrating from D.C. into the increasingly affluent county caused an almost vertical growth in crime statistics, and most cops on the force were usually less than gentle when conducting a bust. Charges of racism and police brutality emanating from the growing black population became common, but Bricker had always emerged unscathed. He considered the PG police force much like the U.S. Marines, with whom he had served in Nam, and wholly believed that a cop's first duty was to protect the back of his fellow officer, whether in the field or during an inquiry. And now, ever since he had been assigned to the Homicide Squad, that sense of mutual loyalty and support among fellow officers had become imperative.

When the phone rang in his Hyattsville office, Bricker let it ring three times. He was superstitious about picking up a phone before three jingles, believing that only bad things come in threes. On the fourth ring he lifted the receiver.

"Homicide. Detective Bricker."

"Charlie baby. This is your old buddy Eddy Chauvanne. I got to talk with you if you got a moment."

"Hey, Ed, long time no talky. How you been?"

It was something like fate that Detective Charles Bricker of the Homicide Squad of the Prince George's County Police Department and Ed Chauvanne had known each other and even maintained a friendly, albeit distant, relationship for nearly thirty-six years. As a child, Bricker had lived in Lane Manor a block and a half down the street from Ed and Ellen and they had been acquaintances as kids before the murder. He had also known the O'Riley girls, and a few years after the murders had attended St. Mark's Elementary School in Hyattsville with Cathy. Later Ed and he had been teammates on the Northwestern High basketball team. Though after school their ways had parted, Ed and Charlie had maintained a loose connection through mutual friends and even downed a beer or two from time to time, but always with the murder as the one commonality shared by both. One had been the victim's brother, and the other had been drawn to law enforcement, an attraction that began with that first contact with officers at the crime scene police line — literally providing a shred of evidence in the form of a patch of blue gabardine he found while watching the investigation. One man's tragedy had provided motivation for another man's career course.

"Been okay, myself. Took an early out at the Washington Suburban Sanitary Commission a few months ago, and I'm just playing now," said Ed. "But I heard, oh Mighty One, you got promoted to detective in Homicide. Congrats."

"Yeah," chuckled Bricker. "Thanks a lot. But you can cut the 'Mighty' crap. What'd you really call for?"

"Well, I just got off the phone with a guy who says he knows for certain who killed Ellen and Mikie. I first thought he was a nut job and hung up on him, but then I got to thinking. Something in his story had the ring of truth. Said he has already talked with you guys. Name's Trueman. William Trueman. Lives out in Cheverly."

"Eddy," Bricker responded, "that jerk's been down here half a dozen times before I came on Homicide, and they always kissed him off as a kook. I've seen the files."

"Did anybody really listen to him? Did you ever speak with him?"

"I don't know. My predecessor, Timmy Bevens said the guy called incessantly, and when he finally came in, uninvited, I believe about the beginning of this year, he got all riled up and was obviously paranoid. He demanded to know why more wasn't being done on the case. The fact that it was more than three decades old meant nothing to him. Timmy said he starts off quiet and controlled, but runs off the ramp in a few minutes. He pegged him as just another one of those conspiracy nuts, but to answer your question, I personally never met him."

"But did anyone actually listen to what he had to say about the car?"

"What car?"

"The one," said Ed in exasperation, "he saw over on Riggs and Ager right after the murders, with a driver that looked like the guy in the Pancho Villa sketch and a .22 Marlin in the trunk."

"Bevens never said or reported anything on that. Just that the guy is a Fruitloop."

"Well, then, how about taking a quick look yourself, for me... and for Ellen. For old times sake. There might be something there after all. Besides there's a free six pack in it for you. Come on out and pitch a few horseshoes and we can talk some more about it."

"I never like to play on the other guy's turf, home court advantage you know, but when you put it like that..." laughed Bricker. "I first have to check my boss, and I have a number of other cases I'm working on. You know, when Ellen and Mikie were killed, there were only two or three murders a year in the county. This year we are about to hit 250. But I don't think there'd be any harm in getting Mr. Trueman down here in a couple weeks from now for a few questions. Maybe you would like to come in and take a look at this guy as well. Would you want to do that?"

"Is the Pope Catholic?" answered Ed.

"Good. Then it's a deal. You know, I might even try to get one of the O'Rileys in here for this one."

It was late July before Charlie Bricker finally approached his boss about Trueman and the Chauvanne-O'Riley cold case. "Hey, maybe we ought to really, you know, talk to this guy," he had said to Chief Thomas Blanchard. The Chief looked at him from beneath a heavy sheaf of eyebrows.

"You are well aware that the chances of this guy Trueman panning out as anything but a pain in the rectum is about 99.9 percent?"

"Yes sir," Bricker said crisply.

"You almost never close an unsolved murder case after a year, and this one's thirty-five years old. That's like trying to figure out who snuffed Hoffa! Many of the key witnesses and original investigators are quite probably already dead. The chances of finding new evidence are slim to none, and even a confession would require corroborative evidence that is probably impossible to find."

Chief Blanchard looked down at his wristwatch. He was already late for a meeting with a reporter from the *Washington Post*. "You know, of course, that most of the case files that old have either already been thrown out or have been microfiched, which means they're as good as lost, since nobody can figure out the cataloging system except... what's his name? Murphy, that damned library science egghead at Archives. And that which is left is probably rotted. Charlie, you still want to look into this one?"

"Yes sir."

"Then, detective, she's all yours."

"Sir, just one more thing. I'd like to bring that contract psychologist, you know, Harry Silverberg, in on this one, if it's okay with you. I think a profiler like him would be of use."

"Knock yourself out," Blanchard stood to leave, "but don't waste too much time on this one. You know," he laughed, "people are dying now that never died before! And Homicide already has its hands full."

Chapter 17

HEAD SHOT

The Landover police headquarters, though built in the 1970s, had a 1950s look about it, from the external brickwork and low-bid siding to the grey and brown metal tables, chairs, and drab interior. Only the spiffy brown-and-black police uniforms looked relatively new, having been recently redesigned along with the motif of departmental signage, the paint jobs on the cruiser fleet, and the myriad information pieces it circulated through governmental agencies. This had been a deliberate makeover attempt to improve the department's public image, which had grown exceptionally tarnished thanks to recent bribery scandals and charges of racism and police brutality.

Ed Chauvanne had never been inside this particular station, although he was not a stranger to the genre, having in his time experienced a few modest brushes with the law, usually related to drinking or brawling. But he had always emerged unscathed and, with the exception of several misdemeanors, escaped conviction, a fact in which he took some pride. He called them his "bragging rights."

Almost a month had passed since his last conversation with Bricker and owing to a serious family problem he had almost forgotten the whole Trueman thing. Only two days after his call to Charlie, his mother, Lucille, suffered a debilitating stroke and would be in a seesaw fight for life for more than two weeks thereafter. Since then she had stabilized somewhat, but the downward spiral was evident to all. When Ed offered to inform Terry in California, Philip had forcefully objected, thinking that his daughter was, after seven years, still coming off her divorce and was probably in spite of everything quite fragile. Philip had always been protective of Terry, and now more than ever. Ed decided to call her anyway after talking with the police.

Detective Bricker's call late on a Wednesday evening, asking Ed to come down the next day, had come at the worst possible time, but having started the whole thing, Ed felt obliged to follow through. Bricker informed him that he had just talked to Trueman, who had readily consented to a conference, but could only do it on Thursday evening. Dutifully, Bricker had also notified the O'Riley family, and both Elaine and Cathy were flying in all the way from Olympia, Washington, to be there as well, albeit they would watch the interview from behind a one-way mirror. Ed would be asked to do likewise.

The O'Riley women were already there when Ed arrived, a bit after 7 p.m., half an hour before Trueman, to avoid being seen by him entering the station. Bricker and a second man, well-dressed, in a tailored brown business suit, and another officer, were there to greet him. The second man was tall, dark-complexioned, and Clark Gable handsome with a thick matte of black hair. After a brief hello, Bricker introduced him.

"Eddy, Cathy, Elaine, I'd like you to meet Harry Silverberg. He's our police psychologist, a trauma specialist. I brought him onboard in hopes that we can see what makes this guy Trueman tick." Then, he introduced the second officer, a boyish looking, freckled face redhead. "This is Sergeant Marvin McQueen, one of the best officers on the force. If there is any real footwork to do on this case, he's our best man."

Reaching out to shake Ed's hand, Silverberg said, "Actually, I'm in private practice and work under contract from time to time with the FBI, DEA, and the PG Police Department, among others, doing what we call profiles. And we think there may be more to this man Trueman than is on the surface."

"Harry and Sergeant McQueen are going to sit in on the interview," Bricker added as he escorted Ed, Cathy, and Elaine into a soundproof chamber next to the conference room. "We think it best, however, that you watch the proceedings from behind the one-way mirror, like we have already discussed. We don't want this guy to get off track just yet. Later we want to bring you all in — especially you Ed, since he has already talked to you — for a personal meeting to test his reaction."

"What do we need a shrink for?" asked Ed.

"I'm a psychologist, not a psychiatrist, Mr. Chauvanne," Silverberg corrected with a forced smile. "Let me explain. Many people who suffer traumas early on in their lives, criminals and victims alike, usually experience ripple effects from them throughout the remainder of their lives. After reading the files, I believe this case is a veritable human earthquake, with aftershocks, even after the passage of thirty-five years, reverberating on and on. It is my opinion that the killer suffers from intense guilt — especially if he or she was once or is a very religious person. The killer feels a mighty need to confess, to come to terms with himself. Just imagine what it must feel like to commit a horrific crime like that and get away with it. In his own mind, the killer may well have walled off his action, but continues to experience emotional seepage that, given the right circumstances, eventually drives him toward a confession. In every case the killer needs to find forgiveness, from God, a confessor, or even from one of the victim's relatives."

"You will have to excuse the tight confines in here," interjected Bricker apologetically, "but it is air-conditioned, and there is a pitcher of ice water and some cookies I brought in to keep you occupied till he gets here."

"Nice touch with the cookies," laughed Ed, attempting to make light of a most serious situation, "but a few cold Budweisers would have been nicer. Now, what's the plan, Mr. Detective?"

"Okay. Before our boy arrives," Bricker responded, "I want to let you know that we have some new information. Not on the murders directly, but on Trueman himself."

"No shit!" Ed said in amazement. "Excuse me ladies, I didn't mean to be so crude. But what have you got?"

You remember the mysterious 'In Memoriam' that was placed in the *Washington Post* this past February?"

"Of course," Bricker's three guests uttered in unison.

"Well, last month, after Cathy got the crime reporter from the *Post* to try and run it down, they found the guy's business card, which had slipped from his wallet. It was lying on the floor right after he posted the notice. Fortunately some intern there picked it up and for some reason or other held on to it, not knowing how important it was. To make a long story short, a reporter named McClennahan ran it down and it was Trueman. Of course, he didn't call him or anything. In fact, he called my boss, Chief Blanchard, the day before Ed called me, which, given the circumstances, is why we have decided to formally reopen the case. And Mr. Trueman may just be a prime suspect."

"Thanks be to heaven!" exclaimed Elaine. "I can't tell you how happy that makes me."

Cathy and Ed agreed instantly.

The door opened and an officer stuck his head in the room. "Detective Bricker," he said, "there's a guy named Trueman here to see you."

Bricker looked at Ed, rolled his eyes heavenward, and said with a smile, "Let the games begin."

It was precisely 8 p.m. when Bricker, Silverberg, and McQueen ushered Trueman into the conference room. Dressed casually in a blue blazer, gray slacks and loafers, he had the appearance of a slightly portly, middle-aged Sunday school teacher, and a voice that reminded the detective of Walter Cronkite. Bricker and Trueman sat at opposite sides of the table, which was bare except for a plastic water pitcher and several paper cups. Silverberg sat in a corner with a note pad on his lap, with McQueen standing nearby.

"Thanks for coming down, Mr. Trueman," said the detective. "This is my number one, Sergeant Marvin McQueen, and this is Dr. Harry Silverberg, one of our experts on homicides. We thought it might be good for him to sit in on our meeting. I also want to apologize for whatever treatment you have received from the department in the past. I assure you I am quite interested in what you have to say about the Chauvanne-O'Riley murders. So why don't we start from the beginning. You talk. I'll listen."

"I appreciate your interest, detective," Trueman said, ignoring Silverberg and McQueen entirely. "As you probably know I've been in to see the police several times before this, and called countless times, beginning way back in 1970. In fact, I think I even spoke with you once or twice several years ago."

"I don't recall any calls except over the last few days, but perhaps I'm mistaken," said Bricker, doing his best to avoid an early confrontation.

"You already know, from when I spoke to you yesterday, about my encounter with the fellow in the gas station, I think back in '55 it was called Woody's Esso — you know, the guy with the .22 in his trunk — so I will not reiterate it again. And as you also know, it is my belief that he was the killer. From my research on the car after I retired from the CIA — I keep my own files on it — I am certain of his identity. I've talked to a lot of people over the years regarding the murders, many of whom were never interviewed by the police. I even tried to speak with Bernard Breese, the serial killer who was sent up for that double homicide in '59. You know, the guy who was briefly a suspect in Ellen and Mikie's murders. I tried to telephone him at the federal prison system medical facility in Springfield, Missouri, where he's doing life, but the guy's got cancer and was too sedated to talk. You know, Charlie — may I call you Charlie?"

"Let's keep it formal, shall we, Mr. Trueman. I prefer Detective Bricker."

Trueman squirmed in his seat uncomfortably.

"Okay, Detective Bricker it is. I have gone to great personal pains and expense on this case since 1970. I have even seen a psychologist and had myself hypnotized in an effort to recall every detail I could about the guy in the sedan at the filling station and the sketch in the papers on the Pancho Villa character. You know that sketch isn't around anymore."

"Did you try the microfilm copies of the newspapers at the Library of Congress? They have both the *Post* and the *Star* back to the nineteenth century."

Trueman blushed.

"So you are certain you know who killed the girls?" said Bricker, attempting to get back on track.

"Yes. I checked the tag number and car make, a 1938 Packard sedan, and found out it was owned by one Alexander V. Dubinski, a construction laborer, who lived just down the street from both the Chauvannes and the O'Rileys. He was a Polish immigrant, a devout Catholic, who came over before World War II with his wife Helena and extended family, including several sons, all of whom were spitting images of the old man. During the war he volunteered as an infantryman in a Free Polish unit, and suffered extreme shell shock, as it was then called, during the liberation of France. For months afterwards he was in a veteran's hospital undergoing psychiatric care. The Dubinskis knew the Chauvannes, but Philip Chauvanne was not too hot on anyone who spoke with a foreign accent, Catholics, or had really dark tans, if you know what I mean. He certainly wasn't crazy about Ellen palling around with a devoted Irish Catholic girl either, but she always had her way."

"So why would a Polish immigrant want to wait for the two girls, and put eleven bullets in one of them and three in the other?"

"For someone to do such a thing, he must have known Ellen and was waiting for her. Why? Maybe she disrespected him," Trueman answered. "Maybe laughed at him or his family, their accents, or Old World ways. You know some of those Eastern European types have a thing about honor. The whole family was big on guns, even the boys. The youngest, Johnnie, had even been on the school rifle team for a while until they found he was fourteen, a year under the minimum age for membership, and was booted out."

"Do you think it was a sex crime?" questioned the detective.

"No, because from my research—and I have done an enormous amount of it—sex offenders who are killers never use rifles. They always kill their victims with their hands, a knife, a pistol, but never a rifle. Besides, how many rapes occur at 8:15 a.m. in the morning?"

"Who said anything about rape? And why do you say it was 8:15 a.m.?"

"It was in all of the papers," answered Trueman sharply.

"I don't think so. We never released the precise time. Tell me again, Mr. Trueman, why you have done all this research."

"Well, I became fascinated with the case while I was in college, at the University of Maryland, the same time as the killings, and have been ever since. Kind of a hobby, you might say. I couldn't really focus on it, though, till I retired, you see. I've got a wife and eight children, most of 'em grown now, and now I've got the time. Once thought I might write a book or something."

Bricker leaned back, took out a pack of Marlboro Lights and offered one to Trueman, who refused. As he lit up, he asked him to demonstrate, from his research, how he thought the killer actually carried out the crime.

"I want you to tell me exactly how you think it was done."

"Sure. That's easy. First he finds a suitable rifle rest. He finds himself a young cherry tree down by the bridge, right where the girls will round the path into the clearing. You know, that tree's still there now. He's using a Marlin Microgroove repeater, with Revelation bullets. Long and lean. The slug produces a very small entry and exit wound. He waits until the girls, who are walking side by side, come to within about 180 to 200 feet from him."

Behind the one-way mirror, Ed squirmed in his chair.

"He calls out loudly, 'Ellen.' Both Ellen and Mikie turn slightly to their right to see who is calling them. He spits off two shots and hits Ellen in the right thigh, which spins her to her right, and then he peels off another shot that hits her square in the stomach. She, of course, is stopped dead—forgive the pun—in her tracks. Somehow she doesn't fall. She looks down in disbelief at her belly and is absolutely stunned as the blood spews out. He fires again and hits her in the chest, just to the left of center. She belatedly brings her left arm up in a defensive move which blocks his next shot, and she takes the hit in her forearm. In an instant, he pops another off at Mikie, who is standing frozen with horror off to Ellen's left, misses once and then again, both of which strike the ground near the girls. But a third shot hits her above the left ankle just as she turns to run. She falls to her left and instantly grabs at her wound. While the gunner's attention is briefly on Mikie, Ellen struggles to escape, half standing, half dragging herself along on the grass. It's futile, of course, and she is bleeding like a stuck pig. As she somehow manages to stand and turns to the right on her wounded thigh, the gunner shoots again and hits her under the jaw, which throws her head back. Two more shots rip into her uplifted left torso. As she fall to the ground, his last shot hits her left calf."

Bricker looked at Silverberg, and then back to Trueman. "What happened then?"

"Well, obviously he wasn't quite finished. Mikie was by now sitting upright, holding her wounded ankle with both hands and crying."

"How do you know she was crying?" Silverberg asked.

For a moment Trueman was quiet, considering his answer. "If you were a child who had just been shot, wouldn't you be bawling? Anyway, he can't let Mikie go. He leaves the tree and walks to within maybe twenty-five feet of the two girls. He finishes the job on Mikie, who is sitting there crying, in utter terror. She is just sitting there with her left side to him, and he pulls the trigger and puts a bullet through her little left tit and into her heart, and as she falls forward, turning away from him, he pops off another that hits her in the back left side. The shot just misses the spine, but she is already dead. He relishes the feeling. He is in complete control and it feels good. It's almost sexual in its intensity. He probably even had a hard on."

"Why do you say that?" pressed Silverberg.

"Men in battle sometimes become sexually aroused by all the fighting and killing. When they hang a man, he usually gets a hard on at the moment he's dropped, and if he's eaten a few hours before, usually defecates and pisses at the same time. Sometimes, even men being bound and tortured can be aroused by the pain. If you've ever been in combat or seen men die, you'd know what I mean."

"So you do think this could have been a sexual thing after all?"

"I didn't say that. I just said that he might have been aroused by what he was doing. Anyway, he isn't quite finished."

"Do you think you can demonstrate for us how you think he finished it?"

Without answering, Trueman stood up, walked around the table, and looked at the floor.

"Okay. He is actually feeling quite satisfied with himself, and he first sits down on a log to survey his handiwork. After a minute or two he realizes he had better hide the bodies before anyone else comes along, and takes out another clip, just in case someone does. He then leans his gun against the cherry tree, walks over to Mikie's body, grabs her legs and drags her about thirty or forty feet to a briar thicket. Her bloody dress is yanked up around her waist as he pulls her along and he sees she has pissed herself and he likes that. After he dumps the body and hastily throws a few handfuls of leaves on her to camouflage the corpse, he then goes to drag Ellen's body to the same thicket, and dumps it not far from Mikie's, but behind a log in the briar patch. He quickly throws a few handfuls of leaves on her as well."

"What about the head shot?" Bricker asked.

"I was getting to that," said Trueman irately. "As soon as the shooter had dumped both bodies, he goes to retrieve his gun, but hears a moan from behind the log. He picks up the .22 and returns to the log only to find that Ellen is still barely alive and trying to pull herself along the ground. The gunner comes up from behind her on her left. She is already bleeding out. She hears his approach, but is too weak to turn her head or body. Her head and upper torso are barely raised above ground level as she desperately tries to pull herself along with her fingertips. He approaches slowly to within five feet of her, from her left rear. She can hear him and whimpers."

Trueman stood as if holding a rifle to his right shoulder, and placed his right foot forward as if holding something to the floor. "He puts his shoe on her cute little ass to hold her in place and prevent her from crawling further. She is too weak to resist. He points the barrel toward the back left side of her pretty little head. She calls out, 'Please.' He stops for a second, then she says quietly, 'Just do it,' and he pulls the trigger. He stands over the body a few seconds then kicks her over with his foot. Her eyes are open, staring straight at him, with a blue hole right between them. He grabs another handful of wet leaves and sprinkles them over her. Then he sits on a log and just stares, kind of in a daze. When a car drives up on Stanford he doesn't move for a minute or so until he hears someone walking down the path and he takes off."

As he described the coup de grace, Trueman acted out the event with an intensity that was almost stunning, displaying the angle of the gun and its trajectory, the recoil, and a slight smile upon its completion. Bricker notices a bulge in the man's pants.

"My God," gasped Ed from behind the mirror, even as Elaine began to sob quietly.

"And you learned all of this from where?" Silverberg asked darkly.

"From the newspaper reports. Thanks to Panadapoulis, you guys weren't exactly very secretive about your findings. The few blank spots just took a little deductive reasoning to fill them in."

"Mr. Trueman, I have to say that was a most remarkable and interesting performance," Bricker said. "Would you be willing to come in and give us a comprehensive overview of your research, and let us have a look at the case files you have assembled? I think they might prove of considerable benefit to solving this murder."

Trueman smiled broadly. "Of course, I would be delighted. How about next week at this same time?"

"That would be splendid," Bricker declared with a smile, "but there is just one more thing. You say you were able to piece this all together from news releases and from your own footwork. I have to tell you, Mr. Trueman, that some of what you said was never publicly released. You obviously have studied this crime in great depth, and I think we have a lot to learn from you. I would like to ask you to consent to taking a polygraph test. Of course, it would be voluntary and you have the right to refuse, but it would be helpful to us."

Trueman's smile evaporated and was replaced with a look of dismay. "Am I a suspect? My God! Do you think I had anything to do with the murder itself?"

"Well, sir," replied Bricker. "We just want to nail down a few things about where you got your data. Anyway, you have nothing to worry about if what you say is true about where you obtained your information."

"I suppose if I refuse then, I would automatically become a suspect."

Bricker smiled. "Something like that. Shall we, as you suggested, make it this time next week? Right here. And bring your files along so we won't need a court order for them."

"I should have known," Trueman said angrily as he stood up and walked toward the door. "Dealing with you was going to be a dead end. Trying to help cops do their job right for a change was a mistake from the beginning. But I'll be here."

Bricker and Silverberg stood as well, but did not escort their guest out. "And, by the way," said Bricker, "don't hold back or destroy any of your files. That could be construed as a felony in itself."

As soon as Trueman was gone, Ed, Elaine, and Cathy spilled out into the conference room.

"That bastard is obviously the killer," Ed shouted. "You saw how he almost relished the demonstration, like he was reliving the shooting. He even had a hard on. The perverted bastard was getting off just demonstrating how he did it. Why the hell didn't you arrest him on the spot?"

"Calm down, Ed. I think we might have just unearthed a real worm. There are definitely some things he dropped in his story that are intriguing, but we need more solid evidence."

"How so?" Cathy asked.

"The most interesting thing about his story was how he said the killer held Ellen in place to administer the head shot," Bricker explained. "The killer did, in fact, hold her in place with his right foot. We know this because we found a tennis shoe print on the rear end side of her panties. No one but the department knew that the body had been turned over after the head shot had been made. All the public knew was that the body was found lying on its back, which is the way you first viewed it. That information, despite what he said, was never released to the press. He said the shot was made from the rear left side of her head from about five feet away, after she had been dragged to the thicket. That was also confirmed by ballistics and from the powder burns in her hair and scalp but was also never made public. Though seven of the shots that hit her were killing shots, she was still clinging to life to the last when the head shot went through the left back of her skull, passed through her brain, exited from under her forehead between the eyes, and dug into the dirt under her face, from which we retrieved it."

Silverberg stroked his chin. "The man displayed definite characteristics of having enjoyed the demonstration in detail, almost as if he were reliving the event. He certainly suffers from an extreme obsession with the crime—if not its solution."

"Well then, why the hell don't you arrest him?" demanded Ed.

"Because we haven't got any evidence that is likely to hold up—certainly not his own testimony. This isn't 1955. We can't just arrest a man the way they did then, on his looks or our own suspicion. And we never did discover the murder weapon itself."

"Okay, then," said Cathy, "where do we go from here?"

"When he comes in next week," said Bricker, "we are going to hit him with both barrels. Between now and then we'll be doing an intensive background check on him. You know, medical history, any psychiatric or psychological problems, service record, work history, and so forth. Harry is going to work up a suspect profile based on what we already know about the case. And the polygraph technology has improved a lot since the 1950s. Later, I want Ed here to play good guy. Meet Trueman on neutral turf and listen sympathetically to his story, if that's at all possible. Gain his trust. Maybe he will spill more out to you than us."

"If he did it, isn't he likely to just take off?" Cathy asked.

Silverberg answered. "White-collar career guys like Trueman, middle-aged, retired, with a mortgage, two cars, a wife and a flock of offspring and grandkids, rarely take flight even if they are guilty. Most of 'em think they are too establishment to be caught and have too much to lose by running off. Too much invested in the system to give up. That's usually their first big mistake."

"Detective Bricker, do you think he actually did it?" asked Elaine.

"It certainly seems to be pointing his way."

When the phone rang, the last person Terry Chauvanne Anderson expected to hear from was her brother. She and Ed had never been close, and the years and miles had served to further distance them. About the only time he called in the past had been when he needed something. This time was different.

"Hey, Terry, it's Ed."

"Hello, big brother," she answered. "How you doing? Is everything all right back there in good old Maryland?"

"I'm fine, but there's been some serious shit going down here you should know about. First off, I have to ask you not to let Pop know I called you."

"Why? Is something wrong with him or Mom?"

After a short silence, Ed answered. "Pop's all right, I guess, but Mom's had a serious stroke. She's in bad shape."

"Oh, my God!" Terry shrieked. "Is she alive? Is she okay? What happened?"

"Calm down," Ed commanded. "She's hanging on, but still in the IC unit at Shady Grove Hospital, near Gaithersburg. Pop found her in the bathroom, half-naked, lying on the floor. She'd gone in an hour earlier to take a bath, and when she didn't come out or respond to his banging on the door, he had to break it down. You know how she is about her privacy. Locks up everything. They've been married, for what, nearly fifty years, and she still doesn't trust Dad! She busted open her head on the toilet seat when she fell and there was blood all over the floor. Her whole left side is paralyzed, and she's having difficulty breathing because of her emphysema. She can hardly speak coherently because one side of her mouth doesn't want to work anymore. Dad's been staying at the hospital with her since she was admitted. He's a total mess, and in kind of a daze himself. I'm having a hard time handling him. He can't drive and trembles now all the time. I'm beginning to think he's had a minor stroke himself and just hasn't told anyone. He told me not to call you because he was afraid you wouldn't be able to handle it after your train wreck with Carl."

"That's ridiculous, that was seven years ago," she said indignantly. "I'm coming home as soon as possible. I know you can't handle them by yourself."

"Sis, that's up to you. But that ain't all."

"What do you mean?"

Ed related in full the events regarding the "In Memoriam" notice in the *Washington Post*, the Trueman story, and almost word-for-word the meeting with Bricker, Silverberg, and the new murder suspect. "The cops decided to reopen the case. He's their prime suspect, but doesn't know it yet. Can you believe that?"

"Well, that clinches it," said Terry. "My lease is up here in a few weeks and I'm coming home as soon as I can tie up loose ends. I've got to be there for Mom and Pop, and I think I'm going to have to meet this Trueman guy in the flesh. If he's the bastard that killed Ellen, I want a piece of him myself."

Chapter 18

POLYGRAPH

The initial Prince George's County Police investigation of William G. Trueman during the week following the meeting at the Landover station had been revealing but incomplete. In some areas, verification was impossible. He was only six when his father, a milkman, died of a heart attack. He grew up in the two-story house in Cheverly, Maryland, where he continued to live most of his life. His military career, begun after high school, was a matter of official record, and disclosed he had been trained in the Army as a weapons technician/instructor, with a special address to side arms and rapid-fire shoulder weapons. He'd seen action in the Korean War where he excelled as a sniper and was credited with at least eleven verified kills along the Yalu River, and had received the Purple Heart for a head wound during the horrible winter retreat from the Chosen Reservoir, and the Bronze Star for valor in action. After a long period of recuperation in a military hospital, he was sent to Fort Bragg as a weapons instructor. There he was twice turned down for promotion owing to what the military record termed "a proclivity to periodic irrational behavior leading to uncontrollable rages and repeated disciplinary problems." He had landed in the brig several times, but because of his war record received an honorable, albeit early, discharge.

Some circumstantial evidence proved far too tantalizing to ignore. After his discharge from the Army, he enrolled at the University of Maryland under the GI Bill and lived in a rented room in Hyattsville, ironically just two blocks from the home of Bernard David Breese, the convicted serial killer they thought for a while may have murdered Ellen and Mikie. Trueman was in residence there at the time of the homicides. He married after college and, being a devout Catholic, fathered eight children, and now had eleven grandchildren. The CIA refused any comment about the suspect's claims of having worked at the agency. Yet, a search of employment records at Fort Lincoln Cemetery, where Ellen was buried, revealed that a William G. Trueman had worked there for a brief time in 1964 as a salesman, just before the suspect claimed to have gone to work for the agency.

Initial investigation of Trueman's family life indicated little that was unusual other than to confirm, from interviews with neighbors, that he still had a proclivity towards irrational behavior, sudden outbursts of unprovoked rage and, since his retirement, paranoia regarding government and "Big Brother."

On July 22, when Trueman arrived at the Landover station with two cardboard boxes of handwritten notes, old newspaper clippings, Xeroxes of documents, photographs, receipts, and miscellaneous papers numbering in the thousands, Harry Silverberg was convinced of one thing—the suspect was a man obsessed or one heck of a researcher. As Silverberg perused the collection while the polygraph and Trueman were being readied for the interview, he soon realized that the obsession was not with just the murder case itself, but with one of the victims in particular: Ellen Chauvanne. Almost every reference to her in the collection had been underlined or circled. Around several press photos of her were penciled annotations on her beauty, how saintly she appeared, and even one line suggesting that she should be canonized. His obsession appeared to have lasted for nearly his whole adult life.

When the polygraph examination was finally conducted, police examiner Ron Boland was already armed with a wealth of information regarding the subject. For his own part, Trueman appeared to be both relaxed and in control of himself.

"You know," he said to Silverberg, "while I was with the Agency, they routinely gave all of us these tests. It was policy. But anyone who's taken or administered enough of them knows how to foil this baby in front of me. And you know and I know that whatever it spits out the other end, it is questionable in a court of law in Maryland."

"Well then, let's begin, shall we," Boland said.

"Okay by me," replied the suspect. "Fire away."

After a few basic warm up questions about his personal data, birth, marriage, address, religion, family, and such, Boland began to hone in on meat.

"Let's move on to your military career. Were you drafted or did you enlist?"

"I joined up."

"That was on June 1, 1951?"

"Walked up to a recruiter right after I turned 18, on June 1."

"Please just answer the following questions yes or no. Did you enlist on your own free will?

"I wanted to kill the anti-Christs, the commies," Trueman responded. "You know, for God, country, and all that."

"Just yes or no. Did you attend sniper training school, August through September 1951?"

"Yes."

"Were you good, and did you like your job?"

"Damned right I was good," Trueman boasted. "The best. You probably know that by now from my record, which you no doubt have already dug up. And I know where you're going with this line of questioning."

"Great," Boland said without taking his eyes off the strip chart. "Please just answer the questions yes or no. Your record indicates you had eleven kills in combat. Is that correct?"

"They didn't count five more that I had no witnesses or verification for, and another half-dozen or so probables. I did take out a gook colonel though. Put two holes right through his chest at 500 yards, but the bastards dragged his ass off, so I didn't get credit for that one either."

"Once again, Mr. Trueman, just yes or no. Did you like your job?"

"Damned straight. I mean yes. When we were entrenched in the mud not more than five hundred feet from the Chinks, when they weren't shooting or lobbing something at us, they would be broadcasting propaganda and really bad music over a loudspeaker, or taunting us with insults, calling us cowards, and telling us our wives and girl friends back home were fucking our best friends while we were up to our necks in slop. That's when I liked my job the most, making the bastards pay for all that crap."

Silverberg, sitting in a corner of the room, was taking notes as fast as Trueman was talking.

"So," continued Boland, "you enjoy killing—Commies, that is?"

"Yes. And my country gave me the Bronze Star for it. That was right before I got nailed in the head by a grenade fragment. Sent me home and put me in a ward at Walter Reed for nearly six months."

"Is that when you started to have your anger management problems?"

"I don't like your line of insinuation, sir," Trueman said loudly, "or where you're going with this. I remind you I am here voluntarily, and unless you change your address to a more civil line of questioning about my research on this case I'm out of here. Got that?"

"All right. Then, let's move on to your job career. Did you ever work for Fort Lincoln Cemetery?"

"Hell no."

"You did't work as a salesman for the cemetery in the mid-'60s?"

Trueman scowled. "What a joke! I know what you are suggesting, because that's where Ellen is buried. I admit that I have visited the gravesite. That was part of my research."

"We have," Boland said, "reliable information from the cemetery employment records that one William Trueman worked there in 1964. Where were you employed then?"

"Damned if I can recall. Look, there are a million guys named Bill Trueman. And if someone with my name worked there it was sheer coincidence."

"Did you graduate from the University of Maryland in 1956?"

"Yes. I went through on the GI Bill, but worked as a grocery clerk part-time to help pay my way. I graduated with a BS in '56, the year after the murders."

"Did you start with the CIA that same year?"

"No. I started in 1965 and retired two years ago."

"Did you know either of the two murder victims?"

"Again, no. I did maintain an interest in them over the years, however, simply because I believe I know who killed them."

"Did you walk into the *Washington Post* on February 6 and place the memorial notice in the obituary pages," Boland asked further.

"Yes. Because I thought someone should remember those poor girls. Certainly no one else did."

"Why did you feel you had to go down to the front desk of the newspaper and post it anonymously, and pay for it in cash when most folks pay with a credit card?"

"I just did, that's all," Trueman responded.

"Let's try it again," the interrogator said in quiet exasperation. "Tell me once more why you placed the notice."

"Okay. I did it to get somebody's attention. All right?"

"Whose attention? And why did you place the notice on February 11 and not June 15, the anniversary of the murders?"

"Damn it," Trueman retorted. "It was around Valentine's Day, and I figured if anybody was going to read it and remember them it would be then. I know who killed those two girls, but no one here believes me. Not Bricker, or anyone else. You guys are either stupid or mentally deficient. I guess that's why you're just county mounties. None of you could hack the big time if your lives depended on it. You guys can't do anything right but hand out tickets to dweebs in handicap parking spaces at the local hajji-mart."

Boland ignored the rant.

"Thank you for your assessment of our career choices. Now if you're done, could we continue?" he said, in an even voice.

"Sure. Sorry about the outburst," answered Trueman with a cynical smirk.

For the next twenty minutes the questioning proceeded in a similar fashion, with Boland never moving his eyes from the strip chart as he asked question after question in a monotone, his emotionless voice robotically directing Trueman to answer yes or no when he began to ramble.

"Okay," Boland said finally in a rising voice. "Let's just cut to the chase. You've got serious problems with at least eight of your responses. Did you kill Ellen Marie Chauvanne and Mikie O'Riley?"

For a moment Trueman glared intensely at the interviewer, pursed his lips tightly, then ripped away the clip lines running from the polygraph to his fingertips and the bands around his chest. His face reddened and his brows furrowed as he suddenly stood up. "That's it, dammit. I'm done," he shouted, spewing spittle on Boland and the polygraph. "You bastards want to pin this on me, and all I've done is to do the job you should have been doing for the last thirty-five years. I'm getting a lawyer and to hell with you."

With no further adieu, he marched from the room, slamming the door behind him.

"I guess you upset the poor guy," Bricker smirked.

"Guess so," Boland said. "Just when it was starting to look interesting."

"Well, all is not lost," Silverberg chimed in. "He went and left his file boxes behind. I suggest we get them copied before he comes back for them."

"Let's be realistic, guys," said Bricker. "The files may provide us with leads to look into, but it's like any other murder case, you follow them until you come to a stonewall . . . and conjecture and assumptions don't count. What we need is evidence. I wouldn't be taken aback if the result, should this case ever be closed, turns out to be not linked to anything that's been done or learned over the last thirty-five years. You simply never know what's going to transpire in an investigation. It can give the impression of going one way, then turn 180 degrees to the other. Even if we miraculously got a confession from the jerk, it has to be corroborated."

He sighed. "If some actual witness came forth and said Trueman did it, you still need something that would connect him to it. It doesn't have to be that much. It would be nice if it were the rifle but that isn't likely to happen. Yet this I can assure you: short of finding the murder weapon itself and tying him directly to it, or he outright confesses and we have good evidence, even circumstantial, we just can't make an arrest, much less get a conviction. Unfortunately, we have been unable to prove that the victims and this guy ever even met. I believe we are going to have to figure out some other way to reel him in."

PART II

TERRY

"Eternity's a long time, isn't it?"

Chapter 19

STROKE

Theresa Anderson moved quickly to strip herself of her obligations in California, not only paying off her bills, but also securing recommendations from advisors, colleagues, and former employers, for later job applications back home. By mid-August 1990 she had moved out of her apartment at 383 Miramar Street, La Jolla. It took her six days to drive across the United States to Maryland. On August 20, she arrived, replete with a substantial entourage of pets, including dogs, cats, a bird, a ferret, an iguana, and a roof rack spilling over with luggage, in her brother Ed's driveway in Ijamsville, in Frederick County. Her dirty little Honda Civic, which pulled up beside his giant Dodge Ram pickup, was overflowing with every kind of debris, including a good-sized cactus, and a potted eucalyptus. The heads of two dogs were sticking out the Civic's windows, and her brother was more than a little amused.

Ed had always thought his sister was a little off her rocker when it came to plants and animals. He knew she was an animal rights activist and a back-to-nature greenie, but as she drove into his driveway after the week-long cross-country trip from California, he was reminded of a scene from an old Ma and Pa Kettle movie. He half-expected that when she turned off the ignition, her beat-up old jalopy would cough a few clouds of dirty black smoke, collapse with a wheeze, and die where it stood, all four wheels folding outwards in a final prostration to the gods of the Interstate.

"Well, Sis, looks like you finally made it, even if you had to do it in that fucked-up version of Noah's Ark. What kind of piece of shit junker is that anyway?"

"Nice to see you, too, big brother," said Terry sarcastically as she emerged from the driver's side. "I drive all the way across North America and the first thing out of your foul mouth after seven years is more profanity. Nothing changes with you, does it?"

"Sorry about that," he laughed. "I just meant to comment on the zoo and arboretum you brought with you."

Ed, a life-long member of the NRA, considered himself an outdoorsman, at home in the woods hunting deer or fishing trout, as long as there was a cold beer close at hand. He had little truck with environmental types, and less for pets of any sort other than his own two killer German Shepherds, which he deemed necessary "to stop intruders" if his own gun collection somehow mysteriously vanished. If an animal weren't suitable for hunting or eating, he believed, it had little use. As for plants, if you couldn't cook or stir-fry them, they were worthless. The aesthetics of flowing plants meant nothing to him. Once, when his wife Maggie attempted to start a rose garden, he derided her so mercilessly for wasting her time that she finally gave it up.

"Enough of the niceties," Terry said. "How's Mom doing?"

Suddenly Ed turned dour, and averted his gaze from his sister.

"Sorry to have to tell you this," he said, "what with you coming all this way and whatnot, but on the same day you left La Jolla, Mom was totally paralyzed by another stroke, except for her speech and one arm. She's also had at least two minor stokes since I last talked to you, but insisted on going home. The docs say, what with her heart and lungs being in the crappy state they're in, she probably won't live more than a few more months at best."

At first Terry stared at him, tears welling in her eyes. Then she exploded, screaming and crying at the same time, and began pounding on his chest with clenched fists. "Why the hell didn't you tell me, you bastard!" she shrieked. "Why didn't you tell me? Why did you wait until I got here? Why?"

"Calm down, Sis, just calm down."

But Terry couldn't and for several minutes she just kept screaming, "Why? Why? Why?" as a torrent of tears streamed down her cheeks. Finally, she went limp, and Ed helped her to his front stoop with one arm around her shoulder and another on her waist.

"How the hell could I contact you?" he said gently. "You had already left California. I had no idea where you were staying while you were en route or how long it would take."

By this time, Maggie had come out, and helped escort Terry inside. She poured her a double Scotch and consoled her for the next half-hour until, finally, her crying sister-in-law regained her composure.

"Where's Pop now? How's he holding up?"

"Good as can be expected. He's a tough old bird," Ed answered as he popped open a Budweiser.

"So far, I haven't seen him since Mom left Shady Grove Hospital last week. Put up with her for all these years despite her hard edge. In a way I think he's kinda relieved knowing she's only got a short time left. His own emphysema is starting to wear him down, and she's a handful for him, but I suspect he'll be okay, for at least a little while."

Ed paused to take a long swig from his beer. "Right now he's at the house they're renting down in Ridgeland, just outside of Damascus. All he does, between tending to her and fixing TV dinners, is watch the tube. Jeopardy. Price Is Right. Court TV, that sort of stuff. Goes in one ear and out the other. All Mom does is cuss at him and blame him for everything. Worse than she ever did before. I stay away as much as I can. She does talk about Ellen a lot though, but with only one side of her mouth working, it usually comes out all muddled, and sometimes sounds like she's even talking to her. She's gone a little nuts, if you ask me."

Terry shoved her empty glass in Maggie's direction without saying a word. As Maggie poured, and the already consumed alcohol began to take effect, Terry looked a bit more at ease.

"So tell me about this guy Trueman," she said. "The guy they think might have killed Ellen."

"The guy's a loony. Charlie Bricker—that's the detective on the case—thinks he did it, but can't find anything but circumstantial evidence on him. And after all these years, it ain't frigging likely that any of that would hold up in court."

"Bricker? There was a kid you used to know in school named Bricker."

"Same guy," said Ed. "He knew Ellen, too. He's now the big cheese in the PG homicide unit. Couldn't have a better cop on the case if you ask me. He wanted me to warm up the creep and see what I can get out of him since they can't do any more, at least right now, than stick him with a circumstantial."

He drained the beer in a single long chug, crumpled the can in one hand, and threw it into a garbage can. "Sis, I don't think I could do it after how I watched him re-enact the murder down at the police station. I'd probably kill him."

"Listen, big brother," said Terry. "After I get situated, I want you to introduce me to Bricker. And, if you won't, then I personally want to meet this guy Trueman. But first I have to attend to Mom and Pop."

Without warning Terry appeared at her parents' door that same afternoon and by the end of the month had completely moved in, with pets and all. Philip and Lucille, both feeble and frail, at first welcomed her with open arms as the caregiver that their son Ed had never been. For her part, Terry quickly wrapped around her parents a protective blanket of concern and attention that immediately lessened their sufferings. Moreover, she wanted to serve as a buffer between them and any potential revelations regarding the renewal of the murder investigation. After securing a part-time editing job with the local Sierra Club, working from home, she was soon contributing to the family's pitifully small coffer. Lucille's declining condition, however, magnified by her physical helplessness and pain, had only served to make her more irascible than ever, and her blowups increasingly frequent and nasty. Terry's menagerie only exacerbated things.

Yet, somehow, Terry carried on even as the domestic situation began to fray around the edges, owing to Lucille's volatile temperament. Philip avoided venturing into his wife's presence except when absolutely necessary, and Terry did so at her peril even though she had taken over full maintenance of her bed-ridden mother. Never a great cook, the daughter's food preparation soon became the target of the mother's vituperative attacks from the still operative side of her mouth, which seldom seemed to rest.

"You never were worth a damned in the kitchen or at cleaning up," Lucille often slurred in a fashion that seemed to make her words even more poisonous. Then, to twist the dagger further, she would add, "If you were only half as good as Ellen, I could probably eat this crap and the house would be neat as a pin." Neither gratitude nor memory had ever been among Lucille's strong points. In fact, Ellen had never been a good cook (except for pancakes), nor had she been particularly tidy. Terry soldiered on somehow, as long as she could without complaint. But it couldn't last.

By year's end she had moved out, secured a one-bedroom apartment at an Annapolis high-rise complex called Spa Cove Harbor, and a new job with a maritime broker called Interyacht. Except for her parakeet, she somehow convinced Ed to board the remainder of her private zoo until she could find a home for them. From her slim salary at Interyacht, she was able to hire a part-time nurse to tend her parents every other day.

Though calling on Philip and Lucille at least once each evening to personally care for their needs, Terry also began to install a regularity, an order, and a rhythm to her own life. Soon she was finally able to address her own needs, and again to begin pursuit of the elusive law degree started years before in La Jolla, where she received her BA. She registered at the University of Maryland for night school to pursue a Master's Degree in law, but, overriding all, there was the solemn pledge she had made to herself to get personally involved in the slow, ongoing, Trueman investigation.

In all the years since she had left home as a teenager, the shadowy image of her dead sister had remained with her, but always tucked away. Now, with the reopening of the murder case, the shadow began to take on form — a life of its own — and she wanted more than anything to look into the eyes of William Galt Trueman. She wanted to peer face-to-face into his very soul. If he were Ellen's killer, something told her, she would know.

Ellen would tell her.

Chapter 20
SOUNDS LIKE A PLAN

It was not without reason that Theresa Anderson despised delay and obfuscation of every kind. Her late sister's mantra of "just do it" had long ago become her own, and she was more than eager for Ed to introduce her to Charlie Bricker. After several weeks of Ed's excuses, however, she resolved to press forward, and called the detective on her own on a Friday in mid-October.

Bricker was extremely cordial on the phone, in a rough-hewn way. He apologized profusely for not calling her even after Ed had informed him she was back in Maryland. He excused himself by telling her he had been inordinately busy with a spate of gang killings in Capitol Heights, barely ten miles from Capitol Hill, where a drug war spilling over from D.C. was underway. There was little small talk, however, and after their brief introduction Terry got right to the point.

"What's the story with this guy Trueman?" she asked. "Why hasn't he been arrested? From everything I have been told, he's done everything but confess. Probably guilty of other murders as well. He maybe even a Ted Bundy serial killer type."

"Ms. Anderson," said the detective, "we're pretty positive now that the horrible murders of your sister and the O'Riley girl were not the work of a serial killer, the likes of a Ted Bundy. In fact, we believe the murderer was somebody who probably acted once in a state of rage at one of the victims, most likely your sister, as she was the most brutally accosted. The O'Riley girl unfortunately happened to be there with her. Collateral damage, as they say in the military. It was someone who really cared for Ellen, but lost control. This was not an unemotional crime. Moreover, it doesn't fit any patterning of local killings during the mid-1950s, at least in our region, when they were also few and far between. Not like today."

"You know I almost went in Mikie's place," Terry sighed. "It could have been me instead of her. Sometimes I wish it had been."

"You can't mean that," Bricker responded.

"Only sometimes. More to the point, how do you account for the fact that Trueman knew details about the murders that nobody but you guys knew? Why can't you just arrest him on that?"

Bricker leaned back in his chair, which squeaked every time he moved. "We can't, at least not yet. Ms. Anderson..."

"Please call me Terry," she said.

"Okay. Terry. I've got to tell you, I've been interrogating killers for years, usually with more than average success given the difficulties of getting any convictions these days. In most cases it's just a matter of sitting down and seeing what motivates them, what makes them tick, what's going to make them confess. Everybody, from Sadam Hussein to Idi Amin, and whoever killed your sister, has something eating away inside."

"You think you can get this Trueman to confess?" Terry asked.

"Maybe. Why would a man like Trueman, or anyone, confess to a murder? Because murderers who do come clean, usually—albeit not always—breathe a sigh of relief when they finally get it off their chests. Most of them will tell you they feel better when they confess. And I can tell you, this guy's got a load, a big load, whatever it is, that he desperately wants to dump."

From the other end of the line, Terry could hear the squeaky swivel chair.

"You know," he continued, "you can sympathize, or even empathize with the worst of them without endorsing their actions. Some will tell you, 'I feel better know.' And I tell them 'I'm glad you do, and you did the right thing.'"

"But why not arrest him?"

"Proof! Though it's thirty-five years old, and certainly one of the coldest cases we have on record, this investigation is still like any other murder case. You follow the leads until you come to the proverbial brick wall. Speculation, subjective or otherwise, doesn't count without evidence. Deductive reasoning doesn't count without evidence, not in a court of law. And as it stands now, we're pretty much at the brick wall looking up."

"What do you mean?" asked Terry.

"I mean, even if Trueman confesses, unless someone, either a witness or participant, comes forward with fresh evidence it's a dead issue. The confession might be false. We've had three or four of them so far over the years. You have to back up a declaration of guilt with other things. If someone says he did it, you need something, anything that would connect him to it. Doesn't have to be a great deal. Would be nice if it we had the murder weapon, but we don't."

"But if he confessed," said Terry, "wouldn't that at least be a start?"

"Sure," said Bricker, "but, after the first few go rounds, he has stonewalled us. The guy's scared toot-less."

"Mind if I try?" Terry said. "I mean, meet with him. Talk to him."

"Not on your life. The guy's a nutcake, we know that, and there's no telling what he might pull," Bricker replied rather brusquely. "It could be very dangerous. You've got to remember who you might be dealing with. He may be the one who savagely killed your sister and Mikie O'Riley. So don't even think of it. This is a matter for professionals."

"Well, Ed said he'd probably kill him if they met on the street, and you professionals certainly haven't made much progress on your own in the last three decades, have you?" she chided. "And, I suppose, as it's a free country, there's nothing you can do to stop me."

"You're absolutely right. I can't, but we have several new lines of investigation underway already, so I would ask you to hold off, for at least a while. Can you promise to do that?"

After a long silence, Terry gave her answer.

"Yes, but only if you promise to keep me informed of what's going on, call at least once a week, or whenever anything breaks."

"Deal," said the cop. "I'll give you a buzz tomorrow evening. How's about that?"

"Wonderful," she answered. "Wonderful."

For the next three months, Charlie Bricker called Terry Chauvanne Anderson almost daily. The conversations grew longer and longer. As Trueman began to look, in Terry's imagination at least, more and more like the killer, and as the exchanges between two people who had never seen each other began to become personal, a bond of trust began to grow, precisely as Bricker had hoped. Yet it was also becoming quite apparent to Terry that, despite his self-censored accounts of the day-to-day progress on the investigations, there was little if any forward motion in the case.

The call from the *Washington Post* reporter came as a surprise as Theresa Anderson was preparing to thaw a frozen pizza in her Annapolis apartment on the evening of November 12, 1990.

"Ms. Anderson," the voice on the phone began, "my name is Kenneth McClennahan. I'm a reporter with the *Washington Post* and we are interested in a story on the possible relationship between one William Trueman, the fellow who placed an 'In Memoriam' notice in our paper last February, and the Chauvanne-O'Riley murders, back in 1955. I know it's probably a difficult thing for you to do, even now, but I was wondering if I might talk with you about it, at your convenience, of course."

"Well, I don't know what I could tell you that you probably don't already know," she said. "I was only seven when my sister was killed. And I don't know much about this guy Trueman, although I have to tell you my family and I would certainly like to learn more than what the police have told us. They haven't been particularly aggressive, at least to my knowledge, in making any further headway."

"I can appreciate your concern. It's mine as well." The reporter stopped to clear his throat, then continued. "You see, I was the one who discovered that it was Trueman who posted the notice and keyed the police in to him. Like you, we think the fellow is more than a likely suspect, and would like to track the case as it progresses."

"The police didn't mention that," said Terry.

"No. I'm sure they didn't," laughed McClennahan. "Let me ask you a personal question. Do you believe Trueman is, indeed, somehow linked to the killings?"

Cradling the phone between her shoulder and right ear while unwrapping the frozen pizza and putting it in the microwave, Terry chuckled out loud. "You suppose?" she said with more than a trace of cynicism in her voice.

"Like I said, I was only seven at the time so I'm probably not the one you should be talking to. You ought to speak with Detective Bricker of the Prince George's County Police out in Landover. Besides, my Mom and Pop are not doing too well these days, and I'm not certain how all this re-opening of old wounds is going to affect them."

"Ms. Anderson, I have to tell you that the *Post* has been repeatedly stonewalled by the PG Police, and especially by Bricker, even though we were partially responsible for getting the investigation of Trueman underway and the case re-opened," the reporter said. "I personally think the police may not want this story to surface again because it would be more than an embarrassment to them. Over the last two weeks I have interviewed Mr. Trueman several times, and I can tell you, although it's not my place to be so judgmental, it looks to me like he has blood all over his hands."

"Haven't met the man, so I can't say one way or the other," Terry countered. "I'd certainly like to, but the police have strongly advised me against it. But, from all I've learned, I'm with you on this one."

"Listen," McClennahan said, "you live and work in Annapolis, don't you?"

"Yes."

"How about I pick you up at your office tomorrow, buy you a lunch at Middleton's? We can talk more about it there. I think I can fill you in on Mr. Trueman with a little more than the police have told you."

"Sounds like a plan," she responded emphatically. "How about 12:30?"

"Great. See you then."

Middleton's Tavern, an Annapolis landmark since its establishment in 1750 and the oldest continuously operating tavern in America, sits off one corner of the Annapolis City dock and was as trendy as they come in a town that reeked of historic snootiness. Its eighteenth century Georgian architecture was compromised, some purists with the Historic Annapolis Foundation claimed, by a garish wood-and-plastic awning, which spanned the establishment's "open air café" along its frontage. Yet the cuisine, especially its seafood dishes — Maryland crab cakes, rockfish, oysters and clams — were ranked with the best in the Chesapeake Tidewater—along with prices to match. During the summer tourist season and at graduation time at the Annapolis Naval Academy and St. John's College, both only two long blocks away, tables at Middleton's were worth their weight in gold. One wag writing in the *Annapolis Gazette* had even suggested they be traded on the commodities exchange like precious metals. But on the cold, drizzly November day when Ken McClennahan met Terry Chauvanne Anderson at the bar, there was no need for reservations.

McClennahan, a slight, somewhat nondescript-looking man, was not how Terry envisioned a top *Washington Post* journalist. His soft voice was far from the stentorian tones of a Bob Woodward, and his mannerisms were more in line with an accountant than an award-winning crime reporter. Yet, she liked him from the moment he introduced himself and shook her hand.

After being seated in front of a fireplace, in a cozy room with walls festooned with everything from Civil War muskets, old Naval Academy uniforms, marine paintings, and depictions of classic Marylandia, both Terry and McClennahan ordered white wine, and lunch, Crab Norfolk for him and a spinach salad for her. Following the mandatory exchange of pleasantries, the reporter gently edged into the interview by first outlining what he knew about Trueman. Much of what he told her, Bricker already had briefed her on. But some of the reporter's accounts were totally new and often conflicted with the detective's reports.

"I interviewed Mr. Trueman twice," McClennahan said, "once at his home, and a second time at the Bob's Big Boy restaurant in Hillandale, out near the Naval Surface Warfare Center. It was a bit weird, discussing the murder over French toast and coffee."

"What's he like?" asked Terry.

"The guy's not an unfriendly type, but definitely paranoid once he starts talking about the case. And he definitely has no love for the Prince George's County Police Department. His father was a milkman who died when he was just a kid, but somehow his mother held things together. He grew up in the house he's still living in, a two-story job out in Cheverly. Nice place in an old neighborhood that's starting to run-down. His house is probably the last white bastion in what has become a totally black community. He did a hitch in the Army during the Korean War, was decorated, but discharged early because of disciplinary problems, apparently stemming from a personality disorder. I guess what we would call today Post-Traumatic Stress Disorder Syndrome. Attended the University of Maryland on the GI Bill, and helped pay his way by working as a grocery clerk. Started working for the CIA in 1964 or '65 and retired in 1988. Had a slew of kids and even more grandchildren. Like he told both me and the police, he said he knew who committed the murders, and who was also involved with it."

A waitress with long hair and a crisply ironed uniform delivered the meal, and asked if she could do anything more for the two customers.

"No thank you," said Terry cheerfully. "We're set."

"Anyway," continued the reporter, as Terry began eating, "Trueman also said he informed the police several times that he knew who did it, and accused Bricker of being a liar when he said he had checked it all out. When I spoke with Bricker about it, he told me he had already interviewed and cleared Trueman's suspect, an old fellow named Dubinski, who used to live in the neighborhood and had moved to the sunny south with his wife and four sons not long after the killings. He had owned a 1939 Packard at the time of the murders but said he had never owned a .22. Bricker said the case files indicated that Dubinski had been among the many hundreds who were interviewed during the first investigation in 1955 but had a solid, verifiable alibi—he was at his job, as assistant manager at a grocery store over on Kenilworth Avenue, and in the company of at least a dozen of his co-workers before, during, and after the murder. He was clean as they come. Anyway, the old man died in 1980 of a heart attack."

"Interesting," said Terry. "I remember something about the Dubinskis, but only that two of his boys were no favorites of Ellen, and both were inordinately tall for their age. Should have been on the basketball squad but weren't."

The reporter piled into his crab dish, took a bite, and resumed his briefing.

"Here's where it gets confusing," he said, continuing to eat. "Trueman told me that he had seen a picture in the newspapers, an artist's sketch, after the murder, and it looked like someone he knew. He didn't go to the cops because he was afraid the guy would come after him, but he showed it to some of his friends at a pub. They laughed at him, saying he was all wet."

"You're talking about the Pancho Villa sketch?" asked Terry.

"Maybe not. In a later telephone call with our boy Bill, he changed the story and said it was the folks in the pub who showed him the sketch in the first place, and said it was in 1957, not 1955 when we all know the Pancho Villa sketch first appeared. Moreover, he said it was of a guy with a beard but wouldn't give me his name. The acquaintance, his suspect, also had a beard but shaved it off two days after the picture appeared. He then claimed he didn't go right to the police because he feared that if he was wrong, he might destroy the guy's reputation. The story he told me directly challenges what he told the police."

Terry leaned forward on her elbows. "Let's be honest. After thirty-five years even the best of us can forget things, dates, the sequence of events, and such."

"In this case, I am not so sure," said McClennahan. "When I met Trueman the second time, he produced an original drawing of a man with a bearded face. He then claimed he had searched his newspaper files on the murders but couldn't find the 1957 sketch and had somebody draw it for him based upon his own memory."

"Police artists do it all the time," countered Terry.

"He then produced a picture of a 1939 Packard and said it was the same as his acquaintance owned, which convinced him the man was guilty. Ms. Anderson, I did a comprehensive search of the files of The Evening Star, The Washington Post, and The Washington Daily News and found nothing but the Pancho Villa sketch that appeared two weeks after the killings. When I confronted him on it, he confessed to having seen it, and remarked that it bore a striking resemblance to Bernard David Breese, the serial killer, and then stated that he knew someone who looked just like that in 1957—himself. He said: 'That was the look of the 50s, the hairstyle and all.'"

Terry shook her head. "None of this adds up, or makes any sense. Sounds like he's changing his story at the drop of a hat. What is it you want from me?"

"We may never get to do the full story, what with the police roadblocks on the data. However, there is still a human interest angle to this. The murder of Ellen and Mikie was a terrible tragedy that seems to have a life of its own, even today, more than three decades later, a story that just won't go away."

The waitress appeared again. "Would you care for coffee or dessert?"

"No thanks," said McClennahan. "Just the bill."

He drained the last wine from his glass, and then stared at Terry.

"What I would like to do," he continued, "is to work with you, keep in constant touch every week, and when you feel comfortable enough to do so, keep me informed about what the PG police turn up. Bricker likes you, confides in you. He wants you to trust him. He did tell me that. I think he wants to hold you in reserve and maybe use you as a last resort."

"That's okay with me," she said airily. "As long as we can finally put this thing away."

"Look," said McClennahan, "I may need your help too. We have to do something to rekindle this thing. And when we do, you have to be a part of it. This may take some time, several weeks, or more. In the meantime, I'll try to convince our detective friend to arrange for you to meet with Trueman. If we decide to do something on the story, I would like to have a photographer come out and take a picture of you, maybe standing on the Eastport Bridge."

She smiled at the reporter. "I'm not crazy about putting either my picture or name in the newspapers. I'd like to talk it over with my father. Otherwise, like I said yesterday, sounds like a plan."

Chapter 21

BILLYBOY WANTS
TO CONFESS

McClennahan had not exaggerated when he suggested the time it might take to get approval from the PG police for Terry to meet with Trueman. It took not weeks, but months. The holiday season did little to hasten either the ongoing investigation, now stalled, or the newspaper reporter's efforts to dig deeper into the case. Daily, religiously, both Bricker and McClennahan would call to discuss what was or wasn't transpiring and, as the Trueman investigation slowly ground to a halt, the pendulum began to swing in Terry's direction.

The personal visit by Charlie Bricker and Harry Silverberg came unexpectedly on a bright Saturday morning just as Terry was preparing to go grocery shopping. She had met neither the detective nor the psychologist face-to-face, but was aware they had either something important that must be related in the first person, or they were about to tell her they were shutting down the case.

After offering her guests coffee and freshly-baked macadamia nut cookies, all three adjourned to the living room, cluttered with the detritus of her new life in Maryland.

"Why am I so honored in this humble abode by the visit of two such illustrious officers of the law?" Terry joked.

"Well, Ms. Anderson," Bricker replied slowly. "As you by now are aware, our investigation is having some difficulty in moving ahead. Many of the folks we would like to have talked to, witnesses who have been questioned, in some cases several or many times during the 1955 investigation, have passed on. The few others we have been able to find, after all these years, have become uncertain about the events they told our predecessors about in the past. Moreover, our prime suspect, Bill Trueman, has lawyered up, and we've pretty much run out of steam in that direction anyway. Indeed, like I've said before, short of actually finding the murder weapon, or getting a verifiable confession and proving it, I think we're back to beating a dead horse. Our only real prospect is, unfortunately, still Trueman."

Opening a folder, he laid out several photographs of Trueman during various stages of his life.

"I thought you might like to take a look at the fellow, so I brought some of our case file photos of him for you to see," said the detective. "We seem to be getting nowhere with him."

"Does that mean you are calling off the investigation again?" Terry asked.

"Not just yet," Silverberg responded. "As Charlie said, we still believe he is a leading candidate — he's the only good suspect we have. Unfortunately, we can't prove anything more than we already know, namely that he's not playing with a full deck of cards, and is one of the most obsessed men I've ever come across in my professional life. Short of getting him to confess, we've got nothing but circumstantial evidence to go on."

Terry smirked. "So what else is new?"

"Listen," Bricker said. "Harry, here, has worked up a substantial forensic personality profile on our boy Billy, and he feels certain. . ."

"I am almost positive," Silverberg cut in, "that Trueman actually wants to confess, but doesn't know how. He wants to get it off his chest, and we think we can get him to do it. That's where you come in, Terry."

Bending down from her chair to scratch her ankle where a tick had bitten her a few days earlier without her knowing it, Terry seemed surprised.

"I'll do anything to get this creep. What can I contribute?"

"Can I smoke?" Bricker asked.

"Appreciate it if you didn't. I've been trying to stop for the last month or so. And you'd just be tempting me," Terry said coyly.

"Oh yeah. Sorry," the cop replied sheepishly. "As you are probably well aware, Terry, from your talks with the folks at the *Washington Post*. . ."

"How did you know about that?" she queried with some indignation.

"We've been in touch with them since this whole Trueman thing began. They're pushing to get something in print. Until now we've tried to keep a lid on it with them, because we're afraid that if they prematurely did a story on him or on the ongoing investigation, he would clam up tighter than Fort Knox."

"Seems to me he's pretty uptight right now," Terry said.

"That's the point," Bricker responded. "We think our only hope is to pry a confession from him. To open the floodgates, which is, hopefully, going to also provide us with the evidence we need. And we have a two-part plan to do it."

"Do tell!" Terry said in her best impression of Scarlet O'Hara.

"Okay. The first part is to let the *Post* do their thing. Their crime reporter, Kenny McClennahan, has been beating down our doors for months on this, to do a big piece on the 'Murder That Would Not Die,' something like that. Hang it all out, the whole story of the unsolved murders, and the recent intrusion of Trueman into the story, replete with the circumstantials that seem to point in his direction. He's already so paranoid that we think this will drive him bonkers. It'll make him feel even more guilty than he probably already is, and he won't be able to take it. He's a devout Catholic and it's probably eating him up inside. So, in effect, we're going to let McClennahan and the newspaper be the bad cop."

"What do you mean?" said Terry.

"Billyboy wants to confess so badly that it hurts," Silverberg said, "but he can't trust anyone, especially after the story breaks, not even the reporter he bared his soul to. That's where you come in. You know how you said you wanted to meet him? Well, this is where you get your chance. You get to be the good cop."

"I don't get it."

Bricker stared her in the eye. "We want to set up a meeting between you and Trueman. Arrange it through McClennahan before the *Post* does the story, while he still has access to our boy. Timing is everything. We can have you meet him in a very public place with a wire, surveillance camera, the whole bit. We will have several armed, plainclothes officers there to protect you if he gets irrational."

"Why should he put any more trust in me than anyone else?" Terry asked.

"He desperately needs release, and I believe that you can win his confidence. I can personally attest to that after speaking with you on a regular basis over the last few months. You are a very persuasive and charming woman."

"Thank you, Charlie, but, again, why should he trust me?"

"You're Ellen's sister. And it's clear that Trueman has the mother of all obsessions with her, obsessions that only you can jar loose. Of course he might not bite or agree to even one meeting. Even if he does, it may take more for him to start warming up and trusting you, confiding in you. Aside from your sister, you're the closest one of all he can come to, and say 'I'm sorry,' probably the only one he can or will confess to. And if he does, you might even be able to find out where the murder weapon is. Either one is a hundred percent better than where we are now. And with both we might even get a conviction."

"It's a shot in the dark, Terry," Silverberg said, 'but it's all we've got left. What do you say?"

At once frightened but giddy with hope, she smiled at the two officers. "I want to talk to my father first," Terry replied, "but I think I know what he will say."

"What's that?" Bricker asked.

"I think he'd say, 'Honey, go for it, as long as they got someone to protect you. It's now or never.'"

She looked at Bricker and, while struggling to hold back her own tears, smiled. "My inclination is to say 'sign me on', but I'm still going to have to think about this one and get back with you."

April 15, 1991. In a tough, suburban war zone of Miami, Florida, a powder blue Cadillac convertible parked in front of a run-down flamingo-pink stucco hospice facility called Chestnut Hill. The driver, a tall, heavy-set man in his early 50s, with thick graying hair and a worried, craggy face, and his passenger, a skinny woman about the same age but weathered well beyond her years, emerged from the car almost simultaneously. As they walked to the entrance of the facility to check-in, the cheers, hooting, and booing wafting from a racetrack two blocks away blended with traffic sounds on the avenue they had just left.

After signing the visitor's register, they were directed to room 138, at the end of a long, sterile-white corridor. As they walked down the hall, the antiseptic smells from rooms with open doors, subtle cloying odors of the terminal residents therein, and the coolness of the pumped-up air conditioning mingled disturbingly with their senses. The tang of death seemed everywhere. The ribald laughter of a passing pair of plump, middle-aged Hispanic nurse aides, clad in rather dingy-looking tan hospital outfits, jabbering on about the handsome young janitor recently-hired, seemed totally out of place.

As the couple arrived at their destination, the white-haired man knocked on the sill of the open doorway.

"Hey, big guy," he said quietly, almost reverently to the man in the hospital bed. "How ya doin?"

"How the fuck does it look like I'm doing?" responded the patient.

"We drove half way across the United States to see you, dodging cops the whole way, and that's the way you welcome us?" said the white-haired man jovially.

"Sorry, little brother. I'm glad you're here. I ain't got much time left, and there's a lot to do. You bring Kitty with you?"

At that, the woman also entered the room, smiled, and walked to the bedside to hug the patient, carefully avoiding the myriad assemblage of medical life support paraphernalia that was keeping him alive.

"Hi, babe," said the patient with a smile that caused creases in his withered face. "Don't know how long it's been since I've had a pair of ta-tas like that cross my chest."

The woman stood back and laughed. "You dirty old bastard. You're worse than your brother."

"So, how they treating you in this dump?" asked the white-haired man. "Been feeding you enough, keeping you happy?"

"The food stinks, and I ain't been able to talk none of these sweet young nurses to jack me off or give me a blow job, if that's what you mean. Otherwise, the place sucks, but it don't matter none. I ain't got long. That's why I called you. The rest of 'em have already said their goodbyes, but I still have some things I got to do, which is why I had to see you before I bite the big one."

"Don't talk like that," said the white-haired man.

"Listen, little brother, I got some shit I want to talk to you about, without Kitty here. And I got some stuff I got to tell her, alone."

"Hey, man, whatever you have to say to her you can say to me. That's the way it's always been, and that's the way it is now."

"Little brother, just this once, do what I say. Please."

"Okay. Why don't you talk to her first," said the white-haired man.

"Thanks," replied the patient, taking his brother's hand feebly in his own. Little brother left the room, closing the door as he departed.

Kitty pulled up a chair beside the bed and smiled at the dying man. "Honey, we ain't got much time before my old man comes back, and you know how impatient he can be. So if you're looking for a god lay, you'd better make it quick."

Taking the woman's hand in his own, the patient smiled broadly, for the first time in weeks. "That's what I loves about you, Kitty, always able to make light in the worst of times. Sorry I can't comply with you, but I've got some things I have to do before it's all over. You know I've loved you like the sister I never had. You've been the only other confidant in my life, besides little brother, that I have ever trusted. But before I do what I have to do, I got to ask you to swear on the Holy Virgin Mary that you won't breathe a word about what I have to tell you until both my little brother and I are gone."

"I swear upon the Virgin Mary," said Kitty, crossing herself.

"Thanks," said the patient. "Now I've got something to tell you so important and difficult I want you to take notes. Once I've told you everything I wants you to memorize those notes, commit to memory everything I've said, then destroy 'em. What I am about to say to you will be between you, me, and my little brother, who already knows the whole story. And when we're gone, it will be between you and God, until you want it. Then it can be your ticket out when you need it."

"I don't understand," said Kitty.

"You will, Kitty baby, you will."

And when he told her, it sent cold chills up her spine, and she understood.

Chapter 22

CANDID CAMERA

Kenny McClennahan was in a quandary. His editor had given him marching orders to move ahead with the Chauvanne-O'Riley murder story. He had done so with substantial vigor, despite the police refusing to cooperate. Every morning, at the daily editorial meeting, without letup, his boss would ask him, "Where are you on the Trueman thing?" or "Where do we stand on the Chauvanne-O'Riley murder story?" And every morning he would provide a brief summary of what had been learned. And every morning, his boss would then ask, "Do you think we have enough to go with the story?" And, much to his boss's exasperation to each query, he would answer, "Not yet."

McClennahan had spent the better part of a year, ever since the "In memoriam" posting, pursuing every promising new lead, interviewing every possible contact, and visiting the actual scene of the crime several times, only to meet with a solid wall of silence from the Prince George's Police. From time to time he had been assisted by a pair of young reporters, Kathryn Evans-Green and Gayland Wargram, but for the most part had carried the load himself. Now, having just received a call from Bricker in Landover informing him that police would be willing to cooperate on a story if he would smooth the way for a meeting between Theresa Anderson and Bill Trueman, he should have been delighted. But he wasn't.

On the morning Bricker had contacted him, and he informed his editor, Todd Belcher, of the good news, Belcher told him that any story he wrote would first have to be run by the newspaper's attorneys to determine if there might be grounds for a defamation of character or slander suite by Trueman. After all, though the man's actions had been incredibly suspicious, there was still no hard, physical evidence linking him to the actual crime. Within three days, McClennahan had his answer.

"There is absolutely no way we can run this story," said Bernie Heissenbuttle, the paper's senior attorney at a meeting convened in Belcher's office. "I repeat, emphatically, no way we can run this story. This fellow Trueman could sue us eight ways to China if he wanted. Todd, Ken, I realize it's a wonderful story, lots of tragedy, human interest, mystery and what not. Maybe even an award-winner, but it's going to get our hind ends in hot water for certain."

"I know, I know," said Belcher, "but I have to tell you that Kay Graham herself has already been vetted on it, several times. It is her opinion — that is, the opinion of the owner of this newspaper and therefore the only one that counts — that the story is too important not to take a chance on. It was front page for us for weeks back in 1955, not long after we bought out the old *Times Herald* and it helped us finally pass the old *Evening Star* in circulation and advertising. It put a second-rate morning rag back in the race—which we won. And now most folks don't even remember the *Star*. I tell ya, this story's a winner despite the risks."

"Bernie," McClennahan chimed in, "I've been informed by her personal secretary that Mrs. Graham has already been personally contacted by the Prince George's County Police Department. They told her they believe an article will actually facilitate the ongoing investigation and help to jar loose a confession from Trueman. And should it come to a court case for defamation of character, slander, or whatever, they are willing to back us one hundred percent."

"A lot," Belcher added, "is going to depend on how Ken writes around it. That's why he's with us and not with the *Washington Times*. He doesn't make mistakes. He's one of the best we've got, and if Mrs. Graham says she's for it, I'm certainly willing to back the story as well."

"Don't say I didn't warn you," the attorney said as he rolled his eyes heavenward and threw his hands in the air. "I might add that this is going to be one hell of a case to have to defend ourselves on if Trueman does want to drag us to court. We could be taken to the cleaners for millions."

"That's why you get paid the big bucks, Bernie," Belcher laughed. "To ensure that we don't."

"All I can say," said the attorney as he left the office, "is that Ken, here, is going to have to be pretty careful."

The reporter, just backed by one of the most powerful women in the American publishing industry, smiled with delight. "You can count on it," he said quietly.

"Ken," said Belcher, "I know you have a couple of other hot items on the stove, but I want you to put them on the backburner for a while and concentrate on this one. We can't afford any slipups. I want every single source, every line, every word verified and cross-checked for accuracy. I don't want any innuendos, open-ended assertions, or editorials. They can get us in deep trouble. Everything has to literally hold up in court. Got that."

"Yes, sir," said McClennahan.

"Well, all right, what are you waiting for?"

Both the police and the *Washington Post* execs decided that it would be best if McClennahan would take it slow about edging Trueman into a meeting with Terry. The first step for the reporter was to casually mention during one of the irregular telephone conversations with his subject that Terry was back in the Washington metro area and that she had expressed an interest in a meeting. The idea of suggesting that she was motivated by plans to write a book about her sister's unsolved murder and wanted to find out what the man knew was put forward by Terry herself and accepted by both the police and the newspaper.

Well aware of Trueman's skittish nature, McClennahan took his time, sympathetically listening to hours of his often-conflicting theories on the murder, diatribes against the Prince George's Police Department, and miscellaneous tales about his life. It was in early May 1991 that he finally mentioned that Terry was back in Maryland, that he had spoken with her, was considering a book on the murders, and if he was willing to meet with her, wanted to get Trueman's input. As both McClennahan and the police had hoped for, Trueman leapt at the opportunity.

McClennahan acted as intermediary between the two parties. Trueman selected as a fitting and symbolic date — a 9:00 a.m. breakfast meeting on June 15, the thirty-sixth anniversary of the crime. He also suggested a public place where both parties could feel comfortable. A popular local restaurant called Bob's Big Boy, in the community of Hillandale, about three miles west of the University of Maryland and near the sprawling U.S. Naval Surface Weapons Center, was mutually agreed upon. It had been the same site where McClennahan had once interviewed the suspect in person.

Trueman's excitement over meeting with the sister of the dead woman he had been obsessed for most of his life, McClennahan informed Bricker and Silverberg, was palpable. Terry was cool and analytical. She began preparing for the meeting as if it were for a college entrance exam, reviewing and digesting every piece of data the police could provide her, as well as her own family's recollections of that horrific day and the Panadapoulis investigation that followed seemingly a millennia ago. Silverberg was meticulous in copying key documents, including Ellen's diaries, and passing them on to Terry to prep her for the event.

On May 31, Terry attended a planning session at the Landover Police headquarters to discuss the upcoming meeting with Trueman. As she entered the conference room, she found Bricker, Silverberg, and a woman she had never met before. Bricker introduced the woman as Bridget Long of the Maryland Department of Public Affairs, head of a unit specifically charged with facilitating national and regional media development within the state.

Though conservatively dressed in a charcoal gray business suit, red silk scarf, and modest heels as befitted a state civil servant, Long was a sublimely attractive, middle-aged redhead perfect for a public relations front office.

"It's a pleasure to meet you, Ms. Long," Terry said, "but why is DPA involved in this thing? I thought it was a police affair."

"We'll get to that in a minute or two, Terry," Bricker interjected. "But for now, we have to discuss some problems which have come up that we had not anticipated."

Terry's eyebrows raised. "Such as?"

"Mr. Trueman, it seems, pulled a fast one. You see, the place he proposed to meet you, the Bob's Big Boy in Hillandale, is just across the Prince George's County line, in Montgomery County. He undoubtedly figured that the meeting would probably be monitored by our plainclothes officers, but in Montgomery County we have no legal jurisdiction and he knows it. Our requests for both Montgomery and Maryland State Police assistance to fill in for us have been refused on the grounds that the case is too cold to warrant it. The FBI told us much the same."

"Why don't we just make some excuse and ask Trueman to move it into PG?" Terry asked. "Maybe somewhere more convenient to his place in Cheverly."

"That would be a dead give-away that you are, indeed, working with us," Silverberg answered.

"What about the wire you talked about?"

"Setting you up with a wire out of our jurisdiction might be challenged or even prove inadmissible evidence in court. And if he discovered you with it on, and there was no one to protect you, it could be dangerous."

"Like it's not already?" Terry commented caustically.

"That's why we brought in Bridget here," Bricker said, gesturing to the woman sitting beside him. "Bridget, tell Ms. Anderson your thoughts on the subject."

"Certainly, Charlie," Long said, "but before I start, Terry, I have to tell you I am in full sympathy with your personal loss and desire to put a period at the end of this long sentence. I also should let you know that I was a student at Northwestern while your sister was there, although I didn't know her personally. I was a year behind her, but some of my classmates knew her well. So I have some distant connectivity with this case."

Terry smiled. "That's all well and good, but how do you propose resolving our problem?"

"At the Department of Public Affairs," Long answered, "my job is to try to get the motion picture and television industry to come to Maryland to make their films. They can bring to the state big productions, which cost a lot of money to make, which is good for the local economy, and high media visibility, which is good for publicity and tourism."

"What does that have to do with solving this case?" Terry asked.

"We would like to film your meeting with Trueman. Set up a hidden camera unit. You know, like the old Allen Funt show, Candid Camera. We think, once the *Washington Post* story appears, we can get it aired on one of the reality TV crime shows like the one Robert Stack does on NBC. You know, Unsolved Mysteries. Or maybe even Hard Copy. Besides, with a film crew watching from behind the scene, there will be someone there to protect you. We can give you a tape recorder as a prop that he can see. You'll tell him you are writing a book and want to tape the interview. His ego is such that he will probably buy that. If he doesn't, you can simply turn it off, since we are recording it anyway. Your willingness to dispense with the recorder will help convince him of your sincerity and interest in him and his story."

"Let me get this straight," Terry said angrily. "You want to film my meeting with the man who may have killed my sister so that the State of Maryland can get publicity or maybe a few bucks more in state coffers?"

Bricker stood and leaned across the table, looking Terry squarely in the face. "You miss the point, Ms. Anderson. It's the only way we can legally get someone there to monitor the meeting, provide some protection, and record the proceedings."

"That's a crock of bullshit, and you know it. What'll they do if he goes off the deep end, hit him with a microphone?" Terry stood and stared straight at Bricker. "I'm going to go through with this meeting, but without the police, without your candid camera, and without your wire, hidden microphones, or tape recorder. I wanted to get my own sense of this guy, and I will. If Bill Trueman killed my sister, I will know."

Gathering her purse, she stepped towards the door, turned and looked back at Bricker, Silverberg, and Long.

"I know this case is cold to you, but my sister was once everything to me. Still is, now more than ever. I have to do this. I'm going through with it. Not your way, but mine."

Three hours later, Theresa Anderson entered the front doorway of the B&G Sports Center on Route 202 in nearby Bladensburg and purchased a Smith and Wesson .38 snub-nose revolver and a box of ammunition.

Chapter 23

BOB'S BIG BOY

Terry avoided telling her parents about the conference with Bricker, Silverberg, and Long, and of her plan to meet with Trueman in a few days without police protection. Nor did she mention the gun she had purchased.

On the evening of June 14, the night before the meeting, Kenny McClennahan called and spoke with her for several hours. He had learned of her plans from Bricker and, for once, vigorously sided with the police in attempting to persuade her from going through with the Trueman meeting.

"You know," he said, "I could call Trueman myself and cancel, since I'm the only one he will talk to."

"Listen, Kenny," she responded, "the police could not offer me any protection since the meeting site is out of their jurisdiction. All they could do was to get a state film crew to record the whole thing from some hidden spot so they could put it on some stupid television reality show. And they are supposed to protect me? I don't think so. Kenny, I'm 43 years old, a big girl, and I can take care of myself."

"Terry, the man's mentally unbalanced. There's no telling what might happen. For Christ's sake, he was a professional killer during the Korean War. And if he did kill your sister and Mikie O'Riley, and maybe some others we don't know about, who's to say what he might do."

"I repeat, Kenny, I can take care of myself. We're meeting right out in the open in a very public place and in broad daylight. Anyway, if you cancel it, we're not likely to get another chance with this guy."

"Oh, for God's sake. Get real! Bank robberies, where people get gunned down in the middle of a bustling city, occur every day in broad daylight," he responded sarcastically.

"Look, don't try to talk me out of it," she said. "I'm meeting him and that's that."

There was a long silence on the other end of the line. "Okay," Kenny resumed. "You're pig-headed enough that I'm certain I'm not going to change your mind one iota, but do this for me. I've interviewed the man twice and talked to him countless times on the phone, so I think I know him better than most. He is very intelligent, but quite edgy if he thinks he's being pushed, and he can get angry at the drop of a hat. Terry, whatever you do, don't say no to him. Go with the flow. And by all means, do nothing to arouse his dander. Know what I mean?"

"I think so," she said.

"And be careful."

There was seldom much traffic on the Maryland highway system on Sunday mornings, at least until the churchgoers hit the road. Terry made better time than she had anticipated in driving from Annapolis to the Capital Beltway that circumvented Washington, en route to meet with William Trueman. She left the house on Quail Lane at 6:00 a.m., and thus made excellent time, indeed such good time that she estimated she would have an hour and a half to kill before the meeting. For a June morning it was exceptionally cool, and she wished she had brought along a heavy sweater. As it was, she was wearing a tight fitting sleeveless blouse so that Trueman would not fear she was carrying a police wire, and she was getting goose bumps on her bare arms.

As she neared the U.S. Route I south cloverleaf on the Beltway, a sudden thought flashed through her mind. Why not drive through the old neighborhood on West Park Drive, see if the house were still standing, and check out how her old childhood stomping grounds had fared.

There was a sudden pain at the back base of her neck, and she remembered the kiss. The kiss that everyone else thought was little more than a figment of a small child's imagination half a lifetime before. Maybe, she thought, she should take a walk through the park to refresh her memory of that tragic day precisely thirty-six years earlier. Why not?

"Just do it," flashed across her consciousness, even as she turned onto the exit ramp south, almost as if her mind were on automatic pilot. Within minutes she was at the intersection of U.S. I and old University Lane (now University Boulevard) and heading east. In a few more minutes she was on West Park Drive and again in childhood.

The neighborhood was remarkably unchanged, although the years and the constant ebb and flow of residents of myriad, diverse ethnic origins had obviously taken their toll. There were few white faces to be seen on the street, mostly black and Hispanic now. Along the roadside were parked a number of brightly-painted low riders, a few expensive Black Ford Expeditions that seemed out of place for what could readily be termed a low-rent district, as well as a few pimped up Harley's. Despite the early hour, several black teenage boys with do rags and bags wrapped around bottles were sitting on the curb in front of the house Candice Miller and her family once occupied. Her own home, however, looked just as it had on the day she sat on the front stoop picking ticks from her dog Tweedle Dee and watched her sister disappear, arm-in-arm with Mikie O'Riley, cross the street to disappear forever into the park.

She was overcome at first by a feeling of bitter nostalgia, for that last moment of yearning to be with her sister. Then she began to feel faint, dizzy, and the pain at the base of her skull came back stronger than before. She pulled the car over onto the park side of the road and sat there for a few moments, to regain her stability, before getting out. She hardly noticed the powder blue Cadillac convertible with Texas tags parked on the same side of the road just fifty feet ahead. Scanning the park from left to right she could see there had been some changes, but for the most part, everything looked much as it had on that day in 1955. She glanced at her watch. 8:10 a.m. She knew there could be no going back now as she began to walk, slowly at first, down the dirt path toward the glade her sister and Mikie had taken. As in her childhood, the little bridge across the stream was darkly hidden by the trees and groundcover. Her goal, although she wasn't certain just why, was to relocate the cherry tree behind which the killer, or killers, had lain in wait, and then opened fire.

As she entered the woods, and neared the bridge, she could hear the running of the nearby stream, which sounded like voices speaking softly in the breeze. Or were they voices after all? Pressing on, she began to hear the voices more distinctly. Then, in an instant, as her pupils adjusted to the shadows, she saw them: two figures standing, still dark in shade, beside the now mature cherry tree, but clearly silhouetted by the daylight on the opposite side of the stream. Both were tall, but she could not tell if they were male or female. She froze in mid-step and stood statue-still at the very spot Ellen had gone down, and could almost hear the sharp snap of gunfire.

The pain in her neck intensified, and her dizziness caused her stomach to rebel. She vomited, staggered, and vomited again, tripping on an exposed root, and fell. Panic gripped her as she stood again and began to run hard, running toward the beckoning shelter of the woods, the same woods her sister had once struggled towards. Suddenly, she found herself entangled in briars and underbrush. The hem of her dress was torn, and she lost a shoe. There seemed nowhere to flee, as the forest swirled about her and then, as she fell again, all turned to darkness.

When Terry regained consciousness, a little black girl was standing over her, smiling, and a small dog was licking her hand.

"Ma'm, are you okay?" said the child. "Cuffy, here, found you."

Terry looked up at her and pulled herself up on one elbow. The pain and dizziness were gone, and the sky was brilliant blue. She looked towards the cherry tree and the bridge beyond, and both seemed to be somehow lighter, brighter. The shadows had disappeared. "I'm fine, honey. I was just taking a morning nap."

"Certainly is a funny place to be napping," said the girl with a laugh. "Do you often do it with one shoe on an' another off?"

The girl held out Terry's shoe as if it were a sacred offering.

"No, but thanks for finding it," said Terry gratefully.

She looked at her watch. It was 8:30 a.m. There was still time to make her meeting with Trueman. She thanked the girl for her kindness, and walked back to the car. Upon reaching it, she turned and looked again down the path she had just come. Once again, the woods looked dark and foreboding. The powder blue Caddy was gone as well. Twenty-five minutes later she was in the parking lot of the restaurant.

The seven and a half-foot fiberglass statue standing in front of the entrance to Bob's Big Boy in Hillandale, some would say, was bizarre. Others considered it little more than tasteless advertising kitsch exported from California, where the restaurant chain was born in 1936. The figure, a giant fat boy with wavy black hair, wore red-and-black checkered overalls, a white short-sleeve T-shirt with the words "Big Boy" emblazoned in electric blue across the chest, and oversized shoes like those Mickey Mouse wore. He was a well-known trademark west of the Mississippi, but rarely seen on the Eastern Seaboard. His left-hand thumb was tucked under a suspender, pulling it proudly out from his body, while the right hand was raised above his head, holding a plate with an enormous, super-thick fiberglass hamburger. Big Boy's bright blue and black cartoon-like eyes looked down toward his left, welcoming all who entered the front door of the restaurant. And little children loved him as they skipped from the parking lot and along the moss green and black terrazzo walkway to the entrance.

When Terry pulled her little Civic past the empty spaces where carhops wearing roller skates once serviced drive-in customers, she felt a twinge of nostalgia for La Jolla, where she had been an irregular patron of the chain. For a Sunday morning, the place was quite active, mostly with early churchgoers having breakfast after services. "Bob's Sweet-tooth Pancakes" were a favorite draw, but the chain was rapidly losing ground in the fierce battle for market shares with faster-growing competitors such as

Denny's, and more lugubrious ones such as I-Hop and McDonald's. Yet, it was just the open, public place that she felt would make it safe. And if there were any problems, sitting across the table from the man who may have murdered her sister, she had more serious protection in her purse.

As she entered, she saw him sitting near the hostess stand. He looked exactly the way McClennahan had described him—middle-aged, thinning sandy-colored hair, fair complexion, about 5'10", affable, and obviously nervous. He was wearing an expensive thin white cable knit sweater that accentuated his soft blue eyes. For only a moment she thought of backing out, then walked straight towards him, with her right hand out.

"You must be Bill Trueman," she said with a forced smile. "I'm Terry Chauvanne Anderson."

"It's a pleasure, and an honor to meet you," Trueman said as he stood to shake her hand. "Kenny has told me a lot about you. Why don't we get a booth? We can talk over coffee and pancakes. They're excellent here. My treat!"

"Sounds good to me," she responded.

Within a minute or two, the hostess had seated them facing each other in a booth beside the front window, in the shadow of the fiberglass Big Boy. After cups of coffee had been poured and placing their order, there was an embarrassing moment of silence, as Trueman and Terry waited for the other to speak. Finally, after clearing his throat, Trueman cracked the ice.

"I guess you find it a little strange, meeting with me," he said. "I know that Bricker has painted me out as a villainous creep. He's even suggested that I was the one who killed Ellen—I mean your sister—and Mikie O'Riley. I want to tell you here and now that is all Detective Bricker's fantasy."

"Mr. Trueman. . ." she began.

"Please call me Bill," he interrupted, giving her a benign Walter Cronkite smile. "And may I call you Theresa?"

"Terry will do just fine."

He smiled. "I guess the first thing on the agenda is to get a bit acquainted. Why don't you tell me a little about yourself?"

"Works for me," she said. "If you promise to. . .to reciprocate."

"Agreed. Let's start with you."

As Terry sat opposite the man she had schemed for months to meet face-to-face, thinking about what to say next, it suddenly occurred to her: it felt as if she were sitting with someone extremely familiar, but wasn't quite certain who it was. It was then she realized that William Galt Trueman, in his white cable knit sweater with sleeves pushed up to the elbows, his easy laugh, and calming blue eyes, reminded her most of her ex-husband Carl. And for the next hour or so, the hitherto complete strangers, one the sister of a murder victim, and the other a suspect in the murder itself, exchanged their life stories and pleasantries as if they had known each other for years.

It wasn't until about 10:30 a.m. that Terry began to gently press Trueman on his "research" into the murder itself. He was ready.

"Bill, before we talk about Ellen and Mikie and what you may have found out, I wanted to . . . I don't know how to say this . . . I wanted to express my gratitude that you had the courage to badger the police and tell them what you know, and who you think carried out the killings. I guess that's also why I wanted to talk to you in person. I know what they know and what they say about your theory about old man Dubinski, but I wanted to hear it from you myself."

Trueman laughed, but began to noticeably fidget and glance around the room.

"I have to be honest with you, Terry. I don't know if you've come on your own to get poop for a book, like McClennahan told me you were interested in writing, or are just setting me up for Bricker and his boys. You may even be wired. I don't really care, since I've nothing to hide. Hell, I once thought I would write a book about the murders myself. I'm too old for that now though, so I'll tell you anything you want to know."

Terry could feel the tension increasing by the second and recalled McClennahan's advice on Trueman: don't say no to him, and don't get his dander up. She tried to break it with a laugh. "I can assure you I'm here on my own, and I am not wired. You can search me if you want."

Trueman relaxed a bit and chuckled. "That won't be necessary, although frisking a beautiful lady like you might have its rewards."

Terry let it ride, but began to re-gauge the man. After all, Ted Bundy was also a seemingly serene, harmless-looking man who had everyone fooled. "So talk to me Bill. Why is it that you think that this Dubinski was guilty?" And he told in great detail the same story he had recited to Bricker and his antecedents, about the mystery man with the .22 rifle at Woody's gas station, of his life-long effort to bring the killer to justice, and his extreme bitterness towards the Prince George's County Police Department.

"Kenny told me you had given him a different story than you told Bricker."

Trueman began to fidget again. "I like Kenny. I trusted Kenny, and still do to some degree. But I found out through a friend—yes, I have some in the right places—that he had begun to collaborate with the police, though they had stonewalled him earlier. So I figured I'd throw him a curve ball, something to confuse 'em a little. You know, mixing up dates, descriptions, and so forth. Out in McLean, at CIA headquarters, we called it "misinformation." Usually confused the hell out of the enemy during the Cold War. You know, I'm kinda sorry the Berlin Wall came down. I miss the good old days when we knew who the enemy was."

"Well, where in heaven did you manage to find out details on the murder that only the police knew?" Terry asked. "Bricker told me you knew that Ellen's body was face up when they found her, but that she had been shot in the back of the head while on her stomach, held down by the killer's foot on her butt. They ascertained that the killer had then rolled her over on her back, which is how she was found, and why everyone, including the press, except the police, Mom, Pop, and Ed, thought she had been shot in the forehead."

"Like I said," he responded. "I had, and still have, a few friends in the right places. I learned at the Agency never to write such things down, but since I've decided to give up the hunt, I guess I can tell you. You know, I have friends who say I'm psychic."

He looked up as the waitress passed, and asked for another cup of coffee, his fourth. Then, for the next half hour, setting the stage for his response to Terry's question, he recited the events of the murder and investigation, reliving them as if they had occurred the day before and he had been a personal witness to every detail. Finally, he answered the question.

"There was a Parks Department patrolman I'd met in a watering hole, which later became a topless go-go joint, called the Starlight, where the college kids used to hang out, down on Route 1. A nice guy, named Daily. Lester "Reds" Daily. Head of red hair like you wouldn't believe. On campus we all heard about the murders almost as soon as the cops appeared on the scene. Reds was on a patrol that same morning and, of course since he was wearing his uniform and arrived in his cruiser, he had no problem getting through the police line. It was, after all, his turf. He went right over to the body, which was face up, just as she had been found. He saw the dirty shoe print on her backside when they rolled her over and figured out right away how the killer administered the coup de grace. He told me all about it over a pitcher of beer at the Starlight. We still stay in touch, even as he moved up. Now runs the Parks and Recreation Division of the M-NCPPC."

"Why didn't you tell Bricker that?" asked Terry. "Your description is one of the main reasons they suspect you."

"There were several reasons. The first being, believe it or not, like I already said, I wanted to write a book about the whole thing, and I wanted to save some of the best stuff for it. Now that's impossible because the police have all my records on the crime and I doubt if I'll ever get them back. Besides, today Reds is a big cheese with the Park and Planning Commission and it could have gotten him in hot water."

Terry nodded and recalled Bricker or someone telling her that killers often wanted to write about their crimes, as another way of confessing. "I see," she said, "but how did you know the precise time the murder occurred?"

Trueman chuckled. "If the damned cops would have actually read my notes, clippings and such, they would have seen that somebody apparently let it slip or intentionally leaked it to the press soon after the murders. I think it was actually published on June 28 in the *Star* as part of one of the stories they did. You know, they covered it for weeks, like everyone else. It was an easily missed detail, but I caught it. Something that son-of-a-bitch Bricker and his buddy boy Silverberg failed to catch when they stole my notes."

"I thought you loaned them to the police," Terry said.

Trueman's face began to noticeably redden.

"My dear," he said, obviously forcing himself to remain calm. "When I retired from the CIA, I continued to do freelance consulting for the agency, something a lot of former or retired employees do, but when Bricker called and informed them of my research work on the Chauvanne-O'Riley murder case and implied I might be a suspect, I was dropped like a hot potato. They don't even answer my calls now. I lost my freelance income on account of my devotion to solving the case and that bastard Bricker. I have worked on it for the better part of my life and Ellen deserves more than what those damned county mounties are calling an investigation."

Trueman was becoming noticeably angry and tears were beginning to well in his eyes. Terry shifted uneasily in her seat. Without losing eye contact, she moved her purse onto her lap and could feel the heaviness of the gun inside as she did so.

"Then, what about the polygraph you took. McClennahan told me you failed it pretty badly."

"Look," said Trueman in exasperation, "Bricker accused me of the murder and I walked out. From my experience in the CIA I can tell you flat out that corrupting a polygraph test is pretty easy. All you need to do is have someone yell at you, touch you, or get you emotionally riled, all of which they did with me. Cops make mistakes inadvertently — or on purpose — and they usually take pretty bad notes. Guys like me go to the police with the purest of intentions and then get a hassle from them. You're an immediate suspect, and they treat you like one. My lawyer thought I was nuts for doing this. He said, 'Do your friends think you're crazy?'"

"Bill," Terry said gently, hoping to bring him back down, "you've been through a lot, but I have to admit it escapes me why a man like you, a family man, obviously educated, established, and. . .well, pretty much your average Joe. . . would devote so much of his life trying to find the killer of two girls he never knew."

The flush in Trueman's face started to fade and veins in his forehead and neck that had begun to bulge disappeared. After a long silence, he attempted to answer Terry's question.

"The reason why I've been so persistent over the years is because things like this have happened to me before," he said, "and it always circles around death. Remember what I said about someone calling me psychic? Do you know what that means? It means outside the normal mental processes, a second sight. The only time I didn't take action, somebody died."

Terry wasn't certain about how to respond, and said nothing. Though her eyes never left the figure opposite her, she was suddenly conscious that the ambient noise in the room had disappeared as the totality of her consciousness focused on Trueman. Her head felt light, and there was a twinge of pain at the base of her skull in the same place she had felt it earlier.

"There were three times in my life," Trueman continued, "in which I saved someone else's life. Each time it was after getting a strange thought in my head that they were threatened . . ."

Suddenly he stood up and began to leave. "I can't do this," he said. "You'll have to forgive me, Terry, but I can't do this."

She grabbed his left hand with both of hers. It was soft and silky, well manicured. Not, she thought, the hands of a killer. "Bill. It's okay. Sit down. I want to listen. I want to understand."

He stood for a moment, looking down at her. "I'm sorry. You're right. And I believe you."

His eyes were red and puffy. After a sip of water and several efforts to clear his throat, he sat down again and continued. "I get these thoughts in my head about people who are about to be killed. Once I saved two little boys who almost drowned after voices in my brain told me where to go and what to do to save them. Another time, just before they did away with the old D.C. Transit trolley system, I was instructed to go to the Shepherd Park Station, out near Silver Spring, on the D.C. line, and when I got there it was just in time to save an old man from being hit by a streetcar. So I guess you could call me psychic. It's the main reason I got involved in the murder case."

Terry leaned across the table and cupped both of Trueman's hands with her own. "Bill, I don't know whether such things actually can occur. I can't say one way or another that I believe in a sixth sense or anything like that, but I do believe there are things we just can't understand or explain. Things that just happen and we are not meant to know why."

She felt a genuine empathy for the man across the table, a man in pain and emotional discomfort, and who didn't know why. "I don't know how or why you became involved in my sister's case, if it was out of compassion, curiosity, or perhaps something else, but if what you said was true, it could only have been for a good reason."

He looked up and almost smiled, and held her hands tightly. "I didn't always do the right thing," he said. "Not long before your sister's death, I started getting thoughts that hurt my head. They were dark and sometimes unwholesome thoughts as if someone was trying to take over my mind. There was a child I had seen in the neighborhood, and in my head I clearly saw him walking with an older boy, a local tough guy who I knew could only be a bad influence. I kept on getting these images of him and the tough kid hanging around together doing some pretty nasty things, and finally decided I should warn the little boy's parents. Then I started thinking, 'Why should I tell his parents.' It was no business of mine. So I didn't."

"What happened?" Terry asked.

Choking up for a moment, Trueman was unable to continue until he took another sip of water and finally blurted it out. "Two days later, Tommy, who was eleven, was killed, sitting on a railway bridge with the older boy, drinking whiskey. And I knew it was going to happen and did nothing."

For a moment he paused, and regained his composure. "Terry, I also knew what was going to happen to Ellen and Mikie before they were killed — and I did nothing. I was afraid when I saw the guy do it in my head, and even more so when I actually encountered him at Woody's. Of course I couldn't tell the cops the whole story. They already thought I was nuts, but that's why I have spent most of my life trying to make amends. I tell her every night how sorry I am and promise to get justice for her. I've come to know and, yes, love and cherish your sister as if she was my own. Can you understand that? Can you believe me?"

Terry felt a chill, not knowing what to believe, except that the man across from her was sick. He had a death grip on a fantasy past, filled with invented memories and tinctured by an obsession of incredible proportions. She also now knew that he was not the man who killed Ellen, but one who was somehow twisted by a life-long obsession that had perverted the very concept of love. Suddenly she realized he was still gripping her hands tightly — too tightly. She tried to remove them, but he held her even more strongly.

"Bill, we ought to go. We've been sitting here for quite sometime."

"Terry," he said, ignoring her suggestion, "I think we can do this together, you and me, for Ellen. Why don't we meet, maybe for a movie or something, and talk more about it?"

Terry struggled to stay calm, to fend of a rising tide of fear and disbelief. She forced a smile and a lie. "I think that would be something we might consider," she said, knowing she would never see him again, "but you're married and it might look awkward."

"I don't think so," he said. Beads of perspiration were beginning to form on his forehead. "You know, when I speak with Ellen, she sounds a lot like you. In fact I think there is a lot of her in you. Don't you?"

"I don't think so," said Terry, even as she forcefully pulled her hands free and started to stand.

Trueman jumped up quickly and with gentle force pressed her back into her seat and glared down at her with an almost demonic grin. "Listen, Terry, I've spent years getting to know Ellen, getting to know everything about her. Learning to love her, but never being able to touch her. Now that we have met, I would really like to get to know you better. Much better. Even more than Ellen."

Terry grabbed her purse and lunged past Trueman. "I wouldn't do that," she said as she walked swiftly towards the door. "It might make her angry. And you don't want to see Ellen when she's pissed off. Not now, anyway."

Chapter 24

POWDER BLUE CADILLAC

The local landscape along New Hampshire Avenue, onto which Terry exited from the parking lot of Bob's Big Boy, had changed dramatically in the years she had been in California. Apartments, strip malls, gas stations, and shopping centers, unevenly interspersed with private homes, now lined both sides of the highway in the worst display of unrestrained pave-over urban growth imaginable. It represented everything she considered ugly and had sometimes fought to prevent, but today, as she fled from the meeting with William Galt Trueman in a mixture of fear, anger, and disgust, she paid little attention to it. All she could think of was how suddenly consumed Trueman had appeared, how his fixation with Ellen, whom he had never met, had been almost instantaneously transferred to her — and how awful but, in some indescribable way, sinfully delicious it had felt. She could not begin to explain it, but felt guilt for even harboring such a feeling, and angry at herself for allowing it. The anger became all encompassing.

She paid little attention to the traffic as her foot pressed hard against the gas peddle and the Honda Civic's speed crept ever higher, passing other vehicles as if they were turtles on a forest path. She was driving without a seat belt, one of her dogs having gnawed through it long ago. Within a few minutes she was at the turnoff onto the inner loop of the Washington Beltway, then heading east and driving with abandon. By the time she was nearing the U.S. Route 1 cloverleaf, with spurs leading south to College Park and north to Beltsville, she was doing ninety-five miles per hour on the three-lane highway, passing others with little thought of safety or danger. The anger continued to rise, and the pain at the back of her neck again suddenly reappeared, causing her to involuntary flinch, and the car to swerve wildly.

She struggled to regain control, even as she passed to the left of a large red dump truck laden with gravel and bearing the name "John Damilier Construction Co." on the on-ramp from Route 1 to her right. As she passed, she could see in her rear view mirror the truck beginning to weave wildly back and forth.

At that same moment, she saw, almost too late, a powder blue Cadillac with Texas plates and a man and woman inside, the same one she had seen near the park. It emerged from the ramp just in front of her. Instantly, she jammed on her breaks to avoid a collision, causing the rear of her car to swing to the right, even as the front turned left, placing her directly in the path of the oncoming dump truck. In Terry's head, the screaming of tires and smell of burned rubber melded with the noise and feel of the truck as it smashed Goliath-like into the rear of her car, almost as if the whole scene were being shot in slow motion. As the Civic spun round and round down the concrete highway, careened from the steel guardrail along the median strip across the highway to another on the opposite side, and finally came to a halt, she felt nothing. It was almost as if time had been suspended.

For a moment she just sat there, unconscious of the blood running from her forehead. All she could think of, as she watched the powder blue Cadillac disappear over the next hill, was how she should get her airbags fixed. When she turned to see what had happened to the truck, she felt nothing except the pain at the base of her skull. Across the highway, the truck had come to a halt against the median guardrail, but appeared to be uninjured except for a few scrapes. Several cars had stopped behind her and on the opposite side of the highway behind the truck, but for the most part the light Sunday morning traffic continued to wiz by as if nothing had happened.

Suddenly she was looking into the face of a young, long-haired man with a scrubby blond beard. He wore a gold earring and a black leather jacket.

"You okay, Ma'm?" he asked anxiously, peering through the driver's window.

"Yeah, sure. Thank you," she answered. "I'm fine." She looked across the highway and saw a white-haired black man emerge from the passenger side of the truck, even as a small crowd of people from several cars pulled off behind him began to assemble on the median. "How's the guy in the truck?"

"Look's to me from here like he's okay," said leather man. "Maybe you ought to let me help you get off the road. It isn't safe with all these cars going by. Somebody might pile up on you."

She saw the massive Harley that leather man had parked behind her, and thanked him profusely, but declined his assistance, even as a crowd was gathering behind the shoulder of the highway. Within minutes, a state highway patrol car arrived on the scene, sirens blaring, then two or three more, and immediately afterwards an ambulance.

Two EMTs were soon examining both Terry and the truck driver, one Harold K. Washington, a 65-year-old D.C. resident and father of nine. Both accident victims appeared uninjured and refused to be taken to the hospital for further examination; Washington because he had no health insurance and couldn't afford it, and Terry because she simply declared herself to be uninjured. Neither was charged with traffic violations as the few witnesses to the accident placed the blame on the powder blue Caddy that had cut Terry off. Yet, since Terry had been struck from behind, it was probable that the truck driver would be held responsible for at least part of her repair expenses. The Civic, however, had been totaled, and replacement costs were likely to be substantial.

When Terry spoke with Mr. Washington to exchange insurance data, her heart went out to him. If any insurance claims were made against him, he said, he was certain to lose his job, which he had just started and the first one he had had in six months. Taking pity on the man, and cognizant that it was she who had, in fact, caused the collision, she told him not to worry. She wasn't going to file a claim. He could pay her back when he could afford it. Though she knew that was likely never to happen, it seemed like the right thing to do. At the time.

Americanwide Insurance thought otherwise.

The accident was from the outset economically devastating to Terry. The pains in her back, neck, head, and chest didn't start until she returned home, but when they began, accompanied by extreme fatigue and occasional slurring speech, they were brutally unceasing and almost unbearable. Soon afterwards she began to experience severe difficulties with oral communications. Like millions of other low-income Americans, she had no health insurance, and her auto insurance company, Americanwide, whose cheerful advertising jingle noted that the company "is with you all the way," proved to be anything but. Her car had been totaled, but was deemed by claims adjusters to have been worth less than a few hundred dollars before the accident. When she informed the insurance agent that there might be medical back problems resulting from the collision that needed attention, the corporate obfuscation was almost tactile. Yet, as the pain continued to increase almost daily, there was little recourse but a visit to a local doctor recommended by the insurance company, which immediately referred her to a surgeon.

The week of preliminary testing that followed was not only mind-numbing, but also expensive. The results revealed that she had suffered some thoracic and cervical spinal bruises, as well as head and brain stem trauma that might conceivably require expensive surgery to rectify. Immediate address to her injuries, however, was not imperative. All that was needed was a little rest and recuperation. At least that was what the insurance company physicians said.

Within three weeks of the accident, but before any further procedures could be undertaken, Terry's preliminary claims for medical expenses resulting from the accident were answered. Not only would she have to undergo additional medical examination by the insurance company's recommended physicians, but she would also have to be examined by a local clinical psychologist, although the reasons for such an examination were not given.

Precisely one month after the accident, Terry met with the company-recommended psychologist, a Harvard alumnus named Melvin K. Landers, PhD., in Annapolis.

"Please forgive me, Dr. Landers," Terry said after being escorted into his well-appointed office in Annapolis, off Spa Creek, "but I fail to see what a clinical psychologist has to do with my back, head, and chest injuries. Why is it necessary I see you before I can have corrective surgery?"

"Ms. Anderson, I assure you," said Landers, "it is primarily a formality required by Americanwide, which is seeking redress from the trucking company's insurers. Judging from your statements to your agent right after the crash, you were pretty well distraught, and, I understand, you have had some subsequent impairment of your speech and considerable pain. All we want to do is lay a baseline on your capabilities for withstanding what may be some pretty intensive surgical repairs. I'm certain there will be nothing to prevent the work, but it is necessary. All I intend on doing is a preliminary psychological profile particularly as it relates to your communicative capacity. Okay."

"If you say so," Terry responded with resignation, "have at it."

For the next hour Landers questioned Terry on her life history, more in line with the methodology employed by a psychiatrist searching for the darkness of motivation, cause and effect, and hidden meanings within the id. Not until the end of the examination, when he began to probe her early childhood, did mention of Ellen Chauvanne and her tragic end occur, or of Terry's recollections thereafter. When questioned about the actual murder, she at first declined to comment, saying that it was not relevant to the accident on the Beltway. Yet, after repeated and cleverly contrived queries by Landers, she relented somewhat. Then, assured by the interrogator that her response would be held in complete confidence, she told him, albeit guardedly, not only of the murders but of the strange incidents of her walk through the park following the slayings and Ellen's kiss, of seeing what she thought was her dead sister in the window of the hospital after her bicycle accident, and of the mysterious telephone calls from someone wanting to speak to Ellen during the investigation, and later again during other murder investigations. As her train of thought continued to loosen, she apprised him of the fears that had been rekindled when the Brigham-Vanderslice and Lee family murder cases erupted, and the temporary closure that came with the arrest of Bernard David Breese. She also commented, without revealing names, on the more recent trauma resulting from the ongoing Trueman investigation.

Landers although feigning a studied indifference, was excited by these new revelations, which begged further inquiry. This was no simple insurance case. It had meat and he wanted to sink his teeth into it, but, as the hour-long interview was nearing an end and he had patients in the reception room awaiting their own appointments, he was obliged to conclude the meeting. He scheduled a second for the following week.

Terry's second session would be wholly devoted to her life before, during, and after Ellen's murder. Then, following some preliminary discussion on recent events, the psychologist began to hone in on the aftermath of the crime.

"How did you cope with being alone after your sister's death?" Landers asked quietly.

"That's a big one, all right," Terry answered. "I conversed with Ellen a lot, you know, as kids, often just lying in bed talking into the night, after our parents had turned in. Still do. Not as if she's there, of course. After she was gone, I was alone in that little room that we once shared, which still smelled of her Vicks® Vaporub they used to fend off her asthma. I'll never forget that aroma. I recall Pop began to tuck me in every night after her death. He would come in to make sure the sheets and covers were just right, and he'd kiss me on the forehead. After he'd leave I prayed. I'd clasp my hands so tight that I couldn't feel them, and I prayed to God that nothing would happen to him or Mom or anybody else like it did to Ellen. I don't know, you know you, ah, you just . . ."

For a moment she lost track of what she was saying, as if a fog suddenly clouded her train of thought, and was only able to regain herself after prompting from Landers, causing some embarrassment. "After the time Ellen kissed me on the back of my neck, and after my bike accident with Betty Steiner, my outlook, my philosophy on life, I guess, was gradually cemented by my sister's spirit. Her mantra had been 'just do it,' and I adopted it lock, stock, and barrel. I realized from that point on you just do it. You just go on. You just push."

"How do you mean?"

"Not only had I adopted, I guess by osmosis, my sister's attitude towards life," Terry said, "but I was inspired a bit by Mikie O'Riley's mother."

"Just how?" Landers asked.

"After Ellen and Mikie were killed, Mrs. O'Riley tried desperately to get pregnant. I suppose to replace the daughter she had lost. Finally she did. Then, one afternoon, while I was over at their house, playing with Mikie's little sister Elaine, in the laundry room while her mother washed clothes, Mrs. O'Riley let out a horrible scream and fell to the floor. We rushed over to her, only to see a pool of dark red blood spreading from between her legs. It was horrible. It was as upsetting as seeing my sister lying there in the park with blood all over her and her pretty orchid dress."

Terry paused for a moment to regain her composure, which had begun to slip.

"But I remembered," she continued, "what she had taught me. Just do it. So I got my act together and found Mr. O'Riley, who was in the basement drinking, and he took her over to Prince George's General, in Cheverly, in his own car. She'd miscarried, but recovered quickly. Not long afterwards she got pregnant again, and had a little boy they named Chris. I once asked her what made her do it again, even though it might have killed her, and she said, 'You do what you've got to do, what the Lord God himself intended. You can never give up, even when all hope is gone.' And I believed her. I'm not so sure now."

"Do you believe the murder of your sister has otherwise affected your life?" Landers asked.

"Dr. Landers, I know you are just doing your job, but I want to remind you I am here as required by my insurance company as a formality in settling a claim for necessary medical procedures I will have to undergo resulting from an auto accident in 1991, which has nothing to do with my childhood or my sister's murder thirty-six years ago. I think you are going to have to be careful in writing your report to Americanwide, and stick to relevant issues regarding the accident. After all," she said in an uncharacteristic moment of naivety, "it seems to me that unless you stick to the nuts and bolts on medical issues, Americanwide is likely to look at your report as unacceptable. Heck, they might not even pay you!"

"Ms. Anderson, I can assure you, both Americanwide and I have only your well being at heart. I don't think you have anything to worry about, either on my behalf or yours. We are, after all, like the jingle says, 'with you all the way.'"

Unfortunately, that was not exactly true.

Landers's report to Americanwide, which Terry would not learn of for several months, completely ignored her complaints, which her previous physical examinations by the insurance company's recommended physicians expressed were clearly organic in nature. The psychologist's diagnosis of her physical discomforts, the report read, were in fact not a result of the accident, but due to "chronic pain syndrome based on guilt feelings for her murdered sister." The report was filed along with the preliminary medical exam reports, and surgery at Johns Hopkins Hospital in Baltimore was scheduled.

Without the slightest indication otherwise, Pandora's Box was reopened.

Chapter 25

TICK

A lthough she could not have known it, for Terry Chauvanne Anderson the accident on the Washington Beltway had repercussions with far more devastating consequences than the mere loss of her car. Although she had walked away from the crash on her own two feet, bravely proclaiming for all the world to hear that she was just fine, the truth was that she had suffered severe damage to her spine, which would painfully manifest in the days, weeks, and months that followed. Far worse, though, the diagnosis by Dr. Landers would influence the very course of her life.

For the next year and a half, although the police investigation of Bill Trueman's possible links to the murder of her sister had continued in fits and starts, Terry was certain that nothing would ever come of it. She knew in her heart that, although the man had a few screws loose and was morbidly obsessed with poor, dead Ellen, he had not been the one who had pulled the trigger that put a bullet through her head. She was certain the police investigation was bound to eventually peter out, and she was right on both counts.

Kenny McClennahan's long and well-written story on the unsolved murder and Bill Trueman's role in the case, which appeared under the title "The Murder That Will Not Die" in the November 24, 1991 Sunday edition of the *Washington Post*, replete with pictures of Ellen on the Eastport Bridge, the O'Riley family, Terry, Ed, and a map of the crime scene, had caused a brief furor and revivified interest. It did little, however, to forward the investigation itself. Watered down to prevent any possible lawsuit by Trueman, the story soon evaporated from the public's memory. Faced with the proverbial brick wall obstructing any further advancement in the case against the obsessed middle-aged suspect from Cheverly, the Prince George's County Police Department had quietly placed the whole file back in the cold-case mausoleum at Landover. Two years later, Charlie Bricker retired, and with him went the will to continue.

Following her meetings with Dr. Landers, while somehow still managing to attend to her aging parents, Terry had put off for nearly six months visiting another doctor regarding her increasingly troublesome pains. When medical assistance was finally sought, the problem proved far more serious than even she had anticipated. On her second visit to Johns Hopkins in Baltimore for a CT scan, she learned that she was suffering from several herniated discs and a possible cervical disarticulation. In January 1993, on the advice of Drs. John T. Barnes, Kevin Prendergast, Arlan Davies, and Quincy J. Bennett, a surgical team recommended by a friend, she underwent the first of three operations, two on the T8-9 and T9-10 sections of her spine, and another on her upper cervix, each of which would leave her worse off than before, along with medical bills amounting to well over $200,000. During the last operation, one of the surgical team, Dr. Bennett, discovered that the upper brain stem itself was severely compromised as several components of the spinal column had already begun to fuse. Two more operations were soon undertaken.

Immediately after the last surgery, Americanwide informed Terry that the company had discontinued her policy and would not honor her medical expenses. The decision, the formal letter stated, was based upon the assessment by Dr. Landers that her illness was nothing more than chronic pain syndrome based on guilt feelings for her murdered sister, to which was added an assessment that she also suffered from a histrionic personality disorder. In other words, the company claimed that, despite subsequent findings by its own recommended physicians as well as the Johns Hopkins surgeons, she was suffering from a pre-existing mental rather than a physical condition resulting from the accident. That she had walked away from the crash apparently uninjured, and had waited six months before seeking medical assistance on her own, was cited as substantiating the company's justification for voiding the contract. The strategy of the company attorneys was to turn a medical case into a psychiatric one. It was posed in such a way that, if ever taken to court, testimony relating to all intensive medical care, which did not begin for six months after the accident, would be inadmissible, and a jury could be easily swayed by the Landers assessment produced immediately following the crash.

Nevertheless, with now more than a quarter of a million dollars in medical debt hanging over her, Terry had little choice but to take legal action. Two days after receiving the formal cancellation of her policy, she engaged the Annapolis law firm of Polkowitz and Barkdale to sue. Although Landers' diagnosis would eventually be entirely discredited by esteemed Hopkins psychiatrists and neuropsychiatry specialists out of court, it would not be before ending up on Terry's permanent medical record and disseminated to all of her subsequent doctors. Moreover, unable to hold a job owing to the severe and chronic pain in her back and neck, she was forced to delay plans for law school.

As time passed, the medical bureaucracy and legal defense measures by the giant insurance corporation, seeking to avoid or delay payment for as long as possible, took its toll. Years of explaining and defending her progressive disability would be required before further essential testing to completely diagnose the extent of accident injuries and discredit the insurance company's claims would even be ordered. And as time passed, she began to slip ever deeper into a vortex of pain and suffering.

It was, on the advice of her attorney, but with considerable difficulty, countless letters, phone calls, and endless meetings with gray county, state and federal health and human resources officials and nameless bureaucrats, who Terry later noted "all looked and sounded exactly alike," that she was able to qualify for temporary public assistance. After paying a few medical (not including the massive surgical charges) and legal bills, there was little more than $150 a month left for living expenses. By the beginning of March 1994, the independent-minded middle-aged divorcee, who had driven across the United States to care for her ailing parents in their final days, was forced to move back in with them to become their total dependent.

As the days lapsed into weeks and weeks into months, Lucille Chauvanne also continued to decline, assailed by the paralysis of stroke and her worsening emphysema. Philip, weakened by his own considerable respiratory ailments, accelerating loss of mental faculties, and cardiac irregularities, had begun his own precipitous descent. Neither, however, lost an iota of the stubbornness that, through thick and thin, had accompanied them throughout their lives. Despite their difficulties in breathing, regardless of the urgings of their physicians, both refused to slack off from lifelong cigarette habits. Lucille's retort to her doctor was blunt and senseless.

"I've been smoking for sixty-five years, and I'm dying anyway, so it wouldn't make much difference if I stopped now or not, which I have no intention of doing."

On a beautiful spring day in 1994 Lucille died much in the same manner as she had lived, that is to say cursing and fighting all the way. But it was, as with most of her life, not on her own terms. Her three-paragraph obituary was terse. It reported only that she had been a State Department switchboard operator in the 1930s and '40s, a former United Givers Fund federal unit campaign coordinator, and Prince George's County election judge. She had died from emphysema on May 4 at Shady Grove Hospital, and was survived by her husband, a son and daughter. "Another daughter, Ellen Marie Chauvanne," the last words had stated blandly, "died in 1955."

Five people showed up for the funeral, all Chauvanne family members. No one wept, not even Philip. After the short ceremony, Terry walked slowly behind her father, who struggled towards their car pushing his walker before him, and helped him into the front passenger seat. On arriving home, at 3:30 p.m., both went to bed and slept dreamlessly for two days.

By the end of July, after countless visits to Johns Hopkins, Terry's physical condition had begun to degenerate even more noticeably than before. Already weak and unsteady, she began to experience tightness in her stomach and chest, frequently accompanied by strong throbbing in her mid-section, rib cage, hips, thighs, legs, and knees. On August 2, Dr. Barnes administered a nerve block and a prescription for steroids, but to no avail. Within a week it became clear that the effort had produced no positive effects and, indeed, served only to contribute to an increased weakness throughout her entire lower body. By Christmas 1994, Terry had gone through no fewer than four primary teams of physicians, none of whom had been able to provide her with relief from what was becoming a growing list of pains and symptoms. In March 1995, she underwent yet another surgical procedure, a thoracotomy to repair her herniated spine, requiring a rigid six-month period of recuperation and a specially built orthotic back and shoulder brace.

The ninety-minute drive to Baltimore, in itself, had become ever more difficult as the mechanical functions of Terry's lower body seemed to be in an alarming state of decline, despite a short period of improvement after the operation. The veritable blizzard of medical payment notices, reimbursement filings, endless phone calls to automated messaging systems, combats with various physician's offices over mounting charges, indeed, the whole complex and frustrating care system itself, only served to exacerbate the situation. And along with it went patience and trust of anyone in the medical community. Prospects seemed dim for any sort of victory in the lawsuit against the multinational giant that had once insured her. And the bills continued to mount.

Against her own inclinations, and despite her father's arguments to the contrary, Terry stubbornly resolved to continue to take care of him. By now, both were simply too frail to argue. Terry's remedy was to rent an affordable house on the Maryland Eastern Shore, in some rural community where costs were far below that of a single-bedroom apartment on the Western Shore. If the two of them were able to pool their resources, she could take on a few freelance editing jobs that she could work on out of their residence. With the additional revenue, they might just eke by until the lawsuit had been resolved. Moreover, she would again be able to house her disparate, albeit beloved, menagerie of pets, then ensconced at her brother's place, and remove his constant bellyaching regarding their maintenance.

The move was not without some advantages. Philip and Lucille had been living in their rental in the Ridgely Apartments, near Damascus, Maryland, since 1977, subsisting off Social Security, Medicare, and Philip's paltry union pension. Neither could they drive a car or leave the house unassisted. With suddenly ballooning inflation in the cost of rent, food, and especially medicine, it had become increasingly difficult for the old couple simply to survive day-to-day, even with their daughter's financial support. Now, with Lucille's death and the necessity for Terry's long-term recuperation, health and financial necessities dictated a move to a quiet, inexpensive retreat.

By early September 1995, following the removal of her back brace, Terry had located an inexpensive but quite lovely pseudo-Victorian two-story on the outskirts of the bucolic little village of Centreville, the county seat of Queen Anne's County, on Maryland's Eastern Shore. The four-bedroom, three-bath home, replete with two-car garage and a substantial lawn, was in a little suburb called Corsica Landing Estates, overlooking the Corsica River, one of the most scenic little waterways in the state, and barely a mile or so from the rustic town center. Moreover, the owner, a gregarious retired construction contractor named Brian Dean, immediately hit it off with Philip, and was willing to provide a two-year lease at an extremely favorable price, $1,200 a month. It seemed the perfect answer, and the possibility of subletting out a room or two to students from nearby Chesapeake College only added to the prospects.

With considerable physical difficulty, Terry superintended the move, and managed all the logistical and legal details. At the end of the month, she and her father became the newest residents of a little byway called Quail Lane, on a scenic slope overlooking the idyllic Corsica. Celebrating with inexpensive champagne, which Philip drank between taking gulps of oxygen from his portable tank, Terry called for a toast. With a wan smile, Philip raised his glass towards his daughter, and said quietly, "Till death do us part."

Precisely two weeks after father and daughter had moved into their new home, an extremely tiny eight-legged parasitic arachnid attached itself to Theresa Anderson's near-deaf cocker spaniel, Tuffy, and from there transferred unseen to Terry's slacks as she slowly walked her several dogs down by the river, near the intersection of Quail and Dove lanes. The creature, just evolving from its larval state, was a fourteen-day-old juvenile and almost microscopic, so small in fact that it would be barely visible on one's fingernail. It was almost impossible to notice as it slowly worked its way from her pants leg onto her ankle. Its scientific name, *Ixodes scapularis*, commonly known as the deer tick, was frequently mistaken for another little insect of similar appearance called *Ixodes dammini*. Its preferred habitat was in wooded areas, low-lying grasslands, seashores, wetlands, and yards, indeed throughout much of temperate North America. Its life cycle, the time it took to evolve from a single egg to adult tick, was almost two years. And it could be found year round, particularly along grassy waterfronts like the edge of the Corsica.

Terry did not feel the tick's bite; the pinhead-sized vampire first numbed the patch of skin on her ankle from which it then sucked her blood. She did not feel the syrupy tick saliva being injected into the microscopic wound to keep the blood flowing. Several days later she hardly noticed the near circular reddish discoloration that had formed around her ankle. Neither would she be aware for years of the bacterium, the infectious spirochetes, called *Borrelia burgdorfen*, which were transmitted unseen and unfelt into her system. Nor had she heard of the horrific malady that the tick had vectored into her body, a malady as murderous as a Revelation bullet: Lyme disease.

The move to Centreville, ticks notwithstanding, had been a wise one, for the rural environment overlooking the little Corsica had provided a psychological boost both Terry and her father needed. Both seemed to be improving in their health and stamina. Within weeks of moving into the house on Quail Lane, Terry felt strong enough to apply for a position with the Queen Anne's County school system as a substitute teacher, K through 12, and was immediately accepted. At the same time, she began sending out resumes to regional publishing houses, and commenced freelance editing and proofreading for a small publishing establishment directly across the Corsica, within viewing range of her house. Although she had taken out a loan earlier, using her father's pension fund as collateral, to purchase a used car, another Honda, for transportation, everything seemed to be going right for once. That is, until she received a letter from her attorney, Joe Polkowitz. Unfortunately the official missive, dated September 9, 1995, had sat unopened for a week in a pile of mail her father had plopped on top of the refrigerator. Terry's hands began to tremble as she read it.

"Dear Ms. Anderson:

As you know, I have been in continuous negotiations with Dr. Charlotte Delon, lead attorney for the Americanwide Insurance Company, regarding settlement of your claims. I was formally notified this morning that Dr. Delon's client has made a final offer of $45,000. With due consideration of your current fiscal status, or prospects for an improvement of your situation, I strongly suggest that you accept the offer, as an appeal would only increase your already substantial legal expenses.

I fully appreciate your feelings that there is not enough money to compensate you for the horrendous injustice inflicted upon you by Americanwide. However, since it appears that we're fighting over a $45,000.00 PIP claim as well as the possibility of some foreseeable damages for the failure to pay the contracted PIP proceeds and family compensation benefits, it may be wise to settle. As I have continuously related to you, the foreseeable damages in contract are being vehemently opposed by Americanwide. The attorney for Americanwide refused to even discuss those damages. Americanwide has consistently taken the position that they will oppose and forever more oppose those types of damages arising out of the contract. Although Judge Horn has allowed consideration of those damages up to this point, in the case, he has demonstrated in the past that he does change his mind on his rulings. I am afraid that since the law is not strong in these regards in Maryland he may very well reverse his previous rulings.

I look forward to your decision.

Sincerely,

Joseph S. Polkowitz, LLD."

Terry felt drained of everything. All of the forward motion of the previous weeks, and the prospect for removing the massive medical debt load that had accumulated over the last few years had been for naught. She was well aware that after her attorneys had taken their share of the settlement, she would have less than $25,000 to see her through, or to begin to repay the quarter million she still owed the myriad doctors, hospitals, and caregivers who had attended her since the accident.

The letter proved to be a definitive benchmark in Terry's life, for what was to follow would become as tragic as the murder of her sister four decades earlier, and would eventually become as one with it.

The only reasonably good news was a short article in *The New York Times* concerning the death of Bernard David Breese, the ill-famed "Sex Beast" serial killer convicted for the 1957 Margaret Henry and 1959 Lee family murders, whom police once believed to have been responsible for the Chauvanne-O'Riley and Brigham-Vanderslice killings. The one-time jazz musician had finally suffered a painful heart failure after more than three decades of imprisonment.

Sadly, the existential sadist killer, who believed in living only for the moment, with moral concerns of no weight beside the extremes of raw sexual violence would, over the coming years, gain a sick following of sorts. One macabre lyricists named Dale Dile, was even reported to have written a song called Scarlet Concert, based upon "his favorite serial killer, David Breese," composed as an "elegy to strange behavior." The three-minute ditty was said to have described slit throats, violins polished with "human butchery," and a grisly craving for human suffering.

On February 14, 1996, her forty-eighth birthday, Terry again drove to Johns Hopkins for an appointment with one Dr. Matthew Amatucci, a leading American neurosurgeon, to begin a new round of treatments. This time the array of weapons intended to address her ailments included opioid therapy for her intractable right thoracic pain, treatment for suspected post-thoracotomy syndrome resulting from the earlier failed surgical attempts, and a neurectomy of her T-8 vertebrae to relieve the pain and pressure in her back and at the base of her skull, and to address recurrent cervical pain, headaches and migraines. After a concurrent psychological examination, which deemed her "a non-addictive personality," she was placed, following the surgical procedures, on a regimen of MS Contin, an opiate, which was soon replaced with Oxycontin, a narcotic analgesic, in increasingly higher dosages, which soon began to impair her cognitive abilities.

Three days after the final operation, and yet another battery of blood and tissue tests, she was informed in an almost nonchalant manner, as if it were little more than a minor condition, that she had also contracted Lyme disease.

"Not to worry," Dr. Amatucci said. "It's just a minor problem caused by a tick bite, and I can assure you it is easily cured."

Nothing could have been further from the truth.

Chapter 26

NORTH POLE

To suggest that the phone call, logged in at Prince George's County Police Headquarters, in Landover, at precisely 2:00 p.m. on January 23, 1997, came as a surprise would be an understatement. The woman on the caller end of the line identified herself only as Kitty, and requested the desk officer, 21-year-old Private LaMar D. Washington, to connect her to whoever was in charge of the Homicide Department.

"Ma'am, could you tell me the nature of your call?" the desk officer asked.

"I want to provide some information on a murder in Northwest Branch Park," said the woman, "but I don't want to speak with some sergeant. Please hook me up with the officer in charge."

With promptitude, the caller was transferred to Lieutenant Marvin McQueen, Jr., the new head of Homicide.

On this particularly cold rainy day, McQueen was not in a mood for receiving crank calls, especially now. Being a single divorcee, he had voluntarily missed both Christmas and New Years celebrations to fill in for some of his married officers who could then take holiday leave. And owing to an uptick in homicides over the last few weeks he had been home only sparingly and hadn't seen his family or his girlfriend in eons. No one but some office staff had even bothered to give him a Christmas present. If anyone had an excuse to be dour, it was Marvin McQueen. Yet the caller had mentioned Northwest Branch Park to the desk officer and the accompanying adrenalin rush told him to receive this one.

Two months earlier, on November 20, 1996, the body of a murdered 14-year-old African-American girl named Taisha Bowers had been found in a wooded area in the park, just south of Northwestern High School. There were no clues, no arrests. Community outrage and the resultant press coverage had brought enormous pressure on the department to find the killer as soon as possible. In a county now experiencing 250-plus homicides a year, most being gang and drug-related and many of which were spillovers from D.C., such demands were easier voiced than solved. For the most part the public had been hardened by such daily statistics, but the Bowers case had touched a nerve.

Picking up the phone, the officer said brusquely: "This is Lieutenant McQueen. To whom am I speaking?"

"For the moment you can just call me Kitty. You the man in charge?" queried the voice from the other end.

"Yes, ma'm. I am told you want to discuss a murder in Northwest Branch Park. May I ask if it relates to the Bowers case?"

"No. And you needn't try tracing this call. I'm in a phone booth a million miles away and using a calling card."

"Okay. Then to which case are you referring?" McQueen asked.

"The 1955 Chauvanne-O'Riley murders," Kitty answered.

The hair on McQueen's neck stood up as he recalled the Trueman interviews nearly ten years earlier. His late father, Sergeant Marvin McQueen, Sr., had been a rookie on the force during the first furtive search for the Chauvanne-O'Riley killer, and participated in the hunt for the Sex Beast Killer, Bernard David Breese, who had at one time been his best friend. And immediately before he was killed in the line of duty during a shoot-out in Capitol Heights, he had been involved in the Trueman investigation. The irony did not escape Detective McQueen. "That case is forty-five years old. How can you assist us with that old chestnut?"

"Easy," said the caller, "I was married to one of the killers."

The lieutenant said nothing for a moment as he tried desperately to summon details on the case from the recesses of his brain, even as he scribbled a message on a notepad and handed it to an aide.

"Detective McQueen," said the caller, "I can tell you everything you need to know about the murder of Ellen Marie Chauvanne and Mikie O'Riley on June 15, 1955. I can tell you who did it, precisely how it was done, and why."

Again recalling the abortive wild goose chase his predecessor, Charlie Bricker, who retired just two years before, had once endured, McQueen responded guardedly. "Why are you telling us now? And how do I know what you have to say is true? What's in it for you?"

"I knew you would ask that. I read all about that nutcase Trueman in the *Washington Post* in '91, and if you will hear me out, I can assure you will find I'm no Trueman. For starters, let me tell you something that was never public knowledge. Something to convince you I know what I am talking about."

"Which is . . .?"

"For starters, the Chauvanne girl was shot in the back of the head while lying on her stomach. The killer turned the body over after he had finished with her, which both you and I know, but the public, to this day, thinks she was shot in the forehead while on her back."

"Pretty good," McQueen said, "but somehow even Trueman knew that."

"Yeah, but he didn't know that it wasn't your clever detective work that found most of the bullets, but an informant, my husband, who phoned in their location to you. And his brother, the one who pulled the trigger, called the Chauvannes and O'Rileys every so often for several weeks afterwards asking to speak to the dead Chauvanne girl just to keep them on edge."

"Okay, Kitty. You have my full attention," said McQueen. "Where do we go from here?"

"I want a trade," Kitty answered. "I want you to call off the Feds, the FBI, who've been on my ass for years. I need protection from prosecution for a few petty offences. In return, I will tell you more about the Chauvanne-O'Riley murders than you ever thought existed. It will help you close the books on it forever."

At that moment several officers entered the room, including Chief of Police John J. Farrell and Sergeant Nathaniel "Nate" Snope, the lead detective in the special cold case unit, only recently formed in the department. Snope quietly handed the lieutenant a note. "The call," it read, "is being made from North Pole, Alaska, probably from a phone booth."

McQueen put his hand over the telephone mouthpiece and whispered to Snope, "You're kidding!"

The sergeant smiled, just shaking his head from side-to-side.

"I can't promise you anything, Kitty," said McQueen resuming the conversation with the caller, while at the same time signaling Snope to switch on the speakerphone. "Why are the Feds after you, and what kind of a deal are you looking for?"

"My husband Johnny and I have been, shall we say, touring the country for the last few years with a few arrest warrants trailing behind us."

"For what?" asked McQueen.

"Name it!" she answered, almost as if bragging. "Fraud, auto theft, forgery, interstate trafficking, and a few others. Let's just say, after I married Johnny in 1972, our lives have been fraught with more than a fair share of difficulties. I should have known that would be the case when I first met the bastard and his brother. Three years ago Johnny was indicted on an insurance fraud charge and we bolted. Been hopping around ever since." There was a muffled sob. "Johnny died of cancer last June in San Antonio and I don't think I can hold out any longer. I need to make a deal. Now. I'm 57 years old and can't keep running. And I don't want to spend what's left of my fucking life in some stinking cell."

The three officers looked at each other blankly.

"I don't know if we can arrange anything," McQueen said, "but if what you say is true about the cold case, I think there is a good chance we might be able to help lighten some of the weight. But you have to come clean and tell us who and where you are. We can't deal with a ghost."

"You have been for years," Kitty answered. "You just didn't know it. I'll call you next week at this same time. Let me know what the Feds will agree to."

"Can I bank on that, Kitty?" asked McQueen quietly.

"Absolutely." Then she added, almost as if an afterthought before hanging up, "Oh, by the way, my name is Kitty Dubinski. And if you don't already know it, I'm in one of the four phone booths in a miserable little burg called North Pole, Alaska, right outside the gates of Eilson Air Force Base. But I can assure you, I won't be here for long, so don't bother trying to send someone."

"Well, well, well," said McQueen, smiling as he put down the phone. "Santa's given me a belated Christmas present after all, named Kitty Dubinski. And I surmise that she is either not too bright, having given us her name and current location, or terribly, terribly desperate."

Within a half hour of Kitty Dubinski's call, the Prince George's County Police Department had informed the Federal Bureau of Investigation not only of the origins of the call, but also of the caller's overture to leverage information about a long-standing cold case into some form of deal regarding protection from prosecution. Within six hours, Kitty Dubinski was taken into custody while waiting at Fairbanks International Airport for an Air Alaska flight to Seward, with a connecting ticket to Los Angeles. Within twenty-four hours, Sergeant Nate Snope of the Prince George's County Police Department, and two federal agents, were on a plane en route to Alaska, where they would begin to interview Dubinski at the substantial Fairbanks City Police Department, on 10th Avenue and Cushman Street, in downtown Fairbanks.

On the morning of January 25, Snope and several FBI agents convened to discuss strategy before commencing with the interrogation. Snope was given a background briefing on the outstanding federal and various state charges, primarily against Dubinski's late husband John, but for which Kitty was being held as an accomplice. John's rap sheet was indeed extensive, beginning with his first incarceration at age fifteen, in 1956, at a juvenile detention center in southern Prince George's, for attempted auto theft up-county in Riverdale, Maryland. His schoolmates had described him as a "gangster-type" kid who rarely associated with anyone but his three brothers, also reported as thuggish, and all of whom had been in constant trouble.

Soon after his release from the detention center the whole family moved to Hollywood, Florida, north of Miami. John had quit school and left home at sixteen, making a living at petty crime and then graduating into more sophisticated grifting. His arrest record grew in proportion to his age, albeit with few convictions, as he moved from state to state. In 1972, while drifting through a dead-end Texas town called Pflugerville, north of Austin, he had met Gertrude "Kitty" Eisenhauer, a waitress in a saloon, and the daughter of a local immigrant German dirt farmer. Within two days John and Kitty had married, both for different purposes, one to escape loneliness and the other to escape Pflugerville. Both would be on the run for the rest of their lives.

Two years later, in October 1974, Kitty became pregnant while the couple was in the midst of working an insurance scam in Mufreesboro, Tennessee, which, unfortunately for them, had been nipped in the bud before it could be completed. Barely avoiding arrest, they had fled to the only temporary safe haven John could think of, his brother Teddy's place in Hollywood, Florida. They had remained with Teddy until Kitty gave birth to a son, named Roland Theodore, at Miami General on a hot July day in 1975. Less than a week later, John, Kitty, and baby Roland had been obliged to flee to Atlanta to escape arrest on a felony drug charge against John. For the next decade, the family had been on the fly, never staying longer than six months in one place, and always one step ahead of the law.

A Fairbanks City Police Detective named Swenson had been the arresting officer who had picked up Kitty as she awaited her flight at the airport. As federal warrants had yet to arrive, she was booked at headquarters on a charge of transporting an illegal substance, two marijuana cigarettes that had been found in her cosmetic case, to hold her.

Snope examined the long list of criminal felony charges, in six states, against John and several accessory charges against Kitty and smiled.

"Gentlemen," he said to all the federal agents in the room, but to no one in particular, "I think we have a live one here. Maybe, if we're lucky, she can help us put a few old dead ones to rest."

Chapter 27

STEP BY STEP

Kitty Dubinski had once been an attractive woman. The years, however, had not been charitable. Nor had her own attention to her appearance and health. What had once been a bounty of beautiful blond hair was now almost orange scruffy wool with a pincushion of loose ends projecting in every direction. Dental work had not been in the cards for drifters like her and her teeth, many of them chipped, were yellowed from a three-pack-a-day smoking habit begun at fifteen when she had run away from home to take on the world single-handedly. Her once crystal blue eyes were bloodshot and surrounded by a sea of dark sagging skin in a face that still bore the strong Germanic features inherited from her father.

Now, as she sat in the dreary gray interrogation room in the Fairbanks City Jail, wearing an orange prison jumpsuit, and slight indentations in her wrists from a recently removed bracelet of handcuffs, she appeared to be little more than another vagrant bag lady who had lost her push cart full of newspapers and rags and with it her life. An aura of resignation and indifference, invisible but omnipresent, was obvious to the several officers who had gathered to question her, including Sergeant Snope, Detective Swenson of the Fairbanks Police Department, an FBI Agent named McKinley, and a youthful, buttoned-down attorney named Antony Spiring appointed to defend her. Everyone chuckled as the attorney handed out his business card that read: "A. Spiring. Attorney at Law."

"Mrs. Dubinski," Agent McKinley began, "I have to say it's a pleasure to finally meet you face to face. I've been running after you and Johnny for years. Sorry to hear that Johnny isn't here to enjoy the party."

"I wouldn't be here now," she retorted angrily, "if that rat bastard in Maryland hadn't double-crossed me when he said he would try to negotiate a deal, but I'm glad for Johnny that he ain't here to meet the likes of you folks."

Snope offered Kitty a cigarette, which she jumped at, having not enjoyed a smoke in nearly a day. Taking it between two nicotine-stained fingertips, she cupped the cylinder with both hands as he gave her a light. He noticed her nails were chipped and dirty, and her hands, with countless veins showing close to the surface, were mottled with age spots and old needle tracks.

"Look, Mrs. Dubinski," McKinley said, "you have a lifetime of stories to tell us, which, I am sure will help clear up a lot regarding Johnny's criminal activities over the years. And, as you and we all know, most of the time you were just along for the ride. We can make it easy for you, or we can make it hard. Unless you help us now, there is a long list of charges that we can easily nail you on as an accomplice if not chief instigator. Cooperate and we'll do everything we can to help you. Your record indicates you've been in jail several times, and I know, at your age, you don't want to end up with what's left of your life in one."

The old woman began to sob quietly.

Spiring chimed in. "Gentlemen. We all know that my client is being held here, pending charges yet to be filed in court, on a pretty slim allegation. Come on! Two reefers in a 57-year-old woman's cosmetic bag. That's a plant if there ever was one."

Swenson glared at the young attorney. "This woman's husband was wanted in six states, from Florida to Nevada to Alaska, and she has been an accomplice in I don't know how many swindles over thirty years, including a few we think she is implicated in here. Take a look at the needle marks on her wrist, her arms, between her toes. Don't give me that shit about planted evidence."

For the next five minutes the attorney and Swenson exchanged barbs as the FBI agent looked on with amusement, reminding himself of just how common such amateurish exchanges were in the backwoods of America.

Kitty took a long drag on her cigarette, and then interceded.

"Listen. I don't have a lot to be proud of in my life. I do have a fine son, Rolly, who, despite his parents, has made a decent life for himself. Joined the Air Force, got married to a nice girl, and has two great kids, my grandchildren whom I've seen only twice in my life. He's the reason I'm here in this godforsaken place."

"Why's that?" McKinley queried.

"He's stationed at the airbase, got a house outside, and I thought I could stay with him for a bit while things cooled down in the Lower 48. I figured with Johnny dying down in San Antonio, the heat would eventually disappear. No one, I thought, would ever bother to hunt me up, for god's sake, in North Pole, Alaska. I'm not worth the trouble, but I was obviously wrong."

"Then, why did you bother making the call to Maryland in the first place?" Snope asked.

"For two reasons. One, was to do the only good deed I've done in my life, to honor the wishes of a dying man. And two, to save my own fucking skin."

"So you made some sort of pledge to Johnny?" McKinley asked.

"No. To his brother Teddy."

"Well," Snope said, "here we are. And like they say, there's no time like the present. We're all ears."

"Kitty, I would advise against . . ." Spiring said, before being cut off by his client in mid-sentence.

"Johnny always told me, one, never trust a cop or a lawyer. And two, do what you need to do, right or wrong. I've got nothing more to lose now. So, Mr. Spiring, please shut up."

At that, for the next three hours, in a dismal interrogation room in Fairbanks, Alaska, Kitty Marie Dubinski narrated the 45-year odyssey of two killers and their horrific crime on the other side of the North American continent that no one, least of all Nate Snope of the Prince George's County Police, had ever expected to hear.

"I first met Johnny Dubinski when I was waiting tables in a bar in a cesspool of a Texas town called Pflugerville. He was tall, good looking, had wavy hair, and a sexy voice. He was smooth as silk and could charm the skin off a rattlesnake. He was just passing through, but from the moment I served him, I was smitten. I didn't care what he did for a living, I just wanted to be with him and, I 'spose, I was pretty desperate. I suppose I was just looking for anything better than what I had, which was nothing. And he looked like a ticket out."

"Did you know he was on the run from the law at the time?" McKinley questioned.

"He told me some guys were after him. And I guess, like a lot of girls, I found myself attracted to handsome outlaw types, you know, the whole James Dean bad boy persona thing. At the time, I was still very young and stupid. He was tall, lean, mean, and sexy. Didn't take shit from anybody and treated me like I was a princess. And like Johnny Cash used to sing, 'We got married in a fever, hotter than a pepper sprout,' a day or two after we met, and immediately left town. Hardly ever stopped moving since. You guys got his rap sheet, so you can reconstruct things afterwards on your own."

"You're probably right," McKinley said, "but we'd like for you to give us a blow by blow anyway."

"Why don't we start with the Chauvanne-O'Riley murders?" Snope suggested.

"Okay by me," said Kitty. "Kill's two birds with one stone. No pun intended. Could I first have another cigarette?"

After lighting up and taking a long slow drag, hacking out a smoker's cough, and then taking another deep one, Kitty began the odyssey.

"Johnny was the youngest of the four Dubinski boys. The oldest was George, then came Robby, then Teddy, and finally Johnny. All except Johnny had been born in Poland during the '30s, but the family had escaped before Hitler invaded. Their old man, Alexander, always told people he was a builder and landscaper, but from what I could see he was really nothing more than a grocery clerk. Their old lady—we called her Helena, but I never knew her real name—was a stay-at-home wife. Never really saw much of her. They were a pretty nasty bunch, especially the old man. Punched poor Helena around a lot, so I guess she sorta stayed in the shadows for her own good."

"Did the old man hit on the boys often?" Snope asked.

"Sure. That is until they were pretty much his size. At least that's what Johnny told me. All of 'em were tall, and all of the boys had an uncanny resemblance to their father. You'd of thought all five of 'em, pop and his sons, were all brothers when they was growed. I never met any of 'em except Johnny until we moved in with Teddy for a while in Florida where they was all clustered together like bees. Unlike the rest of them, Teddy had a steady job at a local Sealtest Ice Cream processing plant in Miami. It didn't pay much, but he always had some side money book making, so he was doing okay, 'cept for his drinking and drug problem. Johnny told me that Teddy had always been a little light in the head and sometimes didn't see things the way others did. He'd been married since 1961 to a Cuban ex-pat named Roberta Clemente, and had three kids by her, but by '71, the year before we arrived, she'd already divorced him. The Dubinski boys were a pretty rowdy bunch, drinking and gambling a lot, in trouble all the time, but they stuck together like superglue. Kinda like a Polish Mafia. Mess with one and you were messing with 'em all. The meanest was Teddy, who was three years older than Johnny, but for some reason I liked him best of all. I don't know why, but he was always real nice to me. I was pretty good looking then and I think he had a boner for me, but respected his brother too much to make a pass. Or maybe it was because him and Johnny were the tightest of the lot. If there wasn't three years between them you'd of thought they was identical twins."

"What does this all have to do with the murders?" Agent McKinley asked. "Where are you going with this?"

"Just hold them custom-made federal britches and I'll get to that," Kitty answered. "After we left Florida, we didn't see much of Teddy or any of the others. Old man Dubinski died about 1980 or '81, and Helena followed a few years later. We saw Teddy at the funerals, and maybe three or four times later, but that's about it. But Johnny and Teddy stayed in constant contact by phone, almost every week. Then, in early 1991, while we were, shall we say, staying with friends in San Antonio, Teddy calls Johnny and says that he's in a care facility in Miami. Had liver cancer and wanted to see us before it was too late. Johnny about lost it. Then Teddy adds that he's got something very important to tell me. So we grab some luggage and clothes and drive halfway across the country. Sad thing is that at the same time, Johnny had liver cancer too but didn't know it. I guess it was because they were, like I said, almost like identical twins though three years apart. Whatever happens to one happens to the other."

"Where and when did you finally see Teddy for the last time?" Snope queried.

"April 15, 1991. Tax day. I remember it well. When we arrived at the Chestnut Hill Hospice, off Palm Avenue, near Hialeah Race Track, we found him in a deplorable state. You know, he asked to be put in that damned place because it was so near the track, and he loved the horses. Lost a fortune on 'em, too. Only thing he liked better was to go bass fishing in the Everglades, but, if you ask me, the care they gave him at that shit-hole of a hospice sucked."

"Anyway, after Johnny and Teddy spent a minute or two together, Teddy asks Johnny to leave the room so's he can talk to me in private. Says he's got something very, very important to tell me. That's when I learned that him and Johnny weren't just a couple of grifters. They were also killers."

For a moment it seemed the silence could be cut with a knife. No one spoke, as Kitty's forefinger slowly tipped off a quarter inch of ashes from her cigarette into a garish green ashtray.

"You see," she continued, "tough as he was, Teddy was a devout Catholic and still had a conscience. He pulled me pretty close so's I could hear him. Then he told me he had something he had to get off his chest, something he'd been carrying around since he was a kid. He said he wasn't scared of dying, but he was terribly afraid of spending eternity in hell. He never told his story to a priest at Confession, 'cause he didn't just want forgiveness from the Lord. He wanted it from the victims of the horrible crime he had committed. Given that they were dead that was kinda hard to get. But you have to understand that by this time in his life Teddy, like Johnny, was pretty much messed up by all the years of booze and drugs. Difference was, Teddy couldn't tell what was real and what was in his head."

"What, precisely, did he tell you?" McKinley asked.

"First he held my hand and made me swear that I wouldn't breath a word of what he was going to tell me until both him and Johnny were dead. Then he told me that what he was about to say would be like money in the bank for me if I ever fell in with you guys after him and Johnny were gone. Said he loved me like the sister he never had, and that I was the only woman who'd ever been good to him. He then instructed me to not only listen to what he had to say, but to take notes, memorize them, and then destroy them. The information he was about to give me was so important, he said, that it could be used as a huge bargaining chip with the law if I was ever facing the prospect of jail time, and that when I learned what it was that I would understand. And when he told me, it sent a cold chill up my spine, and I understood. And I did just what he told me to do. I took notes, memorized them, and destroyed it all."

"So what we've got is your word on the murders that he allegedly committed," Snope said, "presumably being passed on to us just as Teddy told you!"

"Yeah, I guess you could say that," Kitty declared matter-of-factly. "In the summer of 1955 Johnny and Teddy had moved with the whole family from Scranton, Pennsylvania, to Hyattsville, Maryland. Teddy was 17, a sophomore in Northwestern High, and Johnny was 14 in junior high. Neither of the boys were very popular in school, Teddy because he was a bit slow, a year or two behind his age group in school, and Johnny because he was always... Well, let's just say, he was Johnny. But they all had very slight accents then, 'cept Teddy for some reason, and were obviously different from the rest of the kids. It wasn't that they didn't try to fit in, they just didn't.

"Johnny had been given a .22 Marlin squirrel rifle at Christmas in 1954 just before the family moved from Scranton. The old man was an avid gun collector and had everything from old Colt six-shooters like you see in westerns to German souvenirs he had picked up during the war. He always had at least one relic pistol with him. Loved to show off with them. Once, a few days before the killings, he even ran into the Chauvanne girl's little brother and some other kid in the park. They were carrying BB-guns and when he stopped to talk to them, thinking they were of like mind, he scared the shit out of 'em. He had once encouraged Johnny to join the Northwestern High School Rifle Club, but there was an age requirement. When they found out how old he was, he was booted out, which old man Dubinski, typically, attributed to some fault in his son and smacked him around a bit. About that same time, at Helena's urging, Teddy had joined the Lewisdale Teen Club, but never fit in and usually found himself sitting in the corner at the dances every Saturday night. Like a lot of teenagers, though he was a good-looking boy, his face was covered with pimples, which made him even more introverted.

Teddy was in Ellen Chauvanne's classes, and, according to him, she was the prettiest girl in school, and he developed an enormous crush on her. He worshipped her from afar. Now, when you take a big — I mean nearly six footer — healthy, shy 17-year-old, stir in a few hormones, add some teenage angst, and a heavy dose of rejection, you can create a pretty nasty kid. He was actually a shy boy, but compensated by being obnoxious and sometimes outright mean, with language to match. Both him and Johnny got to be pretty rotten bullies, which only served to distance themselves from everyone even more."

"Was that their motivation for the crime?" Snope asked.

Kitty leaned forward, her hands clasped together.

"You know how kids form cliques? Well, at the teen club, sweet-ass Ellen was queen bee, and held her court every Saturday night. According to Teddy, she surrounded herself with a bunch of toadies. Everyone there who wasn't in "the group" simply didn't count. At the dance on the Saturday night a few days before the murders, Teddy had screwed up his courage to ask Ellen for a dance. He had planned it for weeks and even dressed up for the occasion with a white shirt and tie, which he never did before. He began working up to it by flirting with her across the room, even though she was surrounded by her groupies, including her best friend, Mikie O'Riley, and some kid named Combs, who was kinda her boyfriend of the moment."

"So how did she react?" McKinley questioned.

"How do you think?" answered Kitty. "It was a power thing, if you ask me. She crushed him like a maggot right there in front of everyone. Called him a pimple-faced retard. A Pollock idiot. Right there in front of everyone. And they all laughed. It humiliated him so badly that he fled in tears."

The three law enforcement officers all squirmed in their seats, and almost as if on signal shook their heads from side to side.

"When he got home, he couldn't eat or sleep, and the rage grew inside of him to such an intensity that he could hardly bear it. He certainly couldn't confide in his parents, and was afraid what his older brothers would say. You know, those boys were all pretty hard on each other when it came to the macho thing. They were unrelenting. But Johnny was different in that way. He was always the schemer. When Teddy told him what had happened, Johnny just said, 'If I was you I'd get even.'"

Snope glanced out of the triple pane security window and saw that it was beginning to snow. "I think it's time to take a break," he suggested. "I think Mrs. Dubinski here could use a breather and a cup of coffee too."

Fifteen minutes later the three officers and their prisoner reconvened in the interrogation room. By now what had started out as a light snowfall had turned into a blizzard.

"I suspect we will be here for a while," Detective Swenson noted. "We should have plenty of time for the rest of Mrs. Dubinski's story. Or should I say, Teddy Dubinski's story."

Again they sat at the table, all a bit more relaxed than before.

"Mrs. Dubinski," McKinley began, "we left off with your husband suggesting to Teddy that he get even with Ellen for the humiliation he had suffered. What happened then?"

"Johnny, though he was younger, had usually been the lead when the two of them were together. And he was this time as well. When Teddy asked him how he suggested he might even the score, Johnny told him they ought to surprise Ellen. Ambush her from some hiding place with slingshots sometime when she was alone, maybe while walking to school. As they both got excited by the idea, it escalated from slingshots to BB-guns, and finally to Johnny's .22. At first, Teddy told me, they only intended on scaring her. They lived only four or five blocks from the park, and knew she walked through every day to school. What they didn't know was that she wouldn't be alone."

"And it all got out of hand," Snope interjected.

"I guess you could say that," Kitty replied. "They laid out a pretty elaborate plan. Teddy told his parents he was invited to go camping in the park with some other kids on the night of June 14. He would tell his parents that he would go to school from there the next morning. Johnny would smuggle his .22 out of the house a day earlier and hide it in an unfinished apartment over in a new development called Langley Park, which was then still under construction. After school Teddy would take his rolled up camping gear, you know, bedroll, canteen, belt knife, and such, and head for the park. But first he would double back to Langley Park to pick up the rifle, and then cut across a construction project on University Lane to the north end of the park, and that evening camp out there near the bridge. The next morning, Johnny would leave for school as usual, but instead would join his brother in the park. In the morning when Chauvanne was prancing through, Teddy could have his revenge. You know, scare the hell out of her from some hiding place where she couldn't see them. Then the boys would split up, and Teddy would hide the gun back at Langley Park, hightail it back to the school, and both would attend the last day of school as if nothing happened."

"Sounds like they had worked it all out," Snope said.

"Not quite," Kitty retorted. "Everything seemed to go as planned until after Teddy had picked up the gun and was cutting across the construction project the afternoon before the big day. He had his bedroll strapped around him, and was carrying the rifle under his arm. That's when he was spotted by Ellen's uncle, who was working there."

"You mean Henry Chauvanne?" McKinley asked.

"Yes."

"And thus was born the 'Pancho Villa' story," McKinley said with an 'Aha' sort of smile.

"Teddy spent the night in the park, trying to stay hidden from four teenagers, two guys and their girlfriends, who came in after sunset to make out. He said he watched 'em going at it pretty heavy on a park bench they had moved, you know, to keep out of sight of cars passing up on the road. He had a can of "Kipper Snacks" and a pack of Hostess Twinkies for dinner, but didn't sleep much. He told me the sound of the frogs croaking in the water near the bridge kept him awake most of the evening. Said it felt like they were telling him to go home and forget the whole thing. But he kept telling himself throughout the night that he could do this thing. And by early morning, when Johnny finally showed up, he had convinced himself he was gonna see it through no matter what."

"What time did Johnny meet Teddy?" Agent McKinley asked.

"I don't know, but it wasn't much before the girls started through the park. Teddy had picked a spot on the bridge approach, behind a cherry tree that had a good crook in one of the low branches to rest the rifle. Both he and Johnny, thanks to their dad, were excellent marksmen. When the girls came walking down the path towards the bridge, Teddy called out Ellen's name. Her and the O'Riley girl stopped in their tracks and apparently, having just come out of the sunlight, couldn't clearly make out either Teddy or Johnny, who were standing in the shade."

"Did they say anything to each other before he started shooting?" Snope asked.

"The Chauvanne girl must have recognized Teddy's voice, because she said something like, 'What the hell do you want, Dubinski?' And he responded by telling her to say she was sorry for what she had said at the dance."

Kitty's eyes began to get puffy and red as tears started to form. "She said—and Teddy was very clear when he told me this— 'Kiss my ass, you dumb, pimple-faced Pollock.' The O'Riley girl, mimicking Chauvanne, added her own insults, calling the whole Dubinski family a bunch of retards. Like I said, Teddy had intended only on scaring the Chauvanne girl a bit with a few shots around her, but then he really saw red, and started peeling off shots aimed right at her. The O'Riley girl, who had unexpectedly showed up with Chauvanne, was an afterthought, but when he started ripping shots into one he couldn't let the other go."

Wiping her eyes, Kitty asked to hold off for a minute, but then signaled she was ready to resume.

"Can you tell us what happened then?" Snope asked.

Kitty then responded with a blow-by-blow, bullet-by-bullet description of the gruesome event that followed, including the hasty efforts to camouflage the bodies, the discovery that Ellen was not quite dead, and the grisly coup de grace. The details fit precisely with the comprehensive reconstruction of the crime forty-six years earlier by the Prince George's County Police through tireless fieldwork and forensic analysis. The account Kitty had produced had also answered a few mysteries that had gone unresolved on just how the killers had escaped. "I ought to tell you that the gun wasn't a semi-automatic of any kind like you guys said, just a common old squirrel rifle. But both Teddy and Johnny were very good with it—and fast."

"There were a number of sightings of a single guy carrying a gun, bandolier, and so forth," Snope noted, looking squarely into Kitty's now quite puffy face. "You know, the Pancho Villa character, both in the park, leaving the park, and elsewhere with a substantial time difference relative to the actual time of the murder. There was also a sighting of a boy carrying a gun, walking down University Lane. Did Teddy have anything to say about that?"

Kitty sighed. "How about another smoke?"

"You're gonna die of cancer, too, if you don't watch it," said Snope with a grimace.

"I don't think I'm going to last that long," Kitty responded, before continuing her narrative.

"After they had finished with the girls," she resumed, "Johnny said something — I don't know what — joking about the Chauvanne girl, that made Teddy angry. He didn't tell me why, but they began to quarrel, and Johnny said something about sticking to the plan. But Teddy—one of the things he told me on his deathbed—suddenly felt overwhelmed with grief and fear, and was furious with himself for having done what he had done, even though it had been carried out in a fit of rage. Johnny told him to either shit or get off the pot, and that they had better get the hell out. 'Stick to the plan,' he said again, but Teddy just sat on a log beside the cherry tree and cried. Johnny walked off through the grove, crossed the bridge and headed for Northwestern, while Teddy just sat there in the shadow of the tree, with the gun leaning against his arm, bawling his eyes out. That's when that guy Stokes saw him, and he saw Stokes, who he knew from school, but because Teddy was in the shadows Stokes couldn't identify him by face. In an instant Teddy bolted into the woods, where he hid like a scared rabbit. From his hiding spot he could see Stokes and two girls meeting on the path by the bridge and was terrified that they would see the blood on the ground or the bodies in the nearby briar patch, but they seemed more interested in each other than their surroundings, and soon moved on. He stayed in the woods for the next two hours."

"Where was Johnny all this time?" Snope asked.

"He had coolly put in an appearance on the school grounds, went to class, and got his report card like the rest of the kids, and then when they let everyone go, taking his time, he doubled back to the park where he found Teddy shaking. He convinced Teddy to leave, but separately. Teddy walked along the water until he came to the same construction project he had passed through the day before."

"That's where Henry Chauvanne saw him again," said Snope. "Is that right?"

"Yes, but he never spoke to the man or even came close to him. He did stop off at a water cooler to get a drink. Said a few words to some laborers."

"The laborers reported he said something about being in a mental hospital," McKinley said. "What was that all about?"

Kitty's lips formed into a wry smile. "You see how things get distorted! Teddy was, of course, nervous and tried to make small talk when the laborers started jiving him. He said something about how crazy things were those days. You know, with the threat of nuclear war and all everyday in the papers, and there it was, a warm spring day where everything was as peaceful as could be. He said something about his father being in World War II and how lucky they were not to have to fight like that. That's when he mentioned the old man had suffered from shell shock and had been put in a VA hospital for a while. By the time you guys got the story, it had been garbled beyond belief."

"Did he go home then?" the FBI agent questioned.

"No. He met up with Johnny at a designated spot on University Lane and they walked along the road together for some time heading towards Langley Park to hide the gun. Traffic on the road was heavy and Johnny was becoming increasingly nervous."

"That's when they were spotted," Snope noted, "by that construction man. I believe Forman was his name."

"Whatever," Kitty said, slightly exasperated. "Do you want me to tell it or not?"

"Sorry," said the sergeant. "Please continue."

"Anyway, Johnny was getting cold feet and said he didn't think it was a good idea to be seen walking on a very public road with his gun-toting brother. Suppose someone had already found the bodies? So they split up again. I guess it was about that time somebody noticed Teddy and later reported it. In the meantime, Johnny doubled back toward Riggs and Ager Road. There was a gas station there where he used to hang out, drink Cokes, and watch the girls, and figured he would make his presence there known for some form of ad hoc alibi if anything went wrong. Teddy, however, had regained his composure, continued on with the gun partially wrapped up in his bed roll, and, as planned, ducked into the vacant apartment building on Merrimac Street, in Langley Park, where he had planned to dump it all in the basement. But at the last minute, he saw some woman watching him very intently. He knew right away she was suspicious, so he went into the basement and just hid for maybe ten minutes trying to think about what he should do. He knew he couldn't leave the gun there. Finally, he found a basement window transom on the opposite side of the building from which he had entered, and shoved the gun through. He then left, without the weapon. And, can you believe it, the same woman was still there and watched him until he went around the building."

"Did anyone else see him? You know the area was moderately well populated," declared McKinley.

"I guess someone may have," Kitty answered. "but it was mid-morning, and the women were inside doing their chores. Their husbands were at work or en route. And aside from the short spate of hiking on University Lane, the boys had kept pretty much off to the side."

"What happened to the murder weapon?" Snope asked.

"Oh yeah! That! Well, like I said, he had shoved it outside. After leaving the apartment building, he walked around the back of the building, picked up the gun, wrapped it up in his bedroll, and headed home. By that time the bodies had been discovered by some girl and her dog, and pretty soon the whole neighborhood was down by the police line. When Teddy got home, his father was waiting at the door. He had heard the radio news flashes and knew right off what had happened, grabbed the gun, and beat the hell out of him. Then he told him to get the hell out of his jeans, shirt and shoes, and give him the wallet he had lifted from the body, all of which had bloodstains on them, wrapped the gun up in them, and put the whole lot in the trunk of his car, intending to dump it all at the first opportunity he had."

"Do you know where he disposed of the gun?"

"No. Teddy never said anything about it."

"And Johnny!" said McKinley.

"Like I said, he hung around the gas station for several hours sipping Cokes, till he had to go take a leak. The toilet at the station was closed for repairs, so he headed back home. Pretty soon, however, he couldn't hold it any longer, and just stepped off to the side of the sidewalk and pissed. He didn't know it, but a little girl was standing there watching him. When he took his "tool" out, which even then was pretty hefty, she screamed bloody murder. The kid's mother came racing up and Johnny took off like a bat out of hell, scared she'd call someone, which was the last thing he wanted then. Apparently she did 'cause, according to Teddy, there was a story in one of the newspapers a day or two later, about a child molester up on Ager Road. Johnny liked his sex, but I can tell you he was no pedophile."

"So it was the old man who dumped the gun," Snope said. "Did Teddy say what he did with it?"

"No. But I think it was the old man who that guy Trueman saw at the gas station. At least that was what Johnny and I figured when we read the story about him in the

Washington Post back in '91. I do know that the old man threatened both Teddy and Johnny to beat them to within an inch of their lives if they ever said a word about what they did. He told them they weren't even allowed to talk about it at Confession, because the priest was an Irishman, like the O'Riley girl's father, and he thought he might pass it on to his own kind."

McKinley stood up and started pacing about the room. "So, did the boys keep their mouths shut?"

"I suppose you could say that. That is except for Johnny, who was always pushing the envelope, and who couldn't help but tease the cops. He made several calls to the police from a local phone booth and gave them clues so that he could read about their big discoveries in the papers a day or two later."

"So he was the mystery caller!" Snope declared as if stricken by an epiphany elephant.

"If you mean to the police, yes," Kitty continued, "but it was Teddy who called the Chauvannes and O'Rileys at home. He took some sick delight in calling them and freaking out anyone who picked up the phone. You have to remember, he was not all right in the head sometimes. He really loved to get the little Chauvanne girl, Terry, on the line and ask to speak to her sister, like she was still alive. And in a strange way, I kinda think he really hadn't come to terms with the fact that he had really killed her or that she was actually gone for good. I believe, in a way, even then, he truly wanted to somehow say he was sorry to her. He had really loved her from afar, I think, and after it was all over, still did."

Snope picked up a clipboard with a thick pile of papers attached, with an alphabetical listing of the names and addresses of all 5,000-plus people who had been interviewed during the 1955 investigation. "Says here that one Alexander V. Dubinski, of 642 23rd Avenue, Lane Manor, Hyattsville, Maryland, was interviewed twice, once on June 17, and again on June 28, 1955, by Prince George's County detectives. They examined his gun collection, but found no weapon similar to the one believed to be employed by the killers. Did Teddy say anything about the interviews?"

"Only that the old man covered for both boys, confirming their alibis."

"Were the boys ever interviewed?" Snope asked.

"No."

"Was the fear of being caught what motivated the Dubinskis to move to Florida?"

"Yes. Old man Dubinski never confided in anyone, but it was apparent to Teddy that he waited until the heat was off and he could move the whole family as far away as possible. So within a year or so, they had picked up, lock, stock, and barrel, put everything in their car and a rental truck, and headed south. Sort of like those Okies in that book *Grapes of Wrath,* 'cept they headed to California."

"So Teddy was the trigger man, Johnny was the brains and his accomplice, and old man Dubinski aided and abetted in covering up their tracks by disposing of the evidence," McKinley said with the satisfaction of someone who just answered a 46-year-old mystery. "Must have been the old man Trueman saw at the gas station after all, on his way to dump the gun! How'd Johnny take it when he learned Teddy had told you the whole story?"

"He got real hot. Took a while to calm him down, but he finally saw the logic in it all. Ironically, Teddy held on for the next five years. He finally died on April 26, 1996. Then, two months after we last spoke with him in the hospice, while we were headed for Brooklyn, New York, where Johnny had some friends who wanted to talk about a job, we were bypassing D.C. on the Washington Beltway. On the spur of the moment, I asked Johnny to show me where the murders had been carried out. He wasn't too keen on it, since there was an outstanding warrant for his arrest in Maryland. But he finally agreed. It was a nice Sunday, and as it turned out quite by coincidence, the anniversary of the murders. We got there in the morning, and he took me down to the spot where they had waited for the girls."

She stopped for a moment, as if to consider her words correctly, and then continued.

"Johnny then went through a step-by-step reconstruction of the whole damned thing. It was like I was actually there, and I almost cried, thinking of those poor girls. It didn't matter what they had said. Teddy and Johnny, without the slightest bit of mercy, had killed them dead. And at that moment, the reality of just what kind of a man I had been with most of my adult life hit me. It was then that we looked up the path we'd just taken toward the bridge and saw a woman watching us. Johnny about lost it, like he had seen a ghost or something, but I held him back until she kinda disappeared, and we hightailed it out of there. Afterwards, we drove around to some of Johnny's old haunts, and then left. He was definitely a little shook by the visit to the murder site, and when we hit the Washington Beltway, coming off the ramp, he cut some woman off and caused a pile up that must have backed traffic up for miles. But he wasn't about to stop. We got to New York, but by then Johnny started feeling really sick and backed out of a deal he had been working on, and we headed back to Texas."

"What happened then?" McKinley asked, while still pacing about the room.

"Johnny died of liver cancer, which he didn't even know he had, on June 23 in San Antonio. At the funeral I was told by one of his contacts that the FBI had found we were back in town and some agents were already on their way to pick me up. For the first time in my life since I was seventeen I was completely on my own—and scared. So I headed for the only place I could think of where I would be safe, to my son Roland's place, outside of North Pole. But I knew it was just a matter of time before they found me again, so I decided to use my bargaining chip—for all the good it did me!"

"I have one last question, at least for now," said Snope. "Aside from helping you, why do you think Teddy was so anxious to tell you about the murder?"

"I asked him the same thing," said Kitty. "Believe it or not, he told me that he was really sorry. He'd given up going to church long ago, and never could bring himself to unload at Confession. He had carried the load with him his entire life and had wanted to come clean, but couldn't. He told me he had seen the Chauvanne girl every day of his life, haunting him, his every waking hour. He actually carried her picture, some old press clipping, around with him till the day he died. It drove him into alcoholism and, I think, contributed to his broken marriage. He prayed every night that the Chauvanne girl would listen to his appeals for forgiveness, but felt she never would. He was afraid that unless he was forgiven by someone in the girl's own family, someone who had suffered most from the loss, that God himself would never forgive him. He said even if he died and was stuck in some Purgatory here on earth he would keep on trying. And if he failed he knew his soul would forever burn in Hell. Teddy wasn't scared of anything in this life, but it sure as shootin' terrified him about the next."

Kitty sighed. "I was supposed to be his stand-in and if he died I was supposed to personally seek forgiveness from one of the Chauvannes. Of course I never did, so I guess poor Teddy is either still trying or frying right now."

"I think we can call it a day, Mrs. Dubinski, I am truly sorry for your loss," Snope said in all sincerity. He looked out the security window once again, and saw the blizzard had intensified even more.

"If you continue to cooperate," added McKinley, "I can assure you that we will do everything we can to get you the justice you deserve."

"How's about bail councilor?" Kitty said to Public Defender Spiring.

"I'm working on it," he assured her as he gathered his papers. "It's been set at $70,000."

Kitty sighed. "Guess I won't be making any snowballs for a while." She was wrong. Six hours later, her son Roland had posted bail after putting his home up as security.

Thus it was that on the evening of January 26, 2001, Kitty Marie Dubinski, 57 years of age, was granted bail and released on her own recognizance from the Fairbanks City Jail. As her son went to get his all-weather Ford Expedition from the parking lot, Kitty crossed the intersection of 10th Avenue and Cushman Street amidst the blinding snowstorm and failed to see the big Macawley Construction dump truck, hired by the city for snow removal work, speeding toward her. The impact of the collision produced little more than a thudding sound as the big vehicle rolled over her body, killing her instantly.

When the driver, a black haired woman in her mid-forties, stopped the truck, and rushed back to Kitty's mangled body, the sight proved horrific. Kitty's guts, almost iridescent looking in the falling snow, were coming out of her mouth and anus, and her eyes bulged from her head, still connected by bloody strands of tissue and nerves. Her body was still warm and limber.

Chapter 28

RED RASH

At first the signs of disorder were subtle, a bright red rash around the mouth, chronic fatigue, and flu-like symptoms. The doctors said it was little more than a common and temporary post-operative thoracotomy syndrome, consisting of right chest, right side, and right back pain. No one suspected a neurological disorder, especially one related to a bug bite. In the meantime, Theresa Anderson continued her job as a substitute teacher, freelance copy editor for Johns Hopkins University Press and a Virginia-based firm called Editorial Experts, Inc., putting out monthly newsletters for the local Sierra Club, serving on the board of the county chapter of the Humane Society, and even some volunteer work writing articles and doing media consulting for a local congressional candidate. By mid-1996, however, the symptoms had become more than progressively debilitating, anything but temporary. Her gynecologist suggested she might be suffering from HIV, but the tests came back negative. Simply existing had become a day-by-day journey of uncertainty.

Being on the outskirts of a rural Eastern Shore town like Centreville, and continuing to maintain a large menagerie of pets, now mostly dogs and cats, also had its drawbacks. Terry thought nothing about the endless burrs, ticks, and other hitchhikers of nature she routinely pulled from her animals, and frequently off herself as well. It was just a fact of life. "I thought little to nothing about the many ticks pulled off myself," she would later write in her personal journal, "most of which were imbedded and sometimes just left in, too deep to remove, figuring it was just something one dealt with living in the country, with deer often grazing in the yard, dogs and cats in and out, and as well the many mosquitoes, attracted to a pond close by, and the endless mosquito bites, all while sitting on the patio out back at night. At the time I figured my physical complaints were all associated with the auto accident, which became all the more maddening, and likely related to my brainstem injury as well. And I would soon prove to be entirely wrong."

By winter the thoracic problems and a perplexing array of new symptoms, including severe elbow, hip, and knee pains, had begun to take a toll on Terry's ability to work. She became an almost regular outpatient at Johns Hopkins, and for the next year and a half would continue to face a blizzard of tests, medicines, and therapy sessions, administered by legions of specialists, all providing little satisfaction. Almost every two or three months new symptoms began to appear, including short seizures tentatively diagnosed as myoclonic epilepsy, mild hallucinations, and periods of impaired sense of self and time. Indeed, by February 1998, she had finally become too ill to work.

If there was a single uplifting moment for Terry, it was in a letter from her son Sean, who, ever since her divorce from Carl, had been raised to manhood in California by her ex-husband and his second wife. Sean had attended college there and joined the NROTC to secure an officer's commission upon graduation. It had not been what she had wanted for the boy, having been a witness to the human psychological discards produced by Vietnam, but he been adamant and attacked his new career path with the very panache inherited from his mother.

It had been five years since Terry had last seen her son, but they had stayed in frequent correspondence, at first by letter, and later entirely via e-mail. Despite his career choice, perhaps because of it despite her, she had come to adore her son, albeit from afar, more than ever before. Thus, it had been no surprise when she received a charming hand-written note, accompanied by an elegantly printed invitation, requesting her presence at his graduation from college and formal commissioning ceremony as an officer in the Marine Corps at San Diego in May 1998. The only fly in the ointment, however, was that she was scheduled for yet another very critical operation.

In March Terry underwent a second surgical procedure technically dubbed a "thoracic laminectomy/rhizotomy/T-8 ganglionectomy." The operation was performed by a team of Hopkins neurosurgeons in yet another effort to relieve the post-thoractomy syndrome, and repair thoracic disc herniations and a spinal fracture. Again, the operation proved unsuccessful and the pain, despite trial usage of an experimental drug, continued worse than before. Terry despaired of attending her son's commissioning ceremony.

After a week in the hospital mending from the surgery, Terry was transferred to the Johns Hopkins inpatient chronic pain clinic where, after two-and-a half weeks on Oxycontin and other medications, for the first time since the accident she began to experience relief from pain, and even some cognitive improvement. Though far from feeling healed or even good, with the wounds of major spinal surgery still fresh and relief from pain barely holding its own, Terry resolved to make it to the commissioning regardless of the financial and physical costs. As she would later note, "but for that extended hospitalization and the strong pain medication and other meds prescribed me I would not have been able to make that trip, leaving for San Diego the day after returning home from the hospital."

The seven-hour flight from Baltimore-Washington International to California proved a vexing challenge for Terry. She had been specifically instructed by her doctors to engage in no activity for two months beyond getting out of bed a few times a day and walking around the house. Forty-eight hours later she had boarded Southwest Airlines flight 786 laden with a black carry-on, her purse, and a two-week supply of painkillers and other medicines. Two hours into the flight, as she looked down upon the cloud cover from her window seat perch in the heavens, she was overcome with a bodily feeling of separation from reality. "My sense of myself in real time," she later recorded, "seemed, somehow, much impaired. All I could think of was my long-dead sister. I had experienced similar feelings in the past. All were varying in intensity, but more often than not quite severe. Often they were followed by humiliating experiences while interacting negatively with others. There was usually little or no sense to what I said or did, and I was always imagining the worst after the fact, knowing my behavior and other manners of expressing myself to be in general odd and intense at the same time."

All that she could remember of the flight with any certainty was dreaming of Ellen rolling down her bobby sox, putting on her saddle shoes, and removing her curlers in the kitchen on that warm spring day a million years before.

"When are we going," Terry asked expectantly.

"I'm sorry, doll," replied her sister. "I know I told you that you could go with me, but like mom said, not this morning. Next time, I promise."

To say that Sean Anderson was the epitome of a U.S. Marine would be an understatement. The graduation and commissioning ceremony held at UCLA San Diego on May 8, 1998, was attended not only by Terry, but also by her son's father Carl and

Carl's new wife Miriam, and a small congregation of friends and well-wishers, and was colorful performance art of the highest order. Everyone seemed to be in the best of spirits as Sean Anderson was launched with pomp and military ritual into his new career and responsibilities as Second Lieutenant Sean Anderson, USMC. Everyone, that is, except Terry, who discovered only an hour before the ceremony the first clump of hair falling from her head.

In the months that followed the trip to California, the symptoms of Terry's illness continued to proliferate, as one by one her bodily functions began to degenerate. "I felt so ill, so severely ill," she later wrote, "and so desperate for distraction from how I always felt and feeling as if I was in a race against the clock, before I could not function at all, when things systemically really started taking off wildly." One of her physicians suggested the hair loss was a classic symptom of syphilis, which was soon dispelled by testing. Another, rather circumspectly, suggested that she was either psychosomatic and/or a hypochondriac and that the hair loss was natural. Yet no one could account for the recurring bouts of delirium, disconnectedness, and occasional hallucinations, followed by short periods of relative normalcy, as if all the demons in her body had taken a brief vacation.

Such episodic moments of normalcy could be cruel indeed. By the spring of 1999, during one of the longer periods of freedom from pain and symptoms, Terry's optimism blossomed. She began keeping a daily diary of her thoughts and activities, and an organized archive of her personal correspondence on her computer. Once more she considered law school, and decided to register for the LSAT.

On the morning of the test, Terry was awakened by the resumption of the old familiar pains in her body, yet decided to proceed to the test center at all cost. Days later, she would write of the debacle: "After many close calls driving to the test site and after parking and again losing consciousness, and for some time after coming round but before being able to move, I suffered from a very severe systemic pain and feeling of intense delirium. Nevertheless, I got myself inside the building, found the testing room, and sat down. After a few minutes, while sitting at the desk, I briefly lost consciousness, falling onto floor. Regaining consciousness in a few seconds, I told the monitor I was okay, just clumsy, and began the examination. For at least two thirds of the test period I was unconscious and not really cognizant of anything, not really aware of my surroundings. I felt severe delirium and began hallucinating about my childhood, Mom, Pop, Ellen, the murder in the park. When the test results were mailed to my house, I did not open them. I knew it was not only bad news, but also likely set a record for the worst LSAT test results ever registered, and laughed at the thought. I was right and it made me sick at heart."

It was at that moment that Terry gave up all hopes of a career, and began to entertain darker thoughts.

Chapter 29

SPIDERS ON COFFEE

The back porch patio at 1040 Quail Lane was simple, with a pleasant gray flagstone floor, a low surrounding brick wall with a single walkway through to the yard and down the slope overlooking the Corsica River. On the slope stood a single lovely arched rose-entwined trellis, which shaped the patio view of the river. Alone and asymmetrically out of place, it was a beautiful rebel to the organized and otherwise contoured landscape of the community. Several plastic deck chairs and a ragged chaise lounge were arranged around a small sun table that Philip and Lucille had brought with them from Damascus. In one corner of the patio lay a coiled hose and sprinkler. In the other sat a squat outdoor barbecue grill Philip had purchased at a Walmart a decade ago and at best may have used twice.

On the morning of June 15, 2000, Terry and Philip sat on the patio having breakfast. Philip lay comfortably on the chaise lounge, his oxygen bottle propped by his side, tubes from it running into his nose as he sipped at a cup of coffee. Terry sat beside him with a glass of orange juice in her hand and the morning *Washington Post* across her lap.

"You know, Pop, that stuff will kill you," she joked as he deftly manipulated the cup beneath the oxygen lines to his nose. "Caffeine is a toxin that stresses the adrenal gland and interferes with sleep when the immune system tries to repair itself."

He turned his head towards her and smirked. "Sweetie, you've been sitting in front of that damned computer too much. Without coffee, nothing would ever get done."

"I'm not kidding," she said more seriously. "I read where NASA did a study with spiders on coffee. Their webs were a mess. It's the same with caffeine in soda. And these artificial sweeteners are even worse and it's not only the caffeine. They used spiders to test the toxicity in sweeteners like NutraSweet and Equal, which use an ingredient called aspartame in place of sugar. And the poor beggars died. Aspartame contains formaldehyde, which can cause birth defects, epilepsy, brain tumors, lymphoma, MS, and mental retardation. The stuff they put in diet sodas can kill your brain cells, can cause depression, and one ingredient, methanol, is a deadly neurotoxin that can even cause blindness."

"Sounds to me like all your health problems could be fixed," Philip laughed, "if you'd just gave up coffee and Diet Cokes."

"You never know, do you?" she said, smiling as she unfolded the newspaper on her lap.

Suddenly, she gasped and spilled the orange juice on the table as she read the headline of the lead story: "Deathbed Tale Offers Solution to 1955 Slayings."

"So it was those bastard Dubinski boys!" she stuttered in amazement. "Trueman, sick as he was, was actually on to something after all!"

"What the hell are you talking about?" asked Philip.

Terry handed him the newspaper.

"Well, I guess that ends it," Philip said, after a long, stunned silence. His hands were shaking as his eyes began to water up. "God, I still miss that little girl. If only your mother were here now."

Terry was not as sentimental. "That son of a bitch Teddy and his brother never got what they deserved!" she said angrily. "The bastards lived their whole lives without ever paying for their butchery — and it pisses me off that the goddamned cops never even bothered to tell us what was going on. For three years! Can you imagine that! For three years they knew this and never once gave us a hint."

"Honey, it's over," Philip soothed his daughter. "There's nothing we can do now. It says here that officially the case isn't closed because they never found the murder weapon, but the police are confident it was Dubinski. We've heard this all before."

"I can tell you one thing," Terry rasped, "if I ever, in this life or the next, have an opportunity to somehow get revenge on that monster, to make him pay I'd have him rot in hell for eternity. I swear to God I'll send him to hell."

Throughout the summer of 2000, though Philip's constitution was noticeably failing, Terry's seemed to be stabilizing despite occasional narcoleptic episodes that made her extremely leery of driving to Baltimore for her weekly treatments at Johns Hopkins. In July she began a thirty-day I-V antibiotic therapy that seemed to produce even more improvement, including re-growth of her hair, relief from thoracic pain, and in her mental faculties, although by August new pains had begun to cause problems with her hands and feet. Nevertheless, she felt well enough again to begin aggressively re-engaging the world at large, and in particular the political scene, as best she could from her computer.

The controversial election of George W. Bush to the Presidency of the United States maddened her, but the Republican takeover in Congress and what she deemed to be a serious threat to the environment only reinvigorated her to action. In December she began a spirited letter-writing campaign to have President Clinton, during his last days in office, designate the Arctic National Wildlife Reserve in Alaska a National Monument to prevent the Republicans from opening it to oil drilling.

The vacation from pain, unhappily, proved all too brief.

By January 2001 a new flurry of violent symptoms began to assail her. Pain resumed at the base of her neck and vertex of the skull, in the mid-posterior and anterior chest and rib cage, and in her hip girdle. It fluctuated between sharp, nagging, gripping, pressure-like to radiant and generalized with searing muscle spasms all the way down her legs. Her gait became awkward and unbalanced especially after brief walks. The doctors chalked it up to the onset of rheumatism. Dizziness, nausea, and vomiting were becoming a daily occurrence. Owing to the sudden attacks of vertigo she now kept a bucket beside her chair to vomit into while working at the computer. Flashing scalp pains, sudden onsets of severe drowsiness, a resurgence of narcolepsy and delirium, now assaulted her every sense. Simple eye movements to look peripherally, chewing, or even pushing her lower jaw forward would distort her vision. She became hypersensitive to stimuli, especially noise. Occasional ringing or whooshing and buzzing sounds began to obstruct her hearing, far worse than tinnitus. Occasionally moderate to severe bladder incontinence caused several embarrassing episodes while in public places. And then there were the mental problems.

During her cognizant periods, Terry began, for the first time, to research her own symptoms on the Internet and in medical texts from the local library. She took voluminous notes, categorizing data, evaluating published studies, and digging deep into the origins of the monsters that seemed to be taking over her body. With considerable difficulty, she gradually became versed in the nomenclature of medical regimens, surgical procedures, and pharmaceuticals that might be applicable to her case. Any and every avenue of illness that the symptoms suggested might be afflicting her became the subject of investigation.

Recalling the remark made by one of her doctors in 1996 that she had a minor tick-borne ailment called Lyme disease, she began to probe the history, symptoms, and remedies for the illness. None appeared to be well known or studied. In fact, only a handful of researchers, all of them independent, seemed versed on the subject. There appeared to be no national database on the disease, nor was it recognized as a serious affliction by national agencies or institutions such as the Center for Disease Control, the National Institute of Health, or the American Medical Association.

One thing stood out: many of her symptoms were mirrored by what was already known about the mysterious ailment. She was determined to discuss the possibilities with the doctors at Johns Hopkins on her next visit, and reviewed her notes to insure that she would be able to discuss the possibilities intelligently.

In February, when Terry informed Dr. Buri Amani Naja, a thoracic surgeon and one of the medical team handling her case, of her suspicions regarding Lyme disease, the doctor smiled politely

"You are mistaken, Ms. Anderson," he told her in his soft, clipped Indian accent. "I can tell you without a doubt that all of your complaints are unquestionably and directly attributable to your long standing neck and spinal injuries. Dr. Wilniki has failed to detect any arterial blood flow problems, and Dr. Barnes has told me that your reflexes are all normal. Given past strongly positive BAER and ENG findings, and vestibular and peripheral vision problems we have found at the Wiggner Eye Institute, Dr. Wilniki said this certainly explains your complaints of dizziness and nausea, which you say are exacerbated by looking peripherally. But we will schedule an MRI if you feel comfortable with that."

Unconvinced, in an effort to rule out the disease, Terry sought another opinion and met with a neurologist, reportedly well-versed in Lyme. Yet another in the seemingly endless round of blood and urine tests were scheduled, and on the outside chance Lyme was the culprit, Terry was put on a thirty-day I-V treatment of a new drug called Rochephin.

Still the symptoms continued unabated.

Captain Sean Anderson's call to his mother from Camp Lejeune, South Carolina, in March 2001 could hardly have come at a more inconvenient time. Terry's illness had been getting progressively worse, albeit with what appeared to be the occasional stunning relapse in which normality appeared, only to be utterly destroyed by a new assault. She also had to attend to her father, whose own fragile state was noticeably degenerating, making things even more difficult. For months he had been suffering not only from breathing problems, but also from dizziness and nausea, and a curiously persistent cough.

Yet, Sean's words had given them both a cause for celebration. With proper restraint and dignity becoming an officer in the U.S. Marine Corps, he announced that he was engaged to one Marissa Jacquett, and the wedding was to be held on Saturday, May 18, on the Fort Bragg U.S. Army military reservation, near Fayetteville, North Carolina, where he was stationed as a U.S. Marine liaison officer. It was to be a small wedding, with a larger, more regal affair to be held later in the year in Annapolis, after he was reassigned to the Marine base at Quantico, Virginia. Sean was adamant about both his mother and grandfather attending. His father Carl would be there to serve as Best Man, and Marissa's life-long friend Sandra Webber would serve as Maid of Honor.

Though delighted for his only grandson, Philip, like Terry, was at first leery about the long journey to North Carolina in their current conditions, given the announced plan for a later ceremony in Maryland. As Terry later wrote in her journal: "Pop finally acquiesced to the trip after another call from Sean imploring him to come. Pop could not and would not disappoint his grandson. He went despite how he felt and despite his concern about being away from home should something happen."

Equally concerned about her own ability to make the trip, Terry resolved that there was little alternative but to join her father. "Just do it, as Ellen used to say," she barked out of the blue to Philip one evening at dinner.

During the week before their departure for Fayetteville, Terry managed to drag Philip to his primary care physician twice. On the morning of the flight, he was diagnosed with a respiratory infection, given an oral antibiotic, and instructed to go home and to bed immediately. Against Terry's wishes, he did just the opposite. As they left the house for the airport together, his last words were: "I'm going to my grandson's wedding or die trying."

The expedition in the name of family and marital concord would nearly kill both of them.

The flight to Fayetteville aboard Continental Airlines on the morning of May 17 was uncomfortable at best. The long drive from the Fayetteville Airport to Sean and Marissa's rented home west of the base was horrific. Terry spent the better part of the trip nauseated, suffering from head and neck pains and vertigo, lying on the back floor of the rented car, vomiting into a paper cup. Once at their destination, the slightest sensation of motion, light and sound, would bring on a new round of queasiness.

By evening, as the first planned festivities were getting underway, Terry regained enough of her composure, as she later recalled, "to where I could feign all was well and thus make certain things went that evening as Marissa and Sean planned." Somehow, though feeling poorly, Philip managed to cavort and joke with the guests. Perhaps for the last time in his life he was having a good time. Then he disappeared.

About 11:00 p.m. with the party showing no sign of slowing, Terry suffered another attack of vertigo and nausea and retired, but not before checking on her father's room.

"I went into the front bedroom where Pop was to sleep," she later recalled, "and found him sideways across the bed sound asleep and still in his clothes. It was the biggest indication of his feeling extremely ill, his having not been able to change into his pajamas, which he had done religiously since childhood." At 4:00 a.m. she checked on him again, and he had not moved.

By 11:00 a.m., May 18, the day of the wedding, Terry herself was all but immobilized with pain, and an ambulance was called to take both her and Philip to the emergency room at the nearest hospital. In the ER, the attending physician immediately suspected Terry had meningitis or possibly even enchaphalitis and asked for approval to begin a spinal tap. Encephalitis, he patiently explained, was irritation and swelling of the brain that often co-existed with inflammation of the covering of the brain and spinal cord (meningitis) and in most cases was caused by a viral infection. Terry, who had hoped for a quick fix, perhaps an injection that would somehow allow her to return and the wedding to proceed, refused on the grounds that she would be required to lie flat from twelve to twenty-four hours after the test and delay the ceremony. Her illness deemed otherwise, and though a spinal tap was not carried out, she was obliged to spend the scheduled wedding day in bed, as directed by the ER doctor, avoiding strong light to the eyes. Philip was diagnosed by a pulmonary specialist as suffering from not only emphysema and cardiac problems already known about, but advanced pulmonary fibrosis.

Sean and Marissa decided to postpone the wedding until the following day, even though Marissa's Maid of Honor was unable to stay.

"Lying in bed," Terry later recalled, "all I could think of was having been responsible for postponing the wedding and feeling intensely the need to atone for it, which essentially meant spending time with Marissa's family, to be 'sociable' the next day, even though both Pop and I were miserably sick."

On Sunday, May 19, Captain Sean Anderson and Marissa Jacquett were wedded, as Philip and Terry sat in the front row, father and daughter, supporting each other by leaning shoulder to shoulder.

Upon her return home, Terry was diagnosed at Johns Hopkins with severe meningitis and encephalitis, the cause of which was unknown. One prominent neurosurgeon, Gerald B. Durkee, after extensive examinations and tests, admitted he was baffled.

"I have to admit it was a bit of a confusing medical history," he noted in his assessment. "She has been in the Hopkins systems where she has probably seen about ten different doctors, and had five different spinal operations. She has had a huge number of different kinds of medical trials. With all of this, she still has pain at the base of the skull, in the back of her neck, which is basically playing havoc on her regular life."

Seeking to address possible causes, he suggested continued instability of her C-1 vertebrae, post-traumatic cerebral changes, and post-thoracotomy pains, all of which combined to leave her disabled. Combined with pains in her chest and extremities, a product of what could only be described as chronic pain syndrome, for which she was taking Oxycontin and Bachinofen three times a day, her ailments were still a total mystery.

"I am forced to admit," Durkee wrote in the final analysis, "there is probably not much I can do to help her."

On September 10, 2001, Philip Chauvanne suffered a complete collapse and was taken to Shady Grove Hospital in Montgomery County for specialized treatment. Somehow, Terry managed to drive the sixty miles each way between Quail Lane and the hospital two to three times a week to be by her father's side. Often she would become disoriented and spend hours lost in once-familiar countryside. Once, while pulled over to the side of a rural road to wait out a bout of vertigo, she suffered a narcoleptic attack and woke up hours later, as the sun was setting but nevertheless managed to find her way.

"I kept dreaming of spiders drinking coffee," she wrote in her diary that night of the period she was unconscious. But for Philip there would be no more coffee. On October 16, 2001, between 7:30 and 8:30 a.m., well into his ninetieth year, and after five months of severe pain, refusing any further medication and removing the oxygen tubes from his nose himself, he went to sleep and never awoke.

At the memorial services for Philip Chauvanne, held at Humphrey's Funeral Home in Gaithersburg, Maryland, on October 19, Terry's eulogy was brief: "We can have no knowledge of the end of things, but we have a choice of how we live and how we die. Pop chose his."

Alone again, Terry somehow managed to survive. Sean and Marissa, who had moved to Manassas, Virginia, though not convenient to Centreville, nevertheless began to visit on weekends. There were for Terry, of course, also the frequent visits to Johns Hopkins and the endless tests, two more operations, and constant depression. Finally, on March 20, 2003, the beginning day of the longest war in American history, Dr. Paul Lynch Foster informed her that the root cause of much of her illness, as she had suggested for some time, was Lyme disease. The affliction, already in an advanced stage, was affecting not only her physical well-being, but threatened to challenge her mental capacity to conduct even the basic functions of day-to-day life. He recommended that she secure, as quickly as possible, appointments with Dr. Simon A. Campollo, the leading authority on Lyme disease on the Eastern Seaboard, and Dr. Michael Brownstein, Jr., who was among the pre-eminent American neuropsychiatrists in the country, and a leading scholar on the neurological manifestations of the disease. Both would be inordinately expensive, but, Foster said, probably her best hope for a cure.

As she downed a cocktail of dark black liquid, produced by the Pfeiffer Pharmaceutical Corporation of New London, Connecticut, and costing $280 per dose, she thought again of spiders on coffee.

Chapter 30

THE LODGER

In late July 2003, Terry drove very slowly into Easton, ever concerned about blacking out, to place a "For Rent" advertisement in the local weekly *Easton Recorder*. Ever since her father had died, she had been struggling unsuccessfully to secure some of his pension money from the engineers local in which he had been a member for more than half a century. Unable to work because of her accident and the onset of Lyme disease, and with no revenue other than her Social Security disability payment, she finally succumbed to the necessity of taking in lodgers. Since June she had run through several short-term renters, the most recent being a teenager named Kenny Reager who had left home and apparently had no job other than working on his Harley. Among the several who had taken up temporary residence, mostly migrant Hispanic farm workers, he had been the only one who had stayed any appreciable time, and most of the spare rooms in the big house had remained unoccupied.

Perhaps, she thought, it might have something to do with the animal menagerie: her dogs, Tuffy, a male cocker, and Sasha, a German shepherd, five cats, a cockatoo, a squadron of parakeets, a ferret, and numerous wild itinerants that appeared periodically in the night for free chow at the back door. Or perhaps it was simply that the house had not been cleaned, or even swept, since her father had passed. Philip's hospital bed and oxygen tank were still in the corner of the dining room with the same sheets and blankets lying in the rumpled state they were in when the ambulance arrived to haul him to the hospital for the last time. Magazines, newspapers, and detritus of every kind lay scattered about in dismal profusion, owing to her physical weakness and inability to marshal the slightest effort to houseclean. With the exception of the kitchen table and counter, everywhere the dust was thick and ancient. Cobwebs that could have been eradicated by a simple swish of a broom had begun to cluster in every corner. The garage, with the exception of the corner where Reager worked on his bike, was a dirty cavern, filled with countless cardboard boxes containing the life-time accumulations of her late parents, as well as her own belongings from long ago. One expected to encounter trolls at any given moment.

"I'll get to it when I'm feeling better," Terry frequently consoled herself. "I just need some time."

It thus came as some surprise when, three days after the advertisement had appeared, she received a call from a potential long-term boarder.

"Good afternoon," said the caller in a deep, pleasant voice. "My name is Tristan James Keyes, and I'd like to speak with Theresa Anderson."

"Speaking. What can I do for you?"

"Ms. Anderson, I saw your ad in the paper about having a room for rent by the month in Centreville. I'm interested in setting up an appointment to see it, that is if it's still available."

"Yes, it is," she replied.

"Wonderful. You mentioned in the ad that your house is Victorian. I love that era. What's a good time to have a look-see?"

"Anytime after lunch — I get up late — and before 3:30, when I have to drive into Easton."

"How about today?"

"That would be fine," she answered. "The house number is 1040 Quail Lane, in Centreville, just over the little bridge on the Corsica River. I can give you directions."

"It won't be a problem," he replied. "I know exactly where it is. I'll be over in a few minutes."

Terry was uncertain of what to make of the conversation. How did he know right where the house was? And so quickly! But she hardly had time to contemplate the question when she was summoned to the front door by a heavy knock. The doorbell had not worked in months.

On opening the inner door, she was confronted by a heavy-set bear of a man, about six-four and 220 pounds, standing on the other side of the screen door. His face was flush and his short, blond hair was ruffled, with a cowlick in the back. Though not particularly handsome, he had the most affable face she had ever seen.

"Good afternoon," the man said in a husky greeting. "Are you Theresa Anderson?"

"Yes, I am," she answered. "Are you Mr. Keyes?"

"At your service," he smiled.

It was well that her visitor had come on this particular day, as Terry had not felt as alert or energetic in weeks. She was in one of those now rare moments when everything worked — her mind and her body — and life seemed bearable. This was the first time in three months that she had even felt mildly inclined to put on a dab of lipstick and comb her hair. She wore one of her old toe-length flower-child dresses she once loved to flaunt on the campus while in San Diego. And she enjoyed that rare bit of vanity when, afterwards, she looked in the mirror and saw more than a ghost of her gorgeous old self looking back at her. Maybe there was still hope, she thought.

"Well, come on in, but you'll have to go through the garage, as the screen door is eternally stuck. The garage entrance is to your right."

The visitor made his way through the garage, which had acquired a patina more reminiscent of a city dump than anything else.

"You will have to excuse the mess," said Terry as she held the garage house door entrance open. "I've been recovering from a pretty severe illness, and haven't had time to clean up. Didn't expect you right away. The place is a wreck, but I'd be delighted to show you around anyway. Are you from around here? And how did you know where this was, and how did you get here so quickly?"

"I live in Bethesda right now, on the other side of the Washington Beltway, but I recently bought a waterfront lot right down the street from you, and I'm in the process of building a house on it. So when you gave me your address, I knew right where you were, since I called from the construction site on my cell phone."

"Talk about coincidence! Do you work in the area?"

"I'm an aeronautics engineer and work at Goddard Space Flight Center, that is until I retire, hopefully in January. I plan to have the house done first, though. Been doing most of the work myself, on weekends and holidays. Sometimes my brother Bob lends a hand, but most of the stuff I get to do solo."

Terry had wondered about the building progress down the street. It was a prime piece of property, right on the river, and shaded by several copses of ancient trees. She had walked by the site with Tuffy and Sasha several times in the last few weeks, marveling at how attractive the place was becoming.

"Please sit down," she said almost methodically. "So you say you saw my ad in the paper?"

Before the visitor could find a seat in the cluttered living room — that is one not occupied by one of Terry's pantheon of cats, Sam, Elle, Mo, Mitzie and Bubba — Tuffy and Sasha entered and began barking and running around his feet. At that same moment, the cockatoo started yakking, and the parakeets began singing.

"Your ad didn't say anything about being Noah's Ark," he laughed.

She frowned. "Is that a problem?"

"Heck no. I love critters of all kinds. They're all okay by me. How about showing me around?"

Ignoring his request, she pulled Sasha's big hulk aside and started stroking her stiff, gray-and-black hair to quiet her down. "This little lady once belonged to a local cop I know, who saved her from the Baltimore pound for his kids. Unfortunately, the poor creature had been abused by its former owner, and my friend simply couldn't handle her. It wasn't that she was aggressive, you know. She just has a bad case of nerves. So I took her in, and she's been my darling ever since."

Changing the subject and still ignoring his request, she asked: "What made you pick this particular place to build your house?"

"I have been looking for about a year," he answered, "for a relatively quiet backwater near a small town in the Chesapeake Tidewater, and found the Corsica River and Centreville. I love these waters and everything in them. I already have a small boat, and here I can build a dock on my own property and go fishing whenever I please. You know what old Water Rat said in *Wind in the Willows*? 'There's nothing — absolutely nothing — half as much worth doing as messing about in boats.'"

"Well, you will love it here," she said with a smile, thinking of how fortunate it would be to have a tenant actually able to pay the rent, and charming and literate to boot. "You have the river to yourself. And standing still at dusk, listening to the song of the froglings along the water, is almost magical. I kind of see it as my own personal Walden Pond."

As Terry spoke, she failed to slur her words or stutter as she did regularly only days before. Her voice was as smooth and sweet as it had once been, and its effect on Keyes was magnetic. For the first time in eons, her demeanor was friendly, warm, and welcoming as she talked about her animals, especially Tuffy, a deaf, laid-back cocker spaniel adopted from the Queen Anne's County animal control unit, in a way that charmed her visitor. Her long, red, flower-child dress flattered her tall, slender form, and captivated him. The conversation soon became fluid, and turned personal. Keyes, like Terry, had been born in D.C., and their birthdays were only seven days apart. He had spent most of his life in the District, Arlington, Virginia, and in Bethesda, attended St. John's High School, and finished his undergraduate and graduate studies at Notre Dame. His career in electronic engineering had been spent with the Federal Government, at the National Institute of Health, the FBI, and finally as a project manager at NASA.

Within fifteen minutes the clutter that reigned supreme in the house was completely ignored, and a six-month lease had been signed without benefit of a single room having been inspected.

"It's a pretty long commute from here to NASA," said Terry.

"Well, by the time I finish the house and move in I hopefully will have retired, which will probably be about December or January this coming year."

"What do you intend to do then?" she queried, with the trace of a smile.

"They've asked me to teach a physical science course at Chesapeake College."

"What about Mrs. Keyes. How's that gonna work?" Terry asked, matter-of-factly as she walked her new lodger to the garage door. The sun was setting over the Corsica, and the crickets were beginning their evening serenade.

"There's no Mrs. Keyes. Never has been one."

"How can that be, a strapping successful man like you?" she said with a full smile now gracing her face. "You gay?"

He blushed. "Nope... Just never found the right woman."

Terry laughed out loud for the first time in weeks. "Well, I'm glad to meet a man who is so particular," she said, shaking his bear paw of a hand as he left. "I'm really looking forward to having you as a tenant and then as a neighbor."

"And I'm looking forward to just being here," he said. "I'm sure it's going to be a memorable experience."

Then, noting Keyes's not too subtle glance at the diamond ring on her right hand, Terry smiled wanly, answering the question before it was asked. "The ring belonged to my sister. She died many years ago, but I wear it always."

He smiled back. "I understand."

And for the first time in the last few miserable years of her life, the word "kismet" flashed through Terry's mind.

The first few weeks after August 1, when Terry's new tenant moved in, seemed an easy transition. Tristan Keyes was usually up and out of the house every weekday by 5 a.m. His commute was tedious, a daily 58-mile-long trek across the Chesapeake Bay to the Goddard Space Flight Center in Greenbelt, Maryland, via the Governor Preston W. Lane Memorial Bridge, affectionately known to most travelers simply as "The Bay Bridge." He worked late many evenings, but was usually in bed by 10 p.m., at least in the beginning. Conversations between landlord and tenant were at first rarely more than a passing "hello" or "see ya." On weekends, he usually worked dawn till dusk on his house down the street.

Not long after Tristan had taken up residence, another boarder also took up lodging at 1040 Quail Lane. Joe Pugh, a service manager for a local yacht company, claimed to have an MBA from Purdue. In later years, Keyes spoke of those early days as Terry's tenant, and his fellow boarder, with fondness, for it was indeed the beginning of the most memorable part of his entire life.

"He was a nice guy," Tristan later recalled. "Unlike me, he'd come home from work and cook dinner. I used to just pick something up on the way or skip it. He'd buy something nice at the A&P outside of Centreville, and sometimes he and Terry would cook dinner together and talk. Often, from my room, even with the door closed, I'd hear them talk late into the evening. Nothing special, just about his job and things like that."

Tristan didn't see much of Terry those first few weeks, little more than an occasional glimpse. Then one day, on a Saturday evening, coming home from work on his own house, he entered through the garage and saw Terry sitting at the kitchen table with Tuffy by her side, lying on his mat, and all five of her cats wandering around her. She was smoking her Virginia Slims 120 Menthol cigarettes and writing something on a yellow legal pad. At that moment she looked like a queen surrounded by her loyal subjects. After the usual hello, she surprised him.

"Why don't we get a pizza from Shakeys?" she suggested. "Joe's gone home for the weekend to his family in Allentown, and I can't stand my own cooking, when I dare cook.

I've been down for the last few days in my room — the Lyme disease, you know — and I need to get out into civilization. How about it? I'll buy, but you'll have to drive."

Tristan noticed her hands were trembling, her cheeks and eyebrows were twitching, and her complexion and lips appeared waxy-looking.

"You're on," Tristan responded with a bear-sized grin, "but I insist on buying."

For both Terry and Tristan the evening was as comfortable as two old shoes together in their closet space, with the couple getting to know each other, and after returning home, talking well into the night. Tristan was amazed at her depth and intellect, her up-front candor, life, and no-nonsense views of politics (she being a liberal Democrat and he a conservative Republican) and the world at large. And once she started to talk, there was usually no interrupting her. She loved Do-Wop and dancing, though she had done precious little of the latter in the last few years. She was once into vernacular architecture and later landscape design, and had even contemplated writing a book on Andrew Jackson Downing, the eccentric traveler and nineteenth century Father of American Landscape Design. At another time in her life she had been into Roman history and literature, Cicero, Vergil, Suetonius, and the like. She even regaled him with a dramatic reading from Book VI of the *Aeneid*, which she considered the most beautiful and impressive epics, recounting Aeneas's descent to Hades, where he finds the shade of his father Anchises in the Elysian Fields and receives encouragement and counsel for the tempestuous days that lay ahead. She seemed to be fascinated with his crossing of the River Styx on Charon's ferry, which she said was her favorite part of the work. For the most part, Tristan sat and listened, and was deeply attentive. For Terry it was like releasing a steam valve.

She told him about her accident, her Lyme disease, her bouts with depression, her hallucinations, and the loss of her physical and mental capacities. She told him of the tricks she used to mask her illness in public. She told him of upcoming, and long-awaited appointments with two leading Lyme specialists she had made on the advice of Dr. Foster and the fear they engendered in her. And he listened — and listened attentively — for he was at once fascinated, sympathetic and admiring. She was cynically humorous, bleak, strong, and fiercely honest, a dynamic, unsettled character trapped in a grim, horrendous world not of her own making. For Terry, all bets were off on faith in a clockwork universe. Her dominating traits were a sense of self-worth and free will that would either prevail or perish.

That same evening, after retiring to his room, Tristan booted up his computer and looked up Lyme disease on the Internet. For the first time he felt a deep sense of sorrow and pity for his landlord, and a great sense of admiration for her courage and pluck. It was then that he resolved to help her in any way he could.

The short respite from her symptoms had lasted barely two weeks before a new wave of darkness began to consume Terry's days, and then invade her dreams at night. She started to experience memory lapses and difficulty reading. The most minor disruptions of common progressions in her daily regimen, or the introduction of unfamiliar sounds, would drive her into fits of anger. While typing at her keyboard she would become confused and place her words and even letters in the wrong sequence in a sentence. She began to again suffer from bowel incontinence and soiled herself several times without knowing it. The worst was an increased proclivity to suddenly, without warning, fall into a deep sleep, and occasionally at any given moment to hallucinate. The attacks could happen during both day and night, regardless of whether she was standing, sitting, or lying down. Bouts of the narcolepsy now lasted anywhere from a few seconds to several hours or more, and repeated falls began to take an increasingly physical toll on her body. She no longer dared take a bath for fear of drowning, and was forced to resort to showers, which she had always hated, but even then, of necessity, sat in the tub to wash. Repeatedly collapsing, or falling into a motionless stupor, sometimes for several hours even while sitting at her computer, she began to suffer facial bruises from hitting the keyboard when, without warning she lost consciousness and fell forward. The hallucinations and short-term memory loss, which sometimes accompanied the attacks, became existential nightmares. One of the medical team at Hopkins suggested the possible onset of Alzheimer's disease, and another that she was simply manic-depressive. Occasionally, while writing letters at her computer, her words became uncharacteristically vitriolic, replete with foul language and evil insinuations, even threats, as if some devil had temporarily commandeered her soul. Friends and foes suffered alike on the keyboard, but fortunately, she rarely seemed able to finish a communication, hit the send key, or complete a fax. She felt, as never before, a deep, and increasingly horrible erosion of life itself. And no one seemed to understand why, or particularly care. Except Tristan.

The long-awaited visit to the nation's leading Lyme doctors, she now thought in a more lucid moment, could not come fast enough.

To prevent automatic cancellation, it had been necessary to confirm Terry's office appointment, made months earlier, in March, with Dr. Robert Campollo, in East Hampton, New York, precisely ten days before the actual visit. Fortunately, her son Sean thought, his wife Marissa had taken care of that, given his mother's increasingly erratic management of her own affairs. During her most recent episodes of delirium, she frequently lost all perspective of time, the ability to care for her own physical well-being, and most important, the capacity to take her medications in the doses and at the times prescribed. Sean drove from his home in Manassas every week or so, a round trip of nearly 180 miles, simply to set up her daily medications in a little red compartmentalized plastic pillbox that was clearly marked with the proper dosage for each day for two-week periods. But owing to her blackouts and an increasingly fractured sense of time even that had failed to keep her on track. This was all the more difficult when she harangued him for trying to remind her to follow his instructions.

"I can take care of myself," she shouted during one such altercation. "I know my body better than anyone else ever will," she screamed, "and I know what has to be done. I can manage my own dosages and I don't need you or anyone else to tell me when to take them. I can read the prescription labels just as well as you."

Such bitter confrontations became more frequent as the summer wore on and Terry struggled to maintain control of her own life. On a cloudless Sunday afternoon only a week before the appointments with Drs. Campollo and Brownstein, Sean, Marissa, and Tristan had taken her to dinner at Pusser's Restaurant in Annapolis to plan for the all-important four-day trip. Everything had started out fine. The day was sunny and pleasant, and Terry, for once, was in tolerable spirits. Then, not long after they had been seated at a table overlooking "Ego Alley," the historic waterfront area of old Annapolis where nouveau-riche yacht owners preened and strutted their plastic boats, and wannabes gawked and wished, she started to drift.

At first she merely began to talk quickly, then in a clipped, abbreviated form, which soon digressed into an incoherent ramble. It was, at the outset, nothing new to Sean, but then a sudden diversion into an extremely darker area than he had ever witnessed, stunned and horrified him. For the first time she spoke of her need to die, to commit suicide, to free herself from the torture she was enduring, to never have to grow old with pain. Then, almost as quickly as she had begun her descent, she began to speak lucidly, as if she had been totally coherent all along, which made what she said even more disturbing to everyone at the table. "I don't think I could do it myself," she stated matter-of-factly. "I would more likely get better results by placing myself in a deadly situation or location, like maybe the worst crime area in D.C. at night, so someone else could kill me. A bullet to the brain would do it. You know, right between the eyes. But then, I really wish I had been in the car with Thelma and Louise when they went off the cliff in the movie. Quite dramatic, don't you think? That's how I want to do it. But then again," she said wistfully, "a slug through the old gray matter has its simple appeal."

Sean, Marissa, and Tristan could only look on stunned, and then to feebly pooh-pooh Terry for such talk, even as she again began to reiterate her wish to end it all, slurring her words, with long silences between attempts to speak.

The dinner, of course, was a disaster, but worsened afterwards as they walked to the parking lot. Terry had been shuffling along slowly, steadied by Tristan's bear-like hands, when she suddenly started twisting her head from side to side as if dodging something. In an instant she escaped from Tristan's grasp and raised her hands and arms as if to shield her face and body from some unforeseen projectile. "It's hailing," she shouted. "Goddammit, it's hailing and it's stabbing me everywhere." She fell to her knees, crying, shouting, and then screaming. "Make it stop. Please, God, make it stop. My skin hurts all over. The pain, oh the pain. Please, please. I want to die."

Sean wrapped his arm around his mother's shoulder and pulled her toward him. "You're not going to die. We're going to New York and we're going to make you better, whatever it takes. I swear it."

Then she started to weep, quietly and with a strange dignity, as if she had been fully cognizant of her descent. This was the first time Tristan had seen her tears and he would never forget them. With her face barely inches from her son's, she whispered, "You just don't understand, do you? At least Ellen does!"

"Yes, mom," Sean said sweetly. "I do. But Ellen's dead and you're not. And we're going to New York to make sure you're with us for a long time to come."

Chapter 31

TOAD HALL

A ugust 20, 2003. Sean Anderson knew that taking his mother on the nine-hour drive from Centreville, Maryland, to her appointment with Dr. Campollo in East Hampton, New York, and then the next day down to Dr. Brownstein, in New Jersey, was not likely to be an easy chore. Not only were the turnpikes tedious, but also the necessarily frequent rest stops for Terry's needs had become more time consuming than he had expected. And his mother was more fragile and combative than usual.

Sean had recently been promoted to captain, but had spent most of his life on the West Coast, and had certainly never visited the legendary Hamptons, playtime residence of the rich and famous. He knew little of the domestic lives of the Steven Spielbergs and Jerry Seinfelds of the world who had homes there, but he had some clue when he read with considerable shock the pamphlet Campollo's office, Greater East Hampton Medical Associates, had sent to prep all new patients, especially the part about billing.

"All fees must be paid in full at the time of each visit," it read. "The customary charge for the tick-borne disease consultation is $750. Any additional tests, procedures, and medications will be extra. We do not accept insurance for office charges and under no circumstances will we accept Workmen's Compensation cases. We do accept VISA, American Express and Master Cards, checks, and cash.

Please be prepared to pay at the time of the visit. Office policy dictates that all outstanding balances be paid in full by the time of each visit, for it is difficult for us to provide ongoing services to our patients who are behind in their obligations. All cancellations of appointments must be made no less than ten days in advance. Failure to cancel within the required time guideline will result in a billing for the full fee for all missed appointments."

"Welcome to the Hamptons," he had said to himself. "No wonder the rich get fat and the poor die young. At least the son-of-a-bitch accepts Medicare!"

The memory of the recent dinner and his mother's suicide talk frightened Sean immeasurably. Fortunately, as frequently the case, his mother had no recollection of her ravings at all. But the mere thought that she had uttered such things required that he do something, anything. She was a danger to herself. More than the Lyme disease and all its evil that had changed her life so horribly. He had pondered it for nearly two weeks before deciding what action to take. It would, he knew, anger his mother no end, but it had to be done. He would have to inform both Drs. Campollo and Brownstein about what had happened — and he would have to tell his mother as well what she had said.

As they approached the tollbooth for the Verrazzano Narrows Bridge from Staten Island to Brooklyn, he resolved to broach his concerns and what he intended to do when they met with Campollo. It would be difficult to bring it up outright, so he decided to ease into it ever so gingerly.

"You know, Mom, I've been reading Campollo's material as to what we have to do when we get to his office."

"What do you mean 'we'?" she replied sullenly. "I'm the guinea pig."

"Well, it's just the procedural stuff anyway. The pamphlet said you would initially be interviewed by a nurse, and that should take about fifteen minutes to a half-hour. The nurse is supposed to review your medical files and discuss your history. After that either a physician's assistant or a doctor will meet with you to conduct the exam and review your status. Then you talk with the big cheese, Campollo himself. That's supposed to take anywhere from an hour to three hours, depending on the complexity of the history."

The car stopped at the tollbooth and Sean forked over a $10 bill.

"I suppose," he continued, "after that, your exams are likely to take the better part of the day for the doctors. They may need to conduct some additional tests and other stuff. While that is underway, I am supposed to meet with Dr. C. as well."

Terry looked at her son intently. "What the hell do you have to do with it?"

"Well, they're going to ask a bit about some of you're history, the family, and so forth. You know, standard procedure."

"The family's got nothing to do with it. The last time that sort of thing happened, a damned psychiatrist tried to pin all my ailments on some psychobabble about my supposed feelings of guilt and my sister's murder. You just stay the hell out of it."

"Mother," said Sean sternly, "I will talk with the doctor. He needs to know all about you, and even about what you won't tell him about yourself."

"What are you talking about?" she replied.

"I'm talking about you're threats to kill yourself."

"How dare you!" she screamed. "You'll do no such thing. The next thing they will want to do is put me in a psycho ward. There's a lot of goddamned darkness out there, but my life isn't over, not until I say so. I am still worth something as a human being and nobody can strip that away from me except me. I'm calling this appointment off right now. I want you to turn the damned car around, instantly. Do you hear me?"

At that moment Terry did want to die. She felt utterly betrayed by her own son, her own Judas. She now wanted nothing more than to be forgotten, for no one to remember the way she had been for the last few years, her pathetic life, the degeneration of her body and mind. Some people could come face to face with their personal disasters, diseases, and losses, then let go of the debris, turn their backs on the past, and survive. She had tried, Lord knows she had tried, but had failed miserably. She once had illusions of rationality. Reality, she told herself, won't let you down, so you could deal with it. But now her illusions had been sloughed away. And now there seemed to be nothing left.

"Mom, you're depressed. Sometimes you're in the dark and refuse to recognize it. When you talk about killing yourself in that cold, calculating way of yours, what do you expect me to do? I'm your son and I love you. I can't let you just wander down the pathway to self-destruction. You're worth something, worth a lot to me, to Tristan, Marissa, and everyone else who loves you. I have to tell the doctors everything so that they can help you. I can't take you home. Not now. You have come this far. We have to continue."

Terry did not respond, but looked out the window over New York Bay as the car pressed eastward across the seemingly endless span. Clusters of seagulls glided below, diving onto a garbage-laden barge, being pulled along by a gray and red tug, bound for the offshore dump ten miles out in Absecon Channel. She knew that protest was useless, but she raged quietly against her son.

"If you inform either Campollo or Brownstein about anything in my life, I swear to God I'll never speak to you again."

"Mother, I'm your son. I have no choice. If I have to lose you, I'd rather lose you alive than dead."

For the next two and a half hours, silence reigned in the battered, blue '97 Honda pressing eastward along the south coast of Long Island.

As the car entered the East Hampton city limits, Sean simultaneously scanned the directions brochure provided by Campollo's office and drove on slowly.

"You will know East Hampton not only by the signs," read the pamphlet, "but because the road makes a sharp left adjacent to a park with a small pond. This is the beginning of 'Main Street'. Continue past the town center. After the traffic light and immediately ahead the road forks — take the right fork, to the right of the scenic pond. After you go under the Hampton Bridge the road forks again. Take the right fork — this is our road, Thrush Nest Lane. The office is nine-tenths of a mile ahead, on the right. It is a large tan building, and you will see our mailbox with '139' and 'Campollo' on it. Welcome!!"

By the time Sean and his mother had arrived at the offices of Greater East Hampton Medical Associates, neither was in a pleasant mood. The appointment was for 2:00 p.m. and they had miraculously arrived ten minutes early. The receptionist congenially welcomed them. A nurse immediately ushered Terry into a brightly painted office replete with expensive Italian leather and cherry wood furniture, walls tastefully covered with the latest Howard Behrens paintings, and parquet floors mantled with expensive Persian rugs. On the doctor's elegant desk was a life-sized sculpture of a frog with his tongue half uncurled, about to lunge for its next meal, squatting on a gray marble base bearing a gold-rimmed cartouche. In the cartouche, inscribed in Elizabethan script, were the words: "Welcome to Toad Hall, where anything can happen."

The nurse excused herself for a moment to fetch the new patient's case file sent up from Johns Hopkins by Dr. Foster, and Terry took the opportunity to explore the elegant and expensive office. On a magazine table beside the waiting couch she saw the 14th edition — published the previous November and prominently displayed — of Campollo's 'Diagnostic Approaches, Treatment, and Support Guidelines for Lyme and Other Tick Borne Illnesses,' a treatise that had become the seminal study to date on the subject. It had earned the doctor an international reputation for his work in treating patients with tick-borne illnesses and with late stage and chronic disseminated neurological Lyme disease and its co-infections. He was, indeed, one of the top three Lyme specialists in the nation and vice president of the Lyme Disease Association of America.

What Terry had learned about her sickness had largely been a result of the doctor's research. As she sat quietly in his office waiting for the nurse to work up her history, she began to forget the tedious drive up from Centreville, the argument with Sean, his decision to inform her doctors of her suicide threat, and the multitude of pains and illness that wracked her body. Gradually, her mind began to drift back to that day, many years before, when she saw her smiling sister looking down from a hospital window, waving to her that all was right. And she felt, for the first time in ages, that maybe there was hope.

An hour after her history had been taken and all of the preliminaries had been completed, including the donning of the mandatory paper attire, and the battery of blood, urine, and other tests, Dr. Joseph Campollo finally appeared. He was almost handsome, with a lean face, dark hair precisely coiffed, and thick black glasses, about 5'11, Terry guessed. He wore a dark suit, which set off a pink tie, perfectly held in position on his chest by a diamond tie tack. Terry noticed his hands, slender, with long thin fingers and perfectly manicured nails — the flawless look for an internationally reputed pianist, but not exactly what she had anticipated in a tick doctor.

"Good afternoon, Ms. Anderson," he said with a clipped Brooklyn accent, which ran counter to his European appearance. "I hope your trip up here was pleasant and Alice has taken good care of you."

"Yes, she has, thank you," replied Terry.

"I have already studied the blood work and other test data sent up by Dr. Foster. He tells me that you have already become extremely familiar with the symptoms and progress of your disorder, which, I have to say, is admirable but not uncommon with Lyme sufferers. Indeed, many patients, believe it or not, know a good deal more than their own doctors since it is a relatively new beast."

"Well, I have read up on the subject quite a bit, including your research," Terry said, "which is one of the reasons I'm here."

Campollo smiled. "I'm flattered. Thank you for the compliment. I guess, then, that some of what I'm going to tell you may be redundant, but it is necessary to lay it all out. To begin with, when someone contracts Lyme, there is not one thing wrong but many. Thus it is necessary to fix everything otherwise you don't get back to normal. No one treatment will do it all. Lyme is the totality of many infections at one time, which we call co-infections. The Lyme spirochete, a corkscrew shaped fellow called *Borella burgdorferi*, or simply Bb, is the most complex bacteria know to science with over triple the genetic material of any other germ that's ever been found."

"I knew it was complex, but it has hit me from every angle. Sometimes I feel like my body has become a magnet for pain."

"Then let's start with the bad news first. Lyme bacteria infects not only your immune system, but it also produces neurotoxins that can damage the brain, cause nutritional problems, affect the metabolic rate, and damage organs, tissue, cells, and even DNA. It can also cause serious hormonal disturbances and affect one's libido big time. With chronic Lyme, these little beggars can even rewrite their own DNA and undergo genetic shifts on a month-to-month basis to protect themselves against the array of antibiotics that are usually thrown at them. In my view, it is a national epidemic, yet it's not even formally recognized as such by the AMA, FDA, the WHO, or any other of the establishment institutions. There is no national database on the disease, and not likely to be one as long as the insurance lobby on Capitol Hill refuses to recognize the disease even exists. Indeed most cases, like yours, are ignored or entirely misdiagnosed during Stage 1, when oral antibiotics can have a major effect on, if not completely cure, the disease. More often than not the early aches and pains are simply attributed to Chronic Fatigue Syndrome, the Epstein-Barr virus, and dozens of other causes. Within six months, most sufferers have experienced a parade of symptoms that are usually misdiagnosed. Lyme and syphilis share many of the same symptoms, such as rapid pattern hair loss. Both are deep tissue diseases, although Lyme is a far more complex bacteria. We do not know how many tens of thousands, or even millions, of Lyme sufferers there are in the United States. So my treatment, which is called 'experimental' by some, is based upon more than twenty years of my own research on tick-borne diseases. I hope you can feel reasonably at ease with that."

"Thanks for the comforting news," said Terry caustically. "Maybe I should just pack it in after all."

Campollo, who was sitting on the edge of his desk, stood up and then pulled up a chair to sit directly in front of his new patient.

"Not just yet, my dear. Not just yet. From your record and the history workup, it looks like you began to suffer the first symptoms about eleven years ago, is that right?"

"Yes," Terry answered. "About 1991, after an auto accident that injured my back, I started getting fatigued, aches all over, neck pain and stiffness, headaches, which I first chalked up as a side effect of the accident, and then to some virus. Then the joint pains set in, which one of the docs said was nothing more than arthritis or a byproduct of my countless spinal operations. Then I started having blackouts, occasional hallucinations, weakness all over, digestion problems, nausea, vertigo, and so forth. Every doctor I saw had his own idea of the problem. One said it was Post-Traumatic Stress Disorder, and another said it was due to simple depression. Not until I got the Lyme diagnosis from Johns Hopkins did anyone put a finger on it. And you're right about the libido bit, which has been all but non-existent for several years. Sometimes I would go for weeks feeling perfectly healthy, only to have the symptoms and pain start again all over again. But worse, the symptoms now not only seem to wax and wane, but they shift from one problem to another."

"That, Ms. Anderson," the doctor responded, "is because the bacteria is constantly mutating. It does that about every sixty days to protect itself from attack. Based upon what we already know from your preliminary diagnosis, at least from what I see here in your history, and the time that has already passed, I suspect you are suffering what we call Stage 3 Chronic Lyme, which is, I am afraid, not good. We could run a number of tests on you to confirm that, but in Stage 3, your immune system is either breaking down or has already crashed and blood tests are no longer reliable, and serologic tests are less so."

"Is it treatable at all?"

"I will be frank. It is extremely difficult to treat the infection, or should I say infections, in very late Stage 3. Bb is extremely good at finding secreted spaces, protective niches in the human body, and erecting superb defenses against attackers. Our bodies are all a complex geography. Bb is an expert at finding hiding places in that realm. These germs can live within their own body cells, they can live within your ligaments and tendons where there is little or no blood supply except through small capillaries, and they can live where antibiotics can't get at them. They can morph a protective shell about themselves when they are finally found, which requires a different approach to destroy the armor before we can even get at the beast itself. They can hide from the immune system, in the brain, even the eyes, and quite often in the skin. They love skin because it's cool and a long way from major blood supply. And they rapidly grow in number, and obviously the more of them, and the longer they are there, the greater and more insidious the effect."

"My God, all because I didn't vote Republican! Is there any hope?"

Campollo laughed. "Only if you can carry Florida. Seriously, though, your illness will indeed be a challenge, but it is one I suspect from what I have been told about you, that you are willing to take head on. I will again be frank. From your history, the tests you have already taken, and what your son has told me while you were going through the physical, you are also suffering from severe chronic Lyme encephalopathy, that is neuropsychiatric Lyme, which, unfortunately, effects the brain. It has, besides all of the physical symptoms you have been experiencing, including severe narcolepsy, sleep paralysis, and cataplexy, multiple side effects that masquerade as numerous other illnesses that many, if not most doctors unfamiliar with Lyme, are likely to misdiagnose. In about thirty percent of Stage 3 cases, patients even experience suicidal tendencies."

Both of Terry's hands had fisted, and her jaw had grown taut. There it was: thanks to Sean, Campollo was undoubtedly now aware of her thoughts on suicide. "Is there a cure?"

"From what we know now, chronic Lyme encephalopathy is not curable."

Terry flinched, and her neck began to stiffen as the familiar pain began to invade the base of her skull.

"Now the good news. I don't think it's that important if there is a cure or not," the doctor said. "What do I mean by that? First you have to understand that in our bodies, in our systems, we have a balance. We all have germs in our systems that potentially could cause disease, but don't because they are counteracted by our natural immune system. But in chronic Lyme we have the germs coming up, and the immune system beaten down. So the goal of addressing chronic Lyme is not so much curing — because we can't do that yet — but to get the germs down with our treatments and the immune system up with our supportive therapy till we pass a self-management threshold. And eventually you do get to the point where there may be spirochetes left, but you don't need to stay on antibiotics to keep them down, to do without the antibiotics so you can live with it. You can't get rid of them, but you can live with them and a minimum of symptoms. It is much the same as having diabetes. You can't lick it, but you can live quite comfortably with it if you do everything you are supposed to."

"So there is hope," she said sternly. "We Democrats can coexist in a world with such microscopic monsters. We might even be able to throw some of them out of office!"

Again, Campollo smiled.

"Terry, I have to tell you, again quite frankly: you are more ill in many ways than almost any patient that I have treated since the mid-1970s. But I believe we can make you better. It is going to be extremely difficult to aggressively address the totality of your infections and complaints, and you are going to have more down days than you have up. But if we stick to it, I think we can make some progress. I want to set you up with a physician in Maryland, close to you, who can administer your primary treatment, which is going to be through a permanent I-V central catheter five days a week. I'm sorry to say that the I-V treatment will probably have to last for at least a year. To start with, I am recommending daily four grams each of Rocephrine, Primaxin, and Vancomycin and a colleague of mine, Dr. Christina Quade, down at Talbot General, not far from your home, to administer it. Later you can do it yourself, but for now we will set it up with her. And I will see you in two months."

For the first time in weeks, Terry smiled as she recalled a cynical George Bernard Shaw line from her old English Lit class: "We have not lost faith, but we have transferred it from God to the medical profession."

As she was getting dressed, she failed to notice her son and the doctor conferring in the next room. Nor did she hear the word "suicide" mentioned not once, but repeatedly. She was simply too happy to have a first-class physician who understood her situation. Or so she thought.

Chapter 32

HYPNAGOGIC

The next morning, after spending a night in a Motel 6 in Patchogue, a working-class community in the heart of Long Island, Terry and Sean drove the four hours down to Middletown, New Jersey, for her next appointment, this time with Dr. Michael Brownstein, Jr. Compared to Campollo's office, Brownstein's, set in a quasi-industrial area along Highway 225, was modest. And unlike the New York doctor, Brownstein was almost birdlike in form, skinny to the point of appearing starved. A scraggly goatee hung under his boney chin, and a bad comb-over covered his pate. His thick, black-rimmed glasses made his eyes appear twice their size, giving them a saucer look. Though he wore a white lab coat over his robin's egg blue double-knit polyester suit, there was little to suggest that he was among the pre-eminent American neuropsychiatrists in the country, and a leading scholar on the neurological manifestations of Lyme disease.

His greeting was perfunctory.

"Well, Ms. Anderson," he said, looking through a thick pile of papers on his clipboard. "I see that you have, till now, been employing the services of some of my illustrious colleagues at Johns Hopkins."

"Yes," she replied, "but not with much success."

The doctor chuckled, leaned toward her face, wagged his finger, and shook his head from side to side. "I have to tell you, my dear lady, one does not go to Hopkins to get diagnosed for Lyme. You have made a good decision, however, by seeing my friend Dr. Campollo. There is no one who knows more about your disease than he. That is, of course, with the exception of myself."

Terry looked at him with amusement. He reminded her of the nutcase scientist on the "Simpsons" television program on Fox, who sounded as if he was forever doing an amusing imitation of Jerry Lewis. For such an unassuming-looking gent, she thought, she would have expected a bit more humility.

"I know what you're thinking," he said. "Modesty is a good thing, but it is, in truth, merely an unnecessary social contrivance, an excuse if you will, to console those less prepared to deal with the world than those who are more capable. I have no such qualms or false modesty. I can assure you that Dr. Campollo and I will do everything in our power to get you back to reasonable health."

The conference with Dr. Brownstein was anything but comforting to Theresa Anderson, but it was reassuring that he and Campollo were on the same track. Both took her quite seriously. Unlike the psychiatrists she had met with in the past, he did not commence by probing into her life with inane questions—that would, she guessed, come soon enough—but by providing her with a complete background on what was known about the impact of Lyme disease, and most importantly its effect on the brain in Stage 3, and the impairments of cognitive power of sufferers such as herself. His primary intent was to establish a base and then explore. He spoke both slowly and methodically, as if addressing a ten-year old in class.

"First, you have to understand that some of your symptoms," he began, "may be indirectly a result of a lessening, a degradation, or absence of neurological or emotional functions. It is also possible they may have resulted directly from some other dysfunction of the cerebral cortex, where cognitive processing occurs. Laboratory tests such as MRIs, PET and SPECT scans have demonstrated, time and again, both psychological and anatomical traits associated with the dysfunction of the cerebral cortex in Lyme and other tick borne diseases."

"Sir, that's all well and good," said Terry, "but every doctor I see, with the exceptions of Campollo and Foster, has told me I have everything from arthritis to Alzheimer's or that I'm psychosomatic, a hypochondriac, outright nuts, or just manic depressive. I understand now from Campollo that the physical symptoms can change as the spirochete itself changes, but how about my mind? Am I going crackers?"

The doctor leaned back in his leather chair and continued. "They are wrong. That three pounds of matter that we all have in our heads, the human brain, is the most complex structure on the planet. Your symptoms are very real and must be explained. They cannot simply be discounted as being imaginary. Late-stage Lyme disease has been erroneously diagnosed as everything from psychosomatic, hypochondriasis, malingering, and hysteria to factitious disorders such as Munchausen's syndrome, Somatoform, and conversion disorder. In most cases of late-stage Lyme such as yours, a person is reasonably healthy throughout most of their life, but then there is a point in time where a multitude of symptoms progressively appear. The number and complexity of these symptoms may be devastating and the illness is frequently labeled somatization disorder, hypochondriasis, or psychosomatic. However, both hypochondriasis and psychosomatic illnesses normally commence in childhood and, depending upon the stress factors in one's life, are lifelong conditions that vary in intensity. If a complex illness with both mental and physical components begins in adulthood, the likelihood that this is psychosomatic is very slight."

Brownstein took off his glasses, removed a handkerchief from his pocket, and began to wipe the lenses vigorously. His squinting eyes seemed to have miraculously diminished in size.

"Let me say that the cognitive impairments from Lyme are indeed very different than in Alzheimer's. You see, Lyme is, above all, usually a disease of the white matter. Alzheimer's is predominately a disease of the gray matter. Your memory association occurs in the white matter, but memory itself is stored in the gray matter. That is why you have experienced a slowness of recall and occasionally incorrect associations, because there is a dysfunction in your white matter. Do you understand so far?"

"I think so," Terry replied slowly.

"In contrast, gray matter dysfunction usually results in a loss of the information which has previously been stored. I'll give you an example. An Alzheimer's patient may not recall the word "baseball," while someone with Lyme encephalopathy such as yourself can, but may find it difficult to recall or retrieve a closely related word. Some of the symptoms found in encephalopathies are also associated with illnesses such as lupus, stroke, chronic fatigue, and other diseases that affect the brain."

Brownstein switched on his tape recorder, but continued talking.

"The first thing we are going to do after I finish here is to give you a mental-status exam. It will be the first component of our clinical assessment of your problem, because everyone suffering from LE possesses his or her own unique profile of symptoms. The reason I am going to do that first is because no single symptom or sign can be diagnosed by itself as Lyme disease. The status exam, instead, looks for a cluster or pattern of signs and symptoms commonly associated with Lyme. Are you still with me?"

"Yes." Terry had begun to focus on the doctor's scraggly goatee to maintain her concentration.

"There are numerous methods for categorizing cognitive functioning. Simple mental functions, such as flexing the thumb of your right hand, correlates with comparatively unfussy brain circuitry while more complex functions, such as flying an airplane, require the action of a more integrated neural circuitry. The difference between these two actions is like the difference between playing middle C on a flute versus a symphonic orchestra playing the 1812 Overture."

Terry continued to focus on the goatee as the doctor swept along with his monologue. She was certain she saw something move in it.

"I'm willing to wager," the physician continued, "that most, if not all, of your attention impairments were not present before the onset of the disease, whenever that was . . ."

"As far as we can guess, 1991," she interjected. "I was re-infected several times since then, the last time being only two months ago, probably from the ticks on my dog Tuffy."

". . . and you probably have difficulty sustaining attention, and become increasingly distracted when frustrated. Am I correct?" Without waiting for an answer, he pressed on. "And you have considerable difficulty prioritizing which perceptions are deserving of a higher allocation of your attention. Right?"

She was certain now that there was something moving in his goatee, like a little silver-and-green bug.

"If we equate attention span to the lens of a camera, we require the flexibility to continually re-allocate attention reliance upon the current life condition. As with the camera, we shift back and forth between a wide angle and a zoom lens focus to add to or reduce acuity of attention, of course depending on the needs of the current situation. A loss of this flexibility results in some blend of a loss of acuity and/or disproportionate acuity to the incorrect environmental perceptions, which we call hyperacusis. Hyperacuity can be hearing, seeing, touch, and smell."

Terry was now certain there was more than one silver-green bug in Brownstein's goatee. Indeed, it looked as if the beard were beginning to come alive with the little critters. She debated whether or not to warn the doctor, who seemed entirely unaware of the infestation, but thought better of it. Yet, it might be fun to watch his reaction when he discovered the swarm, but the man just droned on.

"The most common is auditory hyperacusis. Sounds seem magnified and are more irritating, and often unbearably painful. Sometimes it can be selective auditory hyperacusis to specific types of sounds. Visual hyperacusis may result as a response to bright lights or artificial lighting. Tactile hyperacusis may be in response to scratchy or tight-fitting clothing, vibrations, or temperature. Sometimes, merely being touched may be outrageously painful. Some of my patients wear loose-fitting sweat suits all the time. Most all are frustrated that being touched can be so painful because it gets in the way of every familial or social activity, and sexual relationships are difficult, if not impossible. And finally, excessive reactivity to certain smells, such as soaps, perfumes, petroleum products, flowers, and so forth, can result in olfactory hyperacusis. How am I doing so far?"

Terry giggled as she watched a big black bug with a purple spot on its back crawl out of the goatee and leap onto Brownstein's tie, and then into his lab coat pocket. "Just fine, doctor. Just fine."

The doctor seemed mildly perturbed. "I know this can be a tad boring, but I never thought it was amusing."

"No sir, it's not. It's just that your goatee . . ."

Brownstein wrapped his bony fingers around his beard, as if to strain something out of it. Terry stifled a giggle as a score of black crickets fell onto the doctor's white coat and scurried to find hiding places. The doctor noticed nothing. "I've had this since graduate school. And my wife thinks it's beautiful. Can we now continue?" he asked indignantly. "After all, it's my time, but it's your money, and more importantly, your physical and mental health, my dear."

"Yes, let's do continue," she said.

For the next half hour Brownstein rambled on about the influence of Stage 3 LE on memory storage and retrieval, working memory, memory encoding, and short- and long-term memory. And as he spoke the bugs just kept coming, covering his coat, and then his hands and face, but without apparent notice or irritation. Now, a distinct hum began to fill Terry's ears, apparently emanating from the insects, which had begun to spill onto the floor, and scurry about in wild pandemonium.

"Short-term, or recent memory is the ability to remember information for relatively brief periods of time, while, long-term memory is information from years in the past, the collected facts during our lives. In LE, there is usually a failure of short-term memory first, followed almost always quite late in the illness by a loss of long-term memory. Many sufferers display slowness of recall with different types of explicit information, such as names, words, faces, numbers, or geographical or spatial cues. In some cases, a patient may also display slowness of recall of implicit information, of procedural memory tasks, such as tying a knot, or doing other tasks they have done all their lives. Sometimes they have trouble with letter and/or number sequences. This can include letter reversals, reversing the sequence of letters in words, spelling errors, number reversals, or word substitution errors. That would be like inserting the opposite, closely-related or wrong words in a sentence. You still with me?"

"Yes," Terry lied. The bugs had gained her full attention and the doctor's voice had become merely background. The humming had become louder, and Terry's body was starting to stiffen. The floor had become a veritable moving carpet of insects.

"Good! Now, I want to go onto processing, that is, the creation of associations. This process allows us to interpret complex information and to respond in an adaptive manner."

The carpet was literally alive with insects, millions of them, moving almost like waves upon the water, waves that had begun to lap at Terry's feet. In one instance she rationalized to herself that the bugs were little more than another of her hallucinations, and then in another instance she physically reacted, lifting her feet off the floor.

Undismayed, Brownstein continued his verbal dissertation. "Some LE patients, who were never dyslexic or had any learning disabilities, frequently begin to suffer from such handicaps. Their reading comprehension disintegrates, and they sometimes find it difficult or impossible to understand someone speaking to them. They cannot localize the source of sound. Space becomes distorted. Sometimes things seem smaller than they are. Depth perception suffers, and makes even simple tasks, such as driving a car, dangerous."

By now the humming had morphed into a deep droning sound, and the whole room, walls, ceiling, floor, desk, and chairs were covered with black bugs, some with purple spots on their backs, and others that glowed an iridescent green. Terry closed her eyes.

"Think of something else," she told herself. "Anything. Just ignore them and they will go away."

The droning grew louder and she could feel the prickly touch of thousands of spiny insect feet begin their ascent up her right leg, scurrying, looking for an opening. An opening to lay eggs, or place their larvae in. A cut, a wound, any cavity would do. Even the one between her legs.

"They are not real," she said to herself, over and over. She tried to focus on the dark behind her eyelids. Focus on the dark. Focus. Gradually, an image began to emerge from the blackness and then become sharper. As the image took shape, she saw the outline of figures, which soon took on color and definition. She saw herself as a child on the kitchen floor at her old home in Lane Manor, holding her Raggedy Ann doll. Ellen was uncurling her hair and smiling beatifically down upon her.

"What's the matter, doll?" her sister said with a loving smile. "I know you want to be with me, but it's not time yet. Okay?"

"Sure," said Terry. "I understand. But when?"

"I'll let you know, honey. But not now." Then Ellen was gone.

Terry opened her eyes. The bugs were gone, the humming sound had ceased, and Dr. Brownstein was talking as if nothing had happened.

"A problem associated with your visual spatial processing," he continued, "we call optic ataxia, which is a difficulty targeting movements through space. For example, you may have a tendency to bump into doorways, difficulty driving and parking a car in tight spaces, and targeting errors when placing or reaching for objects. You may also suffer from an inability to perceive left from right, to do mathematical calculations without using your fingers or a calculator. You may have a problem speaking smoothly, and you may stutter or slur your words almost like you are intoxicated. And it often becomes impossible to write a complete sentence."

The rest of the orientation went off without a hitch. Brownstein closed with a soliloquy on imagery functions affected by LE that actually proved intriguing to Terry.

"Imagery," declared the doctor, "is a uniquely human trait. It is the ability to create what never was within our minds. When functioning properly, it is a major component of human creativity, but when impaired, as in your case, it can result in psychosis. The ability to picture something, such as a map, in our head can be severely affected. You may suffer from images that suddenly appear, which may be aggressive, horrific, sexual, or otherwise. You may also experience what is called hypnagogic hallucinations."

"Hypnagogic hallucinations!" said Terry. "What the hell is that?"

"It's the continuation of a dream, even after you're fully awake. There is also a tendency towards having vivid nightmares, often in Technicolor. You lose a sense of physical existence, a sense that the environment around you is even there."

"You're right there," Terry interjected. "My childhood dreams were always in monochrome, but now they're in vivid colors."

"Of course," said Brownstein in a serious tone, "your record indicates you have suffered from these frequently. Hearing, seeing, feeling and/or smelling something that is not present. In LE, sometimes this takes the form of hearing music or a radio station in the background. Unlike schizophrenic hallucinations, these are accompanied by a clear sensorium, and you become aware hallucinations are present."

"Don't bug me on that one," Terry chuckled, as she watched an albino caterpillar with long sticky-looking antennae crawl out of the doctor's left ear.

Chapter 33

THE WORSENING

Within three days after returning from the epochal visits with Drs. Campollo and Brownstein, Terry drove herself to Talbot General Hospital, eighteen miles from Centreville, to begin her IV and Bicillin treatment with Dr. Christina Quade. The trip, normally less than half an hour on a perfectly straight highway, took more than two hours because of her need to repeatedly pull off the road to regain her focus or to reorient herself.

When she finally reached the hospital, she was less than impressed with the appointed agent of Campollo's ministrations. A specialist in gynecology, and an acolyte of Campollo's work in tick-borne diseases, Quade had recently joined the board of directors of a local Lyme support group called the Eastern Shore Lyme Disease Association, the very existence of which was exciting news to Terry. The doctor, a heavy-set woman with the arms and torso of a gladiator, had long, dirty-looking hair and a chubby face, and wore heavy teal-rimmed glasses that she should not have. Her peremptory demeanor was anything but warm, and a distinct contrast to her mentor in New York. The doctor-patient chemistry, so evident between Terry and Drs. Campollo and Brownstein, was definitely absent with the lady physician at Easton.

After opening a semi-permanent entry port in Terry's right arm, then administering her first IV medication, Dr. Quade excused herself with little more than a nod. "I'll see you on Tuesday at 10 a.m.," was all she said. All in all, Terry thought, given her luck with the medical profession, that seemed okay, since acquiring two excellent physicians out of three wasn't bad. And as far as she was concerned, the frowzy-looking Quade was little more than a filling station attendant who plugged in the IV tubes to pump God-only-knows what chemicals and microbes into her system. That which doesn't kill you, someone once said, only makes you stronger.

The day following her first Bicillin and Rochephin treatments was accompanied by one of her worse hallucination attacks to date. They increased thereafter, along with the darkness of depression, most notably after each of her injections, along with newer and more menacing symptoms. Her short-term memory began to rupture and fade from moment to moment even more than before. Simple daily chores such as feeding and medicating her sick and older pets, primarily her dogs, were frequently forgotten. She became increasingly unsure of what was reality and what was simply something that had occurred in the fog of a hallucination.

One evening she came across a copy of a long and rambling letter she had written — but couldn't remember having done so — to Dr. Brownstein. The piece was filled with words of despair, hopelessness, dejection, and fear of being incarcerated against her will. The letter embarrassed her deeply, for she was uncertain if she had faxed it or not. Simply reading it frightened her. What might the doctor think and do if it had actually been sent, especially since he was well aware of her talk of suicide and paranoia. The letter read:

"I want to be forgotten. I want no one to ever think of me again, not the way I've been the last several years. This is what I want: I want not to be thought of, so humiliated at what I've become — pathetic. If I ever felt some hope of things turning around soon, I just don't see it now. Please, I beg you, do not have me hospitalized against my will. I have no plans to do anything to myself any time soon. And I don't know if I could, just thoughts of getting rid of all material things, getting in my car and driving west, into the dessert, and from there I don't know. I'm afraid, writing you a letter like this, that you might do something rash, meaning calling someone to my home, to hospitalize me against my will. Again, there's no way I will do anything to hurt myself any time real soon, but something has got to give very soon. I need to be able to function. I have to work. I am without resources or support. I am alone. Alone."

Terry felt obliged to send Brownstein an apology for what she felt was a sniveling, whining correspondence, in the event that it had ever been sent. She also informed him of her latest symptoms and depression, as well as the increase in narcoleptic episodes and bizarre imagery. She closed with a plea to give her something stronger than Bicillin and in larger doses. "I need something, anything," she wrote, "that will give me faster improvement. This nightmare has become unbearable."

Two days later, having forgotten the whole episode, she sent the apology to Dr. Campollo as well. It was on the same day she resolved to disassociate herself from Dr. Quade's service as soon as she possibly could, and then promptly forgot her resolution.

Terry was not eager to drive to the hospital for her next visit with Quade and the treatment, which, in the few weeks since her visit with Campollo, she had grown to despise for their almost guaranteed after-effects. Nevertheless, though still feeling poorly in general, her drive to Easton had this time been without incident, delirium or hallucinations. But that was before her next descent into hell.

The IV hookup proceeded without difficulty, and Terry asked for a blanket and pillow and for someone to turn off the overhead fluorescent light. As usual she reclined in her chair to rest and, she hoped, sleep through the procedure. Then, as the fluids commenced flowing into her body, the anticipated nightmare began immediately.

The descent commenced with the onset of severe and progressively agitating sounds assailing her ears, which had suddenly become sensitive in the extreme. And with every magnified noise, from the rustling of fabric to the dripping of water, her body began to jerk in short, startled responses. These soon expanded into full spasms. Then she began to feel that familiar and almost nauseating dip in and out of consciousness, accompanied by severe and aching chills. From her hips to already painful feet, the cold wrapped about her in paralyzing swiftness. The systemic attack on the nervous system, replete with vibration sensations, tingling and throbbing, came next, followed by a progressively severe neck and head stiffness, and intense visceral and intestinal discomfort.

As the minutes passed during the treatment Terry jerked about in her chair involuntarily with spasms and pain, all the while continuing to drift momentarily in and out of consciousness. At one moment the room seemed to be moving about her fixed position, and at another she seemed to be physically bloated to such proportions that her body was touching all of the walls at one time. Then she shrank back to normal size.

Five doors that had not been there before appeared around the room. She watched with curiosity as five nurses, each emerging from a different door at the same moment, appeared with the sound of a gunshot and began to surround her menacingly, closely, their fetid breath almost overwhelming her senses. Terror swept across her as she looked down and saw her hands and feet bound to her recliner chair. Blood was on the damp pillow beneath her head. Her blouse had somehow disappeared and her naked torso and secret parts were slippery with sweat. Each of the nurses, she now saw, was carrying a bucket filled with blood, which, with mammoth paintbrushes, they began to splash on her and on the walls with ghoulish abandon. Visions of the Queen of Hearts from the Disney cartoon "Alice in Wonderland" passed before her eyes as they began to chant, "We're painting the roses red, painting the roses red." Their mantra was repetitious, piston-like, almost motorized, as they circled about, spattering everything, including themselves, in blood. Up and down the nurse-pistons bobbed, splashing and bubbling the red gore all about. "We're painting the roses red," they sang, "painting the roses red."

Terry's legs now felt not only cold, but also terribly wet. She looked down at them with dread. Was it the blood or had she crapped and pissed on herself again? Once more she looked up, and all but one of the bloody nurses had disappeared. Only Ella, Quade's assistant, remained. Her fulsome mouth was accentuated and fearsomely clown-like with a grotesquely painted-on smile in crimson lipstick. Ella was on roller skates fitted with bat wings, skating roller-derby style around a nurses' station and holding a large whip. At first Ella was snapping the air, and then began whipping patients being wheeled through double doors from the same day surgery unit.

Beyond the doors Terry saw water where the hallway had once been. A gondolier dressed in black was herding the other patients, who each dropped a coin in his outstretched palm as they boarded his boat. One appeared to be a tall teenage boy, in a tee shirt and a blue denim jacket with torn off sleeves. The familiar-looking boy looked back at her as he walked towards the gondolier, his sad gaze meeting hers in mid-flight. His lips seemed to be forming words directed at her, but she could hear nothing before he turned and pressed on. She could make out, through the mist, that the boat soon began to traverse, a giant figure on the distant shore. He too seemed somehow familiar. The grinning head on the figure was over-sized, with wavy black hair. It also appeared that he was wearing blue and white-checkered overalls, and was waving a bloody butcher knife in one hand and a platter above its head with the other. On the platter were severed body parts, dripping gore over the sides. A sudden snapping noise turned Terry's attention back to her own situation. Ella had returned, her attention again focusing on Terry as she began skating directly toward her, cracking her whip and laughing cruelly.

Terry closed her eyes in utter terror and tried desperately to think. The bitch is only an illusion. She's only an illusion. Her next memory was of having awakened, fully clothed, but severely chilled, her legs painful and weak, and that nauseatingly wet and sticky feeling between underwear and flesh running down her legs. She was alone in the room and rang for the nurse. No one came. She rang again with equally negative results. Slowly she attempted to stand to walk to the bathroom a few feet away, but her legs crumbled beneath her. As she fell she grabbed the IV pole, which came crashing down on top of her, just as a nurse appeared.

"Greeeaaat timmmming," she said slurring her words. "My leeeegs are soooo weak annnnnd my ballllllannnnce is so farrrr off, I don't thinnnnnk I cannnn make it toooo myyyy riiiiiiiiide."

"I'm sorry," replied the nurse, "I can't understand you. Could you try again, dear?"

Terry repeated herself, slurring her words and garbling her sentence even more.

"Wait here," said the nurse impatiently, as if Terry were going to lunge out the door. "I'm going to have to speak to the doctor."

Twenty minutes later Quade's Pakistani partner, Dr. Patel, appeared, noted with one glance the puddle of urine and dark liquid matter on the floor, glanced at her chart, and asked with a heavy accent: "Now what's the problem, Miss Anderson?"

The last vague memory Terry had of her IV treatment before she slipped again into unconsciousness was of Dr. Patel giving the nurse Campollo's phone number and the nurse making a call and then handing her the phone as if she would be able to handle the situation herself. Her last conscious thought was, 'If I ever awake again, I swear I will never see Quade or Ella again.' After that all was darkness..

Ironically, for several days following her last treatment in Easton, the light began to shine through, the nightmares and lost moments were again replaced with a respite of normality. The drugs finally seemed to be taking hold and working although the gray cloud of depression seemed an ever-present curse that could not be dispersed. Then, just as quickly, new symptoms, new pain areas, more hallucinations, replaced the old ones. Desperate to maintain a semblance of balance, Terry fought through each night to stay awake, for sleep was becoming just a very real euphemism for nightmares and horror, her visions of death in myriad forms.

On Saturday, October 5, Tristan asked her out to dinner. He had not planned it, for on weekends he had normally gone out with his brother, who usually came down to help him on his house in the mornings and stayed the better part of the evenings. This weekend, though, his brother had other business, and Tristan had finally gotten up his courage to ask her.

"Thanks, but I don't think so," she said. "Tris, I'm totally depressed and absolutely beat."

"We can still go out to dinner," he laughed. "Come on, now. It'll do you good. Please. After all, I don't think you want to eat anymore of that stuff you've been throwing on your table lately — that is when you eat at all."

With a weak smile, she finally consented. "Well, I guess I can be depressed at a restaurant just as well as here."

And so it began, but not just on the weekends. Her favorite haunt had once been the Fisherman's Inn, over on Kent Island, off Route 50, at Kent Narrows, where she and Philip had frequently gone. The haunting recollections of jaunts there with her father, though, had brought back too many sad memories, so she and Tristan usually opted for the next best choice, Annie's Hillside Restaurant, also at the Narrows. And with every outing, she began to warm to her tenant in ways she had not considered possible.

She soon began to e-mail Tristan at all hours of the day and night, even though he was in the same house. The communications, often abbreviated with misspelled or misplaced words were usually positive and full of thanks for his efforts to assist her. Soon he began to take care of her cats, leaving them water and food in the garage when she forgot, which was becoming more frequent. On weekends he would take her into Centreville or Easton to shop, and on occasion to Talbot General for her IV treatments with Quade, whose often insensitive and sometimes "sloppy" treatment convinced her that a replacement must be found. He offered her encouragement when she was down, and even helped her assemble a resume in a worthy but futile attempt to secure a freelance editing stint with a local publishing house.

In late November, just before she departed with Sean on the long drive to East Hampton for her second marathon round of appointments with Campollo and

Brownstein, Terry wrapped her arms around her tenant and hugged him. The engineer had become her right arm, her chief support, and her enabler. With a chuckle he began to refer to himself as "The Terry Slave."

The second expedition north with Sean, this time at the onset of the Christmas holiday season, proved quietly as hellacious as the first. Somehow, her son had neglected to confirm the appointments ten days in advance as he had promised. All that mattered to Terry was that she herself was supposed to make the last-minute corrections. She found it difficult to pull her thoughts and words together cohesively, and pleaded with Campollo's appointment secretary for a reprieve.

She had been totally unaware that Seam had major problems of his own, not the least of which was his wife's pregnancy and a series of major complications of which Terry knew nothing. She had grown irate over what she deemed her son's cavalier, indeed blasé attitude towards the whole episode. This made the drive frosty and solemn, filled with anything but Yuletide cheer. His preoccupied silence during the entire trip only enhanced the awful feeling that she was now little more than a useless burden to him.

By the time they had arrived at Campollo's office, Terry had balled up into a shivering, cocoon-like shell, insulated by a travel blanket, and again in a vacuous mental state. Her right hand was tightly wrapped around Ellen's 1944 dime necklace. By the time the doctor could see her she appeared almost comatose and had started breathing in shallow, short gulps, her body trembling in unrhythmical patterns. More than alarmed at the sudden change, Sean was obliged to carry her bodily into the doctor's office. For once Campollo also exhibited a definite sign of distress as he quickly examined the woman, and instructed an ambulance be called to transport her immediately to the nearby Hospital Center of Northampton.

Within a half hour, as Sean accompanied the EMTs, wheeling his mother into the emergency gate at the hospital, he glanced at the sign above the doorway, which read: "Member of the Peconic Wellness Foundation of America."

For the next month, the Hospital Center of Northampton would be Terry Anderson's home and battleground, as she meandered in and out of consciousness, sometimes shouting or screaming at doctors, nurses, and passersby, and at other times brooding pensively, crying, or occasionally conversing amicably with staff. When the hospital psychiatrist entered the room and identified himself as such, however, any fragile peace that might have hitherto prevailed evaporated as if Satan himself had engaged her for her soul. Campollo, however, did not visit, but left instructions that as soon as Terry had been released to her son's care, he should bring her in for a visit.

There were rare moments of tranquility during Terry's stay at Northampton, usually following brief calls from Tristan, back in Maryland. He had express-mailed her a giant picture of Tuffy, whom he had been taking care of in her absence. "It's her poster," he later told Sean. "She liked that. I'd talk to her by phone, but she really didn't like to converse for long, maybe five minutes. Claimed she had issues with the long distance rates from Long Island or something, but I knew it was really because she couldn't concentrate on anything longer than that."

Terry's retention of some personal details, despite her meandering mind, was sometimes remarkably sharp. February 5 was to be Tristan's fifty-sixth birthday, and somehow, during one of his daily phone calls, she unexpectedly brought up the subject. "Well," she said without warning as he apprised her, in a running commentary of what was going on back home, "what do you want for your birthday?"

Tristan was stunned and replied slowly.

"How about you come home safely and well?"

After a long silence, she replied, "I'll be home, but I doubt if I'll ever be whole again."

The long hospital stay had accomplished nothing. By March 2004 Terry's periods of insensibility, where everything had begun to merge into a gray incomprehensible blur in her memory, had increased five-fold. Maintenance of her daily prescription dosage intake of Rocephine IV, Klonopin, Provezal, Oxycontin, Coumadin, Zonegran, Provegil, Namenda, and Loutrimin (for a new fungal infestation) was an ongoing problem until Sean arrived to sort it all out. Terry, however, either wouldn't or couldn't comply with his simple system to remind her of how many and what type of pills to take each day, and became increasingly belligerent regarding his instructions.

By now Terry was unable to even write out a simple check. Again her son came to the rescue and began to manage her mail and pay her bills out of his own account, despite heated objections. Dutifully requesting her forgiveness, he continued to take over an increasingly greater responsibility for management of her affairs despite the 180-mile round trip each time he visited, usually four times a week.

The symptom flares continued to worsen.

Once, before her next scheduled appointment with Campollo in New York, she had blanked out entirely for two days while sitting in front of her computer monitor, motionless or walking around her house, from room to room, for hours on end. There were even more bouts of severe delirium, in an out of consciousness, and violent hallucinations, she later noted in her diary, "of auto accidents everywhere, people hanging out of cars, lots of blood." Although now exhibiting frequent chills, a slight fever, and sporadic diarrhea, she had mentally come around by the February 9 appointment date, and again Sean had driven her up. And again, confirmation of the appointment had been forgotten.

This time the trip northward was more contentious than ever, as Terry retreated even further into her increasingly diminutive universe. When her son commented on the irregularity of her medication dosage, she erupted in a fit of pique.

"Do not worry about me," she said sharply. "Whatever I do, I do in order to cope. That means keeping to myself until I am ready to do otherwise. Thanks for caring and wanting to lend a hand, and for what you've already done to help. But I can handle it myself. And in the meantime, I do not want to talk about my so-called 'issues.' Okay?"

Then, during the session with Campollo, she unceremoniously blurted out her outright dislike of Quade and her seeming incompetence and hostility. She had not expected his reaction to her request that he recommend another physician to attend to her IV and prescriptions. Nor was she aware of the many years of deep professional and personal friendship between the two doctors, or that they had gone through medical school and interned together.

Following the day-long examination and tests, Campollo met with her in his office. Her eyes fixed upon the bronze frog on his desk as he spoke.

"Terry, I'm afraid I'm going to have to terminate our care here. You're much too far away for us to be able to continue our treatment here with any regularity. I gather from your son that there is some difficulty in even getting here. Moreover, for the sake of our other patients, we are obliged to stick to our policy of making last-minute adjustments when one fails to confirm appointments."

"You can't do that," she blurted out. "I'm sick and we've just started. You're a specialist and . . . and I desperately need your help."

"I'm sorry, but our policy regarding confirmations is firm, for the sake of all my patients. I'm sure you can understand that. As you apparently find Dr. Quade unfit to assist you, I am recommending that you set up an appointment with Dr. Jorge D'Silva," he said coldly while writing out an address, "at Bay Country Internal Medicine, in Easton. He is perfectly fit to continue your treatment."

Taking her hand in his and shaking it gently, he concluded, "I wish you the very best. You're a fighter and you can lick this. Good day."

And with that, he turned and departed.

Terry was stunned, virtually speechless. Then, as the door closed, she screamed at the departing physician with whom she had been placing so much trust: "Cut me loose will you? I hope your ass rots in hell, you arrogant son-of-a-bitch. All of you doctors think you're gods, but you're nothing more than dog shit."

Suddenly her knees began to shake and the familiar pain at the base of her skull returned. Zombie-like she left the office and said nothing to Sean, who was reading an old *Field and Stream* in the waiting room. Not surprisingly, the drive to Brownstein's office in New Jersey was even more frosty than the trip to East Hampton. Terry felt the relationship with her son had now become strained almost to the breaking point, but being fired by her own specialist, especially one she had to travel nine hours to visit, over a foul-up in confirming her appointment took the cake.

Nor was the appointment with Dr. Brownstein anything like their last time. The funny, birdlike psychiatrist acted more like the shrinks Terry had encountered in the past, asking a few pointed questions here and there, and saying little in response. She discussed her most recent and recurrent symptoms, her depression and anxiety, headaches, fatigue, sleeping problems, and memory lapses, all of which generated little expression from the doctor. At the end of the session, he wrote out a barely readable prescription for four drugs.

"I'm increasing your dosage of Aricept for long-term memory loss to 5 milligrams per day, taken each morning. I want you also to take 12.5 milligrams of Paxil after dinner for one week, then 25 milligrams thereafter. I'm also starting you on Provigil for your cognitive impairment, your fatigue, narcolepsy, and short-term memory loss at 100 milligrams each morning, and then increase it to 200, if you tolerate it, after four days. Once you have stabilized with the Provigil, I want you to start taking 100 milligrams of Depakote ER every night for three days, then increase it to 500. This will help with your sensory symptoms, mood, and your headaches."

"I'm sorry, Dr. Brownstein," said Terry. "I don't know if I can follow all that, even if you write it down. I can barely remember from one day to the next what I should be doing. I'm sure you, of all people can understand that. Please. Don't invade me with fixes and chemistry. Just be me. Put yourself in my place and try to understand."

"I'm sure your son can help you with that," he answered blankly. Then, he too dropped a bombshell. For much the same reasons given by Campollo, Brownstein was also terminating his treatment of Terry. "I am going to recommend another physician,

Dr. Miles E. Sloan, a psychiatrist who is close to you and can take over. He is a world-renowned psychiatrist, and fortunately for you he is in Easton. I will forward all your records to him, and it will be far easier on both you and your son."

Terry was again speechless. She looked hard at the man, hoping upon hope to see a giant Black Widow spider emerge from his coat pocket and crawl onto his face for a good bite, but for once her proclivity to hallucinate failed her.

Chapter 34

ARMAGEDDON OVER MELON AND JUICE

The spring of 2004 was becoming a navigational problem for Terry, and in particular the narcoleptic and hypnagogic attacks. Falling from whatever perch she was on at the time of such seizures was taking a toll on her fragile frame, especially on her face and arms. Her nose, battered from collisions with her keyboard, as she would collapse forward while writing, was now usually swollen and red, with bruises and scabs, often oozing at the bridge and between the eyes. Within the space of two months she had broken three pairs of glasses from slamming into the keyboard or monitor. The attacks, she began to note in her diary, were cyclical, intensifying for three to four weeks, then subsiding over a week or so, before beginning anew. The application of soothing salves, antibiotics, and Band-Aids over her open sores during her now daily visits to the hospital had become almost routine.

Near the end of April, she informed Dr. Sloan, she had experienced several more tick bites, probably vectored in via her dogs. Then, while sitting in her bathtub taking a rare shower (as she no longer dared to stand and it required too much energy), she discovered another bull's-eye rash covering the whole of her right buttock and part of her right thigh.

Darkness seemed to be setting in more profoundly than ever. Although she could still drive short distances, she had become increasingly reliant upon Tristan and Brian, "two good Samaritans," as she called them, to take her to the hospital for her daily IV hookup. On May 1, after a short series of attacks, followed by the death of Sam, one of her favorite cats, she wrote in her diary: "I can't do this anymore. My animals, some sick, others long sick, and I can't care for them, as I can't afford the vet, and now no transportation either. Can't pay rent, Jesus, how much more is a person expected to take? I have no money, and have become financially dependent in no small measure on my son and daughter-in-law."

On May 7, in the midst of an IV treatment, Terry began to suffer another disconnect. "I have a vague image," she wrote in her diary later that afternoon, "of shifting about with sharp pointed scissors, which I intend to cut the sutures holder in the IV line. When the nurse came in she thought I was trying to kill myself, and I shouted at her 'Do not call anyone to my home. I'm not going to kill myself, anytime soon.' All I could think of was getting the damned thing out, going home, and getting my affairs in order, getting rid of stuff."

Not long after returning home, she received a call from Dr. Sloan.

"I understand . . . I am told you tried to kill yourself with a pair of scissors."

"That's nonsense," Terry replied. "I was in one of my mind fogs, and for some reason tried to dig out the IV."

"They told me you kept talking about getting your affairs in order, getting rid of all your belongings, getting ready for the big day, the most perfect day in your life. What does that mean? Are you talking about suicide?"

Terry stared at the phone for a moment, and then hung up without answering.

As soon as the call had ended, Sloan called Sean Anderson to discuss the feasibility of having Terry placed in a psychiatric care facility.

Five days later, during an appointment with Dr. George Marsalek, a member of the new medical team managing her treatments at the hospital, Terry was told in no uncertain terms that she was not suffering from episodes of delirium, hallucinations, and hypnagogic attacks caused by Lyme disease, but was afflicted with epilepsy. Marsalek recommended an extensive sleep study, another series of MRIs, and a complete revision of her prescriptions.

"Dr. Marsalek, with respect, I suggest you read my medical record. It has already been determined that my problem is Lyme encephalopathy, not epilepsy. My last tests, for God's sake, indicated that the Bb spirochete is now even in evidence in my gall bladder."

"Ms. Anderson," Marsalek said, smiling benignly at the patient, "I have read your extensive medical record, and I have discussed at great length your problems with my colleague, Dr. D'Silva, one of the best neurophysiologists around, and we are in agreement that you do suffer myriad problems, many stemming from your auto accident, but your symptoms of epilepsy are quite clear, and needs to be addressed. We are confident that Lyme disease, though in evidence in your body, is not the problem. We, and I include Dr. Sloan, have already discussed it with your son, who has told us about, shall we say, some of your behavioral problems which we believe are related to mental difficulties."

"Thanks for informing me that I suffer from myriad problems," Terry responded cynically. "I had no idea I was even sick until you told me! My God, Dr. Marsalek, I've been poked, prodded, stuck, cut, MRI'd, CT-scanned, IV'd, analyzed, and generally deconstructed and reconstructed and told I'm impossible to deal with so many times and for so many years now that it's all starting to run together. You so called experts have informed me that I have everything from arthritis and Lyme disease to syphilis and Alzheimer's, or I'm a hypochondriac, psychosomatic, manic-depressive, or whatever. I guess adding epilepsy to the list is to be expected. If I would have received the proper treatment from the beginning I wouldn't be in the state I am in now."

She stood up. "Well, let me tell you now," she said as she walked to the door, "so I won't have to repeat myself — you and the rest of the esteemed quacks at this hospital can stick it up your asses."

June 8, 2004. Sean and Marissa arrived early on Quail Lane to take Terry to lunch at the H&G Restaurant in Easton, the day after her vitriolic engagement with Marsalek. Tristan, who had taken her to the appointment and had heard the whole encounter from outside the doctor's office while he waited, arrived a few minutes later.

As soon as they were seated, Terry got up to go to the bathroom.

"You know what happened yesterday," Tristan said in a lowered voice as she disappeared.

"Yes. I got a call from Dr. Marsalek's office. I have also talked with Dr. Sloan. He is of the opinion, as is Marsalek and the rest, that she should be committed for a while. They think she's a danger to herself."

"What!" Tristan said with a look of astonishment. "Sean, you all do what you've got to do. The woman is sick, no doubt about it. But her problems are from the Lyme encephalopathy, not because she's crackers. She doesn't need more shrinks. She needs to fight the symptoms."

"That's not what Marsalek and D'Silva say, and it was Sloan that suggested she be committed for a while because of her recent efforts with the scissors."

"But she said she never intended to harm herself, only remove the I-V line with the scissors while she was in one of her disconnects," Tristan said. "I know what it must have looked like, but I believe her."

At that moment, Terry reappeared from the ladies room. After the waitress took their orders, Sean moved to initiate the discussion again.

"Mom, I have talked with Drs. Sloan and Marsalek and . . ."

"Before you say anymore," she interrupted, "I know what they told you, and I don't want to talk about it now. It would ruin a perfectly good meal. Maybe we can discuss it tomorrow, if you and Marissa would like to stay over for the evening. Maybe you could run by the store and buy a cantaloupe and some orange juice. We could have it on the patio porch for breakfast tomorrow morning while we talk."

"Sound's okay by me," Sean replied with a smile. Maybe, he thought, it wouldn't be that hard after all.

"Oh," Terry said almost as an afterthought, "Tris, would you be willing to come up and referee the match? There's a melon slice in it for you."

"Sure," Tristan responded, rolling his eyes heavenward. "I've always wanted to see what Armageddon would be like over melon and juice."

Terry was up early the next morning. As usual, she hurt all over, and her legs were barely working as she made her way from her room, down the stairs, and onto the patio. The air was still and the morning mist was lying heavy over the Corsica, the sun having as yet failed to cut through with its knife-like rays. She could just make out the frontiers of the water's edge, and a ghostly shadow beyond when Sean and Marissa appeared.

"Morning Mom," Marissa said with a cheerful smile as she laid out the plates, utensils, and juice glasses.

"Good morning honey," Terry replied.

Sean appeared bearing a large cantaloupe and a pitcher of juice. "Sorry about the orange juice," he said. "All they had was apple."

"That's fine," Terry said, almost automatically without really looking. Her attention was fixed on the shadowy form on the river. The mist was lifting, and the figure became more defined.

"That's a waterman and his mate on their work boat," Terry said. "I see them every day, usually in the same spot, working their crab trot lines. They seem to be there from before sunup until after sunset, every day, almost as if they are always there. The old guy is always wearing black, and the kid is always in his jeans. Strange, cause they never seem to move very far from the beach down the hill, almost like their waiting for something to happen."

"Sound's romantic, Mom," Sean said just as Tristan arrived, "but what in God's name ever happens on the Corsica, unless you count fish kills, and maybe some pollution?"

Terry watched as the boat moved lazily back and forth. She waved at the old man, but it was the boy in jeans, whose back had been to her, who turned as if he knew she was there, and waved his right hand slowly from side to side.

"Nice folks," Terry said, "here on the Eastern Shore, with the exception of a few quack doctors."

"I guess that's as good a way as any to get into a discussion on this thing," Sean said. "Mom, you've been my hero all my life. I hope you know how much respect and admiration

I have for you, having to have conducted your life, your independence, your willingness to take care of grandma and grandpa despite being so ill yourself and for so long. You know I love you and I'm trying to do the best I can. I don't know if this is a good move or not, although I think I have thought it through."

"Think what through?" asked Terry.

"I have been talking to most of the doctors, and I have to say, you've been through so many now that I can't remember them all."

"Try remembering with Lyme encephalopathy," she responded.

"That's the point. I know what Foster, Campollo, and Brownstein have told you, but from what this raft of doctors in Easton tell me, your problem isn't with Lyme, it's related to your old spinal injuries, the possible onset of epilepsy, and more seriously mental stress."

"Sean," Tristan interrupted, "some of the best minds in the business, including the folks at Johns Hopkins, Campollo, and the rest, have already determined that Lyme is the villain because its symptoms are usually mistaken for other afflictions. Your mother has Stage 3 Lyme, which is as bad as it gets, for which there is no cure and all you can do is treat the symptoms."

"If that's the case, how come all these treatments she's been enduring only seem to make things worse?"

"Because nobody yet knows for certain what will work," Terry interjected loudly, "and I'm a guinea pig, although nobody will ever 'fess up to that one."

Sean turned to face the water. He saw the boy on the work boat, just standing there now, looking up at the patio, transfixed and motionless, as if he were listening to every spoken word. At this distance, though, that was impossible.

"Mother, I'll be frank," Sean continued. "We, your doctors and I, are concerned that you might take your own life. You need counseling and at a far more intensive level than Dr. Sloan can give you once every two weeks."

"Are you suggesting that I be committed, institutionalized in some nut house?"

"All I am saying," Sean said, his voice growing imperious, "is that you would be getting better care than you are providing for yourself now, and would be safer than you are here in this house by yourself when you have those attacks, and . . ."

"You want me committed!" Terry shouted. "My own son wants to put me away..."

"No, Mom. I want you to be in a place where no harm can come to you, and you can be fed and clothed, and receive the psychiatric care you need."

"You think I'm crazy, don't you?" Terry screamed. "You think I want to kill myself, don't you? Well let me tell you something, buster. If I want to cuss out every quack doctor I meet, I will. If I want to unhitch my own IV with a pair of scissors, I will. If I want to watch Judge Judy twenty-four hours a day, I will. If I want to call that asshole nitwit of a President a jerk in front of the Republican National Convention, I will. And if I want to take my own life, I will. That's my decision, not anyone else's. It's a free country, at least for a while, and I can do any damned thing I like."

"Mother, if necessary, given your medical history, I could legally have you put under long-term psychiatric care right now and . . ."

Terry's eyes were ablaze. "I warn you," she shouted, "if you try to have me committed against my will, you will be as good as dead to me. Now get the hell out of my home. All of you."

Down on the Corsica, the waterman and the boy returned to their trotlines.

Terry was entirely on her own again.

Chapter 35

IN THE STILL OF THE NIGHT

As the Christmas holidays approached, several episodes of near-paralyzing pains in Terry's back resulted in an unexpected visit to the Chestertown Hospital Center in Chestertown, which she had chosen to replace the hospital in Easton that she had grown to despise. On December 12, after yet another comprehensive set of X-rays and MRI exams on her spinal cord were conducted, the presiding physician, a pasty-faced man named Rilinski, pronounced that there was little cause for pain at all. After reviewing her medical case history, from the auto accident onward, he had issued his written opinion in triplicate. "Postoperative changes appear to be without recurrent disc herniation or spinal stenosis," he wrote on the diagnosis sheet.

"There is small focal myelomalacia identified in the right cervical spinal cord at the level of C3. In retrospect, however, this might have been present on the previous study, a vestigial remnant of an earlier auto accident, but the overall size was very small." Moreover, he noted, there was no apparent causal factor for the reported pain. "Without question," he informed Sean and Tristan, "the pain is all in her head!"

Tristan stared at the physician incredulously. "That's your diagnosis? She's just imagining her pain!"

"Basically, yes. I'm going to give her a prescription for a fairly powerful anti-depressant, which she should take twice a day."

"Will it have a reaction to the antibiotics she's already taking?" asked Sean.

"I don't think so," said Rilinski as he left the room, "but if it does, just bring her back in and we'll whip it into shape."

Within days of the exam, the pain was as intense as ever, and accompanied by even longer and more severe periods of what Terry had begun to call her "daily disconnects," moments of insensibility, where everything merged and disappeared into an impenetrable fog. Belligerent to any outside assistance, she outright refused to return to the hospital or speak with Rilinski, and often her own son.

Increasingly Tristan was becoming Terry's only refuge as he ignored every shortcoming and slavishly attended to her needs whenever she would let him. Every two or three days he would take her out for dinner, sometimes waiting for two hours as she struggled to dress herself during the ever-increasing short disconnects. It was but one of the things that brought her close to him, though she feared admission to even that weakness. She trusted him now more than anyone, although even he was unable to help manage the regularity of her prescription drug intact. Later he would recall the constant struggle.

"Terry, let me," he would say, almost daily, watching her as she attempted to put the right pills in the correct sequence in her daily pill case. "I can do that. Let me put them in there." She wouldn't have it, though. "She was stubborn. So, I said, 'You don't want to have Sean driving ninety miles over here to do this, do you?' And she would say, 'I can do it, damn it. I'll do it.' And so, most of the times she'd get it screwed up. So who the hell could know what dose she had?"

The evening of December 23 it was 22° F and gusty with snow beginning to fall on the Corsica River, when Tristan appeared at the house with a small armload of gifts. As he entered the front door he found the house apparently empty. For a moment he panicked, and then began to call for Terry. From the garage came a weak reply.

"I'm out here."

He found her cleaning out—rather re-arranging, albeit very slowly—the clutter in her car, the accumulated debris of months of unopened mail, papers, and the like. Yet she was clearly in one of those rare good days when normality seemed within reach, when she could manage a laugh, and cultivate the simple pleasures of being alive. Attacking the car was the first industrious thing she had done in weeks. The vehicle was a mess, but she had systematically begun to weed out all of the mail, throwing it onto the passenger's side, having determined to sort through it later and maybe even read some of it.

"Well," she said cheerfully, "what brings you here so early in the day?"

"Heap on more wood! The wind is chill," Tristan grinned. "But let it whistle as it will, we'll keep our Christmas merry still."

Terry laughed out loud, perhaps for the first time in a week. "What the hell was that all about?"

"Christmas, my dear. Christmas. A few words from Sir Walter Scott. A few presents for you, and an offer by Ivanhoe himself to take you out to dinner. As I have to leave early tomorrow morning to be with my folks and all in Pennsylvania, I thought we could do Christmas Eve a bit early. Anyway, what in God's name are you doing?"

"Well, sir knight, I kinda expected you. I'm cleaning out my rat's nest because tonight I'm taking you out. We're going down to Annie's Place. I'm buying. It's my treat, and I want you to have whatever you want. And I'm driving. It's my Christmas present to you."

Delighted with Terry's momentary reprieve from her usual doldrums and her offer, but dubious of her impaired driving ability, especially in the snow, he said, "Go get dressed, I'll finish the car." She dutifully accepted and went upstairs to clean and change. He knew that because of the disease and her impaired motor abilities, it would, as usual, likely take her several hours to get ready. After finishing the car, he sat down in front of the TV and patiently waited.

At 9 p.m. Terry glided slowly down the steps Cinderella-like. She was dressed in a simple black-and-red velvet ensemble. Her once-raven hair was combed provocatively down across her forehead. If there was any makeup on her face it was invisible. Tristan was astonished at her metamorphosis, from the haggard, sickly, middle-aged woman she had been only hours before to a veritable replicant of Audrey Hepburn in a scene from *Breakfast at Tiffany's*. Around her neck she wore a simple silver necklace with a 1944 dime pendant ringed by a silver band. On her right-hand ring finger was the small carat diamond ring that had once belonged to her sister.

Despite Tristan's protestation, Terry insisted on driving, and compounded his worry the entire way by darkly joking about running into a ditch, hitting a tree, or simply disappearing into the frozen Corsica River. The ten-minute trip took half an hour, but the dinner was worth it. Terry ordered a bottle of French wine although her medication instructions had forbidden consumption of any alcohol. With the snow falling outside, and a table by the fireplace, the evening neared perfection. For once the conversation was on everything but Terry's illness, and ranged from the works of the late Poet Laureate of the United States, Joseph Brodsky, one of Tristan's favorite writers, recent land preservation efforts on the Eastern Shore by the Sierra Club, and Maryland politics, to NASA's still stumbling Mars program.

After the second bottle of wine, Tristan asked Terry about her necklace, and, noting the diamond ring, whether her sister had ever married before she died. For the first time, she began to reveal something of her past besides the Lyme disease

"The dime necklace I had made from my dead sister's good luck charm, and the ring had been given to her by a boyfriend just before she was murdered."

Tristan was stunned. Terry had never before mentioned anything about a sister or a murder, but now, like a volcano spewing forth its contents on some unsuspecting hillside town, she began to recite the grim tale of her sister's assassination, and how it had affected her family and her own subsequent life, and of the mysterious telephone calls in the night from someone who always wanted to speak to Ellen. She told him of Teddy Dubinski's deathbed confession to his sister-in-law. She told him of how she had started going to the neighborhood teen club with Ed when she was 11, and her first job, a year later, at a local bakery, of her first kiss in 1961, of her job as a Candy Striper at Holy Cross Hospital in Silver Spring. She told him that she had once been almost accosted there by a doctor, and of her short careers as airline stewardess three years later, where she again had to fend off suitors repeatedly. And she told him of her unhappy marriage to Carl Anderson after his graduation from the Annapolis Naval Academy in 1969.

He blushed when she laughingly told him that she usually slept in the nude, against Carl's disapproval, and still did. She became wistful when she talked about how Carl wanted to wait until he was at least thirty-five and a senior officer before having kids, and of how she had tricked him, while he was stationed in the Philippines, into fathering her son Sean.

"You know, I had the doctors tape-record Sean's birth in California. Carl had been transferred to Puerto Rico and I was living there alone at the time. When he was four years old, I think it was about 1978, I played a very small portion of it to him. Sean's expression of relative horror to the sounds of natural childbirth told me pretty quickly it was a mistake." She smiled benignly. "In truth, my intent had been for him to hear just his first cry and the happy commentary following his birth, so actually the mistake was my not first locating and just playing that portion of the tape. I've joked with Sean over the years about having traumatized him for life. And I guess I did. Look at us know. We both seem to have our knives out."

"I doubt it," responded Tristan. "You must have had some wonderful times with him."

"Yes, there were some pretty amazing moments. I remember when we were living in the Annapolis Road House condominiums in 1976. I was 28 then, and Sean was 2½. It was April and we were in the upstairs bedroom."

She gazed into the fireplace, and the golden light of the burning logs played upon her silhouette.

"It was a crystal clear day and the birds were singing outside the open window. Sean and I were talking while I dressed him, talking about our morning bicycle ritual to the Academy where we would say 'Good morning, water' to the water under the little bridge just down from Carl's, and about Daddy being at work, and Sean's practicing saying 'railroad trestle' and saying 'Mommy, open arms,' so he could give me a hug. He babbled on about washing off Daddy's boat the day before. And then, out of the blue, he said 'Mommy, you're lovely.' And ever after he used to say that to me on a regular basis. How it originated I never knew. But I will always cherish the memory."

After ordering a third bottle of wine, about 11:30 p.m., the story was continued, replete with a full, no-holds-barred, almost clichéd account of a degenerating marriage to Carl Anderson, a man married first to the Navy, and secondly to a wife. She spoke of an affair with a tennis instructor named Jerry Bostwick, from Arnold, Maryland, and smiled as she recalled their "first date," in 1977, a breakfast at the Denny's Restaurant on West Street, near Route 2, in Annapolis. She spoke of her life in Utica, and the return to Annapolis, and her on again-off again affair with Bostwick.

"It wasn't just the sex," she said matter-of-factly. "Jerry really cared for me, and Carl's first love was the Navy. But he had long since given up trying to control my every minute."

She sighed deeply, took another sip of wine, and lit a cigarette.

"I just wanted to be free, to try the world on my own," she said. "Can you appreciate that?"

By now it was snowing hard outside and Tristan had begun worrying about getting home. But he was already too wrapped up in Terry's story to really care.

"Fran O'Brien's," she continued, "is right down the street from the Maryland State House, and a lot of the delegates and state senators were frequent customers. I got to know a few of them, and one, a guy named Freeman, was also an attorney with whom I waited on and chatted up almost nightly. He was a big tipper and it paid to be gregarious with the customers. Pretty soon I knew all about him, and he knew about me. And one night he offered to help me with the divorce. He prepared the papers and suggested we go up to my apartment to review them. I agreed but made sure Sean, who was about six or seven then, was around and in plain view so Freeman wouldn't misconstrue anything. I used to wear slacks that were tight in the waist, and sometimes, especially after dinner, I would have to undo the top snap around the waist to sit down comfortably. When Freeman saw that, he kind of smiled and said, 'Are you finally getting ready for me?' I stood up, stared right at him, and pointing to the door said 'I don't think so. Get out, right now.' Never saw him again, but he left the work-up papers for the divorce behind. I used them and handled the whole thing myself. No attorneys. No anything. Did it all myself. Carl and I legally split a month or two later. That was in 1983. He got Sean because of my infidelities, so I decided to start all over again, as far away from my whole life up to that time as I could get."

"Where did you go?" Tristan said.

"I drove out to San Diego with a friend and my dog. I was then in terrific shape, physically and mentally. As soon as I got there I enrolled part-time at the University of Southern California, at La Jolla, and got a part-time job in the Physics Department working under Sally Ride, who would later become the first female astronaut. I was an editor on the campus newspaper. I even tried fashion modeling for a while in what spare time I had, and was actually pretty good at it. It was a wonderful period in my life. Got to meet a lot of guys who wore herringbone, tweeds, and paisley, but for me it was the ones in black sweaters and corduroys. I was usually dressed in jeans and sneakers with holes in them."

She giggled, and took another sip of wine.

"I had decided," she continued, "I was going to be a lawyer. At lunchtime I used to walk down to the beach and back, watch all the beautiful people, and feel like I was one of them. After work I would spend an hour each day running up and down the stairs in the physics building just to keep in shape."

"Sound's like you were a hard-charger," Tristan said.

"Yes, I was. I was taking courses that opened up the world to me. There was one that blew my mind called 'Imperialism and Victorian Literature,' taught by a Professor

Takao Mayoshi. There were only fifteen students in the class at the beginning, and by the end of the term we were down to five or six. I began to think and write like a fiend. One of the papers I wrote for his class, titled 'Arnold's Culture and Anarchy' was even published. It questioned the nineteenth century assumptions of Eurocentricity and the biases built into the twentieth century humanities disciplines."

"Man, is that mouthful!" Tristan exclaimed.

"It was the most stimulating period in my life. Finally got a Bachelors in English and American Literature while still in my thirties. Made a decent living copy-editing and proofreading for the university press, and freelancing as a writer. In my spare time I got involved with a program called Project Wildlife, and was soon deeply involved in volunteer coordination, wildlife rehabilitation, and communication with the public. The world was my oyster. Then Ed called and told me Mom was dying, and that a man named Trueman had crawled out of the woodwork and was a prime suspect in my sister's murder. I had to come home. I had no choice. My biggest concern was for my parents. They've lived with this pain all their lives, and they were elderly and my mother was sick and dying. There were no such things then as victims' rights groups, and no focus on the victims' families. As a consequence, you live in your own jail, your own hell, all your life, and that's just what they did. I decided I was going to have to pursue my law degree here in Maryland and, if Mom passed on, I would probably have to take care of Dad at the same time because I knew my brother was totally incapable. But I knew I could do it. Then everything turned to crap. No gold at the end of the rainbow now, is there."

"There still can be," Tristan said softly, reaching across the table and cupping her hands gently with his own. "All we have to do is pull this monkey from your back. I want to help you do it if you will let me."

"You're a sweet man, Tris Keyes, but I think we'd better leave. It's almost midnight, we're the last ones here, the wait staff has been giving us the evil eye for the last half-hour, and worse, it's snowing out like crazy. I'll even let you drive."

It was almost 1 a.m. when Terry and Tristan reached home, and were greeted by Tuffy as they walked in. "It's late and I guess I ought to be getting up to bed," Tristan said. "But you have to open your presents first."

"That would be wonderful," she replied.

Together they sat on the living room couch, beside a small table-sized artificial Christmas tree, sans ornaments, that had once belonged to Philip and Lucille. Tuffy had jumped up and sat in Terry's lap, nuzzling his nose under her left hand even as Tristan handed her one of the gifts he had brought.

"This first one's for Tuff," he smiled.

"Well," Terry replied as she tore off the ribbons and wrapping paper covering a box filled with yellow tennis balls, "Tuffy says thank you very much."

She threw several of the balls across the floor and the dog tore after them in utter delight. "Tris," she asked quietly, "do you believe in reincarnation?"

"That's a strange question," he answered. "You know, of course, I'm Roman Catholic and believe in the Holy Trinity, and the Resurrection. Why do you ask?"

Tuffy returned with a tennis ball in his mouth as an offering to Terry, which she promptly rolled across floor. The dog set out on another hot pursuit.

"I don't know. When I was living in La Jolla I read a good bit about the great religions of the world, and I was particularly taken with some of the aspects of Buddhism, especially regarding the concept of reincarnation. You know, ever since I was a little girl, after my sister's death, I've always had this delicious feeling that she was watching over me. And after I saw Tuffy as a three-day-old pup and adopted him from the pound, I've kinda felt that she was somehow more here than ever before. I guess that's why I have more empathy with him than any other animal I've ever had. You know, sort of like we're related. He's kind of like my alter ego. Does that sound stupid?"

"Not at all," he answered. "You know the Lord works in mysterious ways, and maybe He brought you and Tuff together for a reason."

"I'd like to think so," Terry said with a satisfied smile. "Thanks for not making light of it. Many others would."

"Okay. Back to the goodies. This one's for you," Tristan said, handing her another present, quite obviously a book by the feel, weight, and shape, wrapped in red-and-silver paper. "I know you haven't been reading many books lately, but this one I think you will find particularly interesting."

The book was the latest by the popular Chinese-American authoress Amy Tan, entitled *The Opposite of Fate: A Book of Musings*. Terry looked at him with a blank expression on her face.

"I know," Tristan said defensively. "It's not your sort of thing, but the last chapter is incredible. You see, like you, Amy Tan also suffers from Stage 3 Lyme disease, and has gone through almost the same difficulties you have. You know, the whole thing, the parade of symptoms, the lethargy, the lost moments, the myriad assortment of pain, with some of the doctors not even believing you, or constantly misdiagnosing, or even thinking it's a psychiatric problem simply because most of them haven't got a clue about the disease and are too God-like to admit they don't know. You and Amy Tan could write a book together!"

"I know I've already said it before, but Tris, you're a dear, dear caring man."

"Yeah, I know," he countered with a facetious laugh. "Why don't you open the last one?"

Within seconds the last present, also instantly identifiable by its square flat shape, was unwrapped. This time it was a four-set CD compendium of Do-Wop songs from the '50s and '60s.

"You once told me," he continued, "about how your family was wrapped up with the local teen center, and how, even when you were a little girl, you used to go there with your brother and how all the boys liked to dance with you. I picked this collection out because—you also once told me that your most favorite slow dance song of all time was "In the Still of the Night" by the Five Satins—it's on here."

"Oh, Tris," she said, wrapping her arms around his shoulders and putting her cheek upon his chest. "It's perfect. You've made me the happiest woman alive."

"Would you please do me the honor of dancing with me?" he asked.

"Only if it's a slow one," she answered, but a few inches from his face. "You know I'm not too fleet of foot these days."

Then, to the sounds of a romantic tune more than a half-century old, they danced slowly around the living room. Bewildered by his mistress's embraces with the big man, Tuffy began to circle around the couple as they moved across the floor. "Gee, Tuffy," said Terry looking down at the dog, "you've never seen me do this before, have you?"

The moment was magical. There was no pain or sickness, no lethargy or stain of darkness, no fear of future or ghosts of the past, only light and tenderness, only the music and the moment itself. Then the song was over, and Terry's legs, which seconds before had been weightless and nimble, began giving out. Tristan helped her to the sofa and sat down beside her. She put both of her hands on his chest and looked into his eyes, still trying to cling to the moment.

"Tris, I love you."

The words came naturally, but he hesitated with the response, fearing what they might mean for both of them, but finally surrendering. "I thought you would never tell me. I love you, too."

She cupped his face in her hands and gently kissed his lips.

At that moment, Tuffy leapt between them and started yelping. The spell was broken. The moment had passed. Terry pulled away, and with a wan smile, said, "Sweet Tristan, we've had a wonderful evening together, and for me one of the nicest in years. But it's really late and I'm exhausted. Why don't you go up to bed? I'll pick up the Christmas wrappings and I'll see you tomorrow morning before you leave."

As he climbed the dark stairway alone, Tristan Keyes, with the euphoria of only moments before evaporating with every step, now knew that whatever happened, he would be with Terry to the end, one way or another. As he reached his room, he again heard, emanating from below, the honeyed voices of the Five Satins singing their lilting love ballad. He could also hear the tender, sad sounds of a woman quietly crying.

Chapter 36

KITTY, KITTY, KITTY

The evening of July 25, 2005, was hot and dry, the fifty-first day along the Corsica River without rain. On such evenings, after sunset, frogs from the nearby shrinking wetlands frequently invaded the well-kept lawns along Quail Lane to bask under the yard sprinklers. This evening was no different except that Terry was now alone in her house. Tristan had completed construction on his own home down the street at the beginning of the month and, having passed inspection, had moved in a few days later. It made no difference, really, because he stayed in constant daily contact, by regular visits and by e-mail every morning and evening. And whenever she needed assistance, he was at her side within minutes.

Theresa Anderson had suffered another difficult day and, as usual, struggled to maintain some form of normality by sitting at her computer and drafting an e-mail response to a query from Tristan on how she was doing. And, as usual, it had taken hours between moments of lapsed awareness, to get anything at all down. She had only recently stopped and then started smoking again, from her stress and frustration, and at least half a dozen cigarettes butts, begun but never finished, had left their ugly burn marks on the desk. She had already gone through three keyboards owing to keys melted down to metal during episodes of losing consciousness with a cigarette in her hand.

"Sorry I can't say more at this time. . ." she began at 6 p.m. "Very, very bad day, and keep losing consciousness here. . ." she had added at 8:15. "By time started this email probably at least an hour, with keyboard tray table keeping. . .to calling in my lap. . .awkeening. . .me good thing, and DAMN. . .cursor thng." She concluded the e-mail at 9:08. "Really do. . .have to go. Love you…too. Terry."

For the longest time she sat there, staring unflinchingly at the screen and her somewhat garbled words, unable to press SEND. From her window she had heard the croaking of the frogs and the night birds singing. Suddenly she was aware of the beauty of the sounds that had begun to swell in her head to a near rapture.

"I should get some water on those poor beggars," she said to herself, as she stood slowly and walked carefully down the stairs. On the patio she found the coiled hose and a sprinkler nozzle and assembled them in the dark, and then laid the sprinkler in the yard and turned on the water. She sat on the dirty, bruised chaise lounge that her father had so often enjoyed, and closed her eyes to bask in the night sounds. For seemingly endless seconds she listened, transfixed to the symphony of the frogs, which seemed to grow louder and louder. Suddenly, she was awakened from her bliss when a frog leaped and landed on her lap, followed by another and another. Surprised by the slippery blobs, she opened her eyes. Shadows moved. The dark seemed alive with an invisible tumult. As her vision adjusted to the moon glow, she could see at her feet hundreds of tiny dark forms blanketing the patio flagstones jumping about in a strange dance. Within seconds they were thousands, leaping everywhere, but seemingly moving en masse towards the open sliding patio door. Their dark bodies glistened in a luminescent blue glow and their croaking had become a cacophony of sound that now frightened her.

Jumping up she rushed toward the patio door, grabbed a broom beside it and began to wage war against the invaders, sweeping back the relentless oncoming tide. Wave after green wave of the horrible little devils assailed her as she protected her home. "Get back, you fucking bastards. Go back to your swamp." And still they came. "Campollo sent you, didn't he? Well, die, you little pricks!"

Her arms and legs, already weak, began to hurt as she swept back and forth. Her knuckles began to bleed. Soon she could no longer discern the patio floor through the bodies of the living and bloody dead frogs, crushed or swept into oblivion during the nocturnal engagement. One of the beasts bounded onto her head and became ensnared in her hair, even as a sharp but familiar pain beneath the back of her neck sent a lightning bolt through her body, causing her to drop the broom. The moon glow disappeared behind a black cumulous cloud, which seemed to be descending from the heavens and wrapping her in a stultifying mantle of darkness. The sounds of frogs slowly dissipated and she closed her eyes in utter relief.

It was about 4:00 a.m. when Terry awoke on the floor beside her computer. Her eyes had nearly swollen shut from multiple bruises, and she felt her head. It was hurting in a hundred places from her face having slammed into the keyboard, and then on the way down hitting the edge of her desk and then on her wooden bed frame, five feet from the computer.

"Can't let the bastards get me," she said out loud to nobody. "Can't let the bastards win." The incident, she resolved, would have to be kept to herself. Nobody could see her face until it healed. Nobody. Not even Tristan.

The sweltering summer of 2005 passed slowly, with grim news from Iraq, "Shrub's War," as Terry called it, broadcast with sickening regularity on television. Everything she abhorred seemed to have seized control of the world. Roadside bombs, rape of the environment, fundamentalist Christian television ministers and ranting Neo-Con talk-show hosts dominating the airwaves, stolen Presidential elections, and government sell-outs to the big oil money men all passed in review as a snickering pseudo-Texan Chief Executive in cowboy boots held sway over the shredding of the Constitution. Throughout her life she had always exhibited a great passion for justice, intolerance for injustice, and a powerful sense of right and wrong. For a liberal activist of the '60s it was all too much. Every world event seemed designed to personally torment her sensibilities, but always, in the back of her mind, she would ask herself time and again: "What would Ellen think?"

By late August, Terry's blackouts and hallucinations had dissipated somewhat, but not entirely. The wounds about her face, upper torso, and limbs had mostly healed, and she had begun to visit with Tristan more frequently. His daily e-mails to her, always mentioning his love and how wonderful she was, had somehow held things together through some of her darkest hours, though she was still unable to completely unveil her innermost self to him. It was best, she believed, to hold him at arm's length to prevent him—and herself—from getting hurt if worse came to worst. But it was difficult.

One Thursday night, about August 25, Tristan brought a pizza and an old Mel Brooks comedy video, which had caused her to laugh so hard that she started to hurt all over. She loved his company, his intellect, and his humor, and especially sitting beside his bearish hulk to suborn her problems for a few hours in cinematic escapism. The next morning she smiled at his corny, clichéd but entirely-from-the-heart e-mail: "You're the most wonderful woman I have ever met. I enjoyed watching "Young Frankenstein" with you last night and hearing your laugh. You are very dear to me. I love you very much!"

Sometimes, after uplifting moments like these, and a few hours without pain and fumbling, life still seemed bearable.

Several days after the Mel Brooks video, Brian Dean stopped by to look in on Terry, who, for once, seemed cheerful and upbeat. Though she was several months in arrears on the rent, he once again overlooked this and spent his few minutes of visit in pleasant conversation on their mutual interest in animals, and in particular cats and dogs, and their membership in the local SPCA. Some had called Terry's affection and concern for stray animals a bit overboard, like that of her late sister. Ever since she had arrived in Centreville, everyone on Quail Lane knew Terry had carted around a cat carrier in her car trunk in the event she encountered an injured stray. During the first few years in the community, when crossing paths with one, she would round it up and haul it into Easton to a vet for immediate care, nurture it back to health, and then either keep it or give it away. Most, fortunately, returned to their wilder ways and simply disappeared. On occasion, however, the cat population of her home had been considerable, with as many as ten or more roaming about the house and yard.

Ever since the onset of Lyme and its degenerative symptoms, however, such humane endeavors had largely been curtailed, though the disease had failed to quell her love for the denizens of the animal world, now with the notable exception of frogs, and in particular stray cats and dogs of every ilk. On days when she was feeling good, and her capacity for physical mobility had temporarily improved, the humane urges for action were sometimes resurrected, but the consequences could be disastrous. And it became so on this particular day as a result of Brian Dean's visit.

"Yesterday I was down in town at the Stop In Go Citgo," Brian mentioned in passing conversation, "and Will Jensen, the owner there, told me he had a stray black kitten show up one night just before closing and it kind of took over the place. You know how they can do that and you know Will! For all his orneriness he's a caring guy and has been feeding kitty himself. But he wants the critter out, 'cause he's afraid a car will hit it. You know his place is down at the bend on the bottom of the hill there on Route 213 where cars just tear through. He asked me if I wanted the little beast, but I have my dog Brownie, and you know how he is with felines."

"Maybe I should do something," Terry said hopefully.

"I wouldn't if I was you," replied Brian as he stepped through the door to leave. "You can barely support yourself much less another stray. You already have too many worry beads on the string to count."

"Yeah, I guess you're right."

That evening, about 10 pm., Terry found the old cat carrier box in the attic and tossed it into her car trunk, along with a tin of Starkist Tuna, and headed for the Stop In Go Citgo. Minutes later, as she drove up to the garage bay, she saw a "Closed" sign on the door, but could also see two men in grease-covered overalls talking inside. One was Will Jensen and the other his assistant Toby Urban. Without hesitation, she knocked on the garage bay door, and Will answered looking a bit bothered.

"What is it, Ms. Anderson? You know we're closed?"

Stop In Go was one of the few remaining filling stations on the Eastern Shore where attendants still pumped the gas and cleaned a customer's windows. It had become the one saving grace for its independent owner in a world of oil giants, station franchises, and self-service quickie marts that also sold gas. Will always appeared to have a perpetual three-day growth of white whiskers on his face, and was a local original, the proverbial tight-lipped curmudgeon who never smiled but had a heart of gold. And he knew and loved everyone in the community.

"Will," Terry said sweetly, "Brian Dean told me you've had a stray cat come in and you want to get rid of it."

"Yeah," replied the old man. "Wandered in a few days ago and now owns the place. But the damned thing just walks anywhere it wants including across the highway, like she's the Queen of Sheba, and I'm afraid she's gonna get nailed out here on the bend."

"Well," said Terry, "I'd be more than happy to take her off your hands."

Will smiled. "That's right kind of you. She's all yours. All you got to do is find her. It's kind of dark now, so you might want to come back tomorrow morning."

"No, I think I'll just walk around a bit outside. Where does she usually hang?"

"Suit yourself," said the old man, as they stepped out into the darkness. "She's usually loitering around the station or in the abandoned lot next door."

"Thanks. I'll find her."

In the dark, Terry began to circle the station and store, cursing herself for not bringing along a flashlight or asking Will for one.

"Here, kitty, kitty, kitty," she called out repeatedly. For ten minutes, though her legs were becoming increasingly wobbly, she walked about aimlessly in the dark. Wearing only a short sleeve blouse, shorts, and sneakers, she soon fell prey to the briar patch in the abandoned lot. "Here, kitty, kitty, kitty," she kept on calling with a syrupy voice that had served her so well on similar searches. After another ten minutes, and already exhausted, she resolved to bring out her secret weapon, the can of tuna. By now, the station and store had been completely closed and locked up, abandoned for the night by the proprietor, and Terry was alone by her car door opening the can of tuna.

Suddenly she realized that she was more vulnerable now than usual, away from the sanctity of her cocoon, her bedroom and computer, Tristan and Brian, her wonderful connections to sanity and security. The night sky was beginning to cloud, with curtains starting to mask the full moon, making the darkness ever more dense. A flickering neon roadside light on 213, pointing the way to the Stop In Go via a 50 yard-long gravel road, provided the only artificial illumination. The hot August air was suffocating, thick with the promise of rain

Terry suddenly felt intensely alone. Darkness seemed to close in on her and the neon light appeared ever more distant. Her weak legs stumbled several times as she walked along, holding the opened can in front of her.

"Here, kitty, kitty, kitty."

A car passed in the dark. Thoughts of Lane Manor began to run through her head. Playing with her spaniels in the yard. Mom. Pop. Northwest Branch Park. Ellen lying in a briar patch in her bloody orchid dress, her arms and legs akimbo like a broken marionette, and the bluish hole between her eyes. Alone.

"Here, kitty, kitty, kitty."

Images of newspapers, with pictures of policemen and soldiers clearing brush from the park, a police chief standing in front of a table filled with rifles, and funerals she never attended. The surrounding shadows and the images began to blend. From the corner of her eye she caught a movement. Someone watching her. A very tall boy perhaps, wearing jeans and a jacket with cut off arms. Familiar yet not. Most likely a ghostly shadow.

Hypnagogic, she thought to her self. Then she heard an almost inaudible mewing from across the road. Her heart began to race faster.

Another car passed, slowing down suddenly, a bump in the night, and then speeding up again.

"Here, kitty, kitty, kitty."

As she approached the blinking neon sign, she discerned a dark spot in the road. An oil stain perhaps. She came closer and was horrified to see a small black cat lying flat in the street. Rushing onto the road, she gently picked up the creature. Its guts, almost iridescent looking in the nightglow, were coming out of its mouth and anus, and its eyes bulged from its head, still connected by bloody strands of tissue and nerves. The body was still warm and limber. The accident had apparently just occurred. Terry pulled the kitten's midsection to her ear to listen for a heartbeat, and thought of how horrible it would be if the poor animal were still alive, and regained consciousness only to suffer such pain.

She began to weep even as a light misty rain started to fall, creating a halo around the neon light above her. The kitten's blood and entrails began to soak her blouse and bra, and coat her breast beneath as she held the corpse close. If there was a God, why did he let things like this happen? Blessed are the children and the animals. Back in Bible school, they used to teach that all things happen for a reason, God's grand plan, some of which mere mortals can never understand. But why this? Why Ellen's murder? Why her own accident? Why the Lyme disease? Why the slaughter in Iraq where Marines like her son were being shredded? Why all the pain and suffering? Was God just having a high old time playing some unending game? With whom and why? What was she to do with this poor animal, one of God's own beautiful creations?

"Just do it," a voice in her head sang out.

Within minutes she had driven down to Ritchie's produce stand, which lay naked on the roadside a quarter mile from the Short Stop. There, in the dark, she somehow found a large flowering bush and with trembling hands placed the kitten's body beneath a leafy overhang to protect it from the next day's sun.

By morning she was again in front of her computer typing out a directive, indeed a plea to Tristan and Brian informing them of the horrific events of the evening and describing precisely where she had left the kitten.

"I can't leave kitty where she is. She simply can't stay there rotting away. Would you retrieve her and place her out in the open, perhaps in a cemetery, where buzzards, birds of prey, could eat and do nature's work? Kitty will obviously not know." Then she added: "Please do not let anyone else know of this. I don't want anyone having anymore reason to think I would do something drastic to myself as a consequence of this event."

It was 8:30 p.m. when Tristan peeked his head in the patio door. "Anyone home?" he shouted as always, and walked in without awaiting an answer. Terry was, as usual, upstairs in her room sitting behind her computer, staring blankly at the screen. He could see her eyes were red from crying.

"What's the matter sweetheart?"

"It's the kitten," she said.

"We did as you asked. Took her to the town cemetery and laid her out in the open."

"No. It's not that. It's only that I feel absolutely. . .totally responsible for the kitten's suffering and death. Obviously she came running to my call when she was hit. I didn't start calling out by the road until I was certain she wasn't around the station or in the vacant lot and I should have crossed to the other side when I heard her mewing and before I started calling her again. But I saw something. Someone I think. Someone I think I know, maybe not. Damn it, I don't know. If it wasn't for this damned Lyme, and my inability to think clearly, the kitten would still be alive."

"Terry," Tristan said gently as he placed his arm around her shoulder, "you did everything you could for the kitten. Even with your illness you still gave it your best. You went out there in the middle of the night and gave your best. I love you for that among a thousand other reasons I can think of. You know, the priests at my old Alma mater, Notre Dame, used to always preach that 'Man proposes and God disposes,' but that He is with us always."

"Well," she sobbed, "just tell me precisely where the hell is your God now?"

Chapter 37

DOLLAR BILLS

The seizures had continued without letup. Dr. Sloan was certain of that. From the visible bruises, contusions, and cuts he could see on Terry's face, head, neck, and exposed portions of her arms and legs, as she took a seat opposite him, it was obvious that some were recent. From the records Dr. Quade forwarded, he was already well aware of the serious head and nose injuries repeatedly sustained during the last few months from the frequent narcoleptic attacks that had assailed her, usually while she sat at her computer.

He also knew that Terry's terminal had become her refuge, her sanctum sanctorum, as her frail frame continued to weaken from the Lyme disease, the sometimes-poisonous antibiotics used to fight it, and pain medications for her spinal problems. Her Macintosh and the Internet, for the last six months, had been her only tunnel to the world at large, as well as the instrument of her anger and intellect that seemed to keep her going against all odds. However, despite persistent warnings from her doctor that she refrain from sitting at her terminal for most of the day and evening, the sequence of seizures were almost always the same. In one instant she was cognizant and typing away, usually on one of her many "hate the doctor" diatribes or "save the animals" mantras. Then in another movement she totally lost consciousness and body control, with most injuries occurring from falling forward onto her computer or slamming onto her hardwood floor. The attacks could last anywhere from a few seconds to six hours. The incidents were usually accompanied by loss of bladder and bowel control, and the consequent befouling of her clothing, furniture, and the floor.

Now, after months of such attacks, the injuries to her face and body began to take on battlefield proportions. Besides the countless black and blue marks, cuts, and scrapes both old and new, bizarre swelling formations on her face and forehead had appeared, including one like a stack of quarters beneath the skin on her right cheekbone. A recent cut under her right eye looked as if it had been inflicted only hours earlier. She had begun to resemble one of the "Damned" in Michelangelo's Sistine Chapel masterpiece. The root cause of her frequent facial collisions with the edge of her computer desk, the keyboard, monitor, or anything else around had originally been diagnosed as myoclonic epilepsy, and not the Lyme disease that Dr. Campollo had said. Sloan now knew better.

"Well, Terry, here we are again," said the doctor gently. "You know I could have said I told you so."

"I know," she replied, "but ever since I have been on that fucking I-V chemical cocktail, horse pills, and the other so-called medicines those quacks at Chestertown Hospital Center have had me on, it's only getting worse. I don't mean just the blackouts and falling. That's bad enough, but the odd and intense behavior, confusion, and frequent numbness in my extremities are becoming unbearable. And always there is a pervasive feeling like I have to be in damage control mode at every moment but can't. For a second I'm normal. Then comes the dim awareness of something off, out of place. Then the truth comes crashing in, and that's usually it for the rest of the day. But the worst part is that the damned hallucinations, if that's what they really are, are worse than ever. What's even more frightening is that I'm not certain what is and what isn't real anymore."

Leaning back in his chair, Sloan tipped his tape recorder on, raised his arms behind his head, furrowed his brow, and closed his eyes. "So why don't you tell me about them?"

Hesitating for a moment while gathering her thoughts, Terry contemplated walking out while the good doctor took a nap. "Pompous ass," she thought to herself. "The first time I told a shrink the truth, I lost my insurance coverage. The last time, I lost the doctor!"

"Well," said Sloan after a few moments of silence. "Can you tell me about it? You don't have to if you don't feel like it. But I think it would help."

"Maybe you're right," she said almost piously. "The hallucination — actually they are now more dreamlike sequences, or should I say nightmares — began again when I stopped taking some of the new meds about two months ago, you know, the Doxycycline, and all the rest, and pulled my PICC intravenous tube. I simply couldn't keep paying the $450 a month for the meds that were making me sicker just to keep the bastards at Pfeiffer Pharmaceuticals driving their Beemers! At first the attacks last month were infrequent, short, subdued and mild, almost like when you're in a half-sleep-half-awake state. You get a sense of what's going on around you but you don't care. Know what I mean?"

Sloan nodded, still rocking in his chair, his eyes closed.

"A week ago, I am not certain, I walked through a dream, all the way down from my bedroom to the foot of the stairs, as if I was floating. There is a floor-length mirror there, and as I looked into it I saw my image, but I was still a child, and shadows of three people behind me were moving back into the darkness. One, however, a female I think, stayed right behind me and was trying hard to speak to me but I couldn't hear her. Then I realized it was my sister Ellen. She was wearing the orchid dress she had on the day she was murdered, and the bullet hole between her eyes was still clearly visible. I turned around to face her, but she too had disappeared. I wasn't frightened. I returned to my bed and went right to sleep again. It was, of course, all a dream, but when I awoke, I felt utterly exhilarated."

Sloan had ceased rocking. "Do you dream of your sister often?"

"Doctor," she answered, ignoring his question, "I can't begin to separate my dreams from reality. Just two nights ago — it was about 1:00 a.m. I think — I was at the computer trying to write a piece for the Eastern Shore Sierra Club newsletter and got up to get a snack. When I went downstairs and opened the fridge, I saw a large piece of chocolate cake left by my dear friend Tris, who often comes in to check on me. He had left a note beside the cake saying he had also left me some ice cream in the freezer. I took down a full half-gallon of vanilla Hagen Daaz, which was rock hard. So I went to the sink to heat up a spoon under hot running water so that I could dip it. While I was at the sink I experienced a pain in the back of my head, like someone was pushing a hypodermic needle into my skull, and then momentarily lost awareness several times. Each time I was brought back to my senses by some outside stimulus, including once breathing in water. My head had been submerged in a large pan that had filled with water while the faucet was on. In the time it took for that last blanked-out episode to run its course, the ice cream had completely melted, covering the kitchen counter and running onto the floor. When I came to on the floor, I was laying in the puddle of melted ice cream, so I had been out for several hours. And I was pissed!"

She stopped to light up a Virginia Slim, and then continued.

"After I cleaned up the mess and wiped myself off, I decided to at least take a piece of cake upstairs with me to bed. I remember the wall clock in the hallway read just a bit after 3:30 a.m. Then suddenly, just as I was starting up the stairs, I felt a severe pain, that god-awful pressure at the base of my skull again. There was a stiffening of my spine and body, and a sensation that I was losing consciousness, and I began to fall backwards. At that same moment, I swear I heard my doorbell ring. Then I blacked out."

"I don't know how long I was on the floor, but the first thing I remember as I lay in that long dark hall was the doorbell ringing again. It just kept on ringing and ringing. And I just lay there. You know, a doorbell is like a telephone. When it rings you just can't ignore it. I tried to get up but couldn't move. My body ached all over but nothing would move, and I felt like I was going in and out of darkness, in and out of consciousness. And above it all, the damned doorbell kept ringing, almost like a scream, and I couldn't answer it. I felt absolutely helpless."

"What happened then," Sloan quietly asked.

"Somehow," Terry continued, "I finally began to feel my fingers and toes, then my limbs. I managed to get up, and noticed I had banged my goddamned knee in the fall and it had swollen up with a knot the size of a grapefruit, but I managed to hobble over to answer the door anyway. It never occurred to me that it was 4:00 a.m. and who in God's earth is going to be out and about at that hour on the Corsica?"

She stopped talking for a minute, dragged deeply on her cigarette, and then continued again.

"When I turned on the porch light and opened the door, I saw a teenage boy. He looked familiar. I am certain I had seen him before. Very tall and lanky, maybe six feet or so. Pimpled face with a few whiteheads, and his hair slicked back on the sides and greasy. You know, that old Brylcream look like in the '50s and '60s. Just plain clothes, kind of ragged looking, jeans and a blue gabardine jacket with the sleeves ripped off, over a T-shirt. His breath, which I could smell from several feet away, was fetid. It seemed... how can I say it... like the air itself was poisonous. I asked him through the screen what he wanted and what was he doing wandering around the countryside at this hour, and if his mother knew he was gone. Was he lost or broke down somewhere? He just stared at me for the longest time, like he was peering right through me. Finally he said, 'I'm looking for Ellen. I have to tell her something. It's very important.'"

"Ellen who," I asked.

"Again he just glared right through me and finally answered: 'Your sister.'"

"Oddly, I wasn't stunned, or shocked, or anything like that. I guess I should have been since she's been dead for nearly half a century! For some reason I just answered him plainly: 'She's not here now.'"

"He looked both angry and scared as hell, and then said, 'You have to give her a message for me.'"

"I told him, 'I can't do that, not now, anyways.' And then he just turned around and disappeared into the darkness, like he had never been there in the first place. In a second or two the reality of what had occurred hit me. Was I still asleep, dreaming? Had the guy actually been standing on my porch? Or was he really some boogeyman from my imagination? As I turned off the light and backed away from the door, I stumbled on the rug and fell again, this time backward, slamming hard into the china cabinet, breaking the glass in the cabinet and cutting my face as I went down. All of a sudden I felt that familiar delirium sweeping over me again, but this time it felt warm and comfortable. Then it was black... black as hell... but serene. I didn't want to leave the darkness. I don't have any idea of how long I lay there like that, but I remember being stimulated by a bright light from somewhere. You know how you can be awakened and fully conscious in the morning and see light through the pinkish membrane of your eyelids without even opening them? I didn't open my eyes. There seemed to be two separate worlds, one under my eyelids and the other beyond them."

She took another drag on the cigarette.

"Somebody out there on the other side was laughing quietly. I knew they were looking down on me, but I still didn't open my eyes, uncertain of what I might see. And everything was so warm and the gentle laughter so comforting. I had no pain, no suffering at that moment. I wasn't sure if I was dead or alive, but if I were dead that would have been okay. Then whoever was laughing said 'Do it.' The voice was sweet and familiar, but I couldn't place it. 'Just do it, Terry,' it said, but I just wanted to stay where I was in this comfortable place. But I had to see if I was in this damned world or the next. It took all my willpower to force myself to open my eyes and peer into that outside world. And it was horrible. There was no one there."

She paused and looked at the bruise on her right wrist before continuing. Her eyes were glistening with tears.

"It was still dark out and I lay there for a few more minutes. Then I realized that I had loosed my bladder, and that the warmth I had been experiencing was probably from lying in my own urine and blood. I hobbled into the kitchen again to get some bandages and a mop to clean up again. Then, as I limped by the kitchen table I saw two wrinkled dollar bills lying there. I knew the bills weren't mine. I picked them up and stared at them for the longest time. 'Maybe Tris left them for me,' I thought. Maybe someone had come in while I was out cold. But then I looked at them closely. One had a brown stain on it, which I think was long dried blood. Both bills had tiny letters marked in red ballpoint ink in the lower left corner. The letters read "EMC." For a minute I was almost paralyzed with joy. They were the two dollars the police never found in my sister's purse when she was killed fifty years ago. I know because she always marked her baby-sitting money with her initials in that spot so our ratty brother Eddy wouldn't steal it. Then, I felt a strange calm about it all. I have long sensed that Ellen has always been with me, watching out for me since I was a little girl, and was often the reason I kept going. Now I knew it."

"I left the bills on the counter and went to bed, almost in a state of ecstasy, just as the sun was coming up. That afternoon, yesterday, when I finally got up again, the bills were gone."

Marissa sat quietly in Dr. Sloan's waiting room, thumbing slowly and without interest through the myriad yachting, travel, and sports magazines to pass the time. If the magazines were any indication of the economic level of the clientele the good doctor enjoyed, he was indeed mining a rich vein of gold. But one thing was for certain: at $250 an hour, Terry's visits were most certainly going to be parceled out sparingly.

When her mother-in-law emerged from Sloan's office, Marissa stood quickly and asked, "How did it go?"

"Well, basically it was like all of my appointments with him and the rest of the shrinks. I talked and he listened, and that was that."

"Did he offer any advice or give you any prescriptions?"

"Like I said," Terry repeated, "I talked and he listened, just like the rest of them. Said to make another appointment in a month, and to see someone about my injuries. There sure as hell weren't any 'Eureka' moments! It was, as far as I'm concerned, just another pointless expenditure I can't afford."

It had, in fact, been a somewhat traumatic experience, with Terry relating her uncharacteristic behaviors, events of awareness, and periods of lapsed memory. She said nothing, however, to Marissa about the hallucinations, if that was what they were, or the inexplicable appearance and disappearance of the pair of dollar bills. Even about her growing wish for release. When Marissa related the events of the day to Sean — as she most certainly would — it would only refortify his belief that his mother be committed, and Terry wished to give him no more ammunition along those lines.

"Don't worry, though. I assure you, there will eventually be an end in sight."

Chapter 38

CRITTER ANGELS

Mary Ann Cross loved animals and said so. "Animals are such agreeable friends," she had written in one of her lesser-known chronicles, Mr. Gilfl's Love Story, under her famous nom de plume, George Elliot. "They ask no questions, they pass no criticisms." Yet, for Terry Chauvanne Anderson it was not so much that they asserted no say over her actions — they maintained an inordinate influence over her life. It was more like they shared a bit of her very being, which, prior to her illness, often dictated the course of her actions. Even after discovering the cause of her disease, which had been vectored into her system by deer ticks carried by her dogs, she had continued to share her life with her pets without the least trace of malice or blame. As the disease progressed and her capacity to care for her once large menagerie was commensurately reduced, she still managed to heap as much care and love upon those that remained as if nothing had changed. In a way, her pets seemed the only thing that now justified her existence.

Yet, as one by one, their numbers began to decrease through natural attrition, escape into the wild, or by occasional accidents on some lonely county road, she had been obliged to face reality and no longer replenished "Terry's family," as she liked to call them.

If there was a hierarchy among her animals, her dogs had always been at the top of the ladder, although her late parakeet Mo and Siamese cat Mitzie came in a close second. Beginning with Tweedle Dee and Tweedle Dum when she was a child (both of which had reached a substantial antiquity, albeit totally blind and dumb when they passed), all the way down through Sasha and Tuffy, she had invested a considerable amount of her wherewithal to their well-being and comfort.

When Sasha, her German shepherd, had been struck by a truck and was taken, bleeding and dying, to the Animal Emergency Clinic in Annapolis, she had grieved as intensely as she had after the passing of Philip. As after every loss, in a fit of extreme melancholy and bereavement, now magnified by her own mental and physical debilitation, she struck out angrily trying to address blame and find justification for her loss in the cosmic order of things, but there was no order, only chaos. When the clinic had sent a large envelope containing a sweet poem concerning Sasha's demise, giving the animal's name as reputed author, signed with a paw print, and accompanied by a lock of her fur and boilerplate information on grief counseling, Terry exploded in vitriol. She called the clinic doctors, savagely trashing them and threatening a lawsuit for malpractice for failure to save her dog, and then broke down and cried for hours.

Once the emotional crisis passed, Tristan quietly reminded her that she still had Tuffy, her male cocker spaniel, albeit neglecting to mention the dog was already in his own dotage, and also suffering from Stage 3 Lyme disease. It helped, but not much.

As early as 2000, the animal had been diagnosed, like Terry, as having Lyme disease; but not until June 2005 had he begun to demonstrate behavioral and intestinal problems, roaming erratically around the yard posturing for a bowel movement, often without success. A prescription of Laxatone did little to correct the problem. Then, as Terry noted with concern in her diary later in the month: "Tuffy has seemed to me for quite sometime just not right, alternating between hyperactivity, panting, regardless of the temperature, unable to get comfortable when lying down, constantly getting up, circling, lying back down, particularly in the evening. It is for this reason he was put back on Acepromazine, which he was first on years ago to calm him during thunderstorms. He has not needed it for thunderstorms for four or five years, since becoming deaf, which I believe is related to the Lyme disease; his becoming deaf around the time he was diagnosed with the Lyme and erlichiosis. His tumors, particularly the ones behind his right leg, force him to favor that area."

Characteristically, Terry had taken several drastic measures on her own to alleviate his suffering. Several times, she later informed Tristan, she had given the animal several doses of her own Oxycontin, and Senokot, a laxative and stool softener, and even inserted suppositories to assist the poor creature.

It had helped, but not for long. Terry had attempted to make light of her concern. "Guess it's just fate," she said. "You know? Tuffy and me, two of a kind! I don't know how I could live without him." And then she had moped for a week.

By late fall 2005, Terry's last remaining dog, her alter ego, Tuffy, lame in one front and one hind leg and unable to climb stairs, was entering his final days. Tristan had cared for the animal off and on during Terry's frequent mental lapses, washing, shampooing, dousing him with prescription ointments, and paying for special medicines for clinical treatment, frequently expensive visits to the Tidewater Veterinary Clinic in Annapolis, and to a specialist in animal cardiology. Once, when obliged to be away for several days, he had, with Terry's approval, "enrolled" Tuffy in a kennel in Easton called "Boot Camp," where, he informed her with a laugh, the dog "received an 'A' in deportment and sociability and a 'D' in math," and joked that "he's going to have to make it in the world on his looks and good behavior." Yet, there was little that could be done about the dog's declining health, and Tristan knew that with Tuffy's inevitable death it was likely to be another serious obstacle to Terry's own physical and mental stability.

By early November Tuffy was eating with difficulty, and had begun falling down with sad regularity, and it soon became apparent that there was also something wrong with his back. After yet another visit to the vets, Terry and Tristan were informed the dog was suffering from a spinal problem. A diagnostic myelogram, the vet said, would be needed to determine the exact cause, but it was probable the animal would need corrective surgery. Before authorizing such diagnostic work, Terry conducted her own Internet investigation of precisely what myelography was and, much to her concern, discovered it to be an important but invasive diagnostic tool with potential liabilities, including possible paralysis and afflictions called "arachnoiditis" and "tetraparesis." Owing to the routine use of highly toxic agents, particularly a number of oil substances, there was the very real potential for causing permanent damage.

As Terry began to waver in signing the consent form approving of the myelogram, one of the surgical technicians inquired: "Has Dr. Prushinski sufficiently explained the risks involved in the procedure?"

Surprised by the question, Terry lied, "I was not aware that there would be any risk. When we talked about the myelogram, he said nothing regarding any possible hazards. What can go wrong?"

The tech pursed her lips and answered. "I am not authorized or competent to tell you. I suggest you talk to the doctor yourself before you leave."

Terry requested the tech to ask the doctor to return to the examining room and personally explain what perils might be involved. A few minutes later, the tech returned with a message from Prushinski, informing her that there was little if any danger. Again, accepting the surgeon at his word was enough—but not for long.

That evening, Terry received a call from the vet.

"Ms. Anderson," he said, "we can't tell exactly, but it looks like there's a lump and some inflammation around the central portion of Tuffy's spine. We believe that there is also resultant inflammation of the brain, although it is not likely the cause of the dog's pain. Do you want me to fix it?"

Terry thought the vet's choice of words was inappropriate. As if "fix it" he was repairing a washing machine.

"How much will it cost?" she asked blandly.

"Three thousand dollars."

Terry turned slowly toward Tristan, tears welling up in her eyes. "He says it will be $3,000. I don't have that kind of money. I can't make it. I'm going to have to let Tuffy go. We're going to have to put him down."

Tristan frowned for a moment, then smiled. "Nonsense! Of course we can get him tuned up again. You want the old Tuffy back. Okay, we'll just get him back in shape, good as new. I'll pay for it and you can repay me later. I'm as attached to that scruffy old mutt as much as you are."

He was well aware he would never see the money again, but reasoned that as long as the dog was around, though the chances of his recuperating were slim to none, Terry would have a reason, a cause, something to hang on to, something to work toward. He shuddered at the thought of what might happen if the dog didn't pull through.

The operation was destined to be carried out on a cold, blustery day in mid-November, and the drive to the vet's office in Annapolis was hindered by a freezing rain mixed with snow, which made crossing the Bay Bridge nerve wracking. Tristan had volunteered to take Tuffy himself, but Terry insisted on going along. The dog was left at the offices of Prushinski, Mastricht and Core, the veterinary surgeons who were to perform the procedure. Terry was informed that she needn't wait, as the surgery was to be carried out the following day, November 21, 2005, and the animal would have to recuperate at the vets for at least several days, until Thanksgiving.

The following day, Terry waited by the phone, her mind wandering in and out of the past like a tourist on the Via Veneto. In the afternoon, she began to stare transfixed, for more than an hour and a half, on a streamlined beige phone beside her computer. Her thoughts drifted back to her childhood and the strange, midnight calls by the mystery voice from beyond asking for Ellen…the same voice of the boy in her hallucinations.

Finally, in the evening Prushinski called to inform Terry that there had been problems, a hitch in the operation, which he chose not to discuss over the phone, but assured her that Tuffy would heal. Upon retrieving the dog, on a miserable Friday evening, after all of the vets had long since departed for the holiday celebrations, it soon became apparent that his suffering had only been increased. Not only was he unable to move any of his limbs, and could barely turn his head from side to side, he was unable to eat or digest the little that he could consume, and was obviously in substantial pain. It took little for Terry to convince herself that the surgeon had botched the operation, which only increased her despair and anger.

Intent on relieving Tuffy's suffering, and after determining in her own mind that his prescription for medication was grossly insufficient to alleviate his pain — 5 milligrams

Acepromazine at 2 p.m., another 5 milligrams at 2 a.m., and one 50-milligram of Tramadol at 10 a.m. and the next at 10 p.m.— she called Prushinski on January 2, 2006, to request a much stronger dosage. The exchange was less than cordial. That Terry was entering one of her mind-fogs at the moment of the call, and began to rant uncontrollably regarding what she believed to be the vet's "flip tone" and a comment that the dog was nearly comatose, did not help matters. Prushinski refused to increase the dosage.

By January 4, it was apparent even to Terry, who had only weeks before been resolutely determined to save her alter ego, that poor Tuffy's pain, evidenced by his pitiful yelping, squealing, howling, and barking, that he would have to be put to sleep.

Two days later, the last of Theresa Anderson's beloved compatriots throughout her life was euthanized at a pet clinic near Easton.

The evening of March 17, 2006, like many evenings before, had in the weeks following Tuffy's demise, began with Terry sitting at her computer, attempting to compose an accusatory letter, this time directed at Drs. Prushinski, Mastricht, and Core, whom she now blamed for the loss of the dog. Tristan, who was off on a several-day trip to Michigan for an alumni gathering, had encouraged her in her letter writing, knowing that she rarely got around to sending them and as long as she was so occupied, she would focus on little of her own condition.

"I was forced," she began, "to put my beloved Tuff to death in early January, his suffering so awful and my distress over his misery so great, because your treatment protocol was grossly inadequate and all my attempts to have you appropriately and otherwise adequately address his agony were in vain. You were the cause. There are only two things that are infinite, the universe, and the condescending egos of doctors like you."

Thereafter followed a three-page, rambling diatribe on the history of the dog's illness, the purported misleading and totally incompetent work of the doctors, their supposed arrogant and patronizing attitude toward Terry, their lust for easy money at her friend Tristan's expense, and how destructive their actions had been to her own health. As she wrote, it seemed the room began to grow dim around her, almost imperceptibly at first and then with increasing intensity.

"I will not let this happen to me now," she said out loud to the imploding darkness and silence. "Not until I have finished."

"Given my pain, distress, grief, and outrage," she continued writing, "so severe, and my need to save other animals and their guardians from what you put Tuffy and myself through, I will speak enough for Tristan and myself."

Now, the sounds of her fingers touching the keyboard seemed somehow to be blending with the disappearing light, as if a cosmic mute button to her senses were somewhere being slowly pushed. For a moment she stopped typing altogether and shook her head from side to side, trying to regroup, to refocus, to fend off the inevitable.

"I will warn you, however," she resolutely continued, "that I fully intend on bringing charges against you."

It was an impossible task, though. The familiar pain at the base of her skull arrived as if on cue, followed by another descent into the abyss of semi-consciousness, and a familiar warm, black obscurity. When she opened her eyes, a millisecond or an eternity later, she found herself sitting on the front stoop of her onetime home on West Park Drive in Lane Manor, pulling ticks from the matted hair of her beloved Tweedle Dee. Funny, she thought, how much the dog looked and acted like Tuffy.

"You ready?" said a voice from behind her. She turned and saw her radiant sister, with an almost angelic glow about her, and the elation was glorious. Ellen was wearing her favorite orchid dress and a huge smile. "This time, you get to go with me," she said. "Here, take my hand."

Exhilarated, Terry wrapped her little fingers around the elegant, slender hand of her big sister. Then they began to skip together across the macadam road towards the park. It didn't matter what lay ahead, as long as she was with her sister, her guardian, her Madonna. She knew now what she had to do. She had to stay with Ellen to the very end. Together forever.

She could barely see the two boys' silhouettes behind the young cherry tree as she and her sister approached the footbridge across the Northwest Branch, but turned her head to the right when one of them called out Ellen's name. It was all so familiar. Suddenly she felt constricted, passing through invisible molasses. Time was shutting down. The sound of the gunshot she knew was coming was almost imperceptible. She watched helplessly as her sister spun to her right and cried out in silence.

"If a tree falls in the forest," she once asked her father, "does anyone hear it?" He couldn't answer her. Why couldn't he? Why was she there? Why was this happening at all? Was this the way to Never Neverland, or just another hallucination?

Another shot, this time to her sister's stomach, and forward motion slowed to a wretched crawl. She watched intently as Ellen looked down in amazement and fear, blood beginning to ooze through her fingers, spewing forth in stop-motion frames.

"Come with me Terry," shouted the victim, as yet another shot struck her squarely in the chest.

Terry watched as the scene played on a variation of the climatic end in the movie Bonny and Clyde, twelve years in the future. Ellen's left arm had reflexively risen to fend off the shot that had already struck her chest, just in time for another to smash into her forearm.

"Come on Terry. . .come on."

Terry, though, was frozen in place. She saw the miniature bursts of dust erupt from the path as two shots hit the ground in front of her. A third bullet struck her right ankle, but felt more like a bee sting that required an instant grasp of her right hand, but little more.

Sloth-like, she turned to her left and watched as Ellen, bleeding profusely, only partially upright, pressed toward a nearby thicket. For a second Terry looked in the direction of the waterway beyond the shady grove, and could discern a boat, with the ancient ferryman she had once seen standing, his hand now thrust outward, palm up, as if begging. The sound of a croaking bullfrog filled the air.

More shots as Ellen fell, in slow motion, for the last time. Looking towards her little sister, she smiled beatifically, the same way she always had, from the hospital window a thousand years ago yesterday, in dreams, and now at the end and near the beginning.

Terry felt warm tears as she watched the two teenage boys leaving the dark shadow of the cherry tree and walk towards her. Both were tall, almost men, one with matted, Brylcreamed hair, the other tousled. They were wearing jeans, gabardine jackets with cut off arms, and tee shirts with sleeves rolled up to the shoulders, one with a Lucky Strike pack inside the roll. The other had a cigarette tucked behind his right ear and both were laughing as they approached. The older of the two casually carried the Marlin .22 in his right hand. It all seemed so familiar now. The boy carrying the gun, she had met many times before, always in her dreams and hallucinations, the phantasm who had asked for

Ellen on the phone and at her door and in the middle of the dim shadows of countless nightmares. She knew him well.

Eight to ten yards from Terry, the two assassins stopped, and the boy with the gun, as in some B-western, suddenly fired at her from the hip. The bullet struck her left chest. She stood there for a moment, looked down slowly as if she was going to button a blouse, and then fell forward, her eyes still open. Another shot smashed into her back left side, but it didn't matter, for she knew she was already dead. . .or dreaming of death.

She listened attentively to the crisp belching of frogs, the raspy noise of cicadas in the grass, and the sounds of the boys as they argued over what to do next. Clammy hands wrapped around her legs, dragging her across the ground, pulling her dress up over her chest as she went. With unclosing eyes she watched as they next pulled Ellen, feet first, towards a briar patch. Her eyes meet those of her sister. "Come with me," they said. Terry watched as the older boy hurriedly began to cover her sister with dry leaves, and then to do the same with her own body.

"Hey Teddy, you dumb shit, you didn't finish it. Look over there," said the slightly shorter boy, pointing back towards Ellen. "The bitch is still moving."

"You don't have to call her that," growled the older boy. "Show some respect." Then they both laughed as Teddy picked up her white purse, took out her wallet with the two dollars earned from baby-sitting, and shoved it in his hip pocket.

Terry listened to the frogs and the wispy sound of the older boy's black-and-white sneakers crushing the grass as he walked slowly towards Ellen. The noise was suddenly deafening, when only moments before even the sounds of the gunshots had been barely perceptible. Auditory hyperacusis. Wasn't that what that bastard Brownstein had called it? Too late now to fix it. Encephalopathy, my ass! Too late to make repairs there. Too, too late for anything.

With eyes that could no longer blink, as time slowed to a veritable crawl, she watched a tick making its eight-legged way up a bloody blade of grass in front of her nose, and then slowly focused on the older boy as he put his right foot on Ellen's butt and pointed his .22 at the back of her head. The unmoving eyes and thoughts of the two almost-sisters met in mid-space. "Please," Ellen murmured to Terry, "just do it."

As the last shot was fired, and darkness clouded all, Terry knew that she must become one with her sister. It had already been ordained.

Chapter 39
ROOM 107

The morning was cold, drizzly, and miserable outside when Tristan Keyes awoke on March 20, 2006. For the last three days he had been in Michigan at a Notre Dame alumni gathering, and had not returned until after midnight the previous evening. He had, of course, begged Terry to go with him. She had refused. Upon his return home he had been so tired from the seventeen-hour drive that he had left his luggage in the trunk and, still fully clothed, fallen onto the bed and into a dreamless slumber.

Now, renewed by nine hours of rest, he trundled into the kitchen, fixed a cup of black coffee, and sat down at his computer. He didn't turn it on to e-mail Terry a 'Good Morning,' as he normally did. Instead, he looked at his black and gold cloth-bound Barnes & Noble desk diary, a gift from her his last birthday.

Perhaps, he thought as he scanned the diary, he was too old-fashioned for the times. As a former NASA engineer he was certainly computer literate, and infrequently used the spiffy, impersonal computer calendar and planner that did everything but tap dance on his hard drive, but he still found reading from and writing on paper far more satisfying. Moreover, he had loved her gift because it was filled with the arcania of the literary world, which he relished, from Plato and Euripides to Pynchon and Wolfe. Every day's entry also featured a wonderful quote from some literary work or play, the name of an author born on that date, and other interesting writer's trivia. Even the stages of sun and moon. Each year had featured a particular significant literary or historical figure, this year's being Benjamin Franklin, one of his favorite icons. A particularly delightful anecdotal story described Franklin plying Governor George Clinton of New York with liquor during the French and Indian Wars and getting him drunk to procure guns for Pennsylvania. A footnote on the bottom of the page indicated that Randolph Caldecott was born on this day in 1846.

As Tristan glanced on the day's entry, he noted it was almost the last quarter of the moon, soon to be the beginning of spring, with the corresponding constellation of Aries symbolizing to astrologers the renewal of life, energy and the creation of heat. The moon, he recalled from Anthropology 101, which he had taken as an elective in college, was associated in ancient superstitions with the periodicity of women, the terms "moon," "month," and "menses" being all from the same linguistic roots, and indicating the early primitive association of the moon's influence upon the biological functions of women. And, of course, the infamous connections with "lunacy."

Then he noted his own pigeon scrawl entries on March 17 reminding him to check in on Terry first thing upon his return. Though he knew, of late, that she had been unable to speak coherently for more than five minutes, he still wanted to make sure she was okay. As he reached for the phone, he saw the message recorder light was blinking. The digital display indicated twelve calls recorded. As he began to play back the tape, he discovered the fourth had been from Terry, made on the day after he left. Her voice quivered and occasionally broke with a muffled sob, and he could tell she was struggling to articulate in whole sentences, but failing miserably. Much of what she was saying was garbled, repetitive, or made absolutely no sense. If he hadn't known better, he would have thought she was totally inebriated. What he could make out was that, having forgotten he was leaving for a few days, she had stopped by his place soon after he had set off for Michigan. However, the call had been made from Ed and Maggie's. She had wanted to give them something, but didn't say what. As they had been drinking heavily when she arrived and Ed was not in one of his better moods, he had all but ignored her, so she was leaving. There were also repeated incoherent references to her late sister, but they made no sense. . .something about taking Ellen's advice.

When she concluded the call, his blood froze. "I just wanted to say thank you for all you have done and goodbye. You're a very dear man. Love you. Terry."

In a panic, he immediately called her home, but there was only a busy signal. For a moment he was relieved, but not much. It might be Joe Pugh, her boarder, on the phone and not her. With no umbrella and still wearing yesterday's clothes, he bolted out the front door, into what had now turned into a downpour. He rushed up the street to her house, used his key, and went in only to find the place damp, cold, and empty. Joe wasn't anywhere to be found. Going into her bedroom, he noted the bed in the usual war-zone dishevel, cigarette butts and ashes, crumpled and torn printouts from the HP printer, and other detritus all about the floor. The computer screen saver, a clip of Tuffy racing back and forth across the eighteen-inch display, was still on. The phone by the printer was off the hook, the irritating beeping sound filling the air. He quickly replaced the receiver and lifted it up again to call Brian Dean. If anyone would know what was happening, it would have to be Brian. When the phone on the other end was picked up, Tristan didn't wait for a greeting.

"Brian, this is Tris. I just got home and had a telephone call on my recorder from Terry, made on the eighteenth. I couldn't make out most of it because she wasn't speaking well. Sounded like she does when she's about to go into one of those hallucinatory states. Mentioned her dead sister several times, but apparently she had enough lucidity before the call to drive up to Ed's place in Frederick County. Christ, given the state she's been in, I didn't think she could drive around the block much less half way across Maryland. But what frightens me is that she said goodbye to me as if she was never going to see me again. Brian, she's in a hell of a state and I think this time she is actually trying to make it terminal."

From the other end of the line there was a long silence before Brian replied. "I know, buddy. She came by my place also, and I wasn't there either. She left a note, which, of course, is almost undecipherable, thanking me for everything and apologizing for leaving her house — my house — in the state it is in. She also said goodbye to me too. I've been calling around and no one seems to have any idea of where she was. Like you, it never crossed my mind she could make it way out to Ed's alone. She gets confused on the road in front of the house! I tried calling him but there was no answer, and because of her break with Sean, I didn't want to get in the middle there and just left it. I had sincerely hoped she might have finally caved in and gone with you."

As Brian was talking, Tristan was writing out a note to Joe, informing him of the situation and requesting any information he might have. He then began thumbing through Terry's rebellion against modern digital technology, her 1960s rolodex.

"I don't think we can wait any longer, Brian. I'm calling Sean."

As an officer in the United States Marines, Sean Anderson had been well trained in crisis management. As soon as he received Tristan's call, he calmly gathered all of the details he could about his mother's disappearance, as well as all her personal data. He then placed a call to a former Marine colleague, now a commander in the Maryland State Police.

After discussing the situation, and coughing up a promise to locate her if she was in the state, the officer told Sean bluntly: "Captain Anderson, we can probably track her down. You gave us her description, car make, license plate, credit card numbers, and where she was last seen, which will be very helpful. Given her health condition, as you describe it, I don't think she has enough wherewithal to just disappear. I have to be honest, though. Even if she intends to harm herself, until she actually does, or displays any effort to do so, she is a free person who apparently, at least for now, is in control of her faculties."

"But, damn it, she's suicidal," Sean shouted into the phone. "She's going to kill herself. And when my mother sets her mind on something, handicapped as she is, she usually achieves her goal."

"I'm sorry, sir, but until she breaks some law or demonstrates that she poses a threat to herself or anyone else, we can't just bring her back without a reason. We need a court order."

Sean remained adamant. "Well, if you can't bring her back, can you at least find her and let me know where she is? I have a lawyer friend and I'll see what I can do to get what you need."

"That," replied the officer, "I think we can probably do. We'll even try to keep an eye on her until you can come up."

The police were as good as their word, and as efficient. By the eve of March 21, they had found Terry ensconced at a Nite's Rest Motel ("Credit cards and cash graciously accepted") at the intersection of State 27 and U.S. 70, on the Old National Pike, near Mount Airy, Maryland, nearly one hundred miles from home. Having apparently regained her stability, at least all appearances of it before their visit, she informed the two highway patrolmen who knocked at her room door that she was simply getting away for a few days in the countryside and wished to stay where she was. She respectfully but firmly refused to state where she had been or what her plans were. "That's my own business," she said peremptorily to the officers, "and since I have broken no laws, it is certainly none of yours."

After the two patrolman departed, Terry remained in her room with the lights out for the better part of the night. She correctly assumed that the police might be watching—just in case. From behind the blinds of her second-story room window, she could just make out the front of the brown-and-black state police cruiser parked beside the motel office. Then, at 2:00 a.m., the cruiser departed. She too immediately left.

At 11:34 a.m., on the morning of March 23, Angelina Tomas Gomez and Maria Remey Santos, hotel maids at the Lockwood Inn in Manassas, Virginia, cleaning as they had done everyday for the last two years, knocked at the door of Room 107 on their daily rounds. Neither Angelina, 23, Mexican, unmarried, and four months pregnant, nor Maria, 49, married, with eight children back home in Honduras, were American citizens or had green cards. Then again neither did more than half the staff of the motel: most were Hispanics working for minimum wage (or less for those the management knew to be illegal immigrants). The place would indeed have been sorely pressed to stay open if they were not on the payroll. As Rob Bailey, the motel's manager, had told them many

times before, there simply were too few whites or blacks in Manassas willing to do what they did or nearly as well. Not surprisingly, for their continued employment in the U.S., for the very survival of their families back home in Latin America demanded it, they all had avoided contact with anyone even remotely official-looking or wearing a badge of any kind. The practice had been paramount in both Angelina's and Maria's daily routines prior to this morning, but paled in comparison to the sight that they would encounter on entering Room 107.

As they stood outside the door, Maria knocked again lightly.

"Room service," she said in her stilted English. No answer.

She could hear the television inside, and could make out the distinctive voice of Whoopie Goldberg, her favorite American comedian.

She knocked again. This time more loudly, but again no response. The door was locked, so she tried the key. Angelina was the first to cross the threshold and see the woman's fully-clothed body lying on the bed.

"Madre Deus," Angelina shrieked as her co-worker entered behind her, "I think she is dead!"

The woman on the bed was wearing a pretty, retro-looking, pleated orchid-colored skirt and blouse to match. In her half-opened left hand lying across her chest, was a plastic cup that had spilled water across the blouse and bed. On the night table beside the bed was an orange CVS Pharmacy prescription container, with a single pill inside. The woman's right hand was draped over the side of the bed, and on the floor beneath was a large clear plastic bag with a drawstring at its open end. It was instantly apparent to the maid that the woman was not asleep in the normal sense. On the dresser opposite the foot of the bed, the television was still on, with a DVD video running.

In the excitement that ensued in Room 107, neither of the two hotel workers noticed the faintly cloying scent of Vicks® Vaporub.

When the Prince William County, Virginia, police and an ambulance from Holy Redeemer Hospital in nearby Haymarket arrived barely fifteen minutes after Rob Bailey placed the 911 call, they quickly ascertained from her wallet and the prescription bottle that the woman in Room 107 was Terry Chauvanne Anderson. Incredibly, she was still alive, but barely. Only minutes before the two housekeepers appeared, she had overdosed on twenty-three 20-miligram tablets of Oxycontin. From all appearances, they also concluded that she had intended to place the plastic bag over her head, a' la Kevorkian, to insure the job was done, but had passed out almost instantly after taking the pills. It was clear that this was no simple suicide "attempt." Terry Chauvanne Anderson had fully intended on ending her life.

"I just don't get it," said one of the EMTs, as he carried one end of the stretcher with Terry on it toward the ambulance. "Why do folks do this to themselves?"

The other EMT grunted as they lifted the stretcher into the vehicle bay. "Depression, debts, brain chemistry, genes, childhood horrors remembered. Who knows? The problem with suicide is that it's a senseless event. There is no why."

"Ironic, isn't it?" said the first EMT.

"What's that?" said the second.

"Did you see the DVD she had had been watching on the TV?"

"No. What was it?"

"That Patrick Swayze movie."

"Which one."

"*Ghosts*."

Chapter 40

ABSORPTION OF A
BLACK EYE

On Sunday morning, March 26, Tristan called Joe Pugh to inform him of the latest news regarding Terry's condition. She had, he said, been admitted to Prince William County Hospital in Virginia for treatment and observation, but a few miles from Sean and Marissa's home outside of Manassas. She had been pumped out and stabilized after the suicide attempt, but, somewhere along the way, had contracted a mild case of pneumonia, which was being treated. Moreover, she was in substantial pain from the Lyme, which the doctors said they were working to alleviate. Although Sean informed him that she was not to receive any cards or gifts, and would be staying at least until the following Monday, he nevertheless called her in her room and spoke briefly, offering to have her stay with him until she could figure out what to do. She had quietly accepted, but informed him that she was likely to be in far longer than Sean said, as she was being transferred to the Psychiatric Ward at Bush General Hospital. Moreover, she said, she had requested Sean to clean out all of her belonging from Brian's house, box them up, and place them in storage.

"I want to finally get Brian's place back to him," she said. "That poor, kind man has carried me for so long, it's the least I should do. Besides, it's about time I start downsizing and getting things in order." She said nothing about where she intended on moving to or how she would support herself. Tristan did not press the issue.

It wasn't until the following Thursday, March 30, that Tristan could screw up enough courage to visit Terry. When he arrived and was escorted into a room with barred windows and extremely bright fluorescent lighting, he found her scuffing along like an old woman, dressed in simple aqua-colored hospital garb and cloth "footies." Her face was drawn and her overall appearance was distressingly gaunt as she shuffled towards him, though her wan smile gave evidence of her delight in seeing him. He had already decided not to discuss the suicide or why she attempted it; the subject nevertheless hung cloud-like over the meeting.

After hugging Terry and kissing her on the cheek, Tristan nervously began to inform her of the goings-on back home, of Sean's progress in moving her belongings from Brian's place, and disposing of the huge amounts of trash in a rented dumpster beside the garage.

"Your son's been a mountain of stamina," Tristan said, "and he's been working without a break."

Terry, in turn, strangely, seemed mildly excited, not by his visit or his news of the day, or his accolades regarding her estranged son, but by her depressing new surroundings and her new friends, many being fellow patients who had also unsuccessfully attempted suicide.

"You know," she said quite lucidly, "ever since I discovered I had Stage 3 Chronic Lyme disease, it's been among my greatest fears to be locked up against my will in a place like this, a mental ward, but here I find there are a lot of other people just like me.

Some have been screwed blue by the establishment and are without hope. Some have lost something, or someone very important to them, or are in the throes of unbearable sorrow and despair. For others there are demons stalking them that they feel only death can stop. I can see that for a few of them, by taking their own lives, they're extracting a form of revenge, an apocalypse, even some repressed assassination they would wish on others who have hurt them. I truly believe that suicide for some isn't just death, but an accusation, a declaration of isolation, of loneliness. It's their only means of release. But me! I'm not crazy. I'm just suffering from the advanced stages of this horrible debilitating disease, from which there will never be any relief or hope of recovery. When Tuffy died the way he did, it was the last straw. And I am enraged that my son, who has no concept of my pain, intervened in what I chose to do of my own free will. I stand alone now."

Tristan took her hand in his and responded gently. "Terry, dear Terry. You are not alone. Despite what you may feel about your son, he has done everything he can to help you. You can't simply repudiate your connection to him, or, God forbid, try to 'get even' by killing yourself. And there are the rest of us who care deeply for you."

He looked into her eyes, now lined with darkness. "Especially me. And as for your suffering, who knows what may lie ahead. Maybe there's a Jonas Salk out there right now working on a cure that's only a week or a month away. But whatever healing is to come, I believe, it isn't going to be a healing of redemption or some epiphany. It's likely to be more like the slow absorption of a black eye or a bruise. You have to give it time, sweetheart. Give it time and I assure you it will come."

"Maybe yes, maybe no," she said. "I don't know. As of now, nobody knows the answers, although there are a hell of a lot of doctors and shrinks who think they do. You bring my cigarettes? They don't mind us smoking here, but — Catch 22 — they won't let us have any matches."

"Sure did."

"As a child," she continued after lighting up, "I used to believe my parents knew everything. But when I began to ask some hard kid questions, like, who were the first person's parents, and how come cops are allowed to smoke in no smoking areas, and they couldn't answer them, I thought they were withholding critical information from me. How could they not know? I once thought the same thing about doctors. Truth is, they simply don't know, but are too fucking self-centered and self-serving to say so. I only know what I feel, and it's usually pain, and they do everything to quantify and qualify it, but seem to never fix it, though it never stops them from sending out the bill. Sometimes, when I close my eyes, I am certain I am going to wake up and see myself lying there on the floor by my computer, or on a sun swept hill surrounded by flowers, and I am in the air above me. And it's a good feeling, free of the pain, free of the calamities. Free of trying to navigate through this fucked up maze of so-called health-care providers, medications, and bills I can't pay. I've talked about it to others here who have also tried to end it. And I've learned from them."

"What do you mean?" Tristan asked.

"You know," she answered with a sardonic smile. "Most all the people walking around have been dumped here for trying to take their own lives. Most of them are not stupid, but they're at the end of their rope. We're all alike in that sense. The patients here, those that aren't locked up, often discuss with each other how to ultimately achieve their mutual goal when they get out. Tristan, this place is a school for suicide and the damned shrinks that run it haven't got a clue. Some poor inmates — and that's what we look at ourselves as — of course, like Naomi, sitting over there in the corner, will never get out. She's failed ten times and now she's in here for keeps. I have to be honest with you, Tris, because I know I can trust you. I'm more reinforced now about my goal than ever before. The next time, however, I won't screw it up."

"My God, Terry. We have got to get you out of here," Tristan exclaimed. "This place, this hole to hell, can do you no good at all."

Terry remained in treatment in the psychiatric facility at Manassas General for thirty days, all that the government assistance program paying for it would allow. Indeed, she was finally released not because of being cured, or was even deemed competent to take care of herself, but because there was no one to pay the bill. Tristan, of course, was there to bring her home, while Sean drove his mother's car to his own home to prevent a repetition the likes of which had just been stymied. Her discharge, however, was authorized on the condition that she secure follow-up treatments at the nearby Talbot Hospital Mental Health Center.

It had been something of a seesaw battle between Tristan, Sean, and Marissa about what to actually do with Terry, now that most of her belongings, and the banged up artifacts of their lives left behind by her parents, were being trashed or moved from Brian Dean's place. Sean was for finding a small apartment in Centreville, but visits to the few dingy rooms that were affordable proved disheartening. After looking at one grim, Dickensian flat, Marissa made a brilliant suggestion:

"Tris," she said, "since you're practically the only one she will listen to or trust, why don't we fix up one of the spare bedrooms in your new house?" And so they did, bringing her sparse personal belongings, computer, and potted plants from her former home. They prepared an upstairs room for her, directly over Tristan's own bedroom. Her computer was set up on a table with rubber edges—to prevent further facial injuries—beside a window overlooking the scenic Corsica, with her bed and night table set to one side of it. A thick shag rug covered the floor to help absorb any damage from falls, and a large and bright bath adjoined the room, replete with handicap railings and cushions for the bathtub and toilet.

Tristan had never lived with a woman before, and wasn't certain how the arrangement would go over with Terry once she was established. He was even less certain how it would be to exist on even a 24-hour basis around her every day as her physical condition continued to deteriorate. He consoled himself, however, with the knowledge that at least with someone like himself around, the chances of her actually succeeding in another attempt on her own life, of taking that final step on the path to self-destruction, was substantially lessened. And any inconvenience to him mattered little, as his sheltering love for her now knew no bounds.

The trip home was somber, and for the third time in his life, Tristan saw Terry cry, as if she were saying goodbye to an old friend. Sean and Marissa had followed, and together they stopped for dinner at Terry's favorite haunt, Annie's Place. Then, upon arrival at Tristan's, Sean and Marissa took her up to show how they had fixed up a room for her. A short time later, as she stood in the doorway of her new abode and watched her son and daughter-in-law leave, the tears again began flow.

"What's the matter, sweetheart?" Tristan asked.

"I've got to have my car," she blurted out.

"Your car?" he said with a look of incredulity. "What's so important about your car? You know you're not allowed to drive now."

"It's got all of my things in it," she answered. "I don't even have my toothbrush."

"Listen, I can get you anything you want or need."

Terry pouted. "I know, but it's my stuff, personal things I've had for years, which I took with me while I looked for just the right cliff. I know it sounds strange, but I didn't know how long it would take me to find one."

Tristan stared at her. "The right cliff? What the heck do you mean?"

"When I left," she sobbed, "I intended on going up to western Pennsylvania, but first stopped off at Ed and Maggie's place to say goodbye. They were on a bender, too drunk to even say hello. I never really liked my brother so it didn't matter much. It did give me an opportunity to call you and Brian, but in my mind-fog I had forgotten that you had gone to your alumni meeting."

"What's that got to do with a cliff or Pennsylvania, of all places?"

"I thought," she answered, "I could just go into some library there and find a book, a map, or something that would tell me where there was a majestic cliff so I could drive my car off it and go out with flare. You know, like in the movie Thelma and Louise."

"You're kidding, right?" Tristan asked incredulously.

"No. I think theirs was a class act. It would be the only classy thing I've ever done in my life. At least till I get to Never Neverland. I just couldn't find a cliff, so I turned around and headed back, thinking maybe I was making a mistake. Then the police located me at some motel up in western Maryland, and I got angry, mostly at Sean, because I knew he had asked them to find me. That's when something in my head said, 'just do it,' so I determined that I would finish it after all."

"Terry," said Tristan, "Sean only did what he did because he was worried sick about you."

"Whatever! Anyway, I left the motel in the middle of the night and headed for Virginia. I figured if I did it there, close to Sean's place, he wouldn't have to go to so much trouble after it was all over. A few months ago I researched several sites on the Internet on how to conduct a painless suicide. I even left the house with several backup plans based upon my research in the event the Thelma and Louise strategy didn't pan out. I was prepared to do a Kevorkian thing, but by the time I got to Manassas I was in such physical pain and verging on collapsing into a heap, that I took a whole bottle of Oxycontin. Before I could get the plastic bag over my head, I passed out. And you know the rest."

"Dear Terry, you're here now with me," Tristan said softly. "We've fixed up a great place for you in my house. I promise to do anything you want, provide you with anything you need, be there for you 24-7 until the end of time. I will be your man Friday, or whatever. But just promise me that you won't try another stunt like that. I couldn't bear to see you back in that horrible psycho ward. And if you succeeded, you wouldn't be just killing yourself, you'd be killing me too!"

She smiled, touching his cheek with her fingertips. "I might agree. . .if you promise to retrieve my car," she said coyly.

"Deal," Tristan responded triumphantly.

Two days later, Terry's car was sitting in Tristan's driveway. Keeping in character with her self-sufficient demeanor, even though she was obliged to shuffle along at an incredibly sluggish but deliberate pace, she insisted that she unload her belongings from the backseat without her new landlord's assistance. "They're my things and my responsibility," she informed him succinctly. "So why don't you make yourself comfortable, watch the ball game and have some beer and pretzels I put out for you."

"Okay," he said, "but if you need me just give a shout."

While Tristan Keyes enjoyed the Washington-Philadelphia game on television, Terry Chauvanne Anderson quietly removed the .38 snub nose Smith and Wesson she had hidden in the car trunk as one of the original backup plans, the same revolver she had purchased an eon earlier, just before meeting Bill Trueman.

This time, she resolved to do everything by the book, but first there were still a few loose ends that needed tending.

Chapter 41

PERIPETEIA

Anxiety is the space between the present and the future, and watching every move, every nuance, every tremor exhibited by his beloved Terry, Tristan Keyes was consumed by it. Knowing her intent, avowed only to him, a trust bestowed on him alone, he was horrified at the necessity of the repugnant preventive measures that would only intensify her misery and her desire to end her life. He now faced each day one at a time. He could no longer allow himself to plan for the future, only to manage the moment. Nurturing and supportive of Terry's every need and action, and negating his own, he outwardly radiated his normal smiling and confident countenance. Inside, though, he felt powerless, frozen with a paralysis that forbade carrying out the aggressive means to prevent the only woman he had ever loved from taking her life.

Tristan took some consolation in Terry's efforts, soon after their return to Quail Lane, to address what she perceived as wrongs resulting in her beloved Tuffy's recent death. Anything that would occupy and redirect her attentions to matters other than her own dismal sufferings would be better than inaction. By early April 2006, despite her difficulties in maintaining an attention span longer than a few minutes at a time, her computer keyboard dyslexia, and recurrent narcoleptic attacks, she somehow managed to mount a cogent case of malpractice against Drs. Prushinski, Mastricht, and Core. The charge, which was formally filed with the Maryland State Board of Veterinarians, replete with written witness testimony by Tristan, was for the alleged bungling of Tuffy's treatment, leading to the necessity of putting him to sleep. The brief was accompanied by a wordy and often disjointed story of the dog's medical history. On April 15, a vigorous rebuttal to the accusations by the three veterinarians was filed with Dr. Jameson Keitel, Acting Chairman of the Board, charging that "once home, she [Theresa Anderson] failed to follow our recommendations and severely overmedicated Tuffy . . . the night prior to his euthanasia."

The response to the findings, which Terry obstinately declared were without foundation, served only to arouse her anger to new heights, and took her but a few days to mount the final, albeit hopeless, assault on the veterinarian medical establishment. Her challenge proved as futile as her past harangues against her own medical caregivers. On April 20, after days of trying to organize a single-paged letter, days punctuated by narcoleptic attacks, memory loss, and pain, she dispatched her own formal request for an appeal and a rebuttal to the three veterinarians' defense, calling the decision "dumbfounding."

The appeal request was immediately denied. The case was closed, and the last reason for Terry's existence, to seek some form of justice and revenge against the perceived perpetrators of her beloved Tuffy's death, was snuffed out in utter defeat. There now seemed to her nothing left but to tie up the last few pieces of unfinished business and move forward with her plan.

For the first time in his relationship with Terry, Tristan Keyes knew in his heart that, no matter who might intervene, there was nothing he or anyone could do to prevent the love of his life from ending her own. He alone would never be able to stop her, or would even try to forestall the destiny she was committed to. He sadly resolved to ease her journey, make the path more tolerable as best he could. He would be her facilitator to the end. Yet, with the loss of Tuffy, and Terry's last proclaimed reason for being gone, the finality of it all came crashing down on him. As he would later record in his own journal, "When that was done, I started getting this feeling in the pit of my stomach that 'Oh shit! This is the end.'" It was all, now, just a matter of time and place.

On April 24, Tristan drove Terry into Easton for her weekly appointment with Dr. Leonard Sprouse, her latest designated counselor at the mental health facility. There, after an hour of psychotherapy and the customary array of urine and blood tests, they returned home with the usual assortment of prescription drugs — Oxycontin, Skelexin, and Lexophin — which were to be administered by Tristan, who had finally been permitted to act as her medical power of attorney.

That evening, after dinner, Terry retired to her room, closed the door, and with trembling hands retrieved an antiquated portable tape recorder, a pair of dusty earphones, and several tapes from a shoebox hidden inside the heating duct. For the next hour and a half she lay on the bed quietly listening to the treasured past. There was the voice of her ex-husband Carl, recorded from his parents' house immediately after their marriage and just before his first deployment overseas. There was the chatter of her son Sean, 2½ years old, recorded at the Annapolis Road House, and another of Terry and the lad in their upstairs bedroom with background sounds of warbling birds outside the window, still clear as day. There was again the beautiful, innocent voice of her astonishing son recorded in Utica in December 1978. Finally, there was the tape her father made at Ellen's sixteenth birthday party in July 1954, more than half a century ago yesterday. The tremulous voice of her wonderful teenage sister — her mentor, her guide, her angel — was filled with the giddiness of life and expectation. How, she thought, could it all have gone so wrong!

At 2:30 a.m., April 26, Terry pulled herself up to her computer and began typing the first of a series of letters of goodbye. The initial would be to Carl, and would take days to complete. After several false starts, she began to write during an unusually long interval of lucidity.

> "This letter, Carl, is compelled by a need to communicate to you on matters pertaining to this illness, which has for so long been devastating my life, to make known how long and how hard I fought to prevent what will shortly come to pass, and to make known the person I am, a person I believe to be of some grit, endurance, fortitude, tenacity, and perseverance. I tell you these things because you will not hear them from our son Sean, whom I love more dearly than life itself, but who has abandoned me, or I have driven away. You will not hear these things from Sean because he has not the slightest clue of any of them; sadly, judging by his conduct, he's not had the slightest interest in having a clue. Except for my dear friend Tristan, I am the forgotten."

Outside, the moon was in mid-sky, surrounded by a pantheon of stars. A warm spring breeze was blowing through the open window, brushing Terry's mottled and bruised skin, tempting her to stop writing just for a moment to reconsider. Slowly she stood and walked to the side of her bed, looked out into the darkness, and felt the tempting caress of endless sleep sweeping through her body and soul.

"Not just yet," she thought out loud. "I'm not quite finished."

Over the next several days and nights, during the short periods of full awareness and semi-consciousness that were sandwiched between mirages, hallucinations, and pain, between the drowning vertigo and stark delirium that had become her life, Terry struggled to write. To those who had been important to her in life, she wrestled to revisit the past one last time, to provide a final history of herself, to try to explain it all and why she had come to such a point in her existence. Now, she knew, there could be no more chance of living robustly as ennui wrapped its fingers about her heart and exhausted her senses. The loss of Tuffy had deprived her of her last feeling of self-worth. There could never be any further pleasure in living. Blueprinting her path to self-destruction would be her last act of free will to challenge the clockwork of the universe. This time there would be no intervention.

Her letters were flashed with both vitriol and love. On April 29, she struggled to compose for Drs. Quade, Campollo, and Brownstein, a long and scornful denunciation of their abilities as greedy, uncaring professionals, and posed to them what a stir it might have caused had she concluded her life in their offices. "The consequence of a bullet to the head, the spraying of brain, blood, skull, about your waiting room," she wrote with morbid glee, "would certainly have been exciting and I very much would have wanted to experience the act in your presence."

None of the letters would ever be sent.

On the evening of May 9, Terry and Tristan watched a movie entitled *The Human Stain*, about an affair between an old man and a young woman ending in downfall and death. Though Tristan could not know it, it would be their last evening together.

"What's the moment called in Greek tragedy?" asked one of the lead characters named Nathan. "You know, the one where the hero learns that everything he knows is wrong?"

"Peripeteia," responded the second character, named Coleman.

Terry formed the words upon her lips as tears came to her eyes for the last time in her life.

"Peripeteia," she said quietly to herself.

It was 3:39 a.m., May 10, 2006 when Terry struggled, amidst recurring moments of disconnect and writing dyslexia, to begin the last of two disjointed letters, each formally announcing her intent to commit suicide, and each an effort to tie up loose ends. The first, revisiting her descent into the abyss, was to her one-time lover Jerry Bostwick, and would take hours to compose.

"I was going through some last minute things…suicide planned this evening… morning now…In any case, going through some things…had wa[nted] to write you a few months ago, before my first and unfortunately unsuccessful attempt at suicide, ly[me] has become [sin]ce so severe, '96 first infection of what would be multiple infections…diagnosed with very severe neuropsychiatric lyme disease, lyme encephalopathy and the like…progressively ill ever since, plan in fact was to not see in 2006, but shit happened, rather, my being so damned conscientious, trying to get stuff done so to not leave my son with so much to have to deal with... in any case, this time bullet to brain planned...first time plan was drugs and then plastic bag over head, but passed out before could get bag secured around neck. Ha. Ha. Really, that is funny. Woke up few days later in ICU, since have been staying with a friend...had left house was in, trying for years to get Brian Dean back his place, to sell property, to retire, too ill...could do nothing, not the most basic of shit, so had to leave all to my son, Sean, to clear house; left house with clothes on back and a few other things mid march...in any case, wanted to communicate something to you before...can't be sure this evening/morning will be it, finally the end of things...cannot/will not do anything in this friend's house, so need get myself somewhere else, this time using gun...please, in the event I am not successful in getting myself out to someplace....please, please do not call....'somebody' about my intent, indeed about my need to finally....have to go. Loved you once very much. Terry."

By 5:30 a.m. Terry had run off a copy on her printer, and painfully, slowly re-read it, before sighing in complete exhaustion, tearing it up, and throwing it into the trash.

There was still one more note to write, which she would not throw away.

Wednesday, May 10, 2006. The Just Good Coffee Shop was a local fixture in Centreville, situated directly across Lawyers Row, obliquely from the picturesque nineteenth century county courthouse, where many professionals and most of the attorneys who had hung up their shingle in town frequented every morning before work. It had become a ritual with Tristan Keyes, ever since he had moved onto Quail Lane, first as a tenant at Terry's place, mostly after retiring, then later as owner of his own home, to drive the half mile to the shop every morning at 8:30 a.m. for a large café au lait. On some warm spring and summer days he would walk. There he'd usually socialize with the morning crowd for an hour or so, exchanging the local gossip and talk politics and weather with a few of the old-timers. That is, until Terry had moved into his house, when the ritual was notably altered. Now he would linger for less than fifteen minutes, exchanging a few pleasantries with the townsfolk, and return with a large latté for Terry. It had become customary, during her darker days over the last few weeks, for him to draw a little heart or smiley face on the Styrofoam cup to help cheer her up.

On this particular morning Tristan was up early. He had taken on a part-time teaching job at Chesapeake Community College after his retirement from NASA. Wednesdays and Fridays he had classes in the morning and on Tuesdays during the afternoon, but this Wednesday seemed somehow different. He couldn't exactly put his finger on why, but something told him to take the day off.

The morning was clear and fair, with a tender breeze blowing, and Terry appeared to be asleep in her room. Tristan determined to walk into town for his morning coffee, but decided against bringing one back for her since she probably wouldn't be getting up until the afternoon. As he crossed the little Watson Road Bridge leading from Corsica Estates over the river, he noticed daffodils someone had planted, blossoming along the water's edge. "You pretty daughters of the earth and sun," he said out loud to himself with a smile, quoting a favorite sonnet by Sir Walter Raleigh. At the coffee shop, he chatted a bit with a few townies and began to walk back about 9:00, arriving at the house fifteen minutes later. As he came through the front door, he encountered Terry coming out, accoutered in the same sinuous, toe-length flower-child dress she had been wearing the day he met her. In one hand she had a pair of earphones and a portable battery-powered CD player. Her other hand was in the deep pocket on the right of the dress, where either her fist or a heavy object seemed to be distending the cloth. Her face was drawn and sallow, and her eyes hollow and gray, no longer the woman he had met three years before. She looked surprised, not unlike a child caught with her hand in a cookie jar.

Tristan was immediately suspicious.

"What are you doing here?" she stammered in a labored speech pattern that had become all too normal. "I thought . . . I thought . . . I thought you were, ah, you'd be out."

"Well, no," Tristan replied. "I took the day off and I'm going to watch a little news on TV before I take you out for a drive on this beautiful morning. How'd you like that?"

Terry quickly corrected course and stuttered uncontrollably. "That. . . that'd be great. But I see you . . . you've been to the coffee shop . . . a . . . a . . . and you didn't bring me any. How callous can you be Tris. . .Tristan. . . Keyes."

"Okay, okay," Tristan responded with a chuckle. "I'll drive in and get you a mocha grandee, how's that? Be back in ten or fifteen. Meantime, get yourself together so we can go for that drive. Now don't go anywhere till I get back, okay!"

She set the earphone and CD player on the foyer table and cupped his right hand with her trembling boney fingers. "That wou. . .would be great Sir. . .Sir Lancelot. That would be swell."

A minute later Tristan was en route back to town, and Terry stepped into the sunlight to finally let free her will forever.

The walk up Quail Lane to Brian Dean's now-empty house was taxing in the extreme for Terry. She approached the yard with a mixture of emotions, both surreal and unsettling on the most beautiful morning of her life. Her whole body ached, and her limbs quivered with every defective step she took, in utter contrast to the glorious perfection of nature surrounding her.

It was now or never.

Finally, after arriving at her destination, the trellis in the back lawn of the house wherein so much black misery of her life had been concentrated, she sat, leaned back between a perfect bower of roses and thorns, and gazed down towards the idyllic Corsica, where the waterman dressed in black and his tall youthful mate were working their crab trot lines from an old work boat. For but a moment she grew light-headed with the smell of the flowers and spring airs. Maybe she shouldn't go on with it after all. Maybe Tristan was right. Then the throbbing pain at the base of her skull returned, and she knew there could be no other way.

"Get a grip," she said to herself, determined not to slip into the uncontrollable she knew would ensue. She closed her eyes and clenched her fists. Count to ten. Do not let this thing carry you away before you are done. Do not descend into the night. Tristan will be back soon. "Time is of the essence." For endless seconds, she seemed to hold her breath until, almost miraculously, the pain subsided.

When she opened her eyes, the world had changed: the bright and clear morning sky had turned to a cold dark orange with threatening clouds moving in from the north. The waters of the Corsica had begun to roil as an angry sea. The air was thick with mulled sounds of no distinct origins and a sickening feeling of indefinable discord that caused her eyes, ears, and soul to hurt. Down by the river the waterman had pulled his boat onto the shore as if awaiting a passenger, while the youth with him had landed and began a slow, almost menacing ascent up the slope towards Terry.

As the spectral young man came closer, Terry began to make out his distinctive features, which she had grown to know and abhor. Slicked back hair, plain ragged jeans and a blue gabardine jacket with the arms ripped off, over a T-shirt with a pack of cigarettes rolled under the right shirtsleeve. The boy with the gun. The boy who had killed Ellen. The boy who had been killing Terry for years.

"You're going to be with Ellen, aren't you?" asked the specter in a flat, monotone voice as he finally stood before her.

"Yes," she replied. "So what!"

The young man looked in anguish over his shoulder towards the water. The man on the boat was waving slowly, almost rhythmically, summoning him back to the river.

"We haven't much time here, you and I," declared the specter as he turned back towards Terry, his face aging with decades as he turned, "and I have a request which I pray you will allow me."

"Which is?"

"To grant me forgiveness for my sins against your sister," he answered. "As you are still of this earth, but have become almost one with her and will soon be with her, only you, in her behalf, can offer me release from this Purgatory, this existence between all time, for all eternity. I have tried, God knows I have tried to say I am sorry, but you wouldn't let me in."

"Wow! Eternity's a long time, isn't it? And if I refuse?"

Again the now-old man glanced towards the black river and the beckoning waterman. The far shore had faded into shadows and the orange sky, rapidly filling with dusky, cumulous clouds, was turning the color of blood. "Red sky at night, sailor's delight. Red sky in the morning, sailor take warning," clicked Terry with raised eyebrows. "It is morning, the start of a new day, isn't it?"

"Please, help me," pleaded the old man. "Please. I beg you. In the name of Christ the Redeemer, I beg you. Forgive my soul. Save me from eternal damnation."

Terry's eyes, her limbs, indeed her entire body grew heavy, as the winds picked up, and small dust devils, which seemed to grow by the second into a violent storm, began to sweep across the hill, obscuring the youth, the waterman, the boat, and the river.

"Never, you fucking bastard! Go to hell!" she shouted above the thundering tempest and the blackness that was setting in. "Go to hell where you belong, and never come back!"

For an eternity, the darkness of the universe swept down, inexorably diminishing life from years to milliseconds, encompassing Terry in its fastness, smells, and metaphors. No more swift repartee now, for she could not keep up. No more habits of the heart. No more good-conquers-evil bullshit, only distorted truths viewed in a mottled mirror. Rhinestone eyeglasses and a ceramic horse on a jewel box lid. Vicks® Vaporub and a 1944 dime. Sister Ellen. Angel Ellen.

Moments later, she opened her eyes and all was right.

No time now. Sitting beneath the rose bower on what she knew would be the most beautiful day of her life, Terry methodically put on the headphones that she had brought with her, plugged the cable connection into the portable CD player, and began to listen to the Righteous Brothers singing "Unchained Melody," the Do Wop classic theme song from "Ghost." Reaching into her right pocket she took out the Smith and Wesson snub nose .38, put it in her mouth, and pulled the trigger.

Chapter 42

E-MAIL

Tristan emerged from the Just Good Coffee Shop, a large mocha grande in hand, and saw the ambulance running up Broadway Avenue. He thought little of it until he crossed the little Watson Road Bridge en route home. As he approached the left-hand turn into Corsica Estates, he saw a small crowd of residents gathered on the bend at Quail Lane. Quickly he pulled off to the side, stuck his head out the window, and asked a neighbor named Cletus Upshur, Jr., what all the commotion was about.

"Gunshots at Brian Dean's place," said Cletus with excitement. "Somebody must have got hurt 'cause the ambulance just went up there a minute or two ago."

In an instant, an array of thoughts passed through Tristan's head. The first was sheer terror. "Oh shit," he said out loud. Despite the knot forming in the pit of his stomach he began to think rationally. He reasoned that Terry didn't even own a gun so it couldn't have been her. Brian's place was one house down from Cletus's. Could it have been Cletus's father, in the last stages of terminal cancer and being taken care of by his son? Had he decided to end it all? Besides, it was a fair hike up the slope from his place to Brian's, and Terry hadn't seemed physically up to the walk. But he had misjudged her grit before; when she set her mind to it, she could do anything.

"Hop in Cletus," Tristan said. "Ride up there with me."

"Thanks. Much appreciated. I am a bit concerned about my father."

As Cletus was getting in, a Medivac chopper from the UMBC Shock Trauma Unit flew low overhead, and they could see it land on Brian's front lawn. A minute or two later, when they arrived, several neighbors had already gathered on the street in front of the house.

"What's happened?" Tristan asked as he pulled up to the curb beside the onlookers.

"Some woman's killed herself," said a teenage boy.

"Do they know who it is?" Tristan pressed.

"They think it's the crazy cat lady that used to live here," said another. "Seems she shot herself in the head out in the backyard."

Three hours after Terry Chauvanne Anderson had taken her life, and an hour after Tristan had completed making the necessary calls to Sean and Marissa, Brian Dean, and other family members and friends, he sat at the kitchen table, alone, staring blankly at his Barnes and Noble desk calendar opened to May 10. The quote of the day, which somehow seemed appropriate, was from Peter Pan: "All children, except one, grow up." His heart was filled with sadness, grief, remorse, and longing, fringed with guilt for having known what was to be, but nevertheless permitting it to happen. It was a mechanical universe after all. God's will. Or not.

Tristan fingered the wrinkled piece of paper he had found on the kitchen table when he returned from the suicide site. An investigation would ascertain all the whys and wherefores of the event, but he knew it would be pretty cut and dried. Just another statistic that would soon be forgotten. It was anything but. He read the note, which was barely legible, written in the discordant style of the troubled woman who had taken her life. The very way the words were etched upon the paper, with obvious pain and effort, were the last words Terry would ever write and were difficult to read. She had saved the last for him.

"If you find me gone, I am at Brian's home…on hill…call police….do not go up there….I'm sorry Tris, so sorry for your feeling for me…I….July sincere…& obviously…already…. So seriously ill mentally & physically while I write this, so…. so sorry for….sloppiness, hurting you & also…. Say more but just can't please apologize to Brian for me…I don't know where else to go to do this thing…love you…my thank you so much & never forget me. You   in hart K"

He sensed now, in an indecipherable way, that Terry had somehow dragged him across the line, from Jesuitical logic into a darker reality, and in the end had won, not lost. Ever the rationalist, he attempted to understand, to assess, and cogently explain to himself what had happened over the last three years. He couldn't. He had loved her for her desire to learn of the infinite possibilities of life, even as her disease and growing obsession with death and her murdered sister, had whittled away her hours. His love for her had been total and he would gladly have taken the bullet in her place if it could have changed things, but hadn't it all been a set piece from their first meeting to their last moment together? Nothing seemed real now. Not the last three years, not the last three hours.

In all practicality, he knew that there could be no avoiding the amount of sheer space Terry's suicide, from the moment of death through the weeks and months ahead, would take in his life hereafter, and in the lives of her surviving family members and friends. She had been a systematic person, methodical in her way even in her own decline. It was clear now that, knowing and planning where she was going, she had, over the last six months, intentionally downsized her affairs, her possessions, her living space. She had tried to wrap up all the loose ends of her life, culminating with the legal action against the vets after Tuffy's death. She had taken the trouble to find a spot where she would produce the least mess for whoever had to deal with her body when she was done. She had apparently even placed the 911 call on her cell phone, announcing her intention to commit suicide, to ensure an ambulance would be on the way in the shortest possible time to haul her body off, so that all the loose ends, to the very last, were tied.

A disintegrating hollow shell of pain and a feeling of worthlessness, even under the protecting shoulders of someone who loved and cared for her without requiring a return, had been impossible to sustain. She had more than once told Tristan she loved him, but had refrained from pressing the affair knowing full well what lay in store, not for her own self-interest but to prevent a greater hurt for the only one who really cared for her.

On Monday morning, June 11, 2006, Tristan had summoned up the will to enter Terry's room for the first time since the suicide. He brought with him the CD player she had carried with her to her death, which had recently been returned to him by the police. He had already attended to most of her affairs, shut off her Internet service and private phone line, and paid her outstanding bills. He had refrained, though, from actually entering her sanctum sanctorum. It was warm and clear outside, and the view of the Corsica through the window by her bed cheered him as he began cleaning out the Aegean stables.

In the trash can were several letters torn into small pieces. Carefully, Tristan gathered the fragments of Terry's last writings, placed them in an envelope, later to paste together. On the bed lay several weeks of old newspapers, already beginning to yellow in the direct sunlight. A brief article on one of the pages, dated May 9, was heavily underlined, apparently the day before she died. "Long Lost Murder Weapon Found in Langley Redevelopment Project" read the headline. Beneath was a brief story of construction laborers accidentally discovering on May 1 an old .22 Marlin Microgroove rifle that Prince George's County Police surmised had been intentionally buried beneath the footings of a garden apartment built more than half a century ago in Langley Park, and currently being leveled to make way for a high-rise office complex. The gun, and a wallet found with it with two moldy one-dollar bills, were believed linked to a very cold case, at least one double homicide, and perhaps more, though no names were given pending further investigation. But Tristan knew.

After making a substantial dent in the clean up effort, Tristan went downstairs to the kitchen for a cold bottle of Wild Duck Beer, Terry's favorite, and returned to the room. He had resolved to shut it off, to leave everything that had once been hers in place as a kind of memorial. One last time, he thought. One last time to savor it, to breathe in her quirky, irascible essence... And then he would move on with his life.

As he sat on the swivel chair in front of her old Dell computer, he noted the décor of her worktable, with pictures of Terry and her family, Philip, Lucille, Tuffy, Sasha, Sean and Marissa, and even one of himself. On the right side of the table, in what appeared to be a special place, was the childhood group portrait of Ellen, Eddy, and Terry in happier days. The 1944 dime necklace was draped off one side. In front of it stood the opened jewel box with the ceramic horse lid. Inside the box was the diamond ring that had once belonged to Ellen.

On Terry's night table he had set the portable CD player. He put on one of the Do Wop discs he had found in her desk drawer, part of the set he had given her on that wonderful Christmas Eve seemingly so long ago, and then plugged in her computer. The Dell was no longer hooked up to the Internet, but it didn't matter. He wanted to see what she had downloaded from her e-mail and saved, whom she had been in touch with during her final days, what her real thoughts had been. And, yes, what she might have said about him.

As the first tune, "Since I Don't Have You," an old Skylarks piece from the late '50s, started to play on the CD, the computer booted up. He watched wistfully for a moment the familiar image of Tuffy, running back and forth across the screen, and then set to opening up Terry's e-mail. All of the files had been wiped clean. He checked the remainder of her files, all of which had also been trashed.

"Not a problem," he thought out loud, "for a computer geek like Sir Lancelot." Within half an hour he had broken into her hard drive, and began to extract, item by item, e-mail by e-mail, the secret lines of Theresa Anderson's world for the last three years. For the next day and a half, he sat transfixed, as the threads of a complex, tragic life became whole fabric. He discovered her extensive research into her disease, the profiles of all the physicians who had attended to her ills over the years, their works and writings. He discovered the myriad letters and e-mails written but seldom sent, the incoming responses, and his own worshipful daily communications. He discovered her continuing devotion to the animal rights movement, and countless other interests that in better times had stimulated her life. He discovered the extensive files she had kept on the U.S. Marines and their role in the wars in Iraq and Afghanistan along with worried notations about her son Sean's possible deployment. He discovered the initial chapters of a book she had started to write on the assassination of her sister, of her own participation in the later years of investigation into the case, and her growing hatred of the Dubinski brothers after the deathbed confession of Teddy had come to light. She had wanted but been denied revenge. Or so he believed. And he discovered her in-depth study into the best ways to commit suicide. Wherever she was now, probably with those who had loved her, including her dear sister Ellen, Tristan consoled himself, she was undoubtedly happy.

The CD player was on the last song, In the Still of the Night, the Five Satins' piece Terry had loved, when the blinking e-mail icon appeared on the screen. "You Have Mail."

For a moment Tristan leaned back in astonishment. "How can that be? The damned computer isn't on the Internet," he said out loud. The icon continued to blink. He hesitated for but a moment longer, and then opened the communication.

Smiley face and heart symbols bracketed a single sentence.

"I love you Tris, and always will. Terry."